Oracle7

A User's and Developer's Guide

INCLUDING RELEASE 7.1

Oracle7

A User's and Developer's Guide

INCLUDING RELEASE 7.1

GÜNTHER STÜRNER

TRANSLATED AND ADAPTED BY

GEORGE STAW AND PATRICIA STAW

INTERNATIONAL THOMSON COMPUTER PRESS
I Ⓣ P An International Thomson Publishing Company

London • Bonn • Boston • Madrid • Johannesburg • Melbourne • Mexico City • New York • Paris
Singapore • Tokyo • Toronto • Albany, NY • Belmont, CA • Cincinnati, OH • Detroit, MI

Oracle 7: A User's and Developer's Guide
Including Release 7.1

A division of International Thomson Publishing Inc.
The ITP logo is a trademark under licence

British Library Cataloguing-in-Publication Data
A catalogue record for this book is available from the British Library

Library of Congress Cataloging-in-Publication Data
A catalog record for this book is available from the Library of Congress

---

First published by International Thomson Computer Press 1995
Reprinted 1995
Commissioning Editor: Liz Israel Oppedijk
Printed by Clays Ltd, St Ives plc.

ISBN 1-850-32118-3

International Thomson Computer Press
Berkshire House
High Holborn
London WC1 7AA
UK

International Thomson Computer Press
20 Park Plaza
14th Floor
Boston MA 02116
USA

www. thomson.com/intilitcp.html

Imprints of International Thomson Publishing

Contents

Preface

Over the past few years it has become increasingly clear that information is developing into one of the key products of the future; more and more private and public organizations are being faced with the need to globalize and integrate their information technology operations not only at a technological level but also at an organizational and geographic level. Information management systems are obviously one of the most important tools for achieving these goals, but how, in purely practical terms, are we to ensure that the right information is available in the right place at the right time? The complex maze of incompatible hardware and software systems which many organizations have built up over the past years is not the least of the obstacles which make it very difficult to implement a flexible and responsive information management infrastructure; the current discussion about 'open' systems is clear evidence of the importance which this subject has assumed.

Of course the key requirement of such open and integrated systems is that they should be able to share *information* with each other and this in turn demands the availability of an information storage technology which is independent of all the different hardware and software systems which may be in use.

Today relational database storage systems are very much 'state of the art' and Oracle's open software architecture is based on a relational database which is available on all current hardware platforms from mainframe computers through the different mid-range systems right down to single-user machines. In addition Oracle supports all standard interface and communication protocols, and provides features which take account of the latest trends in hardware development such as massively parallel systems.

However in many cases it is clearly neither possible nor practical to replace a wide range of different systems with a single database technology, however desirable this may be. For this reason Oracle has made the concept of network computing into one of the cornerstones of its open software architecture, providing integrated solutions which will place the user at the centre of a heterogeneous and physically distributed information processing and communications network.

This book shows how an open and up-to-date database system can be used in the context of an effective and fully integrated information management system.

Franz Niedermaier
CEO, ORACLE Deutschland GmbH

Author's Preface to the German Edition

Oracle7, the newest version of the ORACLE database system, has introduced a large number of new concepts and features, some of which will require database system developers and administrators to radically reassess the way in which they have carried out certain tasks in the past.

This quantum leap in database functionality confirms the commonly held belief that knowledge loses its relevance as soon as it has been acquired, while at the same time emphasizing the fact that more and more complex subject matter has to be assimilated and put into practise in less and less time. The success of each new project or product and the personal success of each individual involved with it, is to a large extent dependent on how quickly and how effectively new technology can be learnt and applied.

This is where this book comes in. Its aim is to present this latest version of the ORACLE database in such a way that the reader can quickly become familiar with its different features in order to understand and, where necessary, make active use of them. My aim is always to present complicated and sometimes extremely complex details clearly so that both the experienced ORACLE user and the newcomer find it easier to become acquainted with all the aspects of this new product range.

I should like to take this opportunity of thanking all those who have given me their support during the writing of this book. These include many colleagues and also readers of my book on ORACLE Version 6 who encouraged me to write a book about the new version.

I owe special thanks to my colleagues Ken Jacobs and Mike Hartstein who not only answered my many questions with great competence but who, on more than one occasion, made valuable contributions which have helped ensure the accuracy of this book.

I should also like to thank the many participants at the various seminars where I was first able to try out many of the explanations in the book. Their feedback has also been a contributory factor to the book's quality.

However my greatest thanks go to my wife who undertook the responsibilities of proofreader and without whose support this project would never have come to fruition.

Günther Stürner
April 1993

Translators' Preface to the English Edition

The task of translating Günther Stürner's German text into English has been both more difficult and more interesting than either of us had imagined when we first started this job many months ago. The challenge of providing an English text which would accurately reflect the contents of the book while still retaining its tone and structure has proved to us yet again that although the English and the German languages may use many of the same concepts and ideas, they put them together in *very* different ways.

We would like to thank Günther Stürner himself for all the help which he gave us throughout the translation process. Many thanks are also due to Liz Israel and Jonathan Simpson from International Thomson Publishing for their unfailing patience and support throughout this project.

We have also been fortunate enough to have had a great deal of personal support from our friends here in Germany who, by taking care of our children at times when our schedule was very tight, have also contributed to the completion of this English edition. We are especially indebted to Adrienne and Freeman Robbins who volunteered such help whenever they could.

However our greatest thanks must go to our three children Thomas, Gregory and Rebecca who, for the past months, have accepted the prolonged absences of their parents and the many weekends spent at home with (almost) no complaint. They have shown a patience and understanding which will remain as one of our most pleasant memories associated with this translation.

Patricia and George Staw
Germany, August 1994

1

Introduction

Topics covered in this chapter

- The significance of databases for information processing systems
- The development of the ORACLE database system
- The key features of the Oracle7 database
- The ORACLE product groups

1 Introduction

During its relatively brief existence the field of electronic data-processing has undergone many transformations: some of these have been revolutionary, condemning to sudden obsolescence structures and processes which were themselves only recent; other changes have been perhaps less sudden and abrupt, but nonetheless just as far-reaching.

Dramatic advances in the technology of computer hardware have made it possible to create new computer systems which offer a tremendous increase in computing power, completely surpassing the capabilities of previous systems.

Far more evolutionary in nature has been the shift towards recognizing the importance of individual data structures and the relationships between them. It is no longer the individual computer program which is of greatest importance, but the underlying data structures and relationships which have now been recognized as one of the most valuable assets of any business organization. Much greater importance is therefore attached to the system which is primarily responsible for the secure and effective management of these data and their relationships, that is the *database system*. The data which are held by any organization, and the information thus made available, are now regarded as a key element of production, with the database management system recognized as the essential prerequisite for successfully managing this vital economic factor. Without a database system and the corresponding development tools it is simply not possible to develop the complex, flexible and portable computing systems which are required by both public and private organizations.

Complex systems are increasingly necessary to provide an adequate response to the many demands which are being made of both business and government organizations.

For manufacturing industry these include the need to maintain competitiveness, to shorten product life-cycles, to implement new, more flexible and sophisticated manufacturing and logistic technologies. It is only possible to achieve these goals through the comprehensive use of up-to-date electronic tools. Here it is not only the computer and networking systems which are important; the individual software components and in particular the database system are crucial factors for the success or failure of a given strategy.

Complex information systems are necessary in order to reflect adequately both the complexity of the inter-relationships which have to be recreated (the data models and structures), and the complexity of the processes which have to be implemented and executed (programs and functions). In addition they must be able to operate on the complex computer configurations which are already in common use. Characteristics of such configurations are:

- a variety of computers and operating systems,
- a variety of networks and network protocols,
- a variety of graphical and non-graphical user-interfaces.

A complex system of the type mentioned above can only be implemented if these various factors can be fully integrated and if the programs themselves are completely independent of the individual computer and networking systems in use. Of particular importance in this context is the database system, which not only has to store ever-increasing volumes of data, but must also allow rapid and secure access to these at all times.

The range of products currently provided by the Oracle Corporation can be divided into five product categories, each of which deals with particular aspects of the requirements posed by complex applications systems. Taken together, the ORACLE database system and its network technology can be viewed as providing some of the primary components required to design and build complex software systems which are independent of specific computer and network systems. The aim of this book is to describe the individual functions of these two product groups and to show how practical use can be made of them.

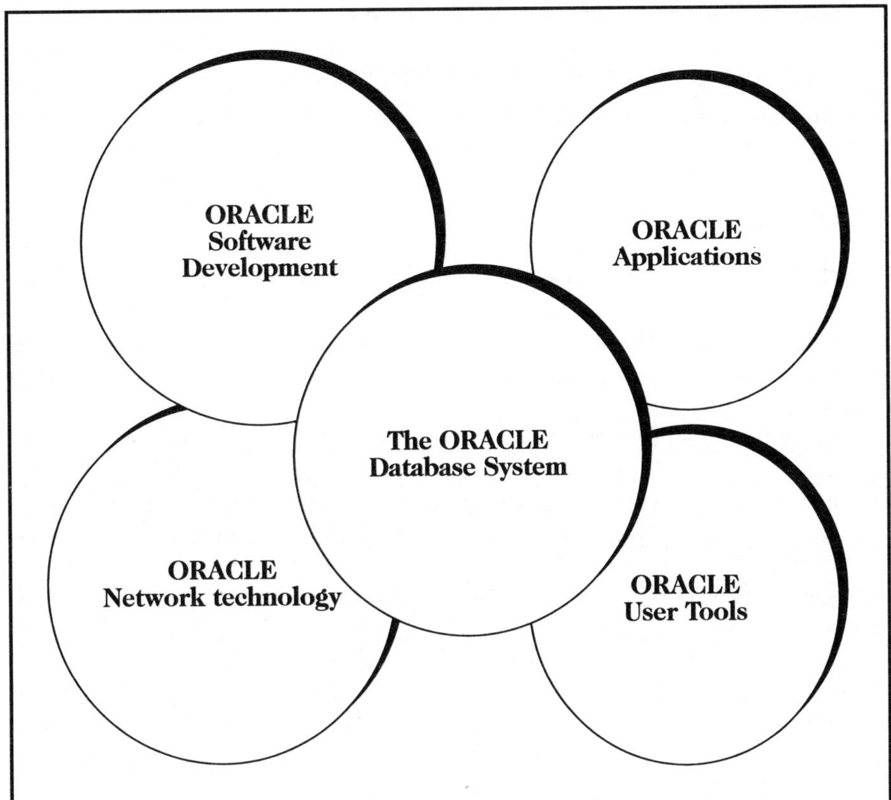

Figure 1.1 The ORACLE product groups

In considering the development of the ORACLE database system, it is possible to distinguish a number of phases, each of which was characterized by different technological and user requirements. These development phases were as follows:

- the pioneer phase (1977-1984)
- the management information system phase (1984-1988)
- the online transaction processing phase (OLTP) (1988-1992)

The OLTP phase in particular saw enormous demands being placed on the database system, requiring a powerful and secure system able to manage both a large number of simultaneous users as well as constantly increasing volumes of data. The ORACLE versions 6.0 and 6.2 (ORACLE Parallel Server) provided the technological basis for OLTP systems which could be implemented not only on traditional single processor and more advanced symmetric multi-processor (SMP) systems, but even on cluster and massively parallel systems. With these two versions of ORACLE a number of technological milestones were set including:

- unlimited record locking without escalation,
- consistent read access without data-locking,
- a fast commit mechanism,
- OLTP in parallel with online backup,
- online recovery,
- support for all relevant computer architectures.

All of these functions, which also became fully available on clustered systems, are essential for the implementation of powerful and sophisticated computer applications systems.

The next stage in this development is the need to implement these systems on a distributed basis, so that they become available to a large number of users. For companies striving to maintain their competitiveness, systems of this type are absolutely essential for improving the response time, flexibility and quality of their production processes or other services. Highly complex in terms of their (in some cases distributed) data structures, processes and configurations, such systems will form the backbone of the organizations of the 90s; by being independent of all computer architectures, operating systems and network protocols and by being able to overcome all the restrictions posed by incompatible user interfaces and different data sources, they ensure the complete integration of all the data and information available within any single organization.

Oracle7 has been specifically designed for the implementation of this type of system and is thus able to fulfil the following requirements:

- the management of a large number of users working in parallel;
- the administration of very large databases;
- unrestricted and uninterrupted system availability;
- a server able to guarantee the complete semantic integrity of all data in the database;
- the ability to configure client/server systems in homogeneous and heterogeneous network environments;
- distributed read and write access which is completely independent of location (that is the location of both user and data sources);
- the ability to manage complex, distributed OLTP systems.

Accordingly the development of Oracle7 had the following primary objectives:

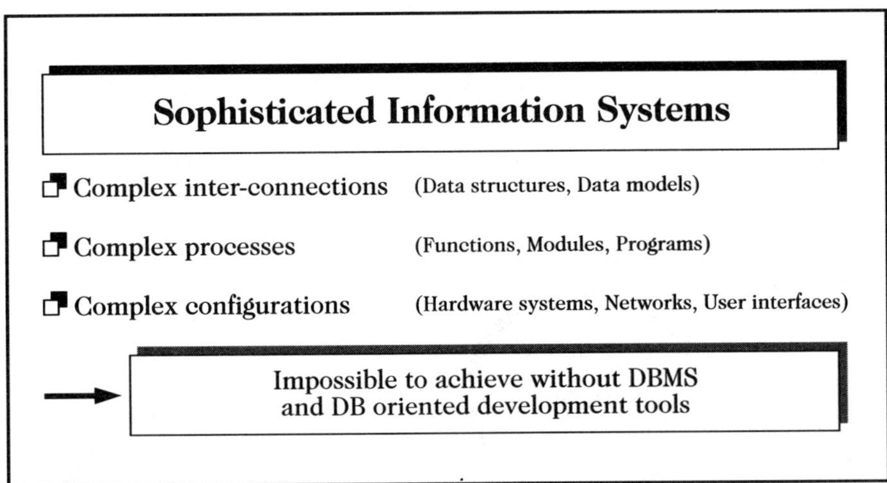

Figure 1.2 The demands placed on sophisticated information processing systems

- The implementation of a new, extended software architecture which would allow even more users or user processes to operate simultaneously on a given computer platform. The newly introduced multi-threaded server architecture (MTS) has been designed for online applications and, in particular, to support computer systems based on SMP (symmetric multiprocessor) architecture. In addition to the MTS functionality, a dedicated server architecture exists to support applications which access the database more frequently; this means that an optimum configuration is possible for each application according to its own specific characteristics (*see* Chapter 3.3). Oracle7 also provides support for clustered and massively parallel systems with the Oracle7 Parallel Server extension.
- The implementation of declarative and referential integrity rules and actions in accordance with the SQL standard as defined by ANSI and ISO. The syntax checking introduced with ORACLE Version 6 is actively supported by the server in Oracle7, but here the same attention has been given to administering these rules as to defining them, thus making it possible to activate and deactivate the rules as required. In addition any conflicts with the rules can be entered and processed in a separate exception table (*see* Chapter 9).
- The implementation of stored PL/SQL programs makes it possible to build software modules which remain resident in the database and are administered by the database server. Such modules are based on three software structures (functions, procedures and packages) and can be implemented in accordance with current ideas on software module technology (based on the Ada module concept). (*See* Chapters 7 *and* 8).

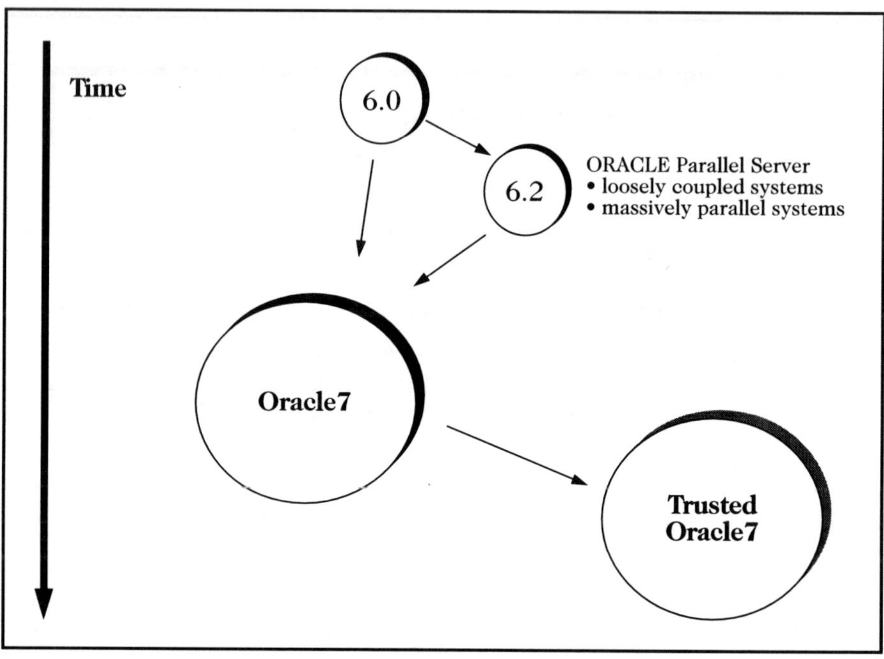

Figure 1.3 Development of the ORACLE database system

- The implementation of database triggers for the definition and integration of complex rules within the database itself. A database trigger is created like a stored PL/SQL program and is always assigned to a particular table. A database trigger is activated and processed when specific DML operations are carried out on the table in question (*see* Chapter 9).
- The implementation of a new database security concept based on the definition of roles and tasks. Thus those system or object privileges which are required to fulfil a certain task are assigned to a specific role. Once these privileges have been granted, the role can then be assigned either to other roles or to individual users (*see* Chapter 10).
- Oracle7 forms the basis for a specialized database system, Trusted Oracle7, which has been designed to deal with highly sensitive data which are subject to very strict security requirements (*see* Chapter 11). As well as providing all the functions available in Oracle7, Trusted Oracle7 provides a range of additional functions to support applications systems which are subject to stricter security requirements (B1).
- The implementation of transparent distributed transactions. By implementing a transparent two-phase commit protocol which is able to secure all distributed transactions without additional programming effort, it is possible to create complex distributed systems (*see* Chapters 13 *and* 14).

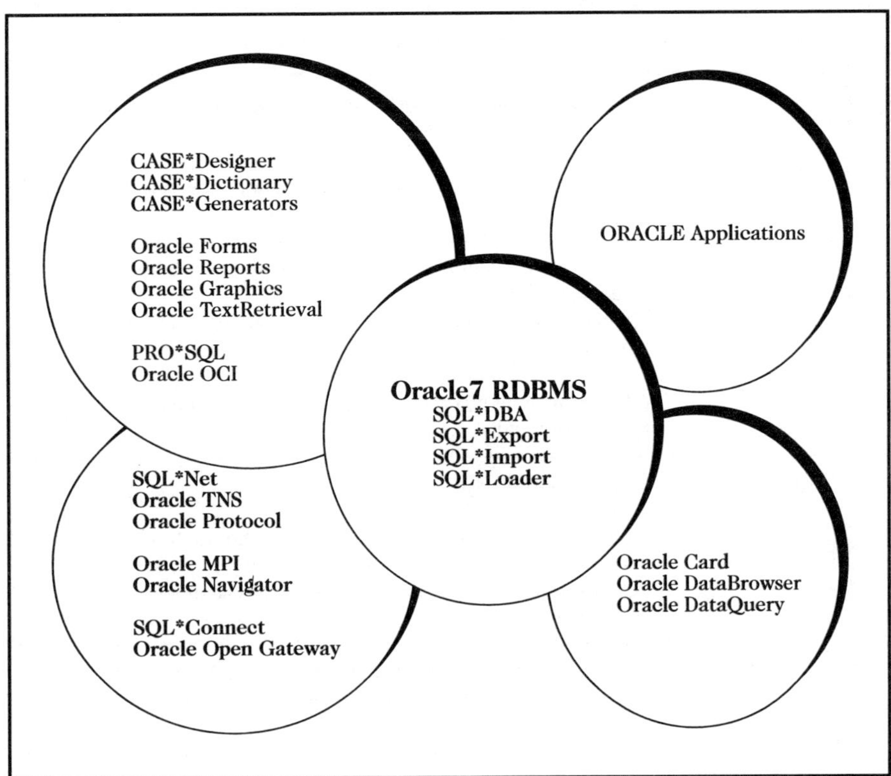

Figure 1.4 The ORACLE products and product groups

- In addition to the functions described above for databases, networks and for creating distributed systems, ORACLE also provides a further range of products; these cover both software development as well as simple and elegant tools which make it possible to work with the database without any knowledge of the database language SQL (ORACLE end-user tools).

Figure 1.4 lists the most important ORACLE products and they are then briefly described in Table 1.1.

ORACLE Programs	Summary of Program Functions
SQL*DBA	Provides the database administrator with all the functions necessary to create, start, stop, backup, recover and monitor a database. The SQL*DBA program can be used both in line mode (command mode) and in full screen mode.
SQL*Loader	Provides the functions to load external files into an ORACLE database. Supports many different file formats including the DXT format used by IBM mainframes. Large volumes of data can be loaded with the 'Direct Path' loader. When this option is used, the SQL*Loader program can process data very rapidly.
SQL*Export	SQL*Export is used to carry out a logical backup of an ORACLE database. The program can be used in different modes, each of which provides a different level of backup security. It is also possible to carry out incremental export procedures. The different export modes are: MODE 1 : to backup individual tables. MODE 2 : to backup all the database objects of a single user. MODE 3 : to backup an entire database (DBA privilege is required).
SQL*Import	SQL*Import is used to load any part of a database which has previously been exported with the SQL*Export program. The program can be used to port data and programs from one computer (operating system) to another.

Table 1.1a

ORACLE Programs	Summary of Program Functions
CASE*Designer **CASE*Dictionary** **CASE*Generators**	This group of products provides support for the database designer through every stage of the database and function design cycle. The design methodology is based on the entity relationship model design. The programs make it possible to incorporate a wide range of referential integrity checks. The structure of a database can be generated automatically. The CASE*Generators make it possible to produce highly developed prototypes for a range of ORACLE programs: Oracle Forms, SQL*Menu, Oracle Reports and SQL*Plus. **CASE*Designer:** Provides a graphical interface for designing a database (developing an entity relationship model), for function and process modelling, for creating dataflow diagrams and matrix diagrams. **CASE*Dictionary:** Provides the central CASE information repository, storing all information which is relevant to a project. This information can be used to generate a complete database. **CASE*Generators:** These can be used to generate complex prototypes for applications programs.
SQL*Plus	This is a comfortable interactive SQL interpreter which allows the user to enter everything from a single SQL statement through to complex SQL*Plus procedures and PL/SQL programs. SQL*Plus is mainly used for developing programs in SQL, allowing the system developer to test SQL statements, PL/SQL programs and database triggers.
Oracle Forms	This provides a means of developing interactive programs on the basis of a visual, event-driven programming technology. All the program objects are stored in the database and can then be used to generate executable programs. A large number of standard settings and the use of the Oracle Forms trigger concept means that applications can be developed extremely efficiently and quickly.

Table 1.1b

ORACLE Programs	Summary of Program Functions
Oracle Reports	This provides a means of creating complex reports. The developer is presented with a graphical interface with which to define the functions and layout of a given report. All the program objects in a report are stored in the database, and are then used to generate the executable report program.
Oracle Graphics	This provides a means of graphically displaying the data in the database. This program can be integrated into Oracle Forms and Oracle Reports. Programs can be written in PL/SQL in order to develop sophisticated graphical applications systems. The functions to develop graphical systems form part of the Oracle Forms and Oracle Reports programs.
Oracle TextRetrieval	This provides a means of managing and processing non-structured data (text and pictures). Texts of unlimited length can be stored in the database and searched through according to their content. 3GL and 4GL program libraries are also provided so that text retrieval functions can easily be integrated into Oracle Forms applications.

Table 1.1c

ORACLE Programs	Summary of Program Functions
Pro*SQL	This tool provides a means of integrating SQL with standard programming languages. SQL commands, stored PL/SQL procedures and PL/SQL blocks can be entered directly into the code of a 3GL program, and these are then converted into ORACLE calls by a precompiler. Dynamic SQL can also be made use of in this way. Precompilers are available for the following programming languages: C, FORTRAN, COBOL, PL/1, Pascal and Ada.
SQL*Module	This tool provides a means of integrating SQL with standard programming languages. The functions in SQL*Module are primarily intended to support the development of program modules and the use of the corresponding program interfaces. The program modules can be written either in a 3GL language or in PL/SQL.
OCI	OCI stands for Oracle Call Interface and represents the call interface for 3GL programs. Program calls which stand for SQL statements are inserted into a 3GL program, which can then be compiled without having to be processed by a precompiler. It is however considerably more difficult to develop programs with the OCI than by using the Pro*SQL or SQL*Module methods.

Table 1.1d

2

Introduction to SQL (Part 1)

Topics covered in this chapter

- The origins of SQL
- SQL and relational database technology
- SQL command types
- The language structures of SQL
- Complex processing with SQL
- SQL environments (3GL, 4GL, ORACLE tools)
- The current status of SQL

2 Introduction to SQL (Part 1)

2.1 Introduction

The database language SQL is the primary means of communication between applications programs and the ORACLE database system. For this reason SQL commands will frequently be referred to throughout this book or will be used to illustrate various operations.

This first section of the introduction to SQL sets out to present the basic concepts of SQL, without in any way aiming to be a complete guide to the language (there are many excellent books available which provide a comprehensive guide to SQL). Part 2 of the introduction to SQL (Chapter 7) deals with ORACLE's procedural language extension (PL/SQL) Version 2.0, which forms the basis for implementing stored procedures, functions, PL/SQL packages and database triggers.

2.2 Historical background

The history of the database language SQL (also pronounced sequel) is directly related to the development of the relational database model, which was first put forward in 1970 in an article written by Edgar F. Codd, a member of IBM's scientific staff. At that time database technology was characterized by hierarchical and network database systems which had proved unable to satisfy the following demands:

- to reduce the programmer's workload,
- to make programs and data functionally independent,
- to make data structures more flexible,
- to allow end-users access to data.

In his work Codd was able to demonstrate that in theory the relational database model could eliminate the shortcomings of the systems available at that time. Put very simply it consisted of two important elements: a data structure comprising two-dimensional tables and a database language which, on the basis of relational algebra, would allow all necessary database operations to be carried out.

This theoretical paper had a galvanizing effect on many researchers in the field of database technology and as a result many research projects were set up in university laboratories and in the research centres of the major DP companies. The goal of all these activities was to develop software which implemented Codd's theory and which would provide a new and usable database system.

One of the most important of these projects was the System R Project which ran from 1974 to 1977 at the IBM Research Centre in San Jose, and which involved a huge commitment in terms of financial and human resources. This project was realized in two phases. In phase 0 System R was conceived as a single-user database system, priority being given to the physical access methods and above all to the definition and development of the relational database language SQL (Structured Query Language), as well as to 'automatic' access optimization (SQL Optimizer). The decisive concepts which still characterize the SQL language today were defined during this period.

In the course of phase 1, System R was developed into a fully functioning DBMS offering multi-user functions and already possessing all necessary backup and recovery functions. A number of important conclusions were drawn from this research project:

1. It was indeed possible to implement a relational database system with the hardware available at the time.

2. As a non-procedural language based on set theory SQL proved able to provide effective support for programmers and to greatly increase their productivity.
3. The automatic access optimization of SQL resulted in a hitherto unknown degree of data independence. Changes in access structures and access paths as well as certain changes in data structures could indeed be concealed from the actual programs which used them.

In 1977 the System R project was completed and the results of its research published; this led to a number of new firms being established, each aiming to develop relational database systems on the basis of SQL. Oracle which was founded in 1977 is a typical example of this type of company.

The present dominance of SQL – there is no other database language of comparable importance or one that is so widely used – is based on the following factors:

- By the end of the 1970s viable SQL database systems were available through independent software houses, ORACLE Version 2 being the first commercially available relational database system based on SQL.
- At the beginning of the 1980s IBM announced two SQL database systems: SQL/DS for DOS/VSE and VM machines and DB2 for MVS machines. This announcement meant that relational systems became 'socially acceptable' for major computer users.
- SQL was submitted to the committee of the American National Standards Institute (ANSI) which in 1986 issued the first SQL standard.

2.3 The internal structure of SQL

The name Structured Query Language would seem to suggest that SQL is merely a query language. This impression has been reinforced by the vendors of SQL database systems and by literature which emphasize the language's query functions. However from the beginning SQL was conceived of as a complete database language which would be able to cover all aspects of database technology.

SQL can be sub-divided in terms of the following functions:

- Data definition (DDL)
  to define data structures within the database.
- Data manipulation (DML)
  to modify data within the database.
- Data retrieval
  to read and present data from the database.

- Data security
  to define access rights to objects in the database.
- Data integrity
  to guarantee operational integrity.
- Data management
  to administer the entire database.

Command type	Command examples	SQL code examples

Data definition	`create table / alter table`
	`create or replace view`
	`create index`
		`create table test (`
		`num number(8) not null primary key,`
		`text varchar2(350) );`

Data retrieval	`select`
	` from`
	` where`
		`select *`
		`from <table>`
		`where num > 4711;`

Data manipulation	`insert`
	`update`
	`delete`
		`update test`
		`set text = 'ABC'`
		`where num = 4711;`

Database security	`create role`
	`grant <priv> to role`
	`create view`
		`create role junior_dba;`
		`grant <priv> to junior_dba;`

Database integrity	`commit`
	`rollback ( to <savepoint>)`
	`savepoint <savepoint_name>`
		`commit;`

Database administration	`create database`
	`create tablespace`
	`create profile`
		`create profile <prof_name>`
		` cpu_per_session <n>`
		` idle_time <n>;`

Figure 2.1 The structures of the SQL language

In the following paragraphs these functions of the language will be presented in greater detail together with corresponding SQL examples. The examples will be based on a simple data structure which is shown in Figure 2.2 as an E/R (entity relationship) diagram.

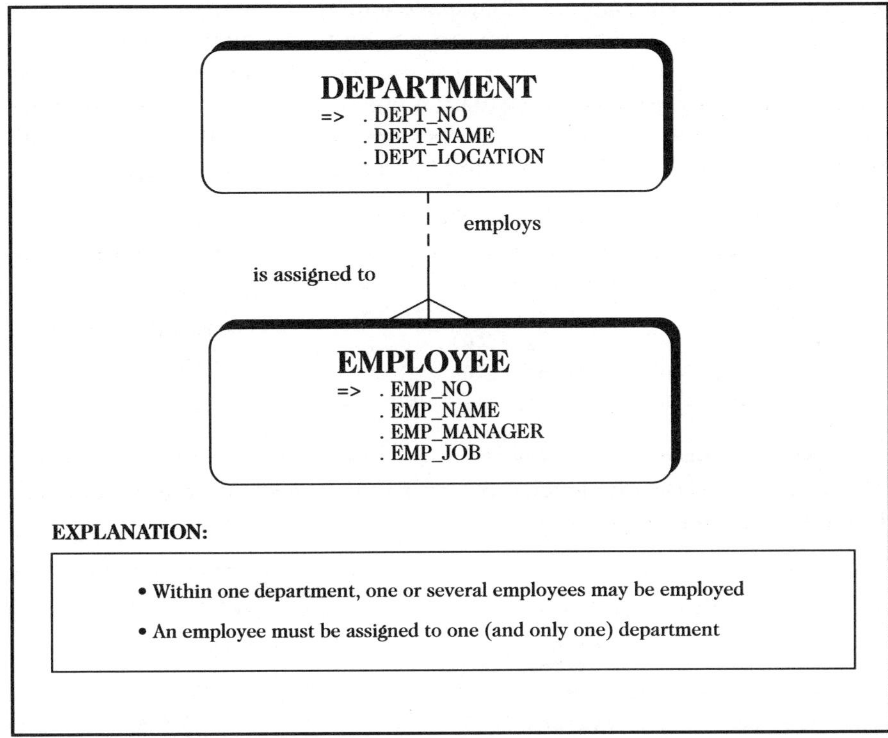

Figure 2.2 Example of a data structure represented as an E/R diagram

2.3.1 Data definition language (DDL)

The commands which are grouped under the term Data Definition Language (DDL) are used to define (CREATE), to change (ALTER) and to delete (DROP) data and access structures. In this case it is possible to differentiate between the following database objects:

- tables
- views
- indexes
- table clusters
- stored packages, procedures and functions
- database triggers
- snapshots and snapshot logs (*see* Chapter 14)
- sequences (number generators)

Data definition operations will be discussed here with reference to tables, views and indexes. Other ORACLE objects such as stored packages, procedures and functions as well as ORACLE database triggers will be discussed in detail in their own chapters (Chapters 8 and 9).

The primary data structure underlying any relational database is the *table* where an object from the real world having been identified by the system design process as an information entity, is given a name and all its attendant attributes and their data types are defined. To define the simple E/R model depicted in Figure 2.2 with SQL the following two SQL commands are necessary:

```
create table department (
dept_no           number(4) constraint dept_pk primary key,
dept_name         varchar2(40),
dept_location     varchar2(40)     );
```

The above command creates the departmental table and the following command creates the employee table with all the necessary requirements of declarative and referential integrity.

```
create table employee (
emp_no            number(8) not null,
emp_name          varchar2(20),
emp_manager       number(8),
emp_job           varchar2(20),
emp_deptno        number(4),
constraint emp_pk primary key (emp_no),
constraint emp_fk
foreign key (emp_deptno)
references department(dept_no)     );
```

Every table is given a name and is made up of a number of different attributes, also called the *columns* of the table, with each column having an ORACLE data type assigned to it. All the ORACLE data types are shown together in Figure 2.3. In addition three explicit, named constraints are defined in this example, `dept_pk`, `emp_pk` and `emp_fk`. These constraints define the primary and foreign keys and establish the relationship between these two objects. Explicit constraint names are of great benefit because, in the event of a constraint being violated, the system outputs the corresponding constraint name as well as the error number, thus making it much easier to identify the underlying cause of the error.

Once the two CREATE TABLE statements have been executed the structures are entered in the ORACLE data dictionary and can then be used to store data.

Data Type	Description	Max Values	Example
`char(n)`	Fixed length character data of length n bytes. All n bytes are used, where necessary filled with blanks.	255 Bytes	`char(40)`
`varchar(n)`	Currently still a synonym for `varchar2`. Oracle recommends the use of `varchar2`.	2000 Bytes	`varchar(80)`
`varchar2(n)`	Variable length character string with maximum length of n bytes. Only uses the number of bytes actually filled.	2000 Bytes	`varchar2(35)`
`number(v,n)`	Numeric data type for `integer` and `real` values. v = Places before the decimal point n = Places after the decimal point	v=38 n= –84 to +127	`number(8)` `number(12,4)`
`date`	Data type for storing the date and time. 7 bytes are used for each entry, 4 for the date and 3 for the time.	31.12.4712	`date`
`raw(n)`	Data type for storing binary data.	2000 Bytes	`raw(1500)`
`long`	Data type for character data of variable length.	2GB	`long`
`long raw`	Data type for storing binary data of up to 2 gigabytes. Column size is variable.	2GB	`long raw`

Figure 2.3 Summary of the ORACLE data types

The structure of a table which has already been defined can be changed using the command ALTER TABLE. In this case two structural changes are possible:

- New columns can be added:

```
alter table employee add (emp_dob date);
```

- Existing columns can be extended:

```
alter table employee modify (emp_name varchar2(40));
```

In order to delete a table including all its data, its indexes and access rights the command DROP TABLE is used. In this case all the data dictionary information is deleted and the storage space occupied by the table is again made available to the database system.

In contrast to a table which is physically present in the database and which occupies storage space there, a *view* is a *virtual* table, which has no physical existence and which apart from the view definition itself occupies no storage space in the database. At runtime the data are made available according to the view definition with the help of the SQL SELECT command. The following simple view is based on a single table:

```
create view employee_20 (number, name) as
select          emp_no, emp_name
from            employee
where           emp_deptno = 20
with check option;
```

In the case of this view the two columns **emp_no** and **emp_name** are selected from the base table **employee** which in view **employee_20** are given the column names **number** and **name**. This can be seen as the *vertical* aspect of the view (the *projection*).

In addition only those records are returned which satisfy the WHERE condition; this represents the *horizontal* aspect of the view (the *selection*). All other rows, which do not satisfy the view's condition, are not returned and cannot be modified.

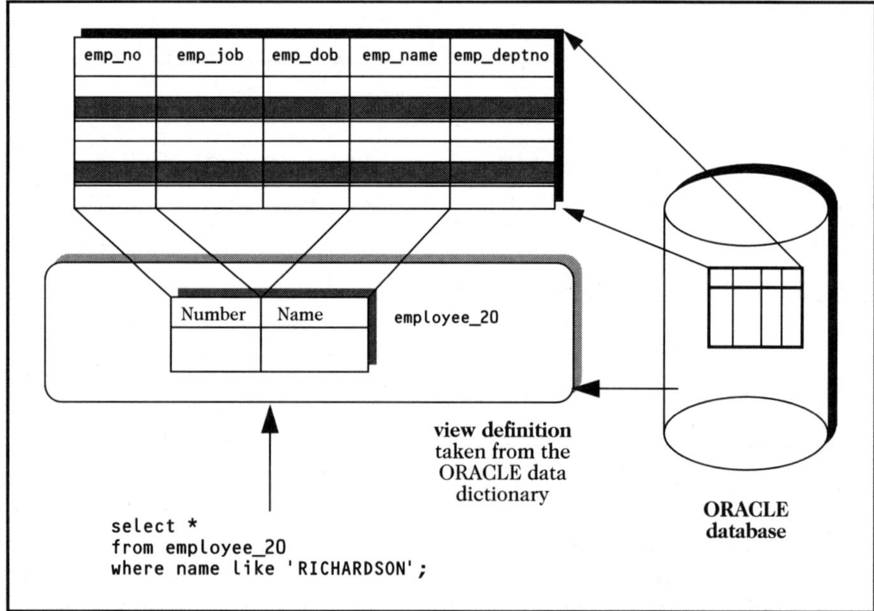

Figure 2.4 Implementing a view

Once the above CREATE VIEW command has been entered the underlying select statement is stored in the ORACLE data dictionary under the view's name `employee_20` and is referenced by SQL commands which use the view's name instead of the table name.

The SQL command:

```
select * from employee_20
where name like 'RICHARDSON';
```

references the view `employee_20`, reading its definition from the data dictionary and linking this to the external conditions specified (`name like 'Richardson'`). *See also* Figure 2.4.

The effect of defining a view is to impose a filter over the mass of available information, so that only those data which satisfy the view's conditions are selected.

The use of views has two main advantages:

1. Views can be used to conceal complex operations such as joins across several tables, groupings or nested sub-queries. Any SQL statements which use these complex views therefore become easier to formulate, more manageable and thus less prone to error.
2. Views are able to provide additional data security, as a user only needs to be given rights to use the view but not to access the underlying data structures. This simple technique provides an efficient means of data security which can also be made user-dependent.

A typical example for the use of views is in controlling user access to the ORACLE data dictionary, which is completely defined by views (*see also* Chapter 3). In this case very complex views are used, often defined across several hierarchies (a view of a view of a view...). A brief look at the definitions file CATALOG.SQL, in which all the view definitions of the ORACLE data dictionary are stored, reveals this complexity and gives some insight into how powerful this technique is.

Whereas the table and view commands serve to create the actual user data structures, indexes are used to provide access paths to the data so that it is possible to rapidly retrieve those records which are defined through the WHERE clause of a SQL command. When a SQL statement is to be executed the SQL optimizer determines which is the best possible (most efficient, fastest) access path to the data. In general we distinguish between two types of indexes, the unique index and the non-unique index. When a UNIQUE index is created the column values on which it is based must be unique throughout the entire table. A UNIQUE index is always automatically created whenever one or more columns are defined with the PRIMARY KEY or

UNIQUE attributes. Additional UNIQUE indexes may however be created at any time, including when the system is operational, by use of the following command:

```
create unique index <index_name>
on <table_name> (column1, column2,...);
```

If more than one column name is given after the table name, this is referred to as a composite index, and can consist of up to 16 columns. A non-unique index should be created for all foreign keys and in certain circumstances for columns which are frequently accessed. The command:

```
create index emp_ind1
on employee(emp_deptno);
```

creates an index on the table `employee`. This index may contain duplicate values.

It is not essential to create an index but in order to achieve acceptable levels of performance the following indexes should always be created:

- a UNIQUE index on the primary key (the ORACLE system does this automatically for all primary key constraints);
- non-unique indexes on all foreign keys;
- non-unique indexes on columns which are often queried and which have high selectivity.

2.3.2 Data retrieval

RELEASE 7.1

As we mentioned earlier the data retrieval command SELECT is one of the most frequently used SQL commands and is indeed often regarded as being synonymous with SQL itself; it is therefore hardly surprising that some DBMS systems claim to be SQL-based simply because they incorporate this command in some form or other. The purpose of the SELECT command is to read data from the database and to present these data in a specified form. Simple though this explanation may seem, the SELECT command is by far the most complex of all SQL commands, capable of carrying out any number of widely differing tasks. Without going into each of these in detail the following list gives some idea of the wide range of functions provided:

- simple queries
- queries with subqueries
- queries with correlating subqueries
- joins
- outer joins
- grouped queries
- representing hierarchical structures such as bills of materials
- sorted results
  - sorted in ascending order
  - sorted in descending order
  - sorted randomly

RELEASE 7.1

A simple query for example could look like this:

```
select * from employee;
```

This statement would display all columns and rows of the table employee. The key word SELECT is always followed by a list of the columns to be returned, with the asterisk standing for all the columns of the table specified in the FROM clause.

If specific columns or rows are to be retrieved the column names are given in the field list of the SELECT clause. Which records are selected is determined by conditions specified in the WHERE clause. Thus the statement:

```
select   emp_name, emp_job
from     employee
where    emp_name like 'A%' or
         emp_job = 'PROGRAMMER';
```

returns the name and job title of all employees either whose name begins with A (% is a wild card for any number of characters) or whose job title is 'PROGRAMMER'. If the result of this statement needs to be sorted according to name then the ORDER BY clause must be added:

```
order by emp_name
```

Data can be sorted in either ascending (ASC) or descending order (DESC), but in practice these two options often prove inadequate to meet user requirements for data to be sorted in a specified order. If for example all employee records must be output so that first all records for Department 20 are returned, then those of Department 10 and finally the employee records for Department 30, then the following statement has to be entered:

RELEASE 7.1

```
select *
from  employee
order by decode(emp_deptno,  10,2,
                             20,1,
                             30,3,100);
```

In this case the SQL DECODE function redefines the weighting of the sort process depending on the employee's department number. For the sorting process the 10 is changed to a 2, the 20 to a 1 and as a consequence the employee data of Department 20 are returned before those of Department 10.

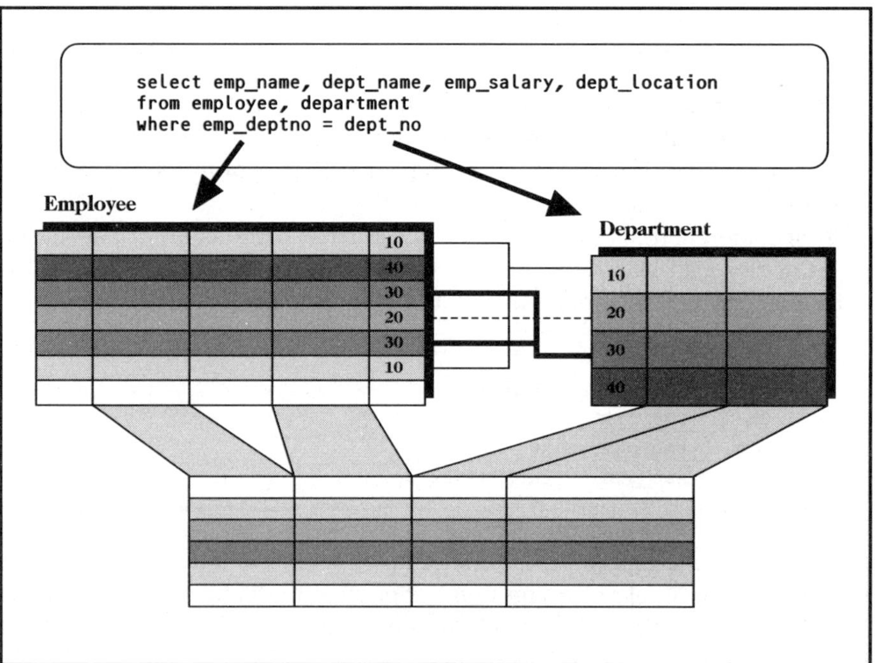

Figure 2.5 Example of an (inner) join operation

A very common database operation is a *join* of several tables whereby the data of two or more tables are returned together. If for example information is required about employees together with data about their departments (from the `department` table), then the following statement has to be entered:

```
select     emp_name, dept_name, emp_salary, dept_location
from       employee, department
where      emp_deptno = dept_no;
```

RELEASE 7.1

In this statement the two tables to be 'joined' are listed in the FROM clause, with the WHERE clause specifying the columns which are to form the link between the tables concerned. The columns specified in the field list are returned whenever the value for department number in the employee table matches that in the department table.

Another interesting application of the SELECT command is its use in representing any kind of hierarchical structure, such as a bill of materials or the structure of an organization. A data structure of this kind can be modelled by simply entering in each record its position relative to the preceding level. Using a simple organigram, Figure 2.6 shows an hierarchical data structure and how this can be converted into tabular form.

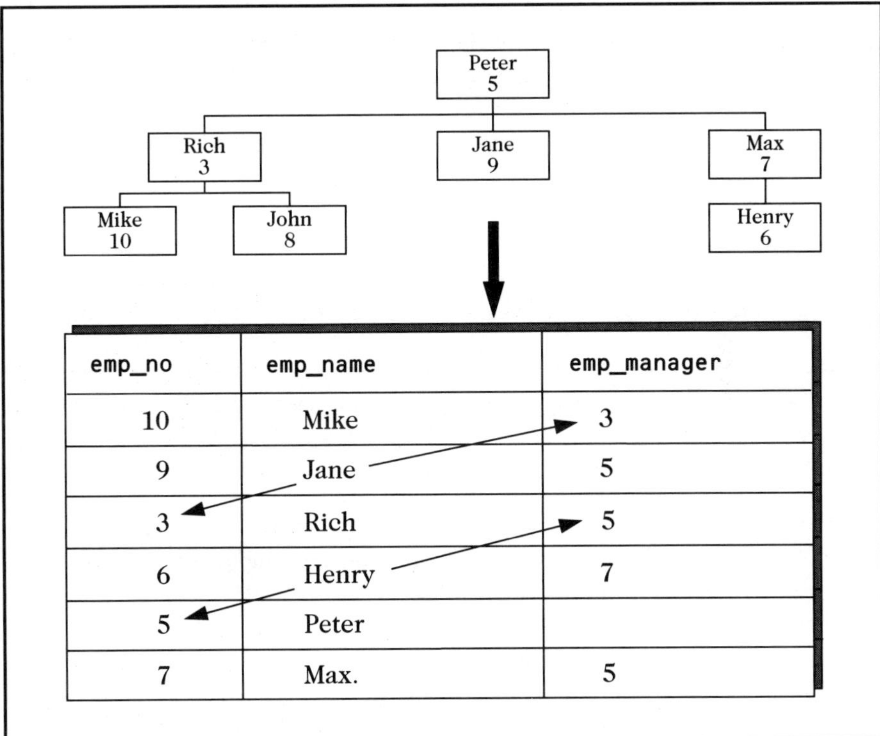

emp_no	emp_name	emp_manager
10	Mike	3
9	Jane	5
3	Rich	5
6	Henry	7
5	Peter	
7	Max.	5

Figure 2.6 Representation of an hierarchical data structure

In this representation the column `emp_manager` contains the number of each employee's respective superior. In order to present this type of data structure with SQL the following statement must be used:

```
select                *
from                  employee
connect by prior      emp_no = emp_manager
start with            emp_no = 5;
```

In this case the CONNECT BY clause describes the hierarchical dependency which exists (*see also* the arrows in Figure 2.6) and the START WITH clause defines the record at which the representation of the structure should begin (the root node). Such hierarchical structures can be represented both 'top-down' as well as 'bottom up'.

2.3.3 Data manipulation language (DML)

Having defined the underlying data and access structures it is now possible to consider how the data stored in the individual tables can be modified using SQL. In this case three basic operations are available:

- Adding records (INSERT)
- Modifying records (UPDATE)
- Deleting records (DELETE)

A single record can be inserted into a table with the following command:

```
insert into department  (dept_no, dept_name, dept_location)
values                  (99, 'DP', 'STUTTGART');
```

Here the column names refer to the corresponding constants in the VALUES clause. In the context of a programming language these constants are usually replaced by program variables.

In the case of the statement:

```
insert into department  (dept_no, dept_name, dept_location)
values                  (:var_no, :var_name, :var_location);
```

the INSERT command takes the program variables (identified by a leading colon) and enters their values in the database. To transfer data from another table or view the following command could be used:

```
insert into employee
select *
from personnel
where pers_job like 'PROG%';
```

This statement transfers records from the `personnel` table (or view), to the `employee` table, taking all rows where the job description begins with `PROG` (`%` is the wild card to denote any sequence of characters). For the purposes of this example it is assumed that the structure of the two database objects `employee` and `personnel` is identical.

Changes to data values within a table are carried out using the UPDATE command, which defines the tables, columns and rows which are to be altered. A rise in salary for all employees of department 30 is programmed as follows:

```
update   employee
set      emp_salary    =    emp_salary*1.10
where    emp_deptno    =    30;
```

The SET clause may contain constants, variables, or any arithmetic expressions. If, within one UPDATE command, different increases are to be carried out for different departments, the SQL function DECODE, which we have already come across, can be made use of.

```
update   employee
set      emp_salary = decode(emp_deptno,10,emp_salary*1.10,
                                        20,emp_salary*1.05,
                                        30,emp_salary*1.15,
                                        emp_salary);
```

In this case the employees receive different salary increases according to which department they belong to: for department 10, a ten percent increase, for department 20, five percent and so on. As this command does not contain a WHERE clause it affects all the rows in the table. In this example the SQL DECODE function is used to determine which arithmetic expression is carried out on the corresponding rows. The DECODE function is one of approximately seventy ORACLE SQL functions (these include SUBSTR, ROUND, SIN, COS, TRANSLATE and INITCAP) which are used very frequently and have proved to be indispensable.

Another interesting use of the SELECT command is within the SET clause of an UPDATE statement. In this case the new value to be set is determined at runtime by a SELECT command (possibly on a different table). This is illustrated in the following example, where the salary for a new employee (identified by the lack of a salary value) is to be set at 10 percent less than the current average salary within the corresponding department. The statement is as follows:

```
update              employee emp1
set emp_salary      = (select avg(emp_salary)*0.9
                    from employee emp2
                    where emp1.emp_deptno = emp2.emp_deptno)
where emp_salary is null;
```

This command is carried out for all employees for whom no salary value has yet been set, these being identified by the external WHERE clause `where emp_salary is null`. For these employees, the average salary (`avg(emp_salary)`) for the respective department is calculated and reduced by 10 percent (`*0.9`). The resulting value becomes the new employee's salary.

The last command available for DML operations is the DELETE command, with which records are deleted from the database. As with the other commands, a WHERE clause can be used to define how many records are to be simultaneously deleted within one statement. If for example all employees older than 65 are to be deleted from the employee table, then the following DELETE command would be required:

```
delete      from employee
where       emp_dob <= add_months(sysdate,-65*12);
```

The effect of this command is to delete all records in which the date of birth is smaller than or equal to (<=) the value returned by the date function `add_months(...)`, in this case the individuals are older than 65. In the above example this function calculates 65 years back (`-65 years*12 months`) from the present date (`sysdate`) and returns the required date as its result.

2.3.4 Database integrity and database administration

Until now database modifications have been looked at mainly in terms of individual commands. Looking at the database system as a whole such operations take the database from one consistent state into another and it is an essential requirement of today's database systems that no situation be allowed to occur in which the database is left in an inconsistent state. It is for this reason that the concept of the *transaction* has been developed. A transaction is an atomic database action which takes the database from one consistent state to another. A transaction may consist of one SQL statement which only changes a single row or of a group of SQL statements in which each single statement changes a large number of rows.

Database transactions are controlled by the following SQL commands:

- COMMIT
  completes a transaction positively so that all changes carried out within the transaction are entered in the database and made 'permanent' there.
- ROLLBACK (TO `<save_point_name>`)
  completes a transaction or partial transaction negatively so that all changes which were carried out within the transaction are reversed.
- SAVEPOINT `<save_point_name>`
  defines a point within a transaction to which it is possible to return with the ROLLBACK command.

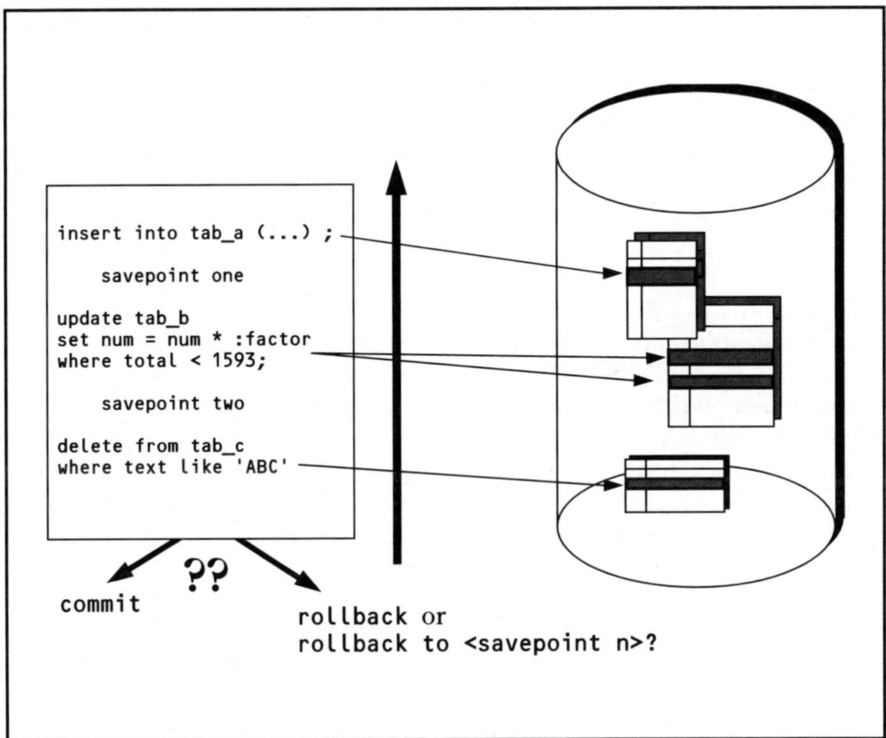

Figure 2.7 Transaction control

Apart from the read, alter and transaction commands there is a further group of SQL commands which can be used for organizing the database. These commands are used to administer the database and cover, amongst others, the following tasks:

- creating and extending a database
- starting-up and shutting down a database
- recovering a database after a hardware error
- checking database activity (monitor)
- tuning the database

2.4 Further uses of SQL

The original aim of the developers of SQL was to design and implement a language which could be used both interactively and could also be embedded within third generation programming languages such as C, COBOL, FORTRAN and PL/1.

A third application of SQL has come with the development of powerful programming systems produced by the vendors of relational databases. Within its own software development environment for example, Oracle offers an integrated range of tools which contains a CASE system with 4GL generators, a 4GL product line as well as a 3GL product line. With the aid of the Oracle CASE generators it is possible to produce a sophisticated applications system on the basis of an initial system specification. This applications system will contain complex SQL command sequences with which an ORACLE (or other) database can be accessed.

Despite the ever-increasing importance of SQL-based programming tools many applications are still programmed in third generation languages such as COBOL, C, FORTRAN, PL/1, Pascal or Ada. If these programs have to communicate with a database and exchange data, then it is necessary to insert SQL commands into the programs. As the programming languages mentioned above bear no relation to SQL (COBOL and C do not have any commands like CREATE TABLE or UPDATE), the SQL embedding procedure was introduced and standardized so that SQL could be used with these languages. When a 3GL program is being developed the programmer can insert SQL commands at any point in the source code, denoting these with the prefix EXEC SQL. Once coding has been completed the program is processed by a precompiler, which transforms the SQL commands into sections of source code in the programming language being used. The source code produced by the precompiler can subsequently be translated by the standard compiler and then linked to the necessary SQL libraries in order to produce a working program. Figure 2.8 shows the typical series of actions in generating a program, with the precompiler forming an additional phase in this sequence.

There are methods for incorporating embedded SQL, the *static* and the *dynamic*. In the case of static embedded SQL (static SQL for short) the SQL command is fixed when the program is written, so that at runtime only the values for the input variables (also called bind variables) remain to be assigned. A typical static SQL command could be:

```
exec sql select   emp_name, emp_salary
            into   :name, :salary
            from   employee
           where   emp_deptno = :d_no
```

The input variable in this example is the variable `:d_no`. The colon in front of the variable signals to the precompiler that this is a program variable and not the column name of a database object. When the program is being run values are assigned to these program variables which are then used in executing the SELECT command. The results of the SELECT statement are returned via the INTO clause to the program variables `:name` and `:salary` and are then available for any further processing within the program. (Outside of SQL commands the program variables are defined without a colon.)

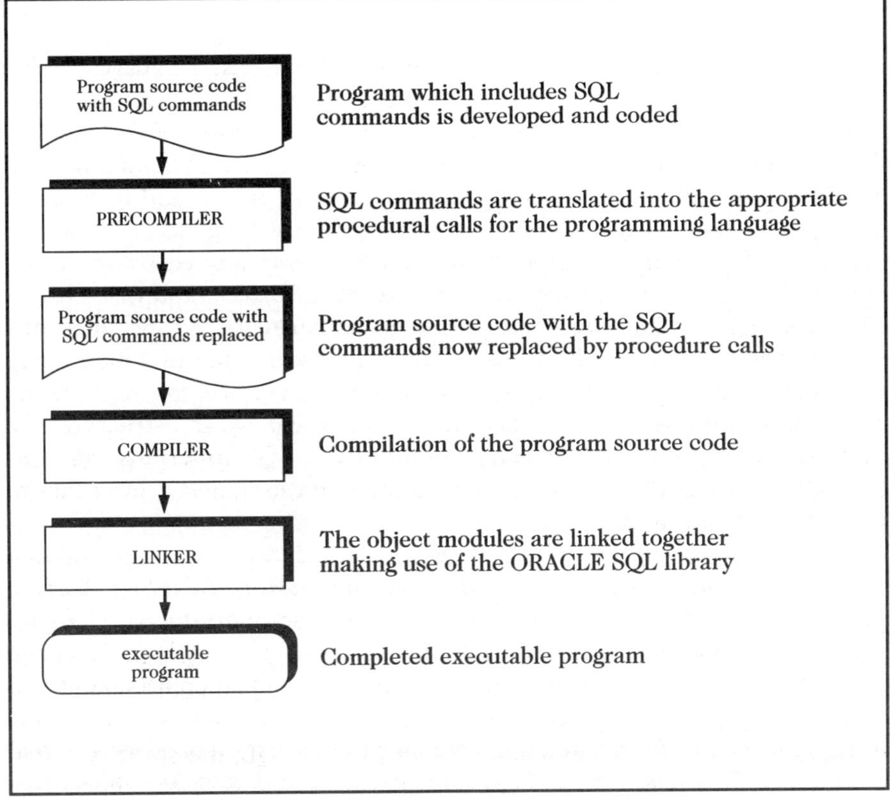

Figure 2.8 Developing a 3GL program with SQL

In the case of dynamic embedded SQL (dynamic SQL for short) the SQL command has not yet been defined when the program is started. Only once the program is running is the SQL command transferred to a program variable and then precompiled, optimized and executed. In comparison with static SQL, it is much more difficult to program with dynamic SQL, however it does allow extremely compact and flexible applications to be produced which, provided that runtime parsing and linking are optimized, are hardly any slower to run than with static SQL. A dynamic SQL statement can be:

- entered interactively by the user
  (using dynamic SQL it is possible to program a SQL interpreter with relatively little effort);
- generated by the program; or
- read from a database table containing SQL commands (allowing program control by means of database tables).

2.5 SQL standardization

The dominance of SQL in the field of relational database languages (today there are practically no database system vendors who are not working on at least one SQL interface) was established mainly as a result of the standardization of SQL in 1986 by the ANSI committee (American National Standards Institute). This decision in SQL's favour put an end to years of controversy about the correct relational database language. The actual standards document which standardized SQL was passed by the ANSI committee in 1986 and bears the title *ANSI-SQL X3.135-1986 (ISO 9075)*. Although SQL became the dominant database language as a result of this standardization, the standard itself is only a minimal one in which many necessary linguistic constructs are not defined. There are, for example, no commands to delete a table (DROP TABLE) or to change the structure of a table (ALTER TABLE). Furthermore none of the SQL functions (such as DECODE, SUBSTR, INITCAP, ROUND) has a place in the standard, even though they are of great practical value.

A standard for embedded SQL was not included either. This situation was not corrected until 1989 with the document *EMBEDDED-SQL X3.168-1989*, which defined the functions of the precompilers for C, COBOL, FORTRAN, Pascal and PL/1, although here too only at a very basic level and without taking account of dynamic SQL. In 1989 a further document was added to the existing standard describing how the conditions for referential integrity should be formulated when defining the tables of a database (*Addendum I X3.135.1*). The current SQL standard *ANSI-SQL X3.135-1989* consisting of the original 1986 standard as well as the two extensions for embedded

SQL and for referential integrity, still does not offer the functionality necessary for the practical use of a database language. For this reason the scope and functionality of the language provided by ORACLE is considerably greater than that specified in the SQL standard. The SQL standard does however form a subset of ORACLE SQL and programmers who only wish to use the ANSI/ISO SQL standard are supported by the ORACLE FIPS Flagger which flags all non-ANSI SQL statements during the precompiler stage and issues an appropriate warning.

As a result of the points mentioned above, the current SQL standard is criticised by both users and vendors of SQL databases, and for this reason the further development of the SQL standard (often called SQL2) is being discussed in a more broadly based committee which is drawn from database vendors and user groups. This standard will contain a large number of functions which are already provided by the ORACLE database system. These include:

- Date/time data types
- Date arithmetic
- Views of UNION/GROUP BY views
- SQL functions such as DECODE, SUBSTR, ROUND, POWER
- INTERSECT and MINUS set operations
- Variable CHAR data types
- Dynamic SQL within precompiler programs
- Representation of hierarchical structures such as bills of materials

3

The ORACLE system architecture

Topics covered in this chapter

- The physical structure of an ORACLE database
- The logical structure of an ORACLE database
- Physical structures used by ORACLE
- Calculating table storage requirements
- The ORACLE server software
- ORACLE processes
- The ORACLE database cache (SGA)
- ORACLE server configurations (multi-threaded server)
- ORACLE Parallel Server
- The ORACLE data dictionary

3

The ORACLE system architecture

3.1 Introduction

One of the primary aims of any database system is to free the system developer from the task of data management, leaving him or her free to concentrate on applications development without also having to worry about how the data is being managed. A database system must therefore be able to completely process any request for data with no special intervention being required from the application program to deal with errors or other unexpected conditions.

The introduction of relational database systems in conjunction with a language like SQL meant that for all practical purposes this objective has been realized. An application program can send off a request for data as a SQL statement which is then processed by the DBMS. This processing covers aspects such as the physical location of the data (or locations, if a number of records is being processed), security considerations, possible error conditions and the final processing of the data as required.

This situation is illustrated in Figure 3.1, where requests are sent to the database system by different applications programs; these requests are processed by the database system which then reports their status and returns data where required. Within this context it is possible to distinguish three distinct levels of functionality:

- The applications programs
  which perform specific tasks for the user such as book-keeping, CAD or production planning and control.
- The database system
  which provides all the data management functions required by its users, such as the means to read and write data, to define new data structures, to ensure data security, to control access in a multi-user environment, as well as providing backup and recovery mechanisms.
- The database
  which contains all the elements which are used by the applications programs and the database system; these include the data and access control structures, the declarative and procedural integrity constraints, the stored database modules as well as the actual user data.

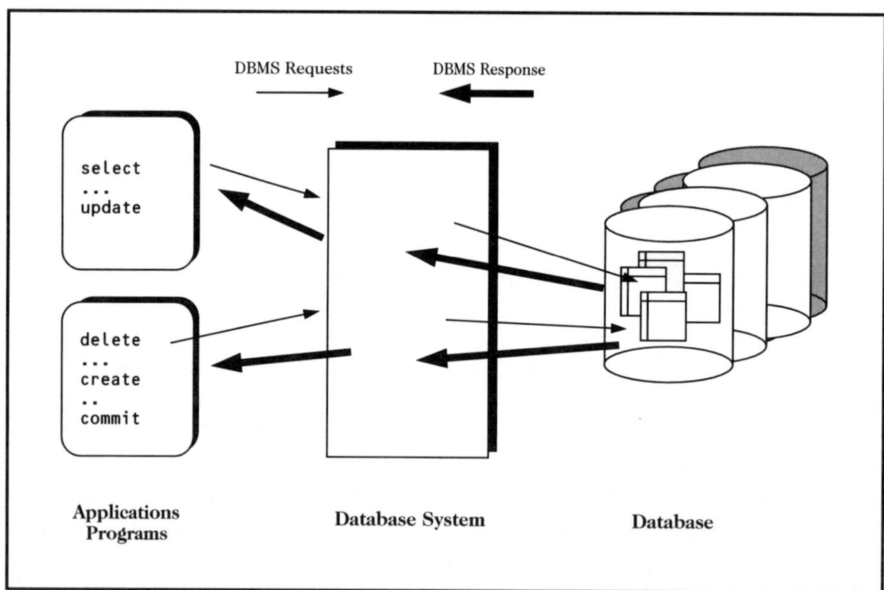

Figure 3.1 The hierarchy of an applications system using a database

Of course these three levels can be encountered in any application which makes use of a database and cannot therefore be regarded as being specific to the ORACLE database system. This chapter will deal with those characteristics which are specific to ORACLE and which distinguish its database system from all others. Section 3.2 will examine the structure of the ORACLE database in terms of what features are needed to provide effective and secure data storage. Section 3.3 will analyse the primary functions of the database system and will deal with the various options available for configuring the system on the basis of user requirements and projected workloads as well as the relevant hardware architecture.

3.2 The ORACLE database architecture

3.2.1 The physical structure

What we have referred to so far as the ORACLE database, proves on closer examination to be a system which consists of three different file types, as shown in Figure 3.2. As we can see, an ORACLE database consists of:

- any number of *data* files, distributed on any number of disk drives;
- at least two *redo log* files;
- at least two *control* files.

Each of these file types contains specific data which are needed by particular database functions.

Data files are used to store all the database objects which are administered by the ORACLE system. As well as the data dictionary we find that user-defined data structures, access structures, procedural objects as well as the actual data are all held here. Whereas data files are used when the ORACLE database is operating normally (creating database objects, read and write operations and so on), the redo log and control files are used above all to deal with any exceptions which may arise while the system is running.

The purpose of the redo log files is to maintain a fixed record of all database changes which are carried out in the course of a single transaction. Any change in the condition of a database (that is a transaction) is not held to have been completed until all the individual changes and the end of the transaction have been recorded in the redo log file.

Figure 3.2 shows the online redo log files, as these would also be present in a multiplexed configuration. It should be emphasized at this point that an ORACLE database will normally also contain a number of archived redo log files. An archived redo log file is a redo log file which has been completely filled and has then been copied (archived) either to another disk or to some other storage medium so that it can be backed up. These files contain in a highly compact form all the changes which have been made to the database and therefore form an essential element for restoring either a complete ORACLE database or individual data files (*refer also to* Chapter 5).

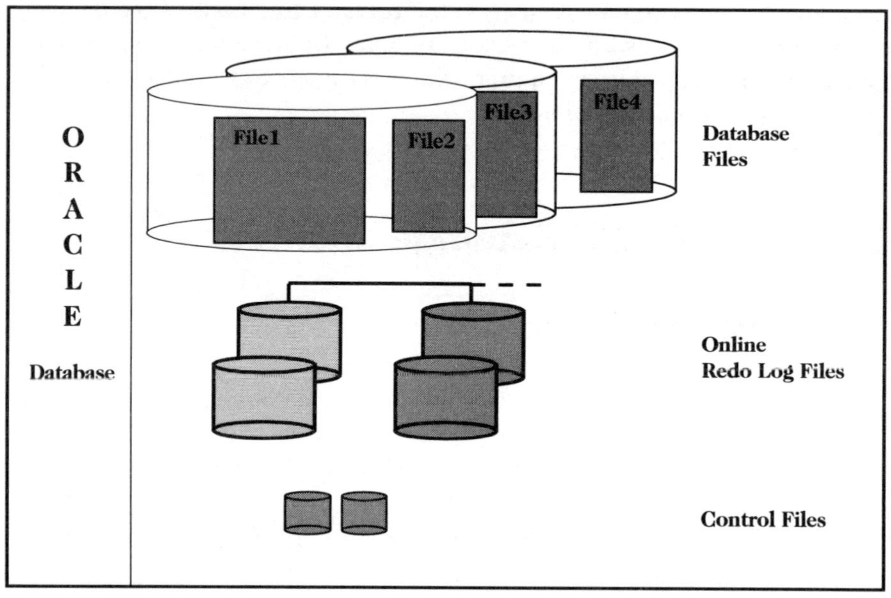

Figure 3.2 The physical components of an ORACLE database

The control files are used to store all the basic information about an individual ORACLE database and how it is structured; this includes the following items:

- when the database was created,
- the names of all data files,
- the names of all redo log files and their sequence numbers,
- the time of the last database checkpoint and the name(s) of the corresponding redo log file(s).

If the structure of the database is modified in any way, for example by the database being enlarged with additional data files or by having files moved to other disk drives, then this information is recorded in the control file. This file type is of particular importance for opening and closing the database as well as for the various recovery situations which can arise.

Up to now we have always referred to data files as though they were individual files which contain ORACLE database objects; however files are only a secondary structural unit for ORACLE and are used simply to provide storage space upon which the ORACLE database system imposes its own specific logical structure.

3.2.2 The logical structure of the ORACLE database

For the underlying operating system, an ORACLE database consists of a number of files in which the data for specific functions are stored.

These data files simply provide ORACLE with the storage space upon which it can impose its own structure – a structure which is geared to the optimum management of large volumes of data.

For the ORACLE system an ORACLE database consists of redo log files, control files and tablespaces. A tablespace consists of at least one and at most 255 operating system files, whose size and location (which disk drive) is irrelevant. Figure 3.3 shows the relationship between the operating system files, which have been created on different hard disks, and the corresponding ORACLE tablespaces.

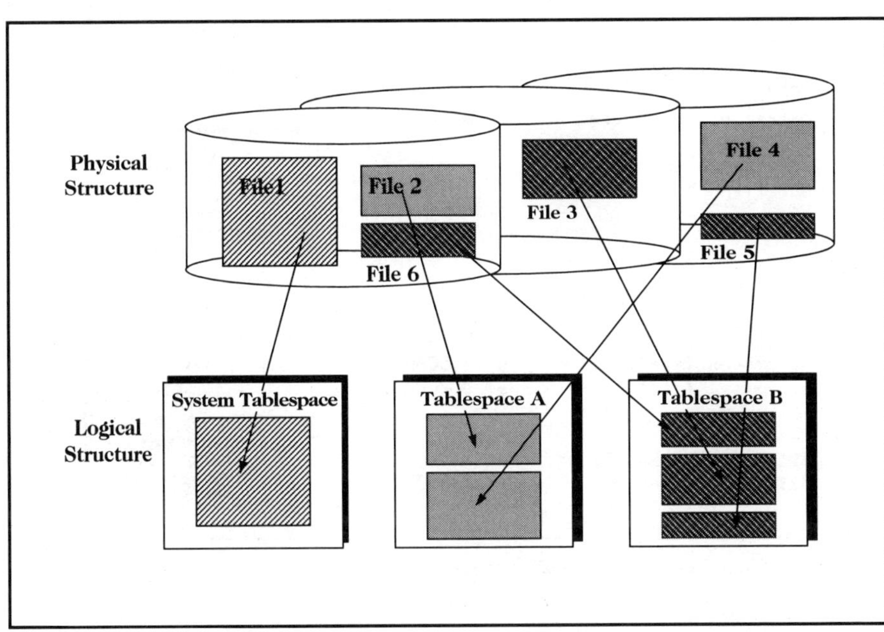

Figure 3.3 Relationship between physical and logical database structures

In this example, the system tablespace consists of one file, the TA tablespace of two files and the TB tablespace of three files, with the second one being installed over two and the third one over three disks. The *system* tablespace with its corresponding files is always created whenever an ORACLE database is installed. What additional tablespaces are then created, and which files are assigned to them, depends upon the overall size and nature of the database being set up. All the database objects which are defined within any ORACLE database must be assigned to a particular tablespace and will occupy some of the storage capacity of that tablespace.

A database object may increase in size within a tablespace, thereby extending beyond the scope of a single file and disk. However a database object may never occupy more then one tablespace.

Figure 3.4 contains the SQL statements required to create the database shown in Figure 3.3. The system tablespace is set up as part of the CREATE DATABASE statement, but as with all other tablespaces its size may later be increased with the ALTER TABLESPACE command. The two user tablespaces `TA` and `TB` are set up with the CREATE TABLESPACE command and tablespace `TB` is then extended with the ALTER TABLESPACE command to also include the file `FILE6.ORA`.

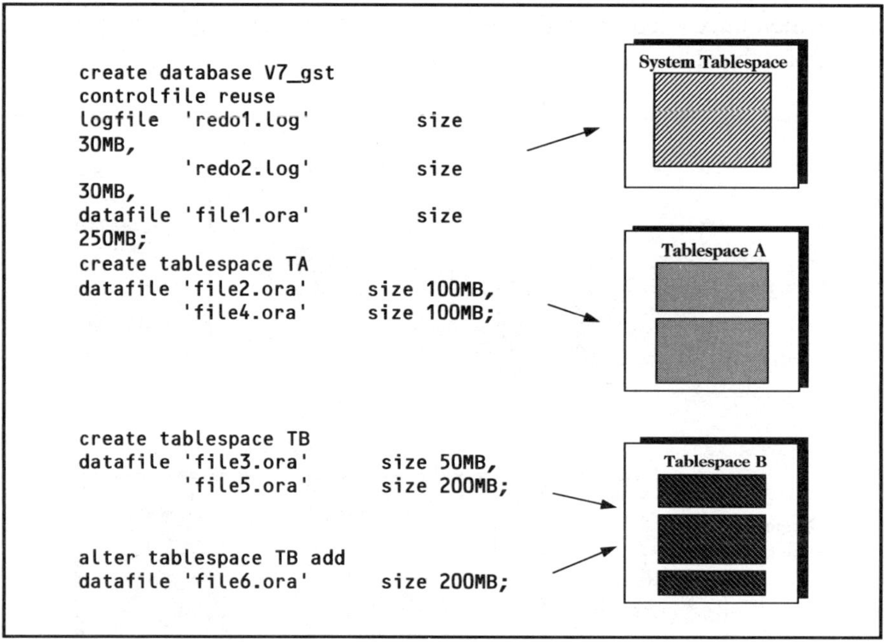

create database V7_gst
controlfile reuse
logfile 'redo1.log' size
30MB,
'redo2.log' size
30MB,
datafile 'file1.ora' size
250MB;
create tablespace TA
datafile 'file2.ora' size 100MB,
'file4.ora' size 100MB;
create tablespace TB
datafile 'file3.ora' size 50MB,
'file5.ora' size 200MB;
alter tablespace TB add
datafile 'file6.ora' size 200MB;
System Tablespace
Tablespace A
Tablespace B

Figure 3.4 Creating a database with three tablespaces

RELEASE 7.1

Once a file has been assigned to a table then it cannot be taken away from it again. It is however possible to delete a complete tablespace from the database together with all its files. The SQL statement `drop tablespace TA` deletes the tablespace `TA` shown in Figure 3.3 and releases all its data files as long as these have not been earmarked for any other database object. If other objects have been assigned to these files then the above SQL statement will abort with a corresponding error message; in this case the correct SQL statement would be:

```
drop tablespace TA including contents
```

This would have the effect of deleting all the objects and data files associated with this tablespace. So great are the consequences of using this command that it may only be entered by users who have the DROP TABLESPACE privilege.

Another option available to the user is to put a tablespace offline for a given period of time, as in the statement `alter tablespace TB offline`. Any database objects stored within this tablespace can then no longer be accessed; all other tablespaces with their tables and indexes are unaffected by this and can be used as normal. RELEASE 7.1

The OFFLINE parameter in the ALTER TABLESPACE command can be further qualified by one of three additional options: NORMAL, TEMPORARY and IMMEDIATE, NORMAL being the default option. Where the NORMAL option is used, a *checkpoint* is carried out for all the files which belong to the tablespace before it is put offline. This in turn means that no recovery is necessary when the tablespace is put back online.

In the case of the IMMEDIATE option, no checkpoint is carried out and the tablespace is put offline without any further processing. However this means that before the tablespace can be put back online it is necessary to carry out a media recovery, which is only possible when the database as a whole is in archive mode.

The TEMPORARY option contains elements of both other options: before the tablespace is put offline a checkpoint is carried out for all its online tables, so that no media recovery is needed when the tablespace goes back online. However a media recovery is necessary for any offline tables in the tablespace.

A tablespace can also be put offline by the ORACLE system as well as by the user; this happens whenever an error condition occurs in the course of a read or write operation. Where a tablespace has been put offline automatically, an error message is sent to the user and the database administrator is notified by means of the ORACLE alert file. Regardless of whether a tablespace is put offline automatically or manually, all other online tablespaces may still be used as normal. In order to put an offline tablespace back online the following SQL statement must be entered:

```
alter tablespace TB online
```

This puts tablespace `TB` back online making all its database objects accessible once again.

It should finally be mentioned that the system tablespace of an ORACLE database cannot be put offline, as this tablespace contains the data dictionary, without which the database cannot function. RELEASE 7.1

The possibility of defining a specific logical structure for an ORACLE database offers a number of important potential benefits for any active ORACLE installation. These include:

RELEASE 7.1

- Increased tolerance of hard disk errors. This can be achieved by setting up the data files on different disk drives and assigning the files of one disk drive (or disk controller) to one tablespace. This means that in the event of a disk failure only one tablespace is affected.
- Improved system performance. This can normally be achieved by placing tables (user data) and their corresponding indexes in different tablespaces and thus on different disks.

3.2.3 The structure of a tablespace

All database objects within an ORACLE database are assigned to a given tablespace, and we can distinguish between four basic object (or segment) types:

- data segments (tables)
- index segments
- rollback segments
- temporary segments

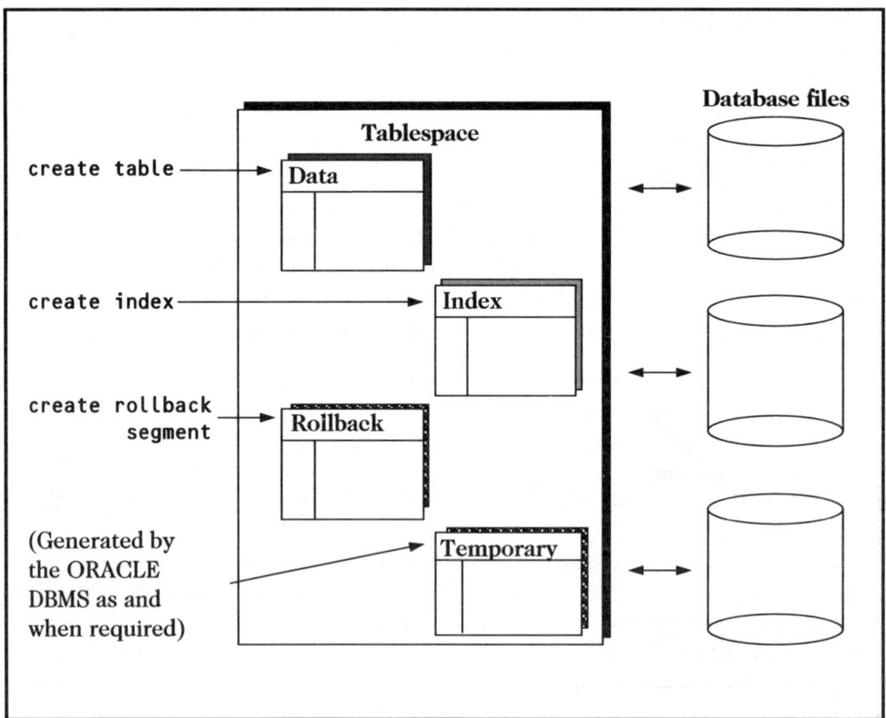

Figure 3.5 The relationship between segment types and SQL commands

Figure 3.5 depicts the relationship between objects and segment types, where each table, index or rollback segment occupies exactly one corresponding segment type (that is a data, index or rollback segment) within its own tablespace. Temporary segments cannot be directly created by the user but are generated by the ORACLE system itself whenever it needs temporary additional storage space in order to carry out specific operations such as sorting data or creating indexes; these temporary segments are released once the operation has been completed.

When a database object with its corresponding segment type is being created, the question of which tablespace is used depends upon the following factors:

- Which tablespaces are available to the user creating the object?
- Which privileges have been granted to the user creating the object?
- Which options are specified in the CREATE statement for the object?

An ORACLE user who has been entered in the system with the CREATE USER command does not automatically have any right to access the system's tablespaces, which means that he or she is not able to define any objects which will take up space within the database. Only by specifying the quota option in the CREATE or ALTER USER commands can a user be given the privilege to use storage space within a particular tablespace.

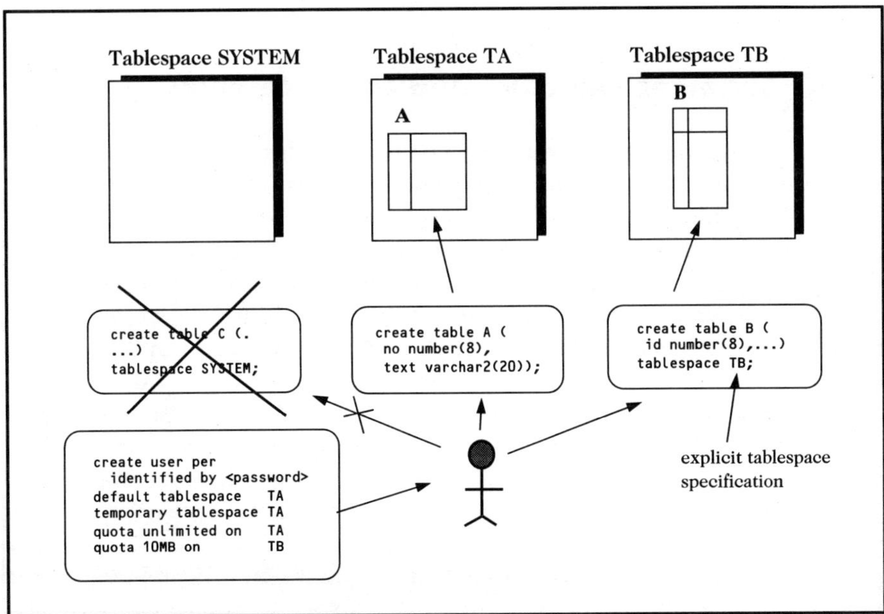

Figure 3.6 Granting access and quotas on tablespaces

Figure 3.6 shows a user being set up with unlimited storage space on tablespace TA and a maximum of 10 megabytes on tablespace TB. At the same time a default tablespace is specified so that whenever this user creates a database object without explicitly naming a tablespace, for example using the CREATE TABLE command, then that object will be placed in the user's default tablespace, as shown in the first example in Figure 3.6. In the second example the same user creates another table but this time explicitly naming the tablespace to be used. If the user's overall quota on tablespace TB is not exceeded by creating table B then the operation completes successfully, otherwise the user receives an error message that the quota has been exceeded. But the user's attempt to create an object in the system tablespace is rejected immediately as no quota has been allocated to him in this tablespace.

Creating the ORACLE segment types (data segments for tables, index segments for indexes and rollback segments) is dealt with in exactly the same way as that just described for tables. Temporary segments on the other hand, which are only generated by the ORACLE system when required, are created either in the tablespace specified with the TEMPORARY TABLESPACE option in the CREATE USER statement or, if this has not been specified, in the system tablespace.

It should be emphasized that all these segment types are completely independent of each other. This means that data segments (for tables) and the corresponding index segments can be located on different tablespaces. By storing data and their indexes on different hard disks in this way, the overall performance of the system is often improved.

3.2.4 Segment structure and characteristics

Each of the segment types we have just dealt with occupies storage space within its tablespace. In order to prevent or at least minimize the fragmentation of individual segments, the system allows us to control the allocation and usage of storage space by means of a number of storage parameters. For this reason it is necessary to examine the segment a little more closely.

A segment consists of one or more *extents,* which in turn are predefined units of storage space allocated to a segment. It is important in this context to distinguish between the *initial extent*, which is allocated when the segment is first created (for example by the CREATE TABLE command), and any number of subsequent *next* extents. These next extents are generated by the system whenever the available storage space is insufficient to store additional amounts of data. In addition to defining the size of the (first) next extent for a given segment, it is also possible to specify (using the PCTINCREASE parameter) the growth factor for each subsequent extent in relation to the previous one. Each extent itself consists of a specific number of ORACLE data blocks, which for most systems is 2 KB in size.

The storage parameters, which are all optional, take the following form:

```
storage  (  initial          20MB,
            next             10MB,
            minextents       3,
            maxextents       3,
            pctincrease      15,
            freelists        3)
```

These storage parameters may be used in the following SQL commands:

```
create/alter   tablespace
create/alter   table
create/alter   index
create/alter   rollback segment
create/alter   cluster
create/alter   snapshot
create/alter   snapshot log
```

The storage parameters defined for a tablespace are adopted as the default storage values for all database objects which are created within that tablespace; these default values can be superseded by entering an explicit storage definition for the object in question.

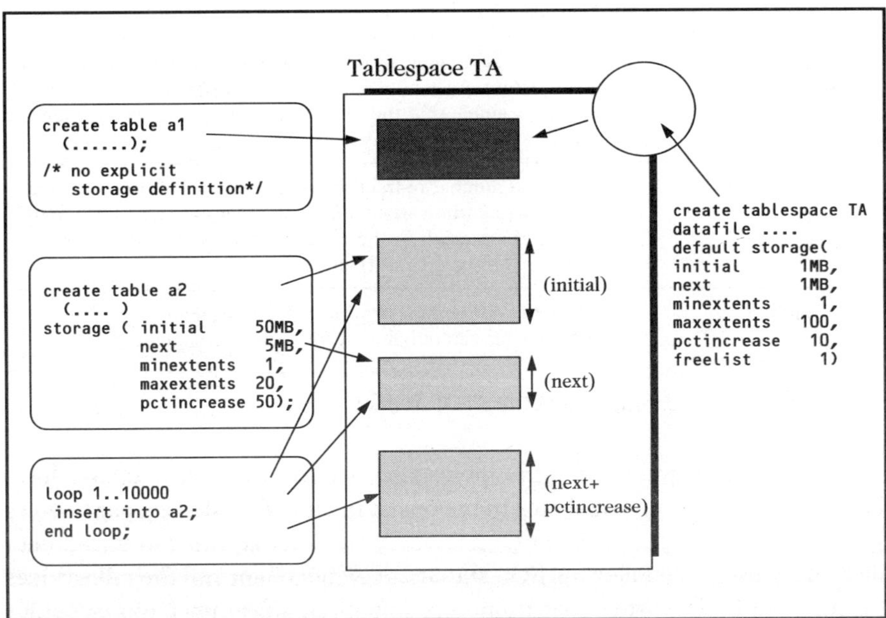

Figure 3.7 Explicit and implicit usage of the storage parameters

Figure 3.7 shows two tables being created in tablespace TA. No storage parameters are entered for table A1 and it therefore assumes the values which were specified for the tablespace as part of the CREATE or ALTER TABLESPACE command.

In the case of the second table A2 an explicit storage clause has been included and the amount of storage space specified in the INITIAL parameter is allocated as soon as this CREATE TABLE statement is processed. Once this storage space has been filled (by insert operations) then the storage extent defined in the NEXT parameter is allocated to the segment within tablespace TA. Once this storage area has also been filled, then a further extent is allocated whose size is calculated using the formula `next+(next*pctincrease/100)`.

Figure 3.8 provides a final overview of all the storage parameters and what they mean.

`initial`	Specifies the size of the first extent of a segment. for example `initial 50MB`, `initial 10KB`. This storage area is allocated when the segment is first created.
`next`	Specifies the size of the extent(s) to be created after the first one (`initial`). This area is not allocated until necessary.
`minextents`	Specifies the number of extents which should be allocated when the segment is first created. If `minextents = 3` for example, then the `initial` extent plus two times the `next` extent are allocated when the segment is first created.
`maxextents`	Specifies the maximum number of extents which can be allocated for one segment.
`pctincrease`	Specifies the percentage by which each new extent grows over the previous extent. A value of 50 for the `pctincrease` parameter means for example that the next extent will be 50% larger than the previous extent.
`freelists`	Specifies the number of freelists for a segment.This parameter is particularly important when a large number of inserts have to be carried out in parallel. In this case the `freelists` parameter should be set to be greater than one.
`optimal`	Specifies the optimum size for a rollback segment. This parameter can only be set for rollback segments.

Figure 3.8 The parameters of the STORAGE clause

In order to examine how the tablespaces of an ORACLE database have been set up, which physical files they consist of and what storage parameters have been specified, it is only necessary to access the ORACLE data dictionary using the following SQL statement, which shows all the tablespaces together with their storage parameters and their current status (whether they are online or offline).

```
select * from user_tablespaces;
```

If the user wishes to find out in which tablespace a particular table has been located and which storage parameters have been specified for it, this information is provided (for all the user's tables) with the following statement:

```
select * from user_tables;
```

The objects USER_TABLESPACES and USER_TABLES referred to here are in fact data dictionary views, which provide information held in the ORACLE data dictionary (*see also* Section 3.4).

3.2.5 The ORACLE data block structure

So far we have looked at those storage parameters which determine the extents of a segment in terms of initial size (INITIAL), the size and growth factor for new extents (NEXT, PCTINCREASE) and their overall number (MINEXTENTS, MAXEXTENTS). It is therefore possible to refer to these as extent parameters, in that they define the extents of a database segment.

But as we now know the smallest unit of a segment is not the extent but the database or data block, which in fact make up the extents. When a database object is being defined (a table, or an index for example) then in addition to defining the extent's characteristics it is also possible to configure the data blocks themselves; this can be done by means of the data block parameters PCTFREE, PCTUSED, INITRANS and MAXTRANS. The first of these, PCTFREE, is used to specify the proportion of the data block that is *not* to be filled when records are inserted into the table, which means that this space is reserved for subsequent updates to those records. The second parameter, PCTUSED, defines the percentage of space which should be filled by inserting records before another data block is allocated by the ORACLE system. Figure 3.9 shows a graphical representation of a data block and illustrates that the block can be divided into two areas:

- the block's header
- the block's data area

The header contains general block information such as the row directory, which occupies two bytes for each record in the data block, and the transaction directory, which contains entries for any current transactions which will modify the records stored in the block. A single transaction entry occupies 23 bytes, and the maximum number of transaction entries per data block is defined by the second two of the four data block parameters INITRANS and MAXTRANS.

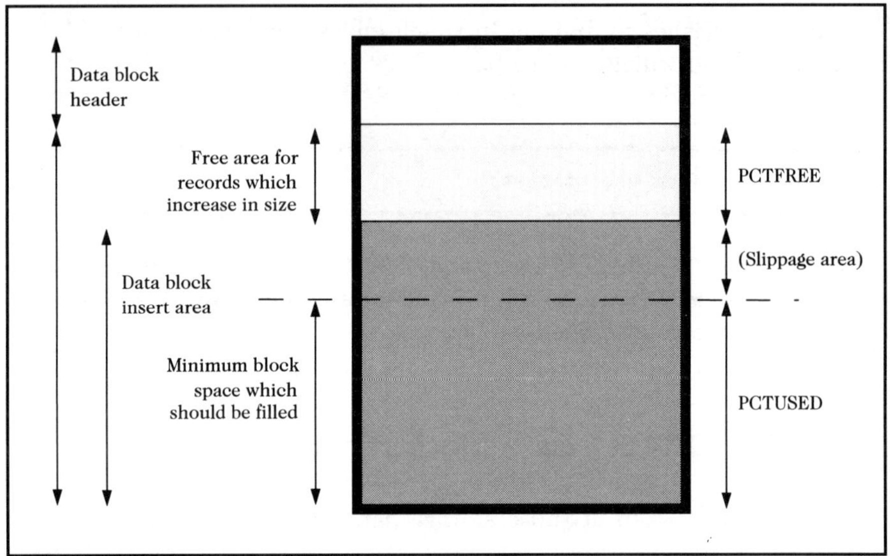

Figure 3.9 The structure and parameters of a data block

The block's data area can be further sub-divided into two other areas:

- The block's *insert* area is that part of the data block which can be occupied by new records which are inserted into the database.
- The block's *free* area is that part of the data block which is reserved for existing records to grow in size.

The free area is of particular importance when the block is being used to store the data types VARCHAR or VARCHAR2, which contain alphanumeric data of variable length. In the case of these two data types, the system will use only the number of bytes actually required for a given value, so that trailing spaces are not stored; this means that subsequent update operations can significantly increase the overall size of a record. A similar increase in size will occur where a number of initial NULL fields within a record are subsequently updated with actual values. The free space in a data block is intended to provide storage space for exactly this situation, so that records can increase in size within the same data block.

This is illustrated in Figure 3.10 where a table has been defined which contains VARCHAR2 data types so that a single record can occupy up to 300 bytes of storage space. However the record which is first inserted into the table contains only the characters 'A' and 'B', which means that only 2 out of a possible 300 bytes are initially being used, although subsequent update operations may take this record up to its maximum size.

If the free area in a data block is not large enough to accommodate a given update operation, then the affected record is moved in its entirety to another block (either a new one or an existing one with enough storage space), and the update is carried out in the new data block. This record is then linked ('chained') to its original data block, which stores the new address (the ROWID) of the record in the same location as that used for the original address. This means that if blocks have to be chained in this way, it is not necessary to alter the corresponding index values.

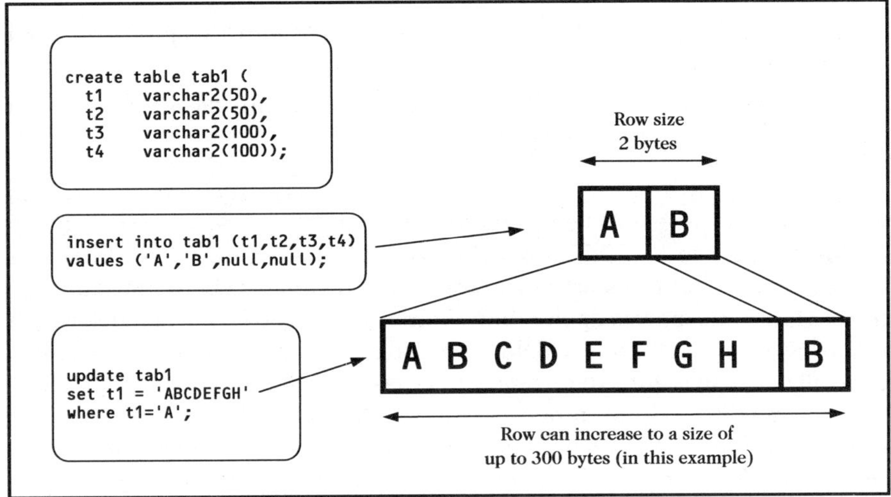

Figure 3.10 Row size increase with variable column size

However it should be emphasized that block chaining can lead to a deterioration in system performance, and in order to prevent this happening the PCTFREE parameter should be set so that sufficient free space is provided for all (probable) update operations in the future: in the case of tables whose records are subject to high growth rates (dynamic tables) a large value, typically between 40 and 60 (percent), is required; for tables which are not subject to many update operations and whose records do not change in size significantly (static tables) a PCTFREE value of between 0 and 30 percent is adequate.

The second important block parameter PCTUSED, by defining the percentage of space which should be filled with new records within each data block, ensures that all the blocks allocated for a particular database object will be filled as evenly as possible. This is because insert operations are always carried out on blocks where part of the space defined by PCTFREE is available, either because this limit has not yet been reached (new blocks) or because space has become free as a result of delete or update operations on the records within the block. All data blocks which fall into this category are entered into the data block *free list* and are thus available for subsequent insert operations. However a block will be chosen from this list only if it can provide enough space to take the complete new record and without taking up any of the block's free area (PCTFREE). As soon as a block's PCTUSED limit has been reached again, the block is removed from the free list so that it can no longer be used for insert operations.

Within the extents of a segment it is therefore possible to distinguish between data blocks in three different conditions:

- data blocks which have been filled with data up to the PCTUSED limit (completely filled blocks);
- data blocks which contain data but are still within the PCTUSED limit (partially filled blocks);
- data blocks which, although allocated to a segment, have not yet been used to store any data (unused blocks).

Of these three it is only the partially filled blocks which are recorded in the data block free list. Whenever, as a result of delete or update operations, the used space in a block falls below the PCTUSED percentage, then this block is entered at the start of the free list. It is important to note that the transaction concept also applies in this situation: space in a data block which is no longer needed after a delete or update operation, does not become generally available until that transaction has been successfully completed.

This means that, in order to reflect the processing within a given transaction, the free list has to be looked at under two different aspects: in addition to the (normal) segment free list an additional (transaction) free list is maintained by the system; this transaction free list keeps track of all the data blocks which have gone below their PCTUSED limit in the course of the current transaction. If in the course of this same transaction an insert statement is executed, then the ORACLE system will first look for the required storage area within the transaction's own free list, using those blocks which are no longer filled to their PCTUSED limit as a result of other operations which have taken place within the transaction.

The transaction free list can therefore be regarded as a sub-free list within the overall segment free list, but which is available only to its own transaction. A transaction free list is set up only if the storage space within any of the data blocks accessed by a given transaction falls below the PCTUSED limit, at which point the block becomes partially used.

If the storage space required for the insert operation exceeds what is available through the transaction free list, then the segment free list is searched for a block with the necessary amount of free space. If this also proves unsuccessful then the system will take the segment's unused data blocks and enter them one after the other into the segment free list. After all these steps have been gone through, it may be that additional storage area is still required, which means that there are no more free blocks left within the current extent. Only in this case will the system generate a new extent within its tablespace's current storage area; the size of this new extent is `(next + (next*pctincrease/100))`.

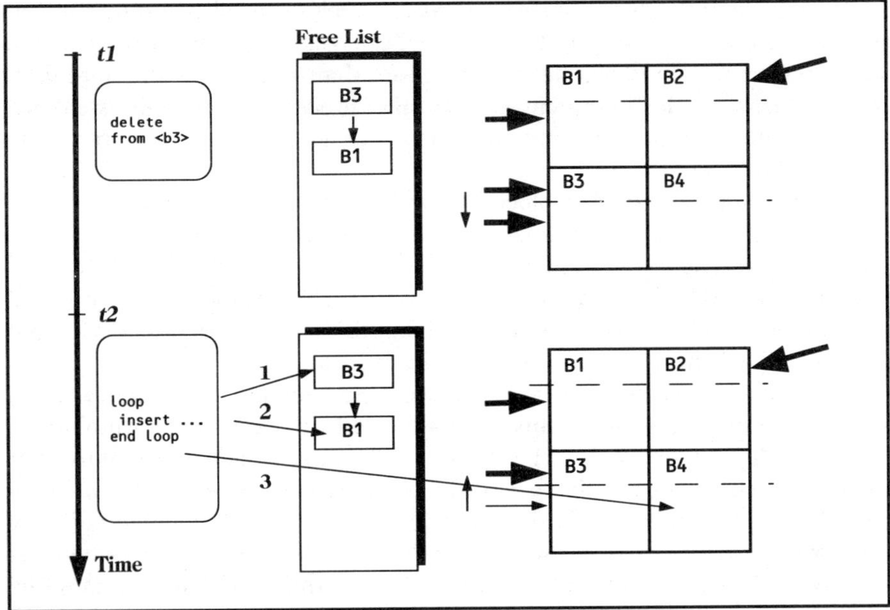

Figure 3.11 Data blocks and the data block free list

Figure 3.11 shows a typical sequence of events within a transaction. This example uses an extent which for simplicity consists of only four data blocks; prior to the start of this transaction these four blocks have the following status:

- Block B1 is partially filled and has therefore been entered in the segment's free list.
- Block B2 is completely filled.
- Block B3 is completely filled.
- Block B4 is unused.

In the course of the transaction illustrated in Figure 3.11 records are first deleted from block B3, so that its available space falls back below the PCTUSED mark. Block B3 is thus entered into the free list and, for the duration of this transaction, is also included in the transaction free list. In the next stage of this transaction a number of records are inserted and, as shown in the illustration, the required storage space is obtained in the following order:

1. Records are inserted into the data block taken from the transaction's free list.
2. Records are inserted into the data block taken from the segment's free list.
3. Records are inserted into the extent's unused data block.
4. Records are inserted into the unused data blocks of a newly created extent.

As this example shows, insert operations make specially frequent use of the free list mechanism, and so it can be a good idea, where tables are subject to a very many parallel inserts (more than 100), to set up more than one free list, in order to increase the parallel processing capabilities of your system. The overall number of free lists can be specified as part of the CREATE TABLE command.

When dividing up the data block into a free and an insert area (by use of the PCTFREE and PCTUSED parameters) the optimum usage of storage space could theoretically be achieved by setting the values for these two parameters so that they add up to exactly 100. This means that records will be entered into the insert area (which in this case is identical with the PCTUSED area) until no more records can fit into it.

However the probability that a data block can actually be filled to the last available byte is very small; this means that all the data blocks which have not been filled up to their PCTUSED limit will of course be entered into their segment's free list for possible use in the next insert operation. Thus we get a situation where the free list contains a lot of blocks each of which has very little free storage capacity but which must nevertheless be examined whenever an insert operation takes place. In order to avoid this situation, a certain free area should always be left to the system as a kind of slippage or open area. A rough guide for calculating the size of this area between PCTUSED and PCTFREE is that it should be large enough to take an average size record for that table. The result will be a considerable reduction in the time any data block has to be kept in the free list, as the next record to be inserted will in all probability be able to make use of a block in the free list (*refer also to* Figure 3.9).

3.2.6 The physical format of a record

The last (and smallest) unit in our examination of the physical structure of an ORACLE database is the database record or row itself. This is made up of two components:

- the row header
- the row body

The row header contains control information such as:

- the number of columns in the row;
- chaining information, where the row is larger than one data block or where a row has had to be moved to another data block because the free area in its original block was too small;
- cluster key information, where the row belongs to a clustered table.

The row header occupies at least three and at most (for clustered or chained rows) five bytes. Figure 3.12 shows a schematic representation of a row's structure.

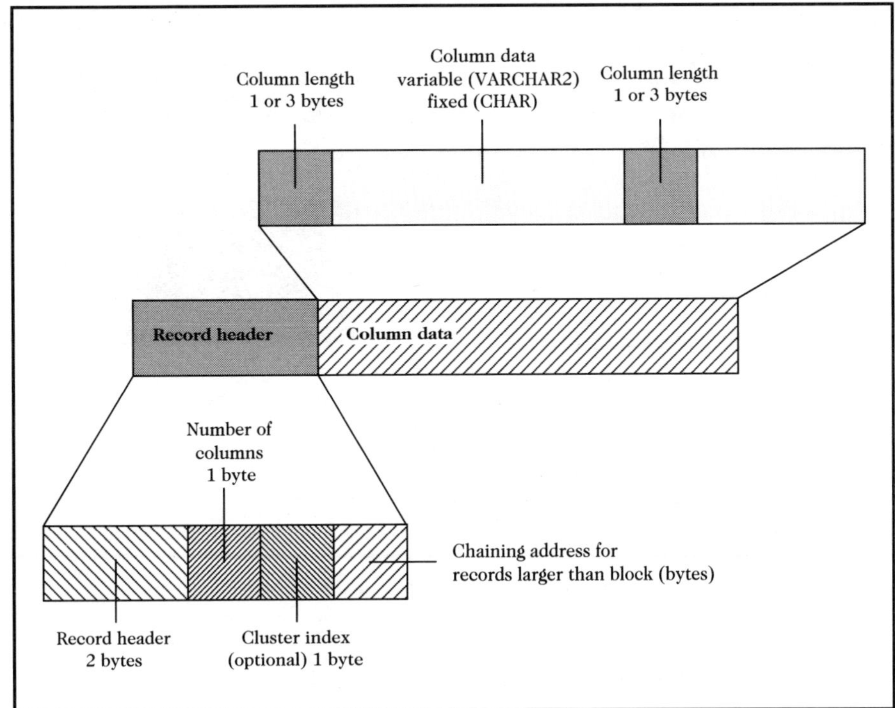

Figure 3.12 Physical record format

The row body contains the actual column data as defined by the CREATE TABLE command, although the physical sequence of columns does not have to correspond with the 'logical' order as set out in the CREATE TABLE statement. A column whose data type is RAW or LONG RAW will always be physically located at the end of the row.

Each (physical) column is preceded by its own column header which is used to record the exact length of the column. The header itself takes up one byte for the data types NUMBER, CHAR and DATE, and three bytes for VARCHAR, VARCHAR2, LONG, RAW and LONG RAW.

Now that we have covered the the parameters which define the extents and the data blocks and have examined the physical structure of a row (record), we can now turn our attention to how these parameters should be set. Firstly it is important to know how many rows of a given table can be stored in a data block and how many blocks must be made available for that table. By working out values for the number of records and the required number of data blocks, it is possible to calculate how the corresponding storage parameters should be set.

How many rows will be stored in a data block can be calculated by dividing the available block storage space by the physical row size, as shown in Figure 3.13. The storage space available is the block size minus the block header and the block free area (PCTFREE). The block header itself consists of both fixed and variable sized elements.

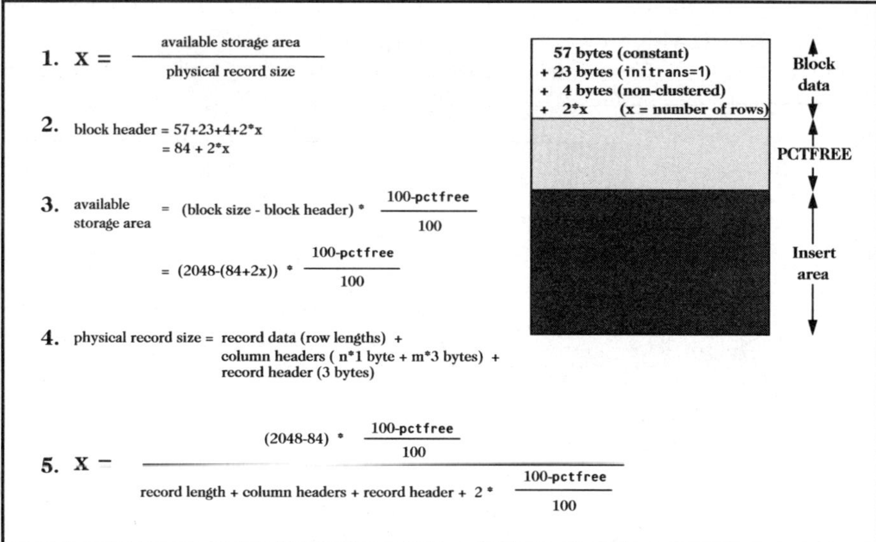

Figure 3.13 Calculating the number of records per data block

- 57 bytes are for general block information.
- 23 bytes are used for each transaction entry; the number of transaction entries per block being defined by the parameters INITRANS, whose default value is 1, and MAXTRANS, which specifies the maximum number of concurrent transactions which may update a data block.
- 2 bytes per row in the block's row directory.
- 4 bytes for the table directory in a non-clustered table; in a cluster 4 bytes of the block header are used for each table.Therefore the number of bytes required for the block header in a non-clustered table is 84 plus 2 times the actual number of rows, and the amount of available space in the block is reduced accordingly. This remaining storage space has to be further reduced by the predefined free area (PCTFREE). In this way the actual amount of space available for inserting data can be calculated, as is also shown in Step 3 of Figure 3.13.

The physical size of each row is determined by the following three elements:

- the size of the row header (3 or 5 bytes),
- the sum of the bytes actually needed for the row's data,
- the number of bytes needed for the column headers (1 or 3 bytes each).

In order to calculate how many rows can be stored in each data block it is very important to arrive at an accurate estimate of the average column size, that is how many bytes are actually going to be used for each row. In Step 4 of Figure 3.13 this physical row size is calculated, and in Step 5 we see the final calculation of the number of rows per block based on a header size of 84 bytes, which means that the value for INITRANS is 1.

On this basis it is possible to estimate how many data blocks will be required to store a given number of records. It should again be emphasized that the accuracy of this formula depends very much on a precise estimate of the average record (row) size.

3.2.7 Summary

In Section 3.2 we set out to examine the physical and logical structure(s) of an ORACLE database. Looking first at its physical structure, we saw that an ORACLE database consists of the following file types: three different types of data files, any number of which can be located on any number of disks, redo log files, of which there must be at least two and which can also be multiplexed, and, finally, the control files, of which there must also be at least two. From this starting point we then went on to examine the successive levels which constitute the logical structure of an ORACLE database and which are illustrated in Figure 3.14.

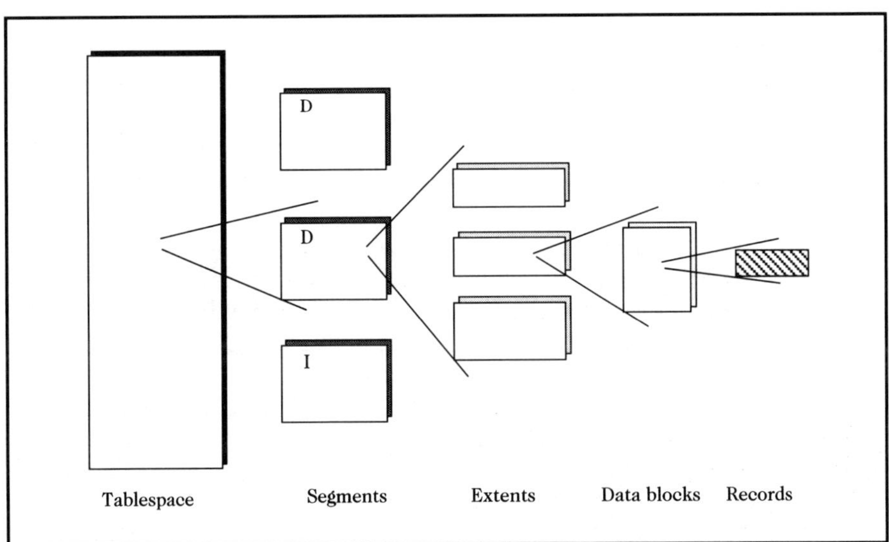

Figure 3.14 The component parts of an ORACLE tablespace

The ORACLE tablespace concept has proved to be particularly well suited to the tasks of creating and maintaining large databases. A system architecture based on tablespaces is able to provide a number of useful and important benefits, making the whole system less vulnerable to disk problems and providing a means whereby one part of a database can be put online or offline (to be backed up or following a disk failure) without affecting the rest of the database. Figure 3.15 illustrates the hierarchy of files, tablespaces, segments, extents and data blocks as an entity relationship diagram.

It is again worth emphasizing that the level of performance achieved by a working ORACLE system also depends on how its physical and logical structures have been defined: which disks are being used for which data files, how the individual database objects (tables and their indexes) have been distributed among the different tablespaces and how the storage parameters have been specified.

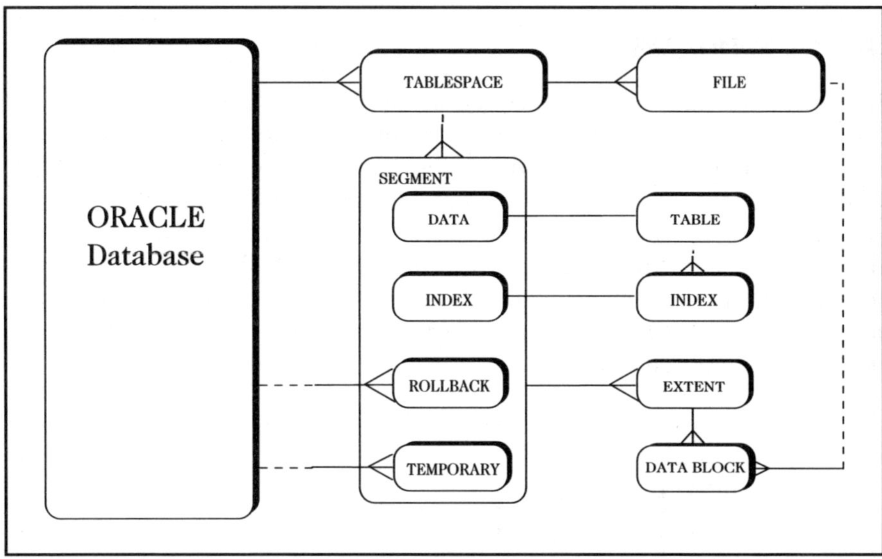

Figure 3.15 An ORACLE database as an entity relationship diagram

The ORACLE data dictionary contains a number of views which tell us a great deal about how an ORACLE system has been structured; the most important of these data dictionary views are listed in Figure 3.16.

Dictionary View	Function
`dba_data_files`	Shows all database files and their status.
`dba_tablespaces`	Shows all tablespaces and their status.
`dba_freespace`	Shows the amount of free space in all tablespaces.
`dba_ts_quotas`	Shows the tablespaces quotas for all users.
`user_extents` `(all_extents` `dba_extents)`	Shows the extents of the tables and indexes belonging to each user, as well as all the tables and indexes (possibly the whole database) to which the user has access.
`user_tables`	Shows all the tables which belong to a user.

Figure 3.16 The structure of a database as shown in the data dictionary

3.3 The ORACLE software architecture

3.3.1 Introduction

The design and implementation of any software system are crucial in determining to what extent that system will be able to meet the sometimes conflicting demands which are made of it by different computer architectures and types of applications. This is particularly true of database systems, which form the basis for a wide range of applications whose scope and functionality are determined first and foremost by the software architecture of that database system. There are currently four basic hardware architectures which have to be supported by the database system's software architecture, and these are listed below.

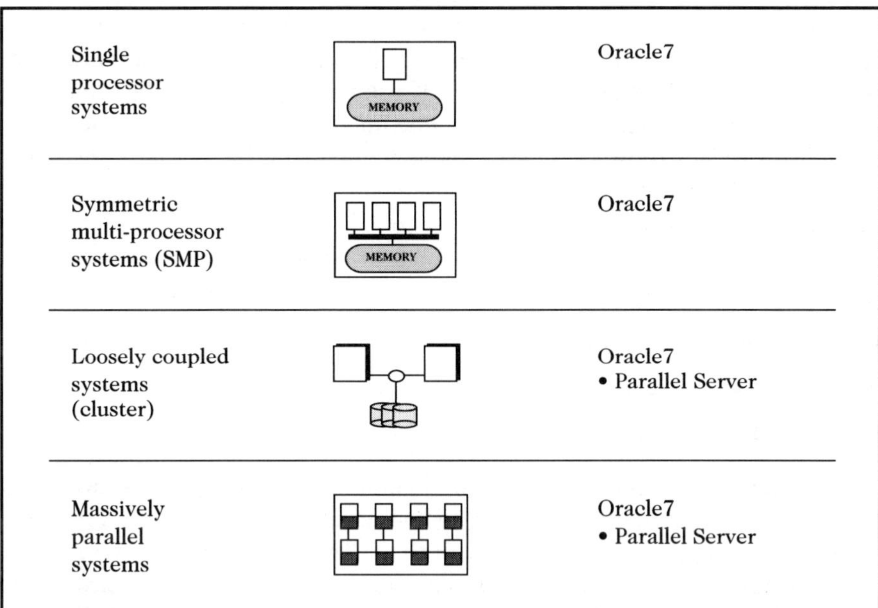

Figure 3.17 Computer architectures with the corresponding ORACLE systems

- Single processor systems:
  these are based on a single processor whose power may vary enormously. Systems of this type are currently used in every area of data processing.
- Symmetric multi-processor systems (SMP):
  these consist of a number of equally configured processors, which all access the same main memory, and are therefore often called shared memory systems. Because of their processing power and their relatively low cost SMP systems are increasingly being used in computers of all types, from PC to mainframe. The use of a common main memory however means that such systems are currently limited to a maximum of thirty-two processors working together.

RELEASE 7.1

- Loosely coupled or clustered systems:
these consist of a number of separate computer systems, which share certain resources such as disk storage. Each individual system within this cluster can itself be a single processor or an SMP system. Cluster systems make it possible to set up powerful computing environments which also provide additional security against system breakdowns.
- Massively parallel systems:
these consist of a very large number of single processors each of which, in contrast to the SMP systems, has its own main memory. Such systems can contain and use several thousand processors in parallel and are therefore capable of providing enormous processing power.

Figure 3.17 shows these different hardware topologies together with the corresponding ORACLE software components.

The software architecture of a database system should be designed in such a way that the software can adapt itself to different hardware architectures, thus allowing the computer's full processing power to be translated into a corresponding level of performance for the system's users. Not until a suitable database architecture is available to make full use of their processing power, will clustered and massively parallel systems find their way into all commercial computing centres.

As shown in Figure 3.1 of Section 3.2 we saw that an applications system can broadly be divided into the following three components:

- the applications program
- the database system
- the database itself

Just as the ORACLE database could be divided in terms of its individual components (file types, tablespaces, segments and so on), so too is it possible to analyse the software architecture of the ORACLE database system.

An ORACLE database system can first be divided into two basic components: the ORACLE instance and a series of related ORACLE server processes. The ORACLE instance itself comprises a variable database cache area, usually referred to as the System or Shared Global area (SGA), together with a series of background processes each of which carries out a specific task within the system. The Database Writer (DBWR) process for example is responsible for writing any modified data blocks in the buffer cache back to disk; similarly the Log Writer (LGWR) process is responsible for writing the redo log files (*refer also to* Section 3.3.2).

The ORACLE server processes are created to handle the requests of users or user processes connected to the instance; usually several of these processes are active at any one time, and they carry out functions such as parsing and executing SQL statements or reading data blocks from file into the database cache.

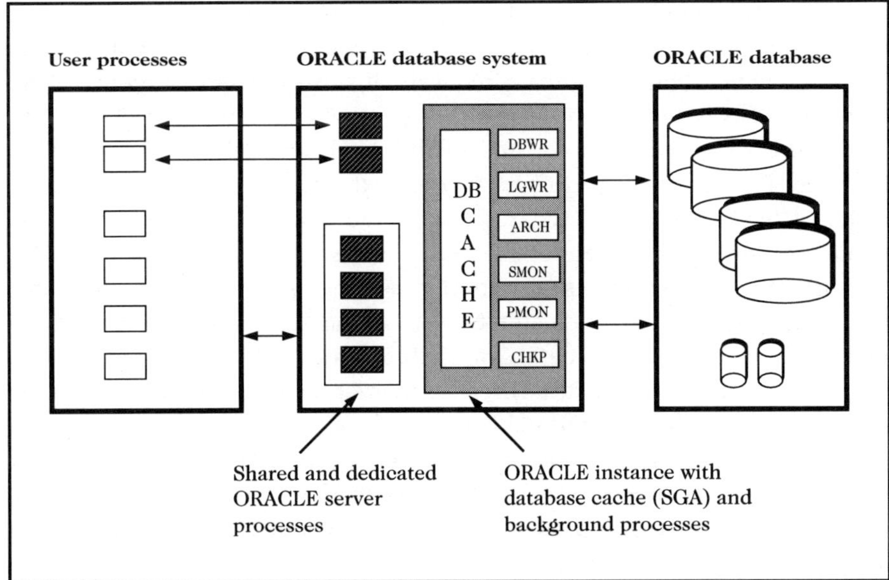

Figure 3.18 The three levels of an ORACLE based applications system

In examining the database's software architecture however, it is not enough just to consider the corresponding hardware architecture, equal attention must be given to the nature of the various applications which are going to make use of the database. All the different types of computing system we have already discussed must also be able to support applications which can have either of the two following characteristics:

- a large number of processes, each of which makes heavy use of the database;
- a large number of users, each of which makes moderate online use of the database.

In order to deal with these different workloads effectively, Oracle7 makes it possible to run two simultaneous configurations of the same system. These configurations are:

- the Dedicated Server (DS) configuration where single processes make heavy use of the database;
- the dynamic Multi-Threaded Server (MTS) configuration for online applications.

Where an application is running under a Dedicated Server configuration, then a dedicated ORACLE server process is assigned to each applications process and is responsible for processing all the database requests which that application generates.

With a dynamic Multi-Threaded Server configuration on the other hand, there are no explicit links between user processes and the ORACLE server processes which handle database requests. Instead a database request from a user process is sent to an ORACLE dispatcher process which places it in one of the request queues located in the database cache of the ORACLE instance. The request is processed by the next free ORACLE server process, which delivers the completed request to the same dispatcher's response queue, so that it can be sent to the user process.

Both these different configuration types can be run under the same ORACLE instance. The Dedicated Server is designed for applications which make intensive use of the database, such as batch jobs or load operations. The advantages of the Multi-Threaded Server become evident in online systems where only a few ORACLE server processes are enough to deal with what is perhaps a very large number of users. In this case the overall number of ORACLE server processes depends on the workload and is adjusted by the ORACLE system (within predefined limits) depending on the actual workload at any one time.

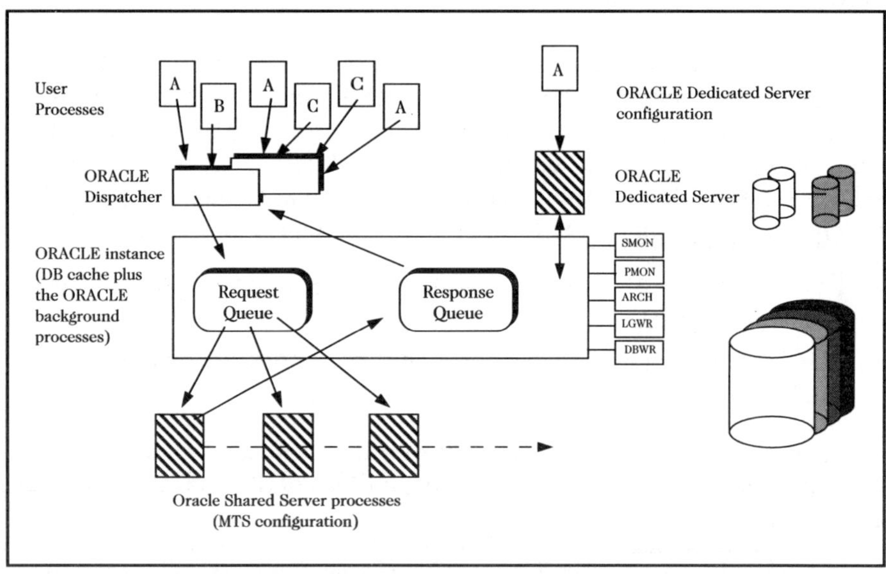

Figure 3.19 MTS and DS configurations with a single ORACLE instance

The question of whether the DS or MTS configuration should be selected is decided by the ORACLE Listener process when a user process first connects to the database. Because a configuration does not have to be selected before connecting to a database, that is to say irrespective of how a program was originally conceived, it is possible to respond very flexibly to changes in the workload of a given program, without of course having to change any part of the program itself. To run an application program with a Multi-Threaded Server configuration the command would be as follows:

```
runform adr scott/<password>$mts
```

In this example the **$mts** qualifier specifies how the connect operation should be carried out and provides the ORACLE Listener process with all the information required to assign a dispatcher process which is then responsible for processing (as described earlier) all the database requests generated by this user process.

The same application could of course equally have been started with a Dedicated Server configuration:

```
runform adr scott/<password>$ds
```

In this case the Listener creates a dedicated server process which deals exclusively with this user process and is for processing all its database requests.

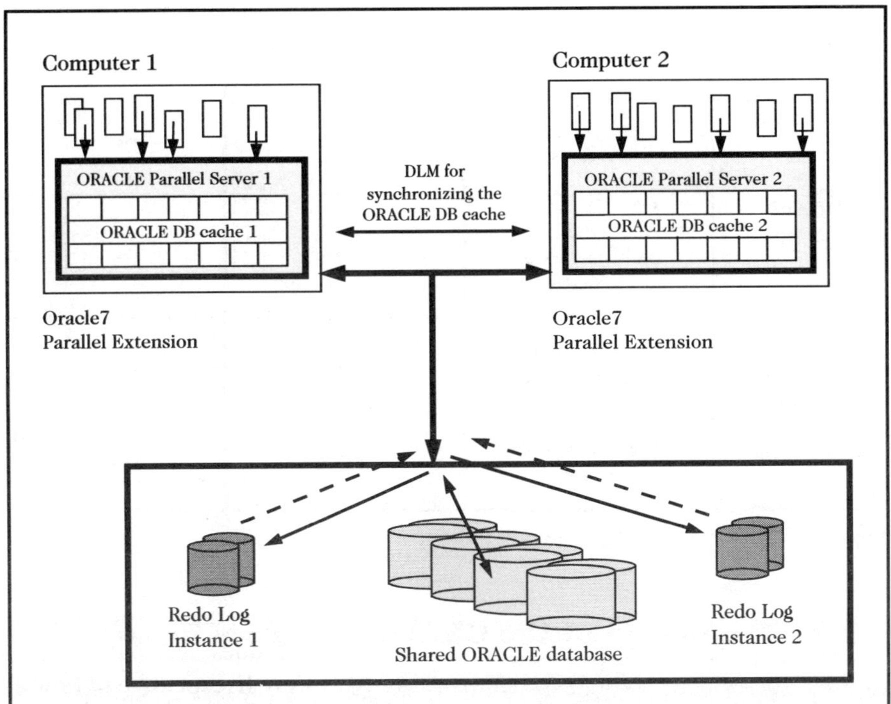

Figure 3.20 Oracle7 in a two node cluster configuration

RELEASE 7.1

Our examination of ORACLE's software architecture so far has been based on the assumption that there is always a one to one relationship between instance and database, that for each ORACLE instance there is one and only one ORACLE database, consisting of any number of files, database objects and server processes. When we come to consider clustered and massively parallel systems however, it becomes necessary to reconsider this assumption. In these systems we find that there can be a number of instances for one ORACLE database, thus producing a configuration as shown in Figure 3.20, where instances are running on each of the cluster's nodes but all these instances are linked to one and the same database. In this environment it is also possible to run the same applications differently on different nodes of the cluster so that, depending on the overall workload of each node, the same program can be run with a Multi-Threaded and with a Dedicated Server configuration.

A clustered system of the kind shown here does however require a number of additional functions in order to synchronize processing within the database caches. This is because it can easily happen that the same data block needs to be accessed and modified in both caches more or less simultaneously. The efficient synchronization of the database caches in this configuration is made possible by Oracle's Parallel Server technology, which is presented in detail in Section 3.3.6.

ORACLE System	System architecture	many online users moderate DB workload	many processes high DB workload
Oracle7	Single CPU systems	**MTS**	**DS**
	Symmetric multi-processor systems	**MTS**	**DS**
Oracle7 Parallel Server extension	Loosely coupled (cluster) systems	**MTS**	**DS**
	Massively parallel systems	**MTS**	**DS**

Figure 3.21 Oracle7 configuration variations

3.3.2 The design of the ORACLE software interfaces

We can examine the design of applications systems which use an ORACLE database from two viewpoints: from the client side, which comprises the actual application program plus all the necessary interfaces to the ORACLE system, and from the server side, which contains the corresponding server interfaces and the server functions.

Situated between these two groups of functions we find the interface programs which allow the client and server systems to communicate with each other. On the client side these interface programs are together referred to as the User Program Interface (UPI), and on the server side as the Oracle Program Interface (OPI).

When for example a SQL statement is generated by any user program (irrespective of whether it is a 3GL or 4GL environment), then it is converted into a series of UPI function calls which can be processed by an ORACLE server process. The UPI calls are generated either by the precompiler or, in the case of dynamic SQL, at runtime. If the application is being run under a Multi-Threaded Server configuration, the individual UPI calls are sent to the ORACLE dispatcher which has been allocated to this application; the dispatcher then places these calls (which we have also referred to as database requests) in the request queue in the database cache, so that they can be processed by one of the shared ORACLE server processes. The next UPI call from the user program (the next part of the SQL statement) can be passed to the dispatcher as soon as the dispatcher returns the results of the first call via the corresponding response queue.

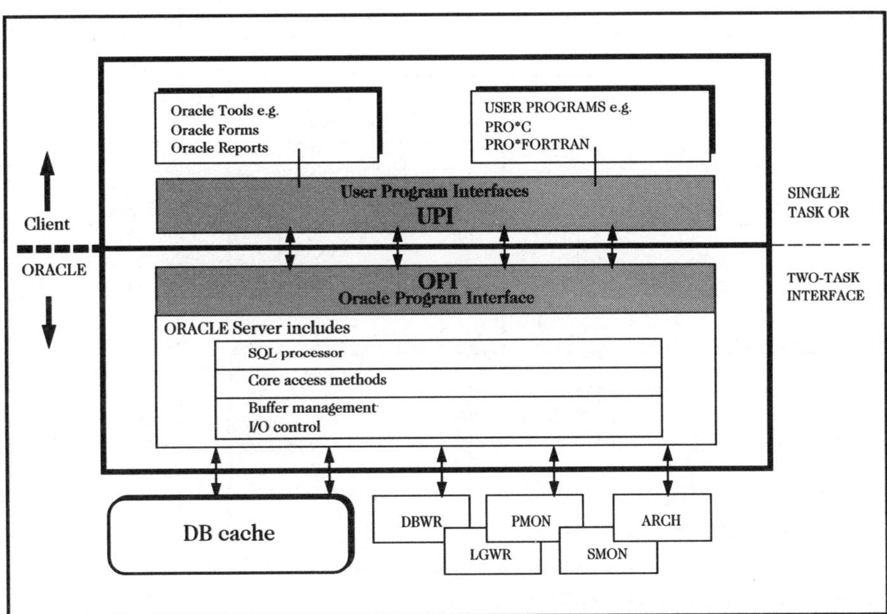

Figure 3.22 The software structure of an ORACLE applications system

The user (client) side of this software complex, which comprises a number of user processes and the user's interface to the system, is illustrated in Figure 3.22.

The design of this user interface is important to any programmer who wishes to make use of the ORACLE OCI interface in preference to the simpler but more limited precompiler (3GL) interface. Programming with the OCI interface demands much greater familiarity with how SQL statements are processed, and involves a number of OCI procedures which have to be programmed or tailored to the users' requirements. As with the other user functions, the OCI routines are also translated into UPI calls which undertake the communication to the ORACLE Server processes.

One of the most important reasons for separating client and server in this way is to ensure that the database server programs cannot be damaged by the user programs in any way, for example by being overwritten. Another important reason is to provide a basis for the implementation of client/server systems, where the user program (the client) has to run on a different system from that of the database (the server). Such systems will clearly be much easier to implement on a system whose architecture already distinguishes between client and server code.

Returning to the Dedicated Server configuration discussed earlier, we find that this can be implemented in one of two ways, depending on what type of operating system is in use, these are the single task and the two-task implementation.

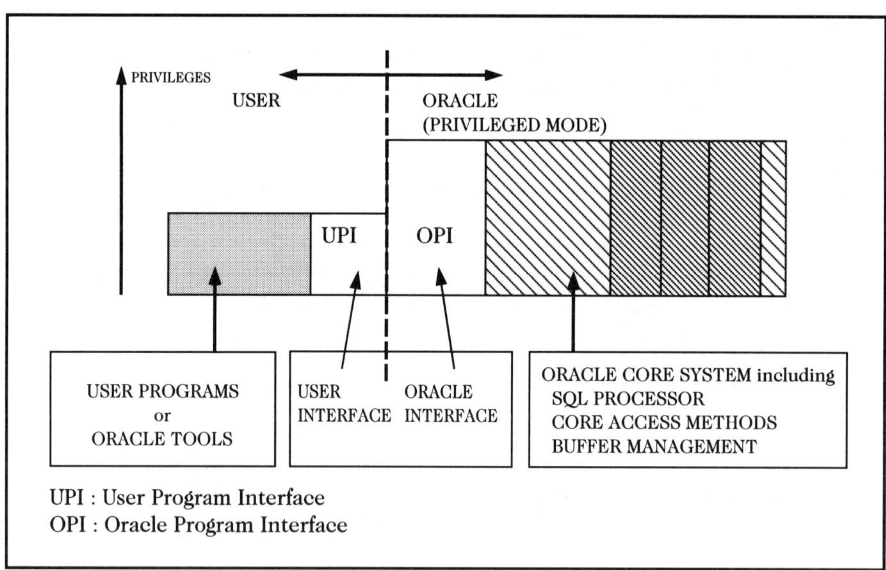

Figure 3.23 Single task configuration

In the case of the single task implementation, the user program and the ORACLE server programs are run within the same process. In order to ensure that the user program does not overwrite any of the memory being used by the ORACLE server, the two programs are run in different modes, with correspondingly different access rights: the server runs in privileged mode so that any of its data held in memory are protected from other programs, which run in a less privileged mode. A typical operating system for this type of single server implementation (*refer also to* Figure 3.23) is VMS from Digital Equipment Corporation (DEC).

With some operating systems however, as it is not possible to run different functions of the same process in different modes, a two-task configuration of the Dedicated Server becomes necessary. In these cases the user program and the server program are run within separate process environments, using some means of inter-process communication such as mail boxes, semaphores or shared memory to exchange messages or data. This type of implementation is usually encountered in UNIX systems (*see* Figure 3.24).

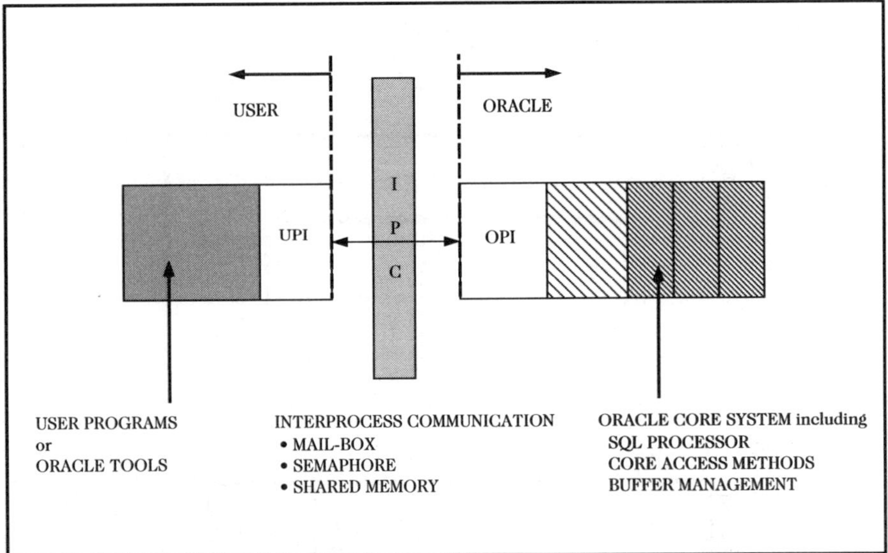

Figure 3.24 Two-task configuration

3.3.3 The ORACLE process structure

As we have already seen, an ORACLE database consists of the following components:

- the ORACLE database cache or System Global Area (SGA),
- a number of background processes,
- a number of files of the following three types:
  - data files,
  - redo log files,
  - control files.

Each one of the ORACLE background processes has to carry out certain specific tasks, and these are co-ordinated by means of the database cache which also acts as a communication channel for the individual processes. In the following sections we will look at the tasks carried out by each of these background processes.

The Database Writer process (DBWR)

The DBWR background process is responsible for writing any data blocks in the buffer cache area which have been modified back to the data files (*refer to* Figure 3.25, line 1). Once a buffer has been modified, it is not written back as soon as the transaction has been completed; instead it is kept in the database cache as long as possible so that other processes can have access to it if required. The point at which it is written back to the data files is dependent on one of a sequence of events or conditions.

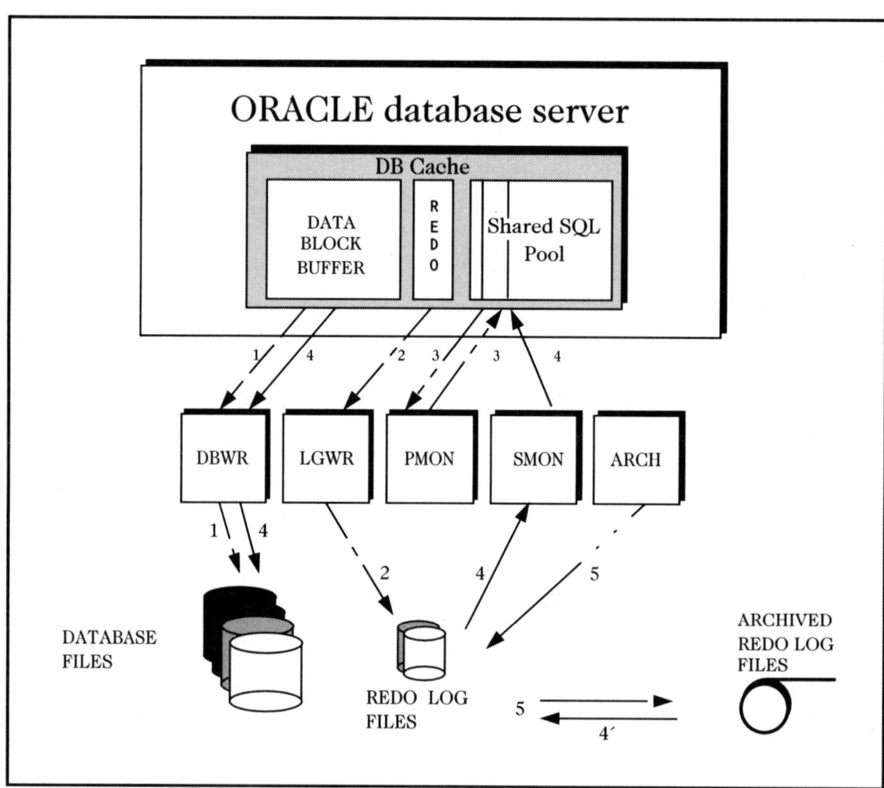

Figure 3.25 The ORACLE Process Structure

The first condition which causes the DBWR process to write all modified data blocks occurs when another process requires space in the database cache area (to read from the data files) but all the buffers in the cache area are at that moment occupied. In this case the DBWR writes some of the modified buffers back to the data files so that the space which has become available can be used by the requesting process.

Other conditions which activate the DBWR process are as follows:

- the number of modified blocks in the buffer cache exceeds a certain, predefined percentage of the overall number of available buffers;
- if the DBWR has not been activated by either of these external events then it automatically carries out a write procedure at a predefined interval; this timeout occurs once every three seconds;
- when a checkpoint occurs, the Log Writer signals the DBWR to write all modified buffers to the data files.

Once this write procedure has been carried out the data files are in a defined state, since any modifications made to the data have now been entered in the files. Whenever a checkpoint occurs it is also entered in the file headers of all data files, in the control file(s) and in the redo log files. If a database recovery subsequently becomes necessary, then the time of the checkpoint is used as the starting point for the recovery procedure.

A checkpoint itself is triggered by one of two events: either by the system switching to a new redo log file (where the current redo log file has been filled) or as defined by the following two INIT.ORA parameters:

- LOG_CHECKPOINT_INTERVAL
- LOG_CHECKPOINT_TIMEOUT

These two parameters specify how often a checkpoint is to be carried out as measured (respectively) in redo log blocks (based on a block size of 512 bytes) or in units of time.

All write operations carried out by the DBWR, irrespective of how they are initiated, must always be synchronized with the Log Writer process. Before the DBWR starts its write procedure a signal is sent to the Log Writer which then writes the current redo log buffer to the redo log file so that it all the data which would be required for a recovery operation are available to the recovery process.

The Redo Log Writer process (LGWR)

One of the most important features of transaction orientated database systems is that when a transaction is completed (by the COMMIT command) all the changes carried out in the course of that transaction should be made 'permanent' in the database, so that the data of a completed transaction cannot be affected by any error situation which may arise. However as we have seen with the ORACLE DBMS, the data blocks which have been changed within one transaction are written to the data files not when the transaction is completed (a synchronous COMMIT), but at some other point determined by the system (asynchronous COMMIT). It is therefore necessary to find some method of preserving the integrity of all completed transactions in case an error, such as a system crash, should occur which destroys the contents of the database cache.

In order to prevent this kind of data loss, all changes made to the buffers in the database cache in the course of one transaction are also logged in the redo log buffer, which forms part of the database cache (*see* Figure 3.26). For all changes which are made to the database, the redo log buffer stores both the current and the previous values (the *undo* data); all redo entries are stored in the rollback segments.

One of the main responsibilities of the LGWR is to write the redo log buffer to the redo log file. The LGWR process is activated by any one of the following events:

- the current redo log buffer is 80% full,
- the end of a transaction is signalled by a user process (irrespective of how full the buffer is),
- the DBWR signals that it has been activated, prior to which a LGWR write operation becomes necessary.

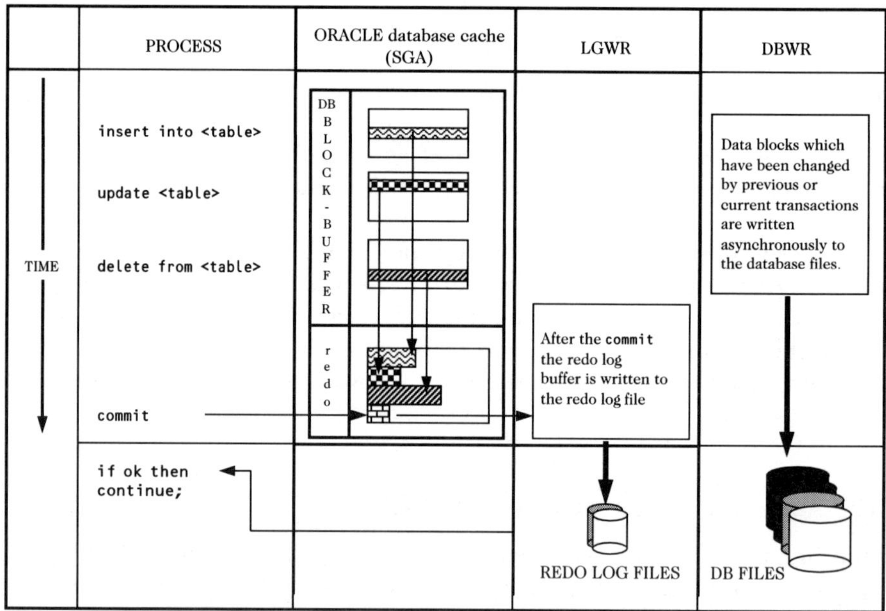

Figure 3.26 Processing a Transaction

When the LGWR has been activated as a result of a completed transaction (COMMIT) then the corresponding user process receives confirmation that the COMMIT was successful so that it can continue with the next stage of its operations. By working in this way the DBWR and LGWR guarantee the following benefits:

- All completed transactions are secured by being immediately entered in the redo log file, thus ensuring integrity of the data.
- All modified data blocks are kept in the database cache (that is in memory) for as long as possible, thus reducing access times.
- All completed transactions can be confirmed very quickly, as it is only necessary for the system to write one redo log buffer to disk, thus improving system performance.

With reference to the third of these three points, it should be added that in a heavily used system it will often happen that one LGWR write will complete a number of transactions, since while the LGWR is writing the current redo log buffer to disk, a number of new transactions will have been entered into the next one (thus grouping the COMMITS). This means that there are a number of commits for each redo log buffer.

Whenever a checkpoint is carried out the LGWR is responsible for the following tasks:

- marking all data blocks in the database cache which have been modified and thus preparing them to be written to disk by the DBWR;
- updating the file headers of all data files with the time of the checkpoint;
- writing the current redo log buffer to the redo log file;
- signalling the checkpoint to the DBWR, which then writes all the data blocks marked by the LGWR back to the data files.

While all these activities are taking place the ORACLE system itself remains fully available. However in the case of a very heavily used system, that is to say a system with a very high number of transactions, a large database cache (more than 20 MB) and a large number of data files, it is possible that system performance will suffer when the LGWR is performing all these additional tasks prior to a checkpoint. In order to prevent this happening, ORACLE provides an additional (optional) background process which will undertake these tasks and which can be started together with the instance. The name of this optional background process is CKPT, and it is started when the corresponding parameter is set in the INIT.ORA file, CHECKPOINT_PROCESS = TRUE. The CKPT process is then responsible for marking the changed blocks in the database cache, updating the file headers and activating the LGWR and finally the DBWR processes.

The Process Monitor (PMON)

Given the large number of user processes which use the database at any one time, it is to be expected that any one of these might suddenly come to a halt, either through being stopped by the system manager or because an error leads to a program crash. If a user process does terminate in this way, it is important to free any database resources being used by that process, row locks must be released for example and all changes made in the course of the aborted transaction must be rolled back. This task, which is usually referred to as process recovery, is the responsibility of the Process Monitor, which activates itself at regular intervals and checks for any failed user processes.

The System Monitor (SMON)

When an ORACLE database instance is started, the System Monitor is responsible for checking for any transactions which have not been completed, either because they are still open or because they have been committed but not yet written to the data files. This situation can arise when a database has not been correctly shut down and all database activity has been halted before ORACLE had the chance to write the contents of all database cache buffers to disk. This can happen as a result of one of the following events:

- the database administrator (the DBA) shuts down the database in IMMEDIATE or ABORT mode, using the commands SHUTDOWN IMMEDIATE or SHUTDOWN ABORT;
- the database system or operating system crashes;
- a hardware failure (but not a disk error) or a power cut occurs.

When the instance is restarted after any one of these events, the SMON undertakes all aspects of the instance recovery without any intervention being required from the DBA.

With the entries in the redo log file, SMON re-creates all the transactions since the last DBWR write operation: all completed transactions are written to the data files and any changes made by incomplete transactions are rolled back. Once this instance recovery procedure has been completed the database is in a consistent state once again, with no 'open' transactions remaining, and is ready to be used.

The Archiver Process (ARCH)

ARCH is an optional background process which is present depending on which mode has been used to start the ORACLE instance. If the database has been started in ARCHIVELOG mode, then automatic archiving is enabled and the ARCH process copies (archives) online redo log files to a separate storage device (for example a tape drive) once they become full. This means that in the event of a large scale loss of data, caused for example by a disk error, it would be possible to recreate the entire database by using backup copies of the relevant database files and archived redo log files (media recovery).

In addition to this ARCH makes all the entries in the control files which are required to complete a recovery procedure.

The Lock Processes (LCK0, LCK1,...LCK9)

The Lock Process LCK0 is needed whenever ORACLE is being run in Parallel Server mode, so that several ORACLE instances are working with the same database. Since the Oracle7 Parallel Server is used on loosely coupled (clustered) or massively parallel systems, we have a configuration where a number of separate instances, each with their own separate cache, are accessing the same database; if this configuration is to work efficiently then some method of synchronizing the cache management will clearly have to be made available.

Communication between the individual instances is made possible by using ORACLE's Parallel Cache Management Locks (PCM Locks) together with the corresponding function provided by the operating system (for example the Distributed Lock Manager). The LCK0 background process then provides the interface process between the parallel ORACLE instances and the actual operating system service which carries out the communication between the individual nodes of the cluster (*refer also to* Section 3.3.6). The LCK0 process itself is responsible for setting and releasing the PCM locks. In the case of systems which have to process very large numbers of transactions, it is possible to set up additional Lock processes, up to a maximum of ten; these additional processes are numbered in sequence (LCK1, LCK2... and so on). It is important to note that all ORACLE instances in a given parallel configuration must each be assigned the same number of Lock processes.

The Recoverer Process for distributed transactions (RECO)

The Recoverer Process (RECO) is required for the automatic recovery of distributed transactions. The process is activated whenever a two-phase transaction cannot be completed due to a failure on one of the system nodes involved, for example where a cluster node crashes just as a distributed transaction was in its prepare phase. In this case the RECO must ensure that this node's part of the overall transaction is properly completed as soon as the node becomes available again: if the transaction has been committed, then the COMMIT must also be carried through on the node that has crashed; the same applies if the distributed transaction has to be rolled back. Further details on the two-phase commit are given in Chapter 14.

3.3.4 The ORACLE database cache

As can be seen from Figure 3.25, the ORACLE database cache or System Global Area (SGA) has a key role in any ORACLE instance. The database cache is an area of memory which can be used by all the user processes which access the ORACLE instance. All the background processes which are necessary for running an ORACLE system make particularly intensive use of this area of memory, both for manipulating data and index blocks as well as for communicating with each other. The database cache includes the following distinct areas:

- The Database Buffer Cache
  The data blocks which have been requested by a user program are placed in the database buffer cache before they can be processed by the user program. Once a data block has been placed in one of the buffers then it can be used not only by the process which first requested it, but by any other user process which has sufficient access rights. An ORACLE installation is regarded as being well tuned when for every nine *logical* reads (reads from cache) only one *physical* read (a read from disk) is necessary. The buffers of the database cache are managed on the basis of a Least Recently Used (LRU) algorithm: that is to say that those data blocks which have been least recently used are first selected by the DBWR to be written back to disk or, if they have not been changed in any way, to be removed from the database buffer cache.

- The Shared Pool
  ORACLE uses this area of the database cache to store parsed SQL statements, compiled functions and procedures, data dictionary information and database triggers. One of the functions implemented for Oracle7 as opposed to ORACLE Version 6 is the ability to use the database cache for storing the parse tree and execution plan of a single SQL statement, so that it can be re-used by other processes without having to be parsed for a second time. Each SQL statement is divided by ORACLE into a *shared SQL area* and a *private SQL area*: the shared SQL area, which can be used by any number of processes, contains the parse tree and the execution plan for the SQL statement; the private SQL area contains information specific to the user process such as the values of the bind variables and the execution status of the statement. A private SQL area is created in the Shared Pool whenever a corresponding user process which is running under the multi-threaded server configuration executes a SQL statement. The database objects stored in the Shared Pool are also administered on the basis of a Least Recently Used algorithm, so that a parsed SQL statement which has not been used for some time will be removed from the Shared Pool to make way for new SQL statements, on the same basis that data blocks are flushed from the database buffer cache.

- Instance Information
  This area of the database cache stores a range of information about the instance, including which resources are currently locked, in which order a queue should be processed, which transactions are currently active and what their status is. This area will also include information on the request and response queues in a multi-threaded server configuration.

The size of the database cache does not have to be defined once and for all, but can be modified to take account of special circumstances. As we have already mentioned, the INIT.ORA file contains all the database parameters which are needed when starting an instance and opening the database. Most of the INIT.ORA parameters can be modified so that the system reflects as closely as possible both the users' requirements and the available hardware configuration. These parameters also determine the size of the database cache; an increase in the number of data block buffers (DB_BLOCK_BUFFERS) in particular will result in a larger database buffer cache which will in turn mean that more memory is needed for the database cache. Depending on the applications programs and the computer being used, the size of the database cache will vary between a few megabytes in the case of a small system up to 50 or 100 megabytes for large systems or where the number of transactions is very high.

The two INIT.ORA parameters which determine the size of the database cache more than any other are DB_BLOCK_BUFFERS and SHARED_POOL_SIZE. The DB_BLOCK_BUFFERS parameter specifies how many data block buffers should be set up in the database buffer cache (the default value is 60). The size of this area depends however not only on the number of buffers but also on the size of the buffer which, depending on the individual operating system, can be a multiple of an operating system block. In addition it is possible to change the database block size through the INIT.ORA parameter DB_BLOCK_SIZE. Typical values for the the database block size are 2 KB for most UNIX, VMS and DG systems and 4 KB for IBM/MVS and VM systems. The larger the number of database buffers, the more data blocks can be held in memory (the database buffer cache) at any one time without having to read from the hard disk. For this reason the overall performance of the system is significantly dependant on setting the right values for these parameters. An analysis of the database cache (*see* Chapter 6) can help to establish the optimum settings for these parameters for a given workload.

The parameter SHARED_POOL_SIZE defines the size of the database cache's shared pool where SQL statements, procedures, functions and database triggers are stored, the default size being 3.5 MB. The same rule applies here as for the database buffer cache, so that the larger the shared pool area, the more compiled SQL statements, procedures and so on can be held in memory at any one time. The optimum setting for this parameter is again very much dependent on the actual user and applications profiles and, as with the database buffer cache, can be calculated on the basis of a careful analysis of the system.

3.3.5 MTS and DS Oracle configurations

When defining an ORACLE instance which will have to run under both Multi-Threaded (MTS) and Dedicated Server (DS) configurations, there are essentially two components of the system which have to be taken into account and configured as necessary. These are the instance itself, which is configured by the parameters in the INIT.ORA file, and the Oracle Listener process (LST), which controls all requests to connect to the database and is therefore responsible for starting an ORACLE session (that is a user process) in either MTS or DS mode.

File Name	Required by	Example
INIT.ORA	**ORACLE Instance**	mts_service = server1 mts_dispatcher = tcp,2 decnet,3 mts_max_dispatcher = 8 mts_servers = 4 mts_max_servers = 25 mts_listener_port = (address=(protocol=tcp)(host=hp1)(port=3001)) mts_listener_port = (address=(protocol=decnet)(object=gst)(node=vax1))
LISTENER.ORA	**ORACLE Listener**	sqlnet listen = (address=(protocol=tcp)(host=hp1)(port=3001))) sqlnet listen = (address=(protocol=decnet)(object=gst)(node=vax1)))
TNSNAMES.ORA	**ORACLE Listener**	mts=(description=(address=(protocol=tcp)(host=hp1)(port=3001))(connect_data=(sid=server1))) ds= (description=(address=(protocol=decnet)(object=gst)(node=vax1))(connect_data=(sid=server1)(**srvr=dedicated**)))

Figure 3.27 Parameter files for MTS and DS configurations

An ORACLE instance can be run in MTS mode when the corresponding parameters of the INIT.ORA file have been defined correctly. These parameters specify factors such as the minimum and maximum number of shared server processes (MTS_SERVERS, MTS_MAX_SERVERS) and the number of dispatcher processes required for each network protocol. In the example shown in Figure 3.27, we see that two dispatchers have been started for TCP/IP and three for DecNet, although each dispatcher is capable of serving more than one user process at the same time. The allocation of user processes to dispatchers is undertaken by the Listener process on first connecting to the database, and the Listener ensures that the workload is evenly distributed between all dispatchers.

In order to carry out its functions the Listener process requires the configuration file LISTENER.ORA, which specifies on which ports to 'listen' for incoming connect calls. A second file, TNSNAMES.ORA, contains alias names for connect strings to any number of different ORACLE instances.

The extracts from the three file types shown in Figure 3.27 show the most important parameters which have to be defined for a MTS configuration. Once the parameters in these files have been defined then the Listener process can be started independently of any ORACLE instance, and is able to serve any number of ORACLE instances. On the basis of the parameters defined in the INIT.ORA file for this example, the ORACLE instance will be started as follows: with two dispatchers for TCP/IP protocol, three dispatchers for DecNet, four shared server processes and with the request and response queues set up in the database cache.

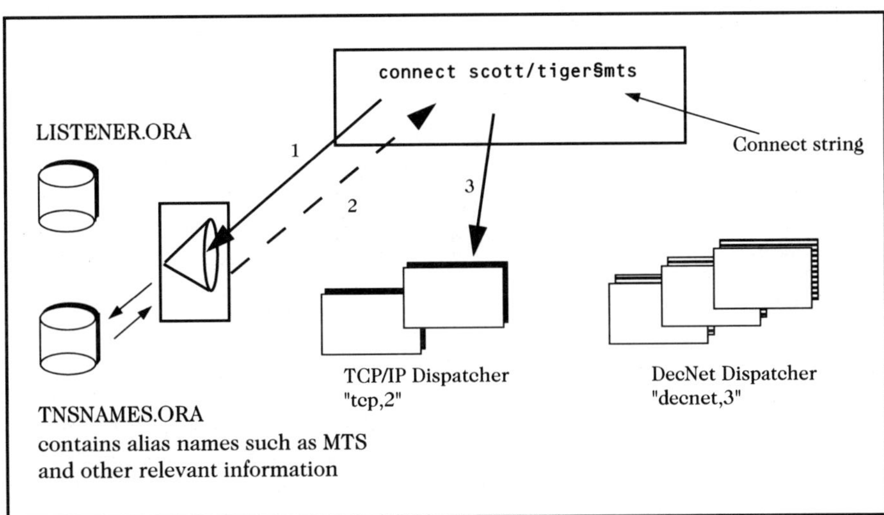

Figure 3.28 Connecting to a database under an MTS Configuration

Figure 3.28 illustrates the processing of a connect request. The incoming connect request (1) from a given user process is detected by the Listener and the connect string is interpreted with the help of the information contained in the TNSNAMES.ORA file. Once the connect string has been correctly processed, the Listener checks the workloads of the available dispatcher processes and the user process receives the address of its dispatcher (2), which then becomes responsible for processing all future database requests

(3) from that process. Once the dispatcher address has been communicated the Listener has no further role in processing the connect request or in managing the session as a whole.

If the Listener receives a connect request as shown in Figure 3.29 (in a DS configuration), then its first two actions are the same as those we have just looked at for an MTS configuration: the connect string is validated against the TNSNAMES.ORA file and is then processed accordingly (*refer also to* Figure 3.27). The alias name used in this example `ds` (the name is not significant) tells the Listener that a Dedicated Server (SRVR=DEDICATED) has to be started for this user process. The Listener therefore starts an ORACLE server process and then passes its address to the user process. This Dedicated Server is then responsible for all database requests from the user process, which thus becomes independent of the shared servers and dispatchers of the MTS configuration.

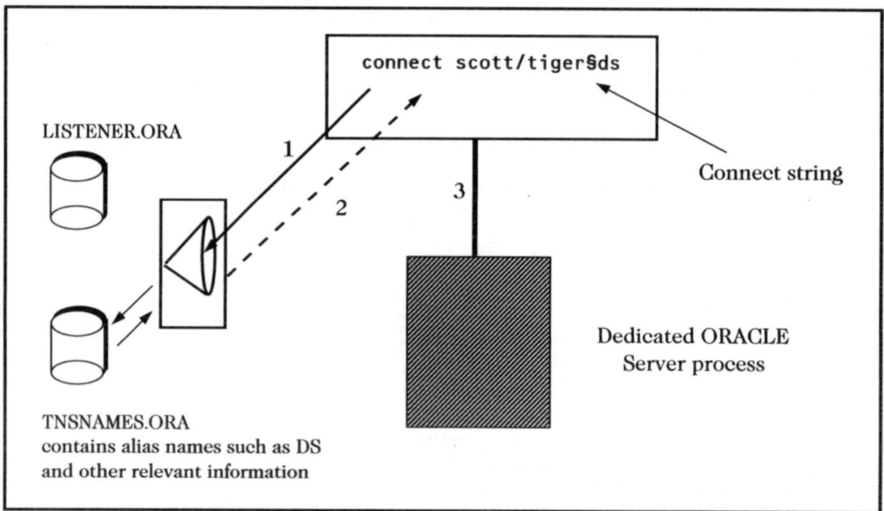

Figure 3.29 Connecting to a database under a Dedicated Server configuration

By using the alternative configurations which are available under Oracle7, it is possible to provide each user process with a configuration which makes optimum use of the available system resources. By using the MTS configuration it is possible to run a large number of online user processes with only a few shared server processes, which means that the overall number of processes in a large online system can be drastically reduced. Whenever the workload for the current shared servers becomes too great then additional server processes are started automatically; similarly the number of server processes is reduced as the online workload decreases. This ability of the ORACLE system to respond dynamically to the overall workload at any one time ensures optimum use of all available resources. It should be emphasized that both the configurations we have looked at (Dedicated Server and Dynamic Multi-Threaded Server) are available on all the hardware platforms supported by Oracle.

ORACLE System	System architecture	many online users moderate DB workload	many processes high DB workload
Oracle7	Single CPU systems	**MTS**	**DS**
	Symmetric multi-processor systems	**MTS**	**DS**
Oracle7 Parallel Server extension	Loosely coupled (cluster) systems	**MTS**	**DS**
	Massively parallel systems	**MTS**	**DS**

Figure 3.30 Oracle7 configuration variations

3.3.6 ORACLE parallel server technology

3.3.6.1 Introduction

RELEASE 7.1

The Oracle7 system was optimized for single processor systems and for symmetric multi-processor systems (SMP). In order to support the specific hardware architectures of the loosely coupled (cluster) systems increasingly found in the UNIX environment, as well as those of massively parallel systems, it became necessary to implement additional functions which would ensure optimum support of these platforms without any loss of database functionality. The ORACLE Parallel Server Technology was developed with this aim and the Parallel Server option of Oracle7 is available specifically for this type of computer architecture.

One feature common to the architectures of both clustered and massively parallel systems is the absence of a common main memory, indeed each node in a cluster configuration is a complete computer system consisting of one or more CPUs and its own main memory. To transform these individual computers into a powerful cluster system in which a number of stand-alone computers are connected together to form a single 'logical' system, it is initially necessary to provide the corresponding hardware and operating system components. However these basic components are in themselves insufficient to make optimum use of the resources which a modern database management system can provide.

If database systems are to be successfully used in a clustered system environment as servers, then it is essential that the database systems on the individual nodes are synchronized as effectively as possible and that they can communicate without restriction.

3.3.6.2 Parallel Cache Management (PCM)

A fundamental requirement in the development of the ORACLE Parallel Server was that ORACLE's online transaction processing (OLTP) capabilities should be retained in loosely coupled and massively parallel system environments. No compromises should be allowed which might limit the OLTP functions, in other words the ORACLE Parallel Server should also offer the following functions:

- fast-commit procedure
- asynchronous data block writes
- an unlimited number of row locks without escalation
- read access without locking
- online backup
- online recovery

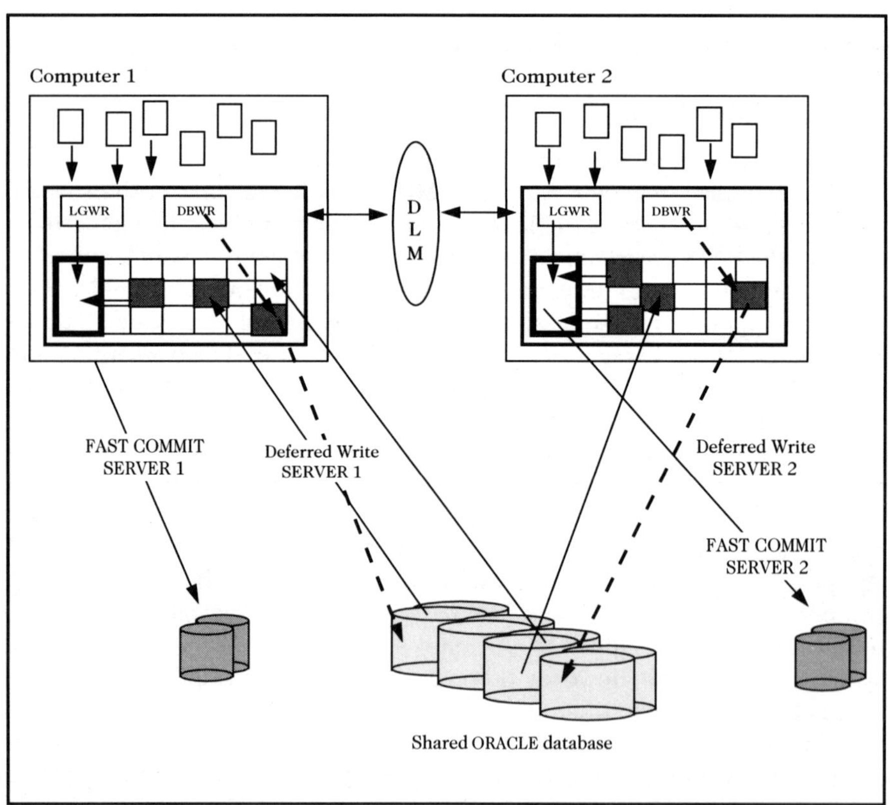

Figure 3.31 An ORACLE Parallel Server Configuration

Figure 3.31 shows a typical ORACLE configuration in a loosely coupled system environment. In this example each node in the cluster has an ORACLE instance with its own database cache and background processes, and both instances work with the same ORACLE database; this means they are both able to carry out the following functions:

- to modify data in the same database objects (the same database files),
- to read data from the same database objects (the same database files),
- to write the protocol for a committed transaction to the redo log files assigned to the instances.

As can be seen from the diagram this configuration presents additional problems with regard to synchronizing the individual database caches and the resulting need of the ORACLE instances to communicate with one another. An ORACLE Parallel Server configuration must therefore have mechanisms at its disposal which enable it to determine the status of a data block requested by a SQL statement as follows:

- whether it is still in the database files,
- whether it is already in the local database cache,
- whether it is in another instance's database cache.

The way in which the database caches are synchronized and the frequency of communication between individual nodes are both of decisive importance in determining the performance of a database in this type of system environment. In order to retain the OLTP functions in the ORACLE Parallel Server while at the same time minimizing the workload necessary for database cache synchronization a distinction has been made between the following functions:

- transaction synchronization,
- database cache synchronization.

Transaction synchronization is carried out with the same functionality and based on the same efficient locking procedures as are used in 'standard' Oracle7 (*refer also to* Chapter 4).

This means that regardless of which instance is involved, every transaction locks only at row level and lock escalation does not occur at any time; the transaction locks are released as soon as the transaction has been completed (COMMIT, ROLLBACK, ROLLBACK TO `<savepoint>`). In this way it is possible for rows from one and the same data block to be simultaneously modified by different transactions in different ORACLE instances.

In order to synchronize the database caches in a cluster configuration (parallel cache management or PCM locking) the operating system has to provide a service to enable communication between the individual cluster nodes. In a DEC-VAX environment this communication is carried out by the Distributed Lock Manager (DLM) and on the various UNIX cluster configurations from Sequent, Pyramid, HP or IBM there are similar operating system extensions which undertake the same communication between nodes. This service is used by the ORACLE Parallel Server only for database cache synchronization, not for transaction synchronization.

Different cluster system resources can be administered with the Distributed Lock Manager, but the database cache synchronization of an ORACLE Parallel Server System is only concerned with data blocks, index blocks and rollback segment blocks and is based on the following pre-conditions:

- The size of a DLM resource (that is the specific number of data blocks per PCM lock) is defined for individual database files by an INIT.ORA parameter.
- The status of a DLM resource, that is of the specified number of data blocks, can be SHARED, EXCLUSIVE or NULL (unknown). This lock on a DLM resource is called a PCM lock in order to distinguish it from a transaction lock.
- A PCM lock is assigned by the DLM to the ORACLE instance and not to a transaction, this means that whereas the transaction locks are released once a transaction is completed, the PCM status of a data block is retained.
- A data block's PCM lock remains assigned to an ORACLE instance until another ORACLE instance requests an incompatible lock. It should be noted that if incompatible PCM locks are requested it is not possible, in contrast to the procedure for transaction locks, for one of the PCM requests to be put into a waiting status. Every incompatible PCM lock request forces the instance holding the current PCM lock to change its status and to carry out a specific action.

In Section 3.3.6.3 we will examine three examples of this type of status change in detail. Figure 3.32 contrasts the two synchronization procedures which have been implemented in the Oracle7 Parallel Server.

The Parallel Cache Management procedure guarantees that the data blocks in the caches of the individual ORACLE instances are always valid. If an ORACLE instance has a data block with a valid PCM lock (Shared S or Exclusive X) then no further communication is necessary to check that the data block's values are valid and that they have not been or are not being being modified by another instance.

ORACLE Parallel Server

ORACLE Transaction Locks (Standard ORACLE Transaction)	ORACLE Database Cache Management (Parallel Cache Management)
Transaction is responsible for holding locks.	ORACLE instance is responsible for holding PCM locks.
Locks remain in force until the end of the transaction.	Locks remain in force until a PCM lock is requested by another instance.
Row-level locking.	PCM locks are held on one or more data blocks.
Responsible for co-ordinating a number of transactions (possibly of several instances) on the same data structure.	Responsible for synchronizing the database caches (which data blocks are being held by which instances).

Figure 3.32 Comparison of Transaction and PCM Locks

Separating *transaction* synchronization and *database cache* synchronization has the following advantages:

- All Oracle7 functions remain fully available even in loosely coupled system environments, for example fast commit, asynchronous write, read access without locking and so on.
- Transactions in different ORACLE instances lock only the rows which are to be modified; this means that parallel transactions in different ORACLE instances can modify different rows of the same data block without access conflicts.
- Communication to synchronize the single database caches is kept to a minimum.
- As the Distributed Lock Manager (DLM) is needed only for database cache synchronization and not for transaction synchronization it is less likely that the DLM will be overworked.

3.3.6.3 Examples

The following examples illustrate the operation of the various ORACLE Parallel Server components both individually and in conjunction with each other. All the examples are based on a simple two node configuration in which the following operations are carried out:

- read operations
- modification operations on separate data blocks
- modification operations on the same data block

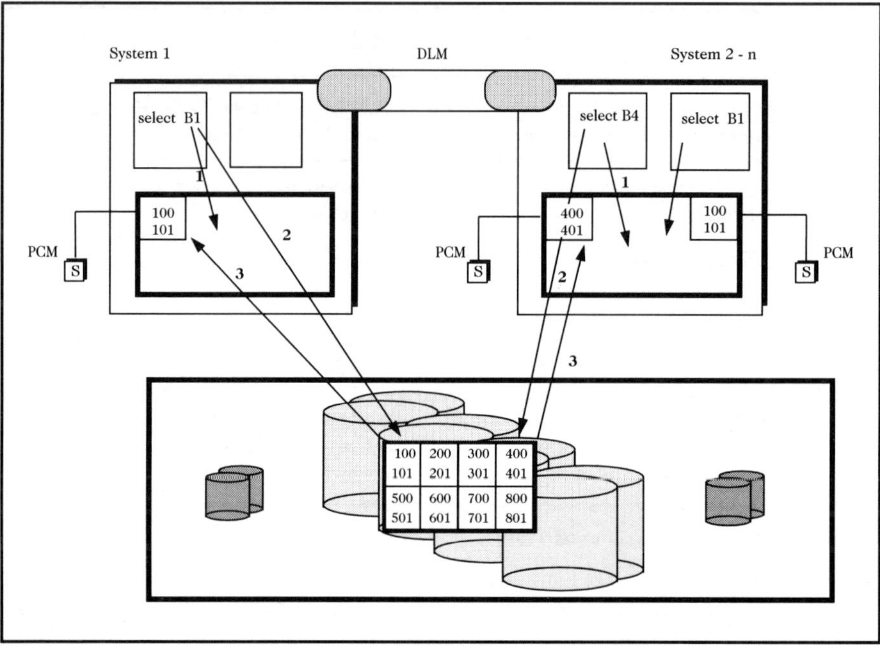

Figure 3.33a ORACLE Parallel Server: example 1 – reading data

Process stages		Description
I. Instance 1	0	ORACLE **Instance 1** generates a read command for data block B1.
	1	PCM checks whether the block is in the local database cache (SGA) with the correct status for this operation.
	2	The block isn't available in the local database cache nor is it being used by any other instance.
	3	The data block is read into the database cache of ORACLE **Instance 1** and a (shared) PCM lock is set.
II. Instance 2	0	ORACLE **Instance 2** generates a read command for data block B4.
	1–3	Under identical conditions the next processing stages are the same as those described in **I**.
III. Instance 2	0	ORACLE **Instance 2** generates a read command for data block B1.
	1	PCM checks whether the block is in the local SGA with the correct status for this operation. The existing PCM lock on the data block from **Instance 1** is detected.
	2	As these two lock requests are compatible the PCM lock which is needed by **Instance 2** can be generated without further communication between the instances. Block B1 can then be read from the database file into the database cache of **Instance 2**.
	3	The data block B1 is read into the database cache of ORACLE **Instance 2**.

Note: *At this point data block B1 is being held for read access in the database caches of both instances, subject to the DBMS paging procedures of the individual instance. This applies for all read operations including (which is particularly important) for the many read operations which are carried out on the data dictionary and the dictionary cache.*

Figure 3.33b Example 1 – processing sequence

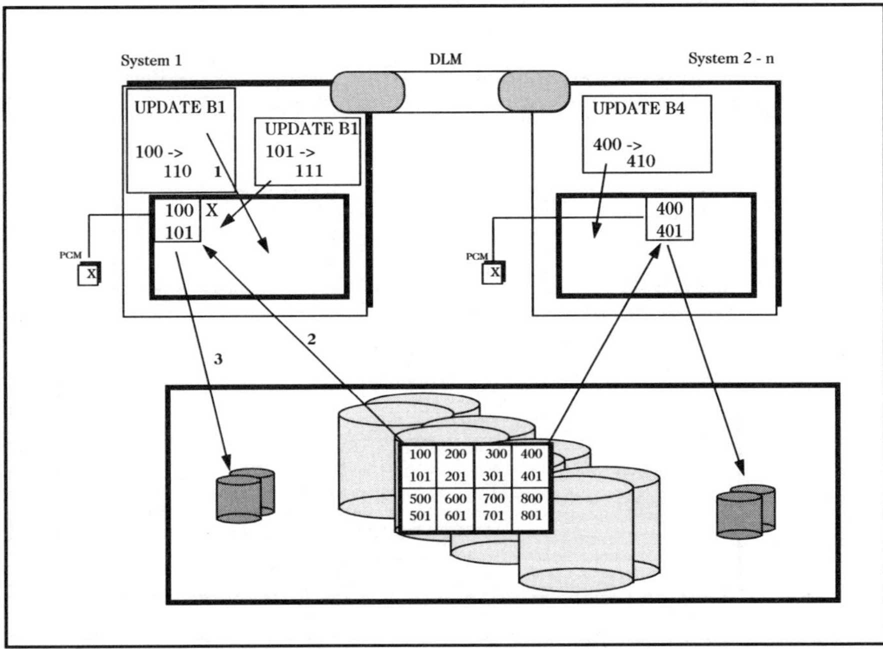

Figure 3.34a ORACLE Parallel Server: example 2 – modifying data (separate blocks)

Process stages		**Description**
I. Instance 1	0	ORACLE **Instance 1** generates a modify (UPDATE) operation for data block B1 (one row).
	1	PCM checks whether the block is in the local database cache with the correct status for this operation PCM(X).
	2	The block isn't in the local database cache and is not being processed by any other instance; it is therefore read into the database cache (SGA) of **Instance1**. The block B1 is then assigned the exclusive status PCM(X).
	3	Once the modification is completed then the redo log block, which contains a full protocol of this transaction, is written to the redo log file and the transaction is thus completed. Block B1 however remains in the SGA of **Instance1** where it can be accessed by the other processes of **Instance 1** without any additional processing being necessary (asynchronous write).
II. Instance 2	0–3	The above procedure is also followed for **Instance 2** and the example with data block B4.

Note: *A data block remains in the SGA of the corresponding instance until it is written to the database files by the DBMS paging procedure or until the block is required by another instance with an incompatible PCM lock request. In this case the data block in question is immediately written back to the database files. Even if a block has been written back to disk by the DBMS paging procedure, its PCM status remains in force.* Refer also to *Example 3.*

Figure 3.34b Example 2 – processing sequence

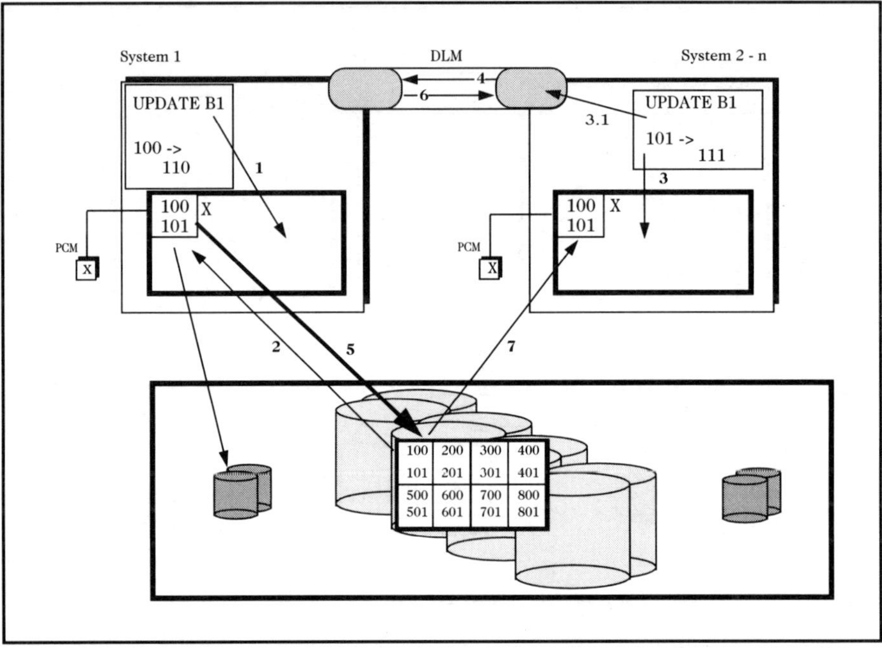

Figure 3.35a ORACLE Parallel Server: example 3 – modifying data (in the same block)

Process stages		**Description**
I. Instance 1	0–2	ORACLE **Instance 1** generates a modify operation for the first record in data block B1. The procedure is then as described in Example 2: • the local DLM is signalled • the data block is read and assigned the status PCM(X) • the modification is carried out but the transaction has not yet been completed
II. Instance 2	3	ORACLE **Instance 2** generates a statement to modify the second record in data block B1, which, however, is still located in **Instance 1**. The local SGA is first searched for block B1.
	4	The DLM of **Instance 2** signals to the DLM of **Instance 1** requesting block B1.
	5	The DLM of **Instance1** causes block B1 to be written to disk and lifts the PCM(X) lock (database cache synchronization). However the lock on the first record in block B1 remains in force (transaction synchronization).
	6	The DLM of **Instance1** signals to **Instance 2** that block B1 can now be read from disk.
	7	**Instance 2** reads block B1 into its SGA and assigns a PCM(X) lock, after which the required modification can be carried out.

Note: *Different records in the same data block can be modified at the same time by transactions which have been generated by different ORACLE instances. The parallel cache management is responsible for synchronizing the database caches (SGAs) of all active ORACLE instances.*

Figure 3.35b Example 3 – processing sequence

3.3.6.4 Increased tolerance to hardware failure

A further advantage of a loosely coupled configuration is its increased tolerance to hardware failure, and this important feature is fully supported by the ORACLE Parallel Server technology. If one of the nodes in a cluster fails while an ORACLE instance is running then this database is automatically restored by one of the remaining ORACLE instances without the intervention of the database administrator.

This feature is achieved as follows:

- Transaction locks held by the lost ORACLE instance are released.
- Rollforward recovery.
  All transactions of the lost ORACLE instance which have been committed but not yet written to the database files are completed by means of the redo log file.

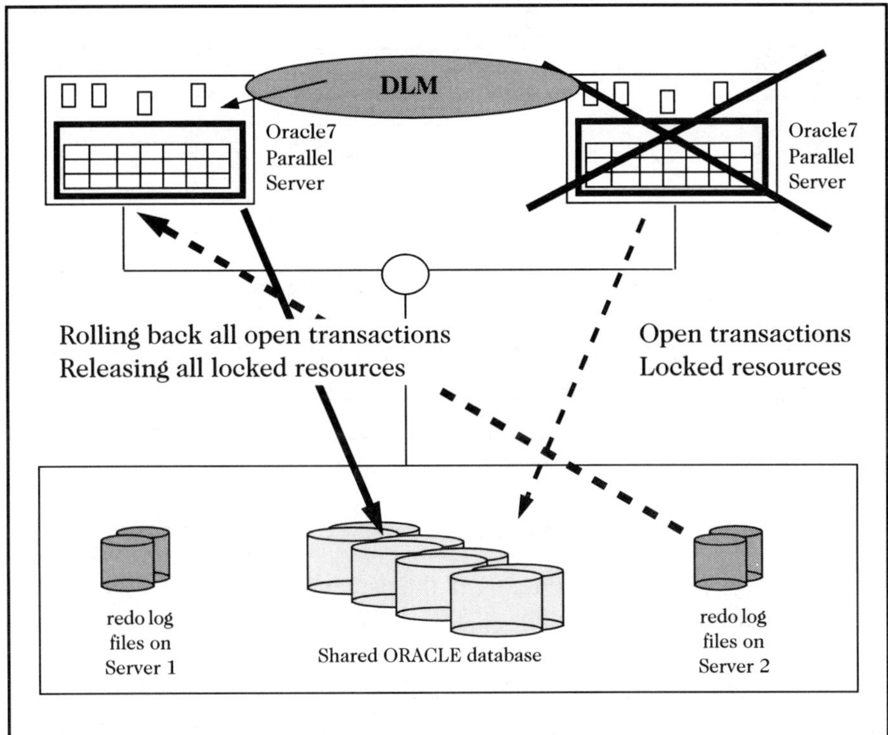

Figure 3.36 Parallel Server Hardware Fault Tolerance

- Rollback recovery.
  All transactions of the lost ORACLE instance which have not yet been committed are rolled back.

3.4 Data dictionary

3.4.1 Introduction

Up until now we have examined an ORACLE database in terms of its constituent file types (database files, redo log files, control files) and how these are logically structured (tablespaces, segments, data blocks and so on). Apart from its physical structure however, we can also look at a database in terms of its contents, as represented in Figure 3.37.

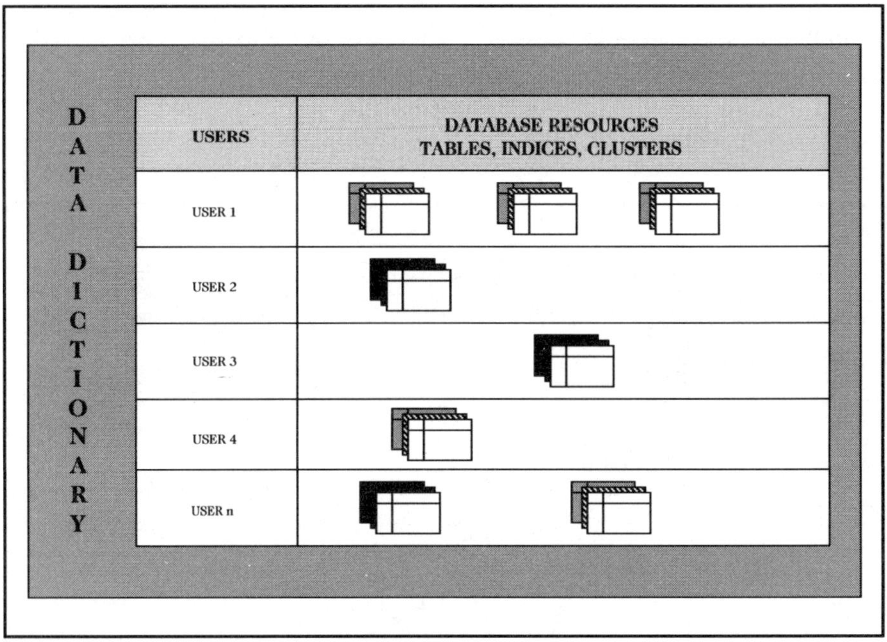

Figure 3.37 The contents of an ORACLE database

Looked at it in this way an ORACLE database always consists of:

- A data dictionary which contains all the data which are responsible for the correct running of the database. The data dictionary forms the basis for the administration of all ORACLE database objects.
- Any number of users with differing privileges.
- Database objects such as tables, clusters, views, indexes, procedures, database triggers which have been created and can be used by the individual ORACLE users.

The data dictionary, which serves to administer the ORACLE database, itself consists of a fixed data structure. In the ORACLE system this data structure is implemented as a set of database tables which can be accessed with SQL. The data dictionary can be divided into two levels: at the internal level we have the actual base tables, which cannot be accessed by an ordinary user; only very highly privileged ORACLE users have direct read access to these data structures. In all other cases these base tables of the data dictionary's internal level can only be modified by the database system itself.

The second level or the external level of the data dictionary contains a large number of views of the data dictionary's base tables and these are available to all ORACLE users to a greater or lesser extent, providing them with a wide range of information. In the following sections we shall look at the internal and external levels in more detail.

3.4.2 Data dictionary tables

For each new ORACLE database three users are always created. The users are:

- SYS
  SYS is the owner of all the data dictionary tables (internal level) and of all data dictionary views (external level).
  SYS is the most highly privileged user in any ORACLE system and should only be made direct use of in the most exceptional circumstances.
- SYSTEM
  SYSTEM is the owner of the database tables which are created for the ORACLE tools such as Oracle Forms and Oracle Reports. SYSTEM is the standard DBA of every ORACLE system and can be used to carry out all the standard DBA tasks which may occur.
- PUBLIC
  PUBLIC is a 'dummy' user, which stands for all of the users in an ORACLE system, and may be compared to the 'WORLD' user classification in many operating systems. This means that any privileges which have been granted to PUBLIC are available to all users of the ORACLE database.

The user SYS is special in that it creates all the tables of the data dictionary. This occurs automatically when the database is set up with the (standard) CREATE TABLE commands which are contained in the SQL procedure SQL.BSQ. SYS is the owner of these tables and possesses all privileges for them. These base tables contain internal system information and may only be modified by the ORACLE server. Read access to these tables is also forbidden to any ORACLE user except SYS and should not be allowed under any circumstances. This is because the internal data dictionary level can change from one ORACLE version to another and this would have an immediate impact on all related read commands. All read access to the data dictionary should be carried out only on the basis of the available virtual tables (views) as the structure of this external level remains constant even when versions are changed.

As we have already mentioned, the data dictionary contains all relevant system information, such as:

- users and their privileges
- tables and their column names and data types
- statistics on tables and indexes
- index information
- access rights to tables
- resource profile information and the corresponding user allocations
- availability of free space

For every SQL statement many items of data must be checked, so that the data dictionary has to be accessed a number of times. Since the data dictionary itself consists of tables, the system generates its own internal SQL statements to check whether each SQL statement entered is valid and can be carried out. Figure 3.38 demonstrates this taking the example of a simple SQL statement.

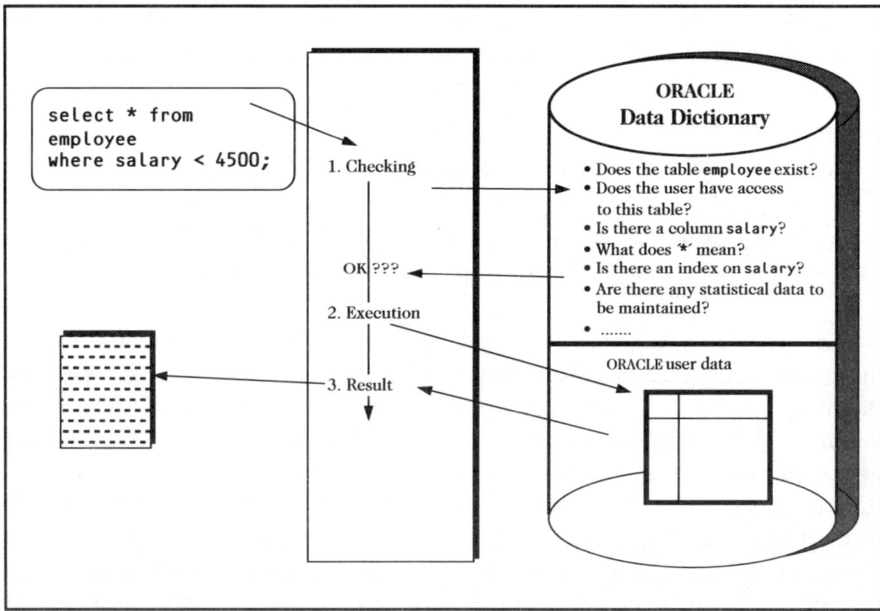

Figure 3.38 Processing a SQL statement

With regard to Figure 3.38 it should be pointed out that not every internal SQL statement has to access the disk since a very large amount of information is held in the database cache. This internal information is also managed with a LRU algorithm, so that data dictionary data which are frequently used remain in the database cache longer than those data which are very seldom used.

3.4.3 Data dictionary views

The external data dictionary level allows each ORACLE user to see all information relevant to his or her work with the ORACLE system. This level is realized by a large number of virtual tables (views), which obtain their data from the real dictionary tables (internal data dictionary level) and display the required information simply and easily. These data dictionary views can be queried by the user with SQL in the same way as any other table which the user has defined. The external data dictionary is divided into three groups, each of which provides a different perspective of the data and the name of each group is used to prefix the names of the corresponding data dictionary views. The three groups are:

- USER
  This designates all database objects which are owned by the current user. Thus the following command will show all the tables which the user has created:

```
select * from user_tables;
```

- ALL
  This designates all database objects to which the user has access. In this case objects are displayed which have been created by other users, who have then granted access rights to the current user. Thus the following command will show all the tables to which the user has access:

```
select * from all_tables;
```

- DBA
  All views with this prefix can only be accessed by users with the corresponding DBA privileges. These views present a global view of the whole database. Thus the following command will show all the tables of all users in the entire system:

```
select * from dba_tables;
```

As these three examples demonstrate, the names of each of these views differ from one another only by their prefixes, but their basic function is the same in all three cases, to present specific information from the underlying tables. This naming convention is a basic characteristic of ORACLE's external data dictionary and is illustrated in Figure 3.39 which lists a number of data dictionary views in tabular form showing how the view's name consists of a prefix and a corresponding appendage.

Prefix Appendage	user_	all_	dba_
tables	Returns the names of all the tables which have been created by the user.	Returns the names of all the tables to which the user has access.	Returns all the tables in the entire system.
tab_columns	Returns all columns for all the tables which have been created by the user.	Returns all columns for all the tables to which the user has access.	Returns all columns for all the tables in the entire system.
indexes	Returns all indexes which have been created by the user.	Returns all indexes on tables to which the user has access.	Returns all the indexes in the entire system.
views	Returns all views which have been created by the user.	Returns all views to which the user has access.	Returns all the views in the entire system.

Figure 3.39 Naming conventions for the ORACLE data dictionary views

3.4.4 Implementation of the data dictionary

As we have already mentioned both the internal and external data dictionary is created by the (especially privileged) SYS user when the database is initialized. As the data dictionary is made up of database objects (internally by tables and externally by views), these objects need to be created when the database is initialized by the appropriate create table and create view commands. The sequence of commands needed to generate the internal data dictionary is in the SQL.BSQ file, and for the external data dictionary in the CATALOG.SQL file; these command sequences are executed when the database is initialized.

The views of the data dictionary consist mainly of complex select commands which provide the user with information from the base tables in a usable form. Taking the familiar USER_TABLES view as an example, Figure 3.40 shows how this view is defined with information from five data dictionary tables, listed in the from clause, being brought together to form the single view. Without making any attempt to analyse this command in detail the following three points should be mentioned:

- The select list also includes arithmetic operations. For example the values for INITIAL_EXTENT and for NEXT_EXTENT are calculated from: `s.iniexts*ts.blocksize` and `s.extsize*ts.blocksize`.
- The ORACLE DECODE function is also used within the select list. In our example this function changes the input value `t.modified`, which can be `0` or `1`, into a `Y` value (if `t.modified = 0`), into an `N` (if `t.modified = 1`) or into a question mark (`?`), if the input value is neither `0` nor `1`.
- The WHERE clause contains an outer join, as is indicated by the inclusion of the outer join operator (+). An outer join means that the row will be included in the result even if there is no match for it in the partner table.

```
create view user_tables
(table_name, tablespace_name, cluster_name,
  pct_free, pct_used,
  ini_trans, max_trans,
  initial_extent, next_extent,
  min_extents, max_extents, pct_increase,
  backed_up, num_rows, blocks, empty_blocks,
  avg_space, chain_cnt, avg_row_len)
as
select o.name, ts.name, co.name,
       t.pctfree$, t.pctused$,
       t.initrans, t.maxtrans,
       s.iniexts * ts.blocksize,  s.extsize * ts.blocksize,
       s.minexts,  s.maxexts, s.extpct,
       decode(t.modified, 0, 'y', 1, 'n', '?'),
       t.rowcnt, t.blkcnt, t.empcnt, t.avgspc, t.chncnt,
t.avgrlen
from sys.ts$ ts, sys.seg$ s, sys.obj$ co, sys.tab$ t, sys.obj$ o
where o.owner# = uid
    and o.obj#      = t.obj#
    and t.clu #     = co.obj# (+)
    and t.ts#       = ts.ts#
    and t.file#     = s.file# (+)
    and t.block#    = s.block# (+)
```

Figure 3.40 Generating the data dictionary view USER_TABLES

Direct access to the data in the data dictionary tables is not permitted but every user has access to them by means of the USER_TABLES view. If an ordinary user (that is one without special privileges) were to carry out the select command given in the view definition directly, he would receive the message that the tables specified in the from clause do not exist. This is because the ORACLE user SYS, which owns the base tables and the virtual tables of the data dictionary, has granted only read access to all users (PUBLIC). All users have access to the database object USER_TABLES but not to the database objects on which this view is based. Because they can only be read indirectly via the relevant views, the highly sensitive base tables of the data dictionary are thus given optimum security.

This situation is illustrated again in Figure 3.41.

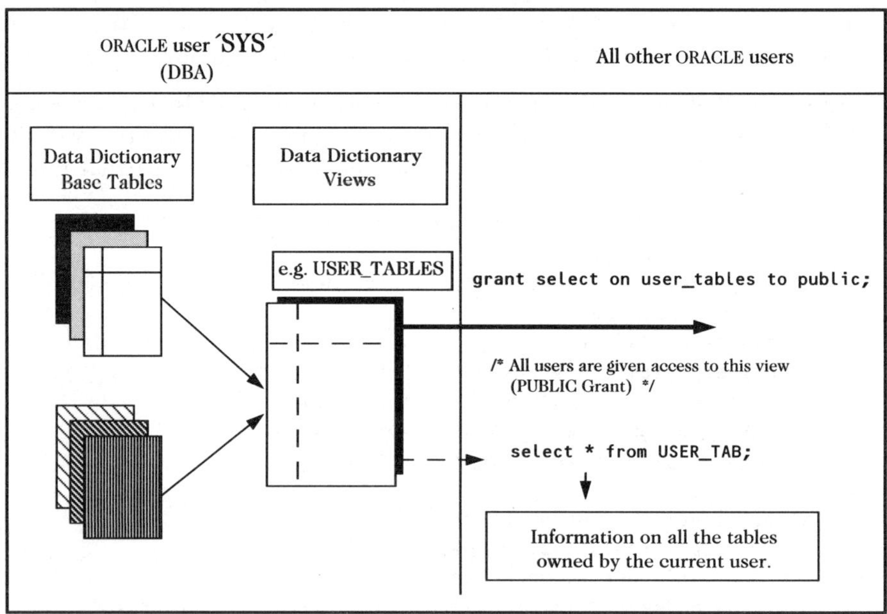

Figure 3.41 The internal and external data dictionary

Protecting database objects in this way is however not limited to this specific case of the data dictionary; defining a view is a frequently used method of protecting all types of database objects.

Operational integrity

Topics covered in this chapter

- The need for operational integrity
- The different types of locking mechanisms
- The transaction concept
- Controlling transaction processing
- Providing consistent read access
- Discrete transactions

Operational integrity

4.1 Introduction

As we have seen in the previous chapter database technology deals with a wide range of system resources such as tables, data blocks and indexes. In any working database system of course these resources have to be shared between a number of user processes which are all trying to access the database at the same time. Therefore the system also has to provide appropriate mechanisms to manage competing processes while at the same time ensuring the integrity of the database, so that if for example two user processes are trying to access the same record in a table, each process will be able to complete its work and leave the database in a consistent state.

To illustrate the problems which can arise in this context we can take the example of two travel agencies, where each one attempts to book places on the same flight using a data management system which is not able to manage 'parallel' changes to the data. This will lead to the sequence of events shown in Figure 4.1.

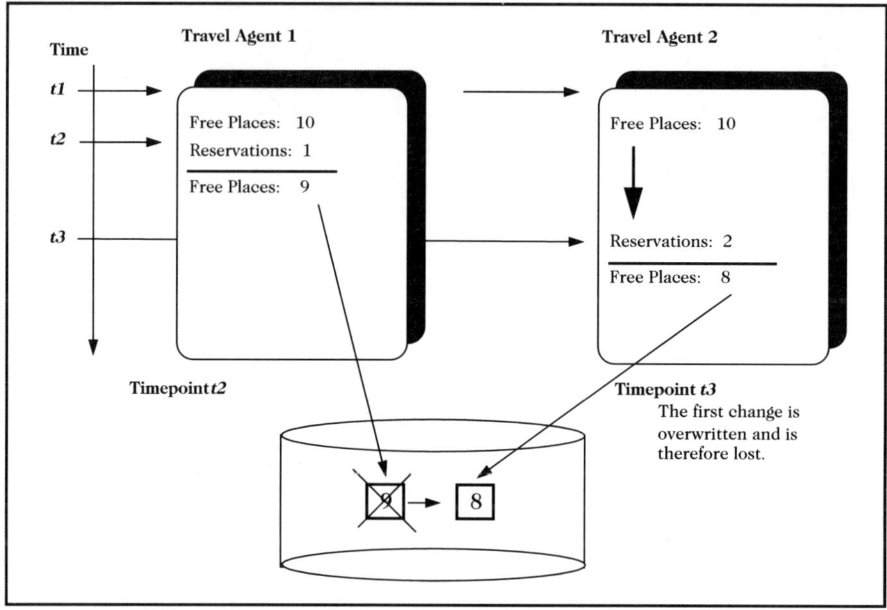

Figure 4.1 Lost update problem

There are initially 10 free places for the flight in question and this information is returned on the terminals of both travel agencies in response to their first queries.

The first travel agency books one seat at timepoint ***t1***, thus reducing the number of free places on this flight from ten to nine. Since the data management system provides no special features to deal with this situation, the second travel agency continues to assume that there are ten places available and at point ***t3*** books two of these. For the second travel agency the number of free places has now been reduced from ten to eight, so that although three places have been booked altogether, according to the data management system there are still eight places available on the flight. The modification carried out by the first travel agency is overwritten by the subsequent booking (***t3***) and is therefore lost (lost update).

In order to prevent this problem of database inconsistency, a database must offer appropriate locking mechanisms and procedures so that two such processes can run one after the other and yet remain independent of each other. In order to examine suitable locking mechanisms we must also look at the question of *lock granularity*.

Some typical levels of lock granularity are:

- Table level locking
  If a process is modifying one or more rows of a table the whole table is locked. Other processes which also want to work on rows within this table have to wait until the end of the transaction.

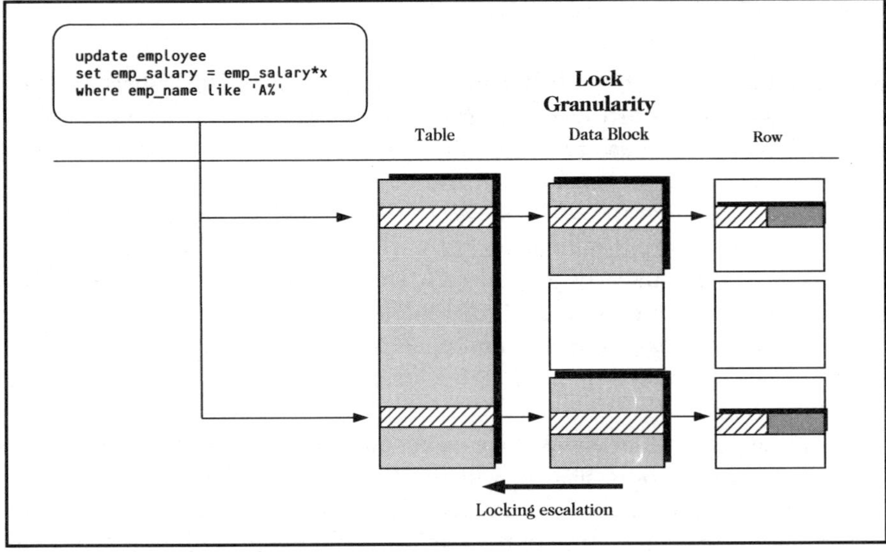

Figure 4.2 The different levels of lock granularity for DML operations

- Block level locking
  If a process is working on one or more rows of a table all the data blocks which contain the modified rows are locked. Other processes can still work on all rows which are in other data blocks.
- Row level locking
  If a process is working on one or more rows of a table only those rows are locked which are affected by the modification. All other rows can be worked on by other processes.

Operation	Locking Mode: Row Level	Locking Mode: Table Level	Comments
`select`	–	–	A read operation does not lock any data and does not prevent any DML operation (`insert`, `update`, `delete`) from being carried out.
`insert`	X	RX	All DML operations lock only at ROW LEVEL !! During all DML operations the table can still be read by any other processes. (Consistent read access)
`update`	X	RX	
`delete`	X	RX	
DDL/DCL commands	–	X	

Figure 4.3 The ORACLE locking modes for the different SQL operations

4.2 Locking mechanisms

We have already mentioned that in order to guarantee the consistency of the database in a multi-user environment, where several users want to access the same database resources, it is vital that the resources being used by one process are protected until the first process has completed. All of ORACLE's DML operations (INSERT, UPDATE, DELETE) make use of row level locking, where only those rows which are the object of a given operation are exclusively locked (X). During the operation the tables themselves are put into ROW EXCLUSIVE (RX) mode.

As the RX lock can be held simultaneously by any number of processes, several INSERT, UPDATE or DELETE operations can be processed in parallel on the same table.

This mechanism guarantees the greatest possible level of data concurrency, since each process only has to wait until a lock is released before it can modify a row which had been exclusively locked by another process. An important and special feature of the ORACLE locking procedure is that read operations do not need locks at all and a read operation will always return a consistent extract of a database table (or, in the case of a read transaction, of several tables) without read and update transactions interfering with one another. This feature, which is of great practical importance, will be dealt with separately in Section 4.4.

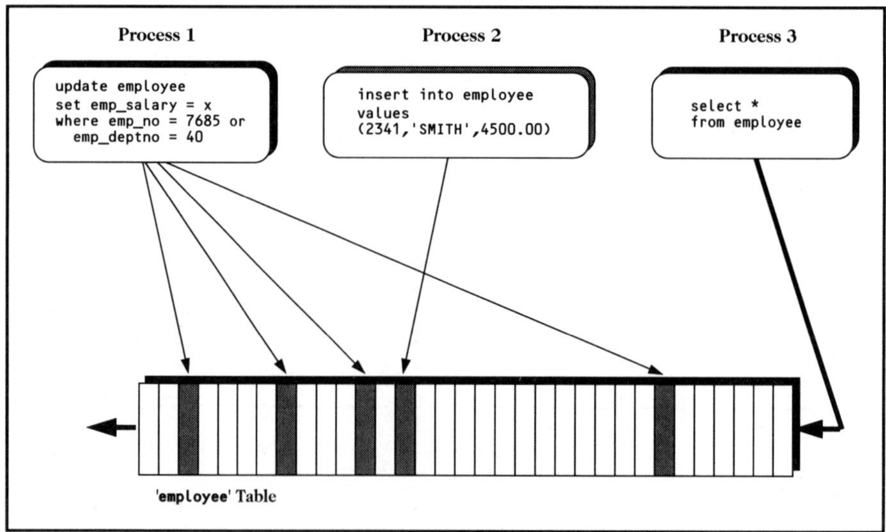

Figure 4.4 Providing row level DML locking together with consistent read access

The consistent use of row level locking for all DML operations (irrespective of how many locks are in operation, thus also avoiding the problem of lock escalation) is the most effective but also the least commonly used procedure to process competing updates in sequence. The procedure as used by ORACLE was introduced with Version 6 as the 'Transaction Processing Option' and now forms the basic locking procedure for Oracle7. An efficient row locking procedure is particularly necessary for systems with high transaction throughput in order to minimize the frequency of access conflicts and deadlock situations. In the area of referential integrity this aspect is also of great importance.

The implementation of the ORACLE locking procedure is based on three fundamental components: the transaction directory within each data block, the system change number (SCN) and the ORACLE transaction table, which is an internal data structure that is held as part of the rollback segment header. Every transaction which is started receives a unique transaction number (the SCN) which is administered within the transaction table. All records which are modified by a transaction are assigned the transaction's SCN (*see also* Figure 4.5).

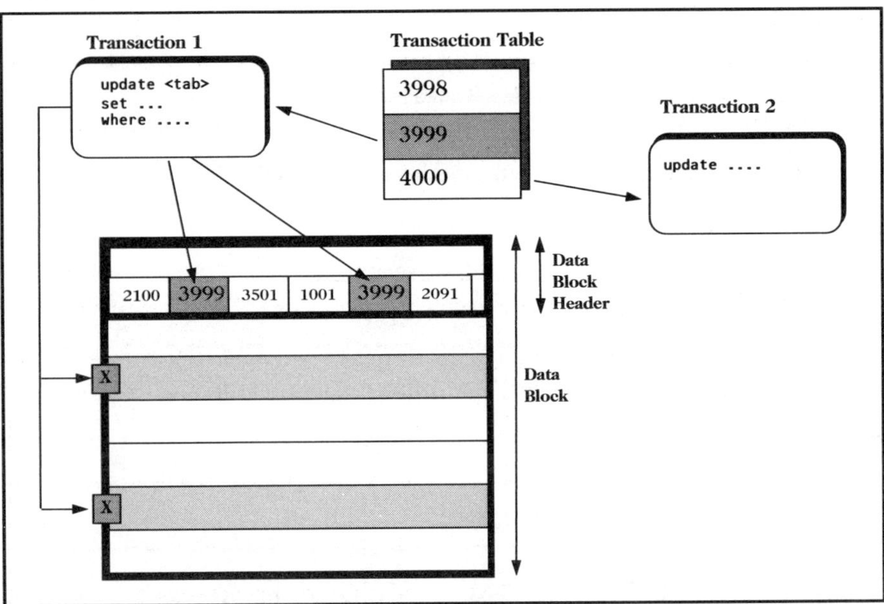

Figure 4.5 Row level locking without locking escalation

A row is locked for any another transaction when its SCN corresponds to an active SCN in the transaction table. Row locks are released at the end of a transaction by deleting the current transaction number (SCN) from the transaction table. This procedure allows any number of row locks to be released by a simple operation in the main memory. This basic procedure is illustrated in Figure 4.5 where transaction `T1` is assigned an SCN of 3999 which is held in the transaction table from the start of the transaction. The transaction table data structure is located in the database cache and is accessible to all ORACLE server processes. In this example the UPDATE command of transaction T1 modifies rows 2 and 5 (for simplicity's sake only one data block is affected) and the transaction's SCN is entered in the transaction directory of the two modified rows. Another transaction which then wants to modify one of these two rows recognizes that it is locked since the SCN 3999 is present in both the transaction directory for the two rows as well as in the transaction table.

When the transaction is ended by COMMIT or ROLLBACK then SCN 3999 is deleted from the transaction table and this causes all row locks for the transaction to be released. The transaction numbers in the transaction directories are not altered at the end of the transaction and remain constant until they are written over by another transaction.

The locking mechanisms described above are always automatically provided by ORACLE, so that in DML operations all modified rows are locked until the transaction is completed. It is nevertheless possible to influence the locking mechanism on one or more tables with the aid of the following SQL command:

```
lock table <tab> in <mode> (nowait)
```

For this command the following modes are available:

- EXCLUSIVE MODE (X)

```
lock table <tab> in exclusive mode (nowait)
```

The table is exclusively locked but other processes still have read access.

- SHARE MODE (S)

```
lock table <tab> in share mode
```

The table is locked in READ ONLY mode. Other processes can also lock the table in SHARE MODE and read its data but no process can carry out modifications on the table.

- ROW EXCLUSIVE (RX)

```
lock table <tab> in row exclusive mode
```

This is the standard locking procedure in Oracle7 which allows any number of processes to generate RX locks on the table and thus carry out DML operations simultaneously.

- ROW SHARE (RS)

```
lock table <tab> in row share mode
```

Allows further processes to apply RS and RX Locks. Other processes can read the table but not exclusively lock it. At the point of update the RS locks are changed into RX locks (exclusive row lock).

- SHARE ROW EXCLUSIVE (SRX)

```
lock table <tab> in share row exclusive mode
```

Other processes can read the table and lock it in RS mode. Exclusive (X) locks or share (S) locks are not allowed.

Figure 4.6 illustrates again all optional lock types and their compatibility. It should be noted that the standard lock mode for DML operations is the RX lock which itself provides the lowest level of lock granularity, that is, locking at row level. This standard locking mechanism should only be departed from in justifiable and exceptional cases so that resources are not locked for longer than is absolutely necessary.

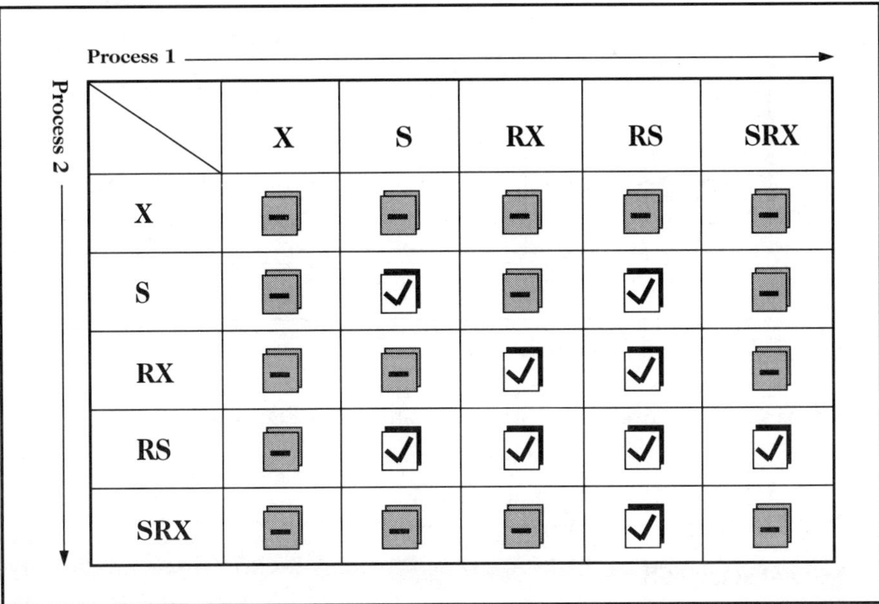

Figure 4.6 Locking compatibilities

4.3 The transaction concept

The locking mechanisms which we looked at in the previous section are just basic rules which serve to prevent conflicts or to resolve a conflict which has arisen without affecting the basic integrity of the data. The next highest unit of the ORACLE system which makes use of these basic rules is the transaction. The term 'transaction' when applied to database technology means a DML operation which changes the database from one consistent state into another. A transaction must always be completed, which means that when a transaction is ended the database is left in a consistent state. If it is not possible to achieve a new consistent state the transaction must be completely rolled back in order to restore the previous consistent state.

The example most frequently used in computer literature to illustrate a transaction is that of a bank transfer in which a certain sum X is to be debited from account A and credited to account B.

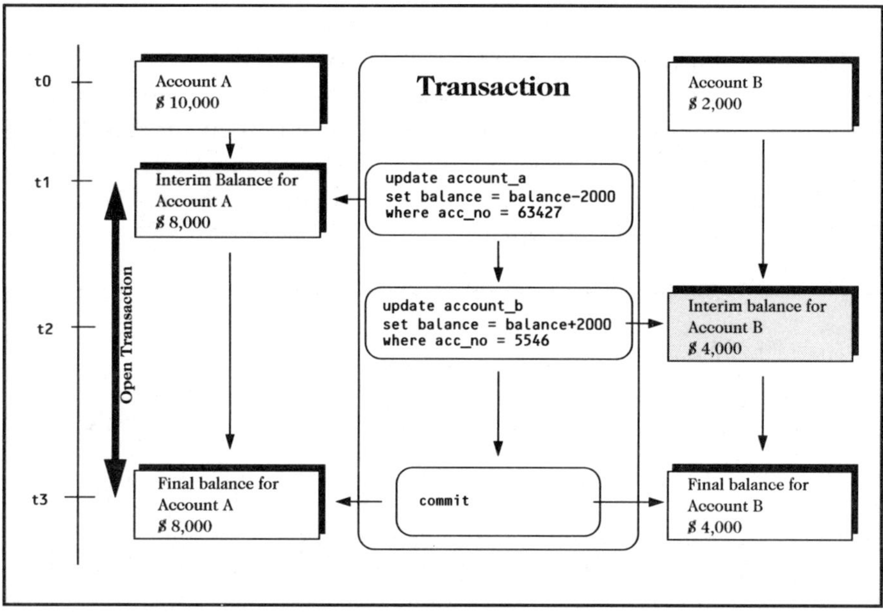

Figure 4.7 Transaction processing

The transfer occurs in two stages, as shown in Figure 4.7.

First stage (*t1*)

Sum X is deducted from account A.
As a result account A has a new balance.

Second stage (*t2*)

Sum X is credited to account B.
As a result account B has a new balance.

Only after the second stage has been successfully executed is the database in a consistent state again (for the purpose of this task) with the transaction having been fully completed. Since the two stages are carried out in sequence, it is of course possible that the program might crash after the first modification. This would mean that the specified amount would already have been deducted from account A but would not yet have been credited to account B.

After the first stage (the point where the program could crash) the database is in an inconsistent state, as the transaction could not yet be completed. In a case like this, as we have already discussed in Section 3.3.3, the PMON background process returns the database to its original condition and releases all the resources locked by the transaction (process recovery).

As a result of this error it is not possible to carry out the required task and this is of course unsatisfactory for both the bank and the customer, however the far greater damage of an incorrect debit, which might otherwise have resulted, is avoided. In Chapter 14 we will see how this single-phase commit protocol, which is sufficient to administer and control local transactions, has been extended to cover distributed transactions as well.

The type of task to be carried out determines which DML operations make up a transaction. A transaction may consist of only one command which modifies a single row of data; equally a transaction may contain many different DML operations, which modify or delete a large number of rows in different tables. The control of a number of single statements to form a complete transaction is carried out by means of the SQL commands COMMIT, ROLLBACK, and ROLLBACK TO ***<savepoint>***.

The COMMIT command has the following effects:

- The transaction is completed successfully.
- All the modifications executed by this transaction are made permanent in the database by writing the redo log block to the redo log file.
- All resources locked by the transaction are released.

The ROLLBACK command has the following effects:

- The transaction is ended unsuccessfully.
- All data modified by this transaction are rolled back to their original values which are retrieved from the rollback segment.
- All resources locked by the transaction are released.

We have already examined (in Section 3.3.3) the sequence of actions which make up the COMMIT command. At this point it is important to emphasize that the modified data are not directly written to the database by the COMMIT, but that only a short entry which describes the transaction is written to the redo log file. Once this has taken place the transaction is complete and the program which initiated the transaction can execute its next command.

The possibility of a ROLLBACK must always be taken into account by a programmer in case anything occurs within a transaction which prevents a consistent state in the database being achieved. If a transaction has to be rolled back, then two options are available to the programmer:

- The transaction can be completely reversed.
- The transaction can be partially rolled back to a predefined savepoint using the command ROLLBACK TO ***<savepoint>***.

When a transaction is rolled back to a savepoint all the resources used within the rolled back section of the transaction are then released. This makes it possible to divide a transaction into smaller 'portions', smaller ROLLBACK units. This benefits both the programmer, as it provides a very flexible method of program control, and overall system performance since in the case of a partial rollback there is less to be undone and subsequently less which has to be repeated. Figure 4.8. illustrates a transaction with savepoints. Depending on an error code the transaction is either completed successfully or is rolled back in discrete stages.

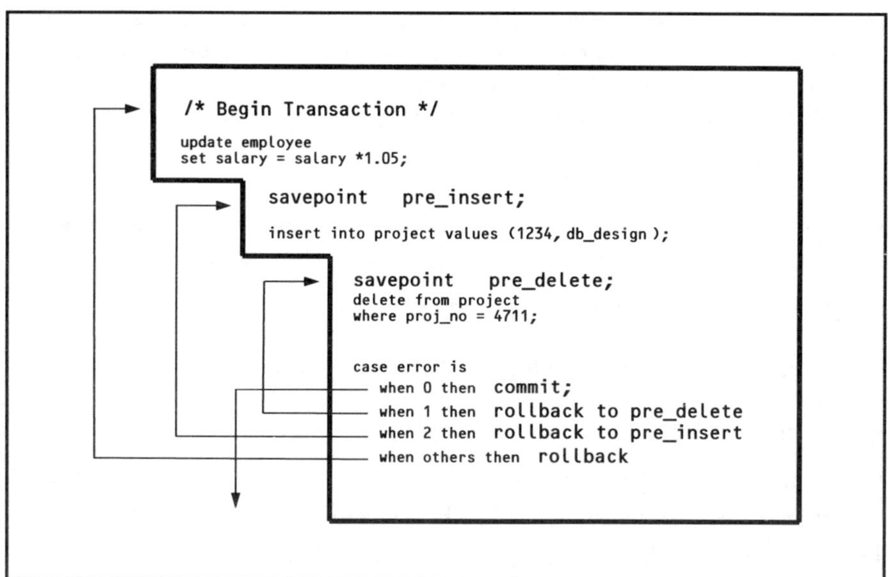

Figure 4.8 Transaction control commands

Please note that the command ROLLBACK TO ***<savepoint>*** only rolls back whatever database processing has been carried out up to this point. Any corresponding changes in the program's control must be explicitly programmed.

4.4 Providing consistent database reads

Considering the demands which are made on a working system it is clear that a given database table is constantly being accessed with read (SELECT) and modify commands (INSERT, UPDATE, DELETE). We have already seen how potential conflicts between parallel DML operations have been reduced to a minimum by ORACLE's row-locking mechanisms and by its transaction concept. However given that a database is accessed to carry out read as well as modify operations we must also consider how read operations are to be dealt with by the system.

Figure 4.9 shows two processes simultaneously accessing the same table. The first process reads the table in full (SELECT) and the second process modifies only some of its rows (UPDATE). When the modification process starts the read process has only read part of the table, since reading the whole table is likely to require much more time than the modification procedure. This could lead to a situation where the read process returns an inconsistent mixture of old and new values. There are several possible solutions for dealing with this basic problem.

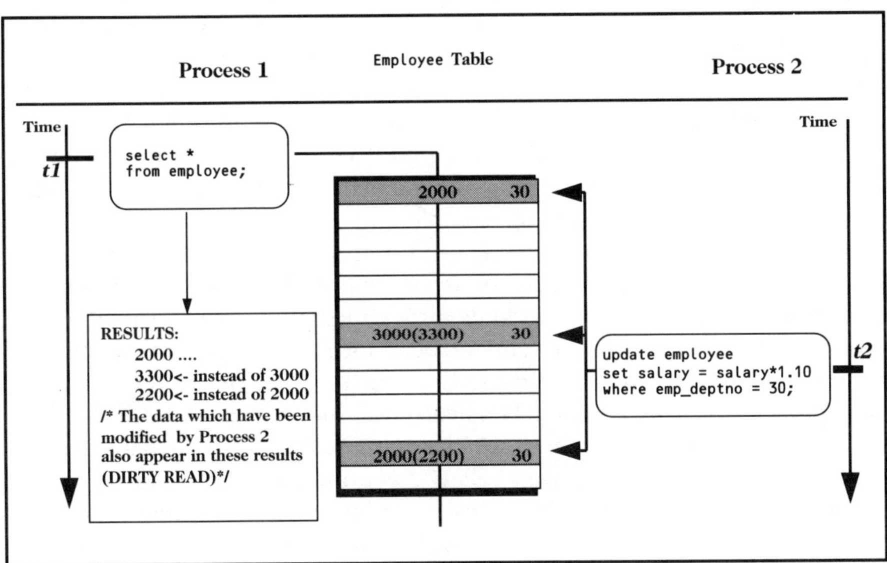

Figure 4.9 Interaction between READ and MODIFY (DML) operations

One way of achieving a consistent result for this type of read operation is to implement corresponding lock mechanisms. One method commonly used is to lock an entire table to all modification operations as long as any read command is active on that table. If read commands are going to be carried out using this method it is important to ensure the following conditions:

1. That no modification operation is active on this table; otherwise the read operation has to wait until this operation is completed.
2. That a table cannot be modified by another process while it is being read from.

These simple locking rules can certainly solve the problem of inconsistent read access, but at the cost of severely restricting the system's ability to process read and modify operations simultaneously, resulting in an overall loss of performance on the whole system.

A second solution to this problem permits any number of simultaneous read and modify operations, with a read operation always taking the current (but not necessarily the consistent) values in the relevant database table. This technique, which is often used in practice, is known as the 'dirty read' method and was described in the example at the beginning of this chapter. Although this procedure has the advantage of a high level of concurrency (since read and modify operations can be carried out independently of each other) it must be remembered that the results of any read operations may contain errors.

Basically both methods must be regarded as unsatisfactory since their respective advantages are offset by major disadvantages. The first method returns consistent read data but with very poor throughput as soon as modify operations have to be carried out at the same time. The second method achieves a good throughput in processing modifications but with the restriction that read operations may return inconsistent data. If we have to choose between the two procedures, then the first is certainly preferable because a system that allows its users to read inconsistent, inexact or even non-existent data is ultimately not acceptable.

Because of the obvious deficiencies in both methods ORACLE has developed the *multi-version read consistency* method, which unites the advantages of the two other methods, providing both consistent read access together with a high degree of concurrency for read and modify operations. As implemented by ORACLE this method ensures that all the data read by a given user process are completely consistent, reflecting the state of the database at the moment when the SELECT command was entered. This method is based on the assumption that at any given moment a table must be in a consistent state, which may of course be superseded by another consistent state (for example after an UPDATE operation which has been committed). Figure 4.10 takes us through the same example as in 4.9, but this time with reference to ORACLE's read consistency method.

Process 1 starts a read command at timepoint t1. At this point the salaries of the three employees in department 30 are respectively $2,000, $3,000 and $2,000. This is the consistent state of the table at point ***t1***. Shortly afterwards (***t2***) **Process 2** generates an UPDATE command and changes the salaries of the employees in department 30 by 10 percent. The read process, which in our example has to read the whole table, comes across a row which has already been changed by **Process 2**. In order to reconstruct a consistent state for the read command (the state at point ***t1***) ORACLE makes use of the rollback segments in which the previous values of all modified data are stored. By making use of the rollback segments to carry out read operations there is no need to implement any additional locking mechanisms (*refer also to* Figure 4.3). Thus it is possible for any number of read and modify operations to access the same table simultaneously without locking each another's resources and without the read operation delivering inconsistent results. The data returned by a read operation are always consistent, reflecting the state of the database at the moment when the SELECT statement was entered.

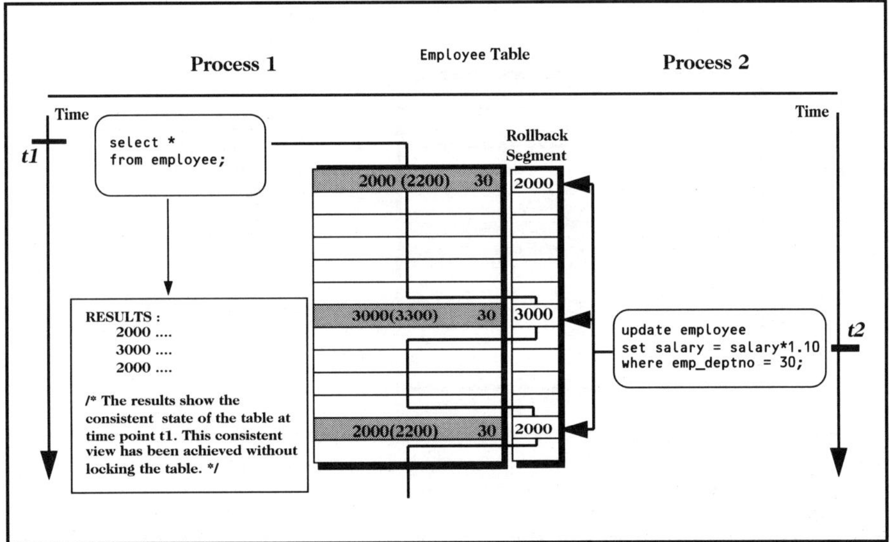

Figure 4.10 The ORACLE read consistency model for read access without locking

In the previous example we looked at the question of read consistency in terms of a single read command. However it is often necessary to return consistent data for a number of separate read operations, possibly on different tables and this can be achieved with an ORACLE *read only transaction*. A read only transaction is initiated by the SQL command SET TRANSACTION READ ONLY which, in terms of our consistency example, defines point ***t1***, so that all subsequent read operations in the course of this transaction reflect the state of all tables in the database at point ***t1***.

A read only transaction can contain any number of read commands on any number of tables (but not the modify commands INSERT, UPDATE, DELETE) and is ended by COMMIT or ROLLBACK. During a read only transaction any other processes can modify the data in the same tables without in any way affecting the results of the read operation. This means that it is for example possible to generate complex reports (which require a series of

SELECT statements) with completely consistent data without having to lock the tables and without preventing modify operations by other processes. For a working database system where multiple read and modify operations are going on all the time, this method allows the highest possible throughput while still ensuring the consistency and accuracy of each user's data.

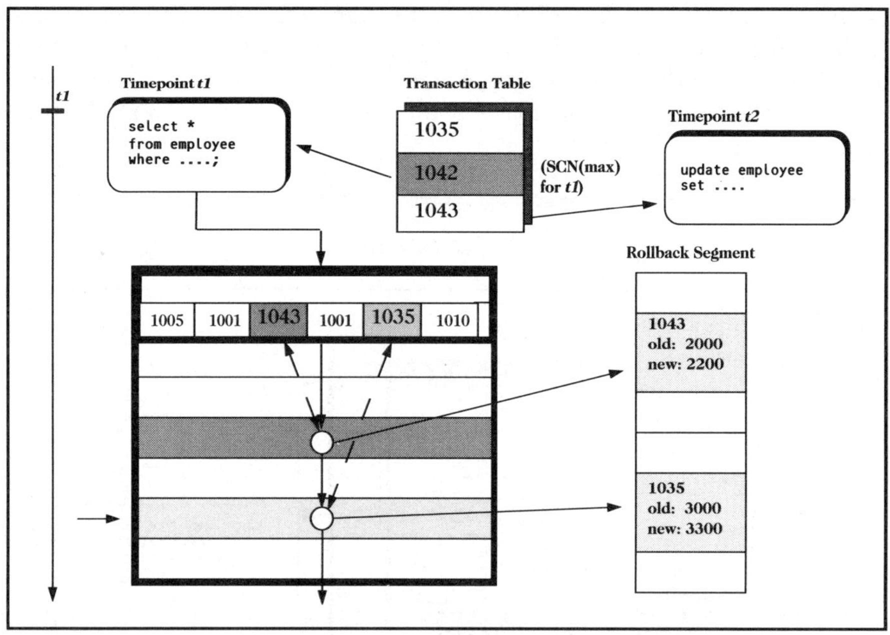

Figure 4.11 The ORACLE multi-version read consistency method

The transaction number (the SCN) which has already been mentioned, has a crucial function in the realization of this read consistency model. When a read operation is started (at point ***t1***) the system determines the highest current SCN (which we will refer to later as `SCNmax`). The transaction with this number was therefore initiated prior to the read operation now being started and all SCNs with a higher value have been started at a later point. As the required data is being read, the system must determine for each row whether it has changed since the read operation's consistency point (***t1***). This is achieved by referring to the SCNs in the transaction directories of the individual data blocks. A row has been changed in relation to the read transaction's consistency point if its SCN is greater than the `SCNmax` value recorded at the start of the transaction.

In our example at least one transaction has modified a row after the read operation started (at point ***t2***), and the original value therefore has to be retrieved from the ROLLBACK segment. In addition all open modify transactions must also be taken into account by the system and the values for any rows whose SCNs were in the transaction table when the read transaction started must also be read from the rollback segment. In all cases it is the state of the database at the moment the read operation begins which is crucial. Rollback segment entries must therefore be retained until a modify transaction is completed and no read operation is active which might require the data from the rollback segment for consistency purposes.

4.5 Discrete transactions

In the transaction model we have looked at up to now a modify operation is always carried out in the database cache using the data block and storing the original values in the rollback segment. This method makes it possible to carry out transactions which can be of any length or complexity, and which may be local or distributed (*see* Chapter 14 on this). The ORACLE read consistency model even allows read access to data whose actual structures are being modified without any resulting inconsistencies.

In addition to this general model, Oracle7 offers a special transaction type for certain transaction profiles: the *discrete transaction*. This type of transaction can lead to considerably improved performance particularly for local transactions which only change a few rows. This improvement in performance is mainly due to the fact that all modifications are not immediately carried out in the data blocks but are deferred until the commit point. As a result of this procedure it is not necessary to generate entries in the rollback segment, since the original value is not actually changed as the corresponding SQL statement is being executed.

However the improvement in performance gained by using discrete transactions must be paid for by accepting certain restrictions on their overall use:

- A discrete transaction must be local (distributed transactions cannot be executed as discrete transactions).
- A data block can be changed by each transaction only once.
- A read command that wants to access a data block which is being processed by a discrete transaction will be rejected. Since a discrete transaction does not generate any rollback segment entries, a consistent read is not possible.

Despite these restrictions the use of discrete transactions can be very effective in certain cases, especially as a programmer can control when this type of transaction is to be used by carrying out the following steps:

1. The ORACLE instance must be configured to allow discrete transactions by setting DISCRETE_TRANSACTIONS_ENABLED = TRUE in the INIT.ORA file.

2. A discrete transaction must be explicitly initiated by the stored procedure BEGIN_DISCRETE_TRANSACTION.

All transactions which are not initiated by this procedure, irrespective of the status of the DISCRETE_TRANSACTIONS_ENABLED parameter, are processed according to the standard ORACLE transaction model and can be executed in parallel with discrete transactions, as shown in Figure 4.12.

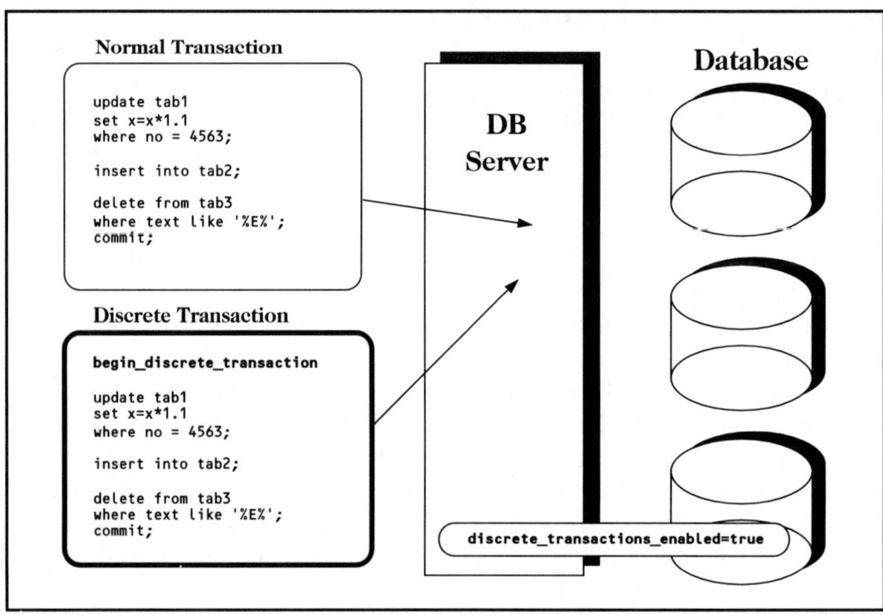

Figure 4.12 Processing normal and discrete transactions in parallel

5

Recovery

Topics covered in this chapter

- The need for database recovery mechanisms
- Recovery and the ORACLE transaction concept
- Recovery and the ORACLE system architecture
- Process recovery
- Instance recovery
- Media recovery
- Backup strategies for an ORACLE database
- ARCHIVELOG vs. NOARCHIVELOG mode
- Restoring an ORACLE database

5 Recovery

5.1 Introduction

The previous chapter was essentially concerned with the co-ordination of competing processes and with the locking mechanisms necessary to keep the database consistent at the row or record level. In this chapter by contrast we will look at the methods and procedures designed to keep the database as a whole in a consistent state, even in the most varied error situations.

The key requirement which our database must fulfil is to prevent any situation in which data or, more precisely, transactions may be lost. The database system must react appropriately to the various errors which can arise under normal operating conditions and must take whatever measures are necessary to maintain or restore the consistency of the database.

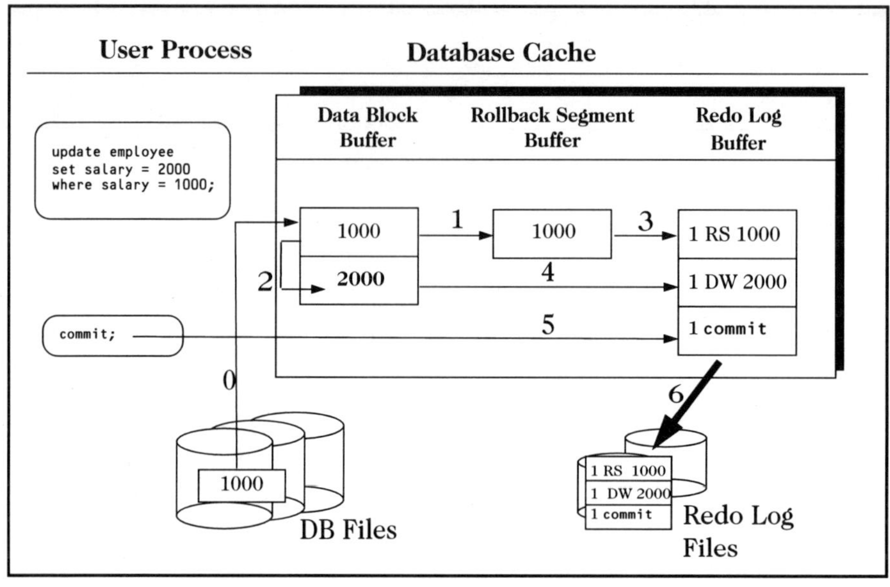

Figure 5.1 Processing a transaction

In general we can distinguish between the following four types of error situation:

1. An unexpected error in a user program which has carried out changes to the database that have not been committed.
2. A failure of the database system (database server crash).
3. A failure of the operating system (operating system crash).
4. The loss of one or more database files due to a disk failure.

On the basis of these four failure types ORACLE provides three distinct types of recovery:

1. Process recovery (where the user program has crashed).
2. Instance recovery (where the database server or operating system has failed).
3. Media recovery (where database files have been lost).

In the following sections we will examine all three recovery types in detail.

5.2 Transaction processing

In Section 3.3, where we looked at the functions of the ORACLE background processes and their role in processing a transaction, we were concerned above all with understanding how these processes actually work. Now we will look at them again but this time in terms of what recovery functions they provide.

When a modify operation (for example UPDATE) is initiated by a user program the following steps take place within the database system (these are also shown in Figure 5.1).

0. The data block is read from the database file into the database cache and the relevant row or rows are locked. This step is only necessary if the corresponding data block is not already in the database cache.
1. The value to be modified (1000) is copied into a rollback segment buffer in the database cache.
2. Within the database cache the required modification is made to the data block, so that the value 1000 is replaced by a new value of 2000.
3. The changes to the rollback segment are also recorded in the redo log buffer. (All database modifications are recorded in the redo log and as the rollback segments are also database objects any changes to them are also entered in the redo log).
4. The new value (2000) is recorded in the redo log.
5. The user program commits the transaction, following which a commit record is entered in the redo log buffer.
6. The COMMIT command causes the redo log buffer to be written to the redo log file. This is carried out by the LGWR background process.
7. After the buffer has been successfully written to the redo log file the process which generated the transaction is notified that the COMMIT has completed and it can then continue with the next stage of the program.

Once these steps have been carried out the transaction is completed and made permanent in the database although at this point the modification has not yet been written to the database file. The data block with the new value remains in the database cache and therefore in main memory for as long as possible (*refer also to* Chapter 6 'Database Tuning'). A data block which has been modified in the database cache is written back to the database if one of the following events occurs:

- Space is required in the database cache for other data blocks. In this case those database buffers which have remained unmodified the longest are written back to the database.
- A checkpoint is carried out in which case all modified data blocks are written back to the database.

5.3 Process recovery

We will continue with our previous example in order to illustrate process recovery, but we shall assume in this case that no COMMIT has been carried out. The user program changes the salary field from 1000 to 2000 with the appropriate UPDATE command (*see* Figure 5.2) but shortly afterwards the user program crashes. Because of this the user program can neither end the transaction positively (COMMIT) nor reverse it (ROLLBACK).

The situation within the database is then as follows:

- The row has already been modified in the database cache (new value 2000).
- The row has been exclusively locked by a user program which now no longer exists.
- Records have already been entered in the rollback segment and in the redo log buffer.

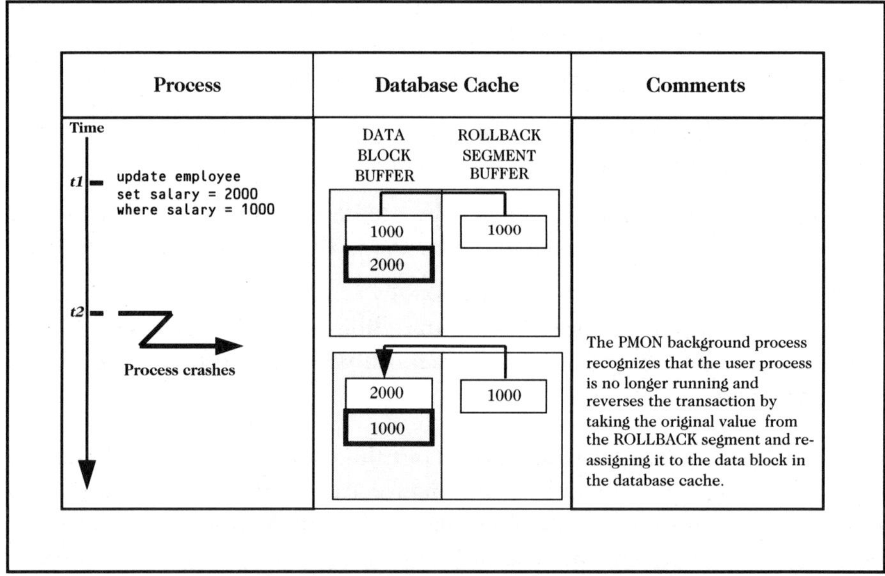

Figure 5.2 Process recovery with the PMON background process

In order to deal with this type of situation the ORACLE Server periodically (approximately every 20 seconds) activates the PMON background process, whose task is to determine whether database resources are being locked by non-existent processes.

In our example the PMON process discovers a process number which exists in the database cache but for which there is no corresponding entry in the operating system.

As a result the PMON process initiates a rollback of the open transaction. The original value (1000) is copied from the rollback segment back to the data block concerned and the exclusive row lock is released. With process recovery the last open transaction is always completely rolled back without any intervention being required from the user or the database administrator.

5.4 Instance recovery

In comparison with the relatively simple case of process recovery we have just looked at, instance recovery is much more complex and will normally involve many more processes. An instance recovery always becomes necessary if the database itself fails or if the operating system crashes while the database is open.

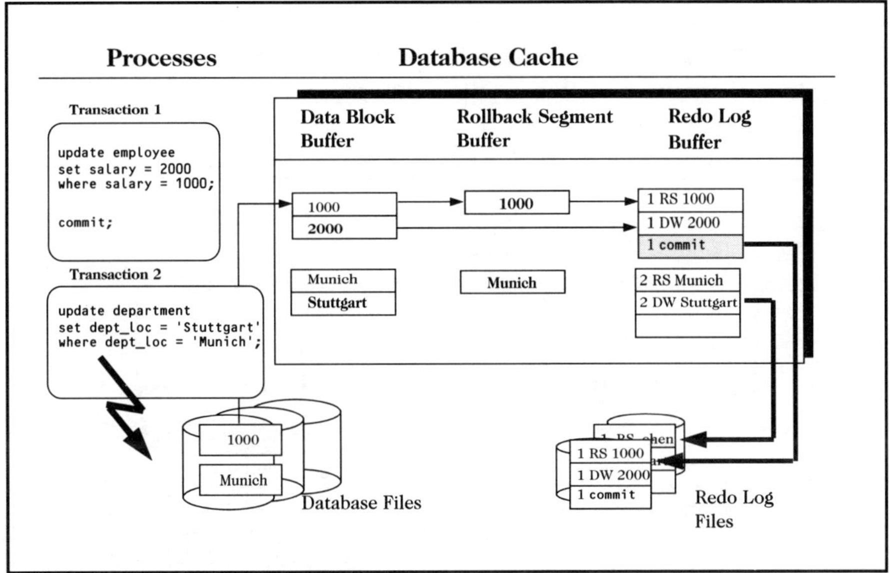

Figure 5.3 Process interaction following a system failure

Figures 5.3 and 5.4 illustrate the separate stages in this process. Figure 5.3 shows two transactions, of which only one has been completed when the system crash occurs. At this point the state of the database with regard to transactions `T1` and `T2` is as follows:

- The database buffer in the database cache
  `T1`: `salary` has been changed from 1000 to 2000.
  `T2`: `dept_loc` has been changed from 'Munich' to 'Stuttgart'.

- The rollback segment buffer
  T1: the original value of `salary` (1000) has been recorded.
  T2: the original value of `dept_loc` (Munich) has been recorded.
- The redo log file
  T1: the data for this (committed) transaction have already been written to the redo log file.
  T2: the data for this transaction have also already been written to the redo log file, but without a 'commit' entry as the COMMIT command has not yet been generated for this transaction.
- The database file
  T1: `salary` still contains the original value of 1000.
  T2: `dept_loc` still contains the original value of 'Munich'.

If we look only at the database file it may seem that it is in an inconsistent state as it does not reflect the committed transaction. However this is not adequate assessment since the redo log file is also an integral part of the database and must therefore always be included in any such considerations. To produce a consistent database the database files and redo log files must be taken together.

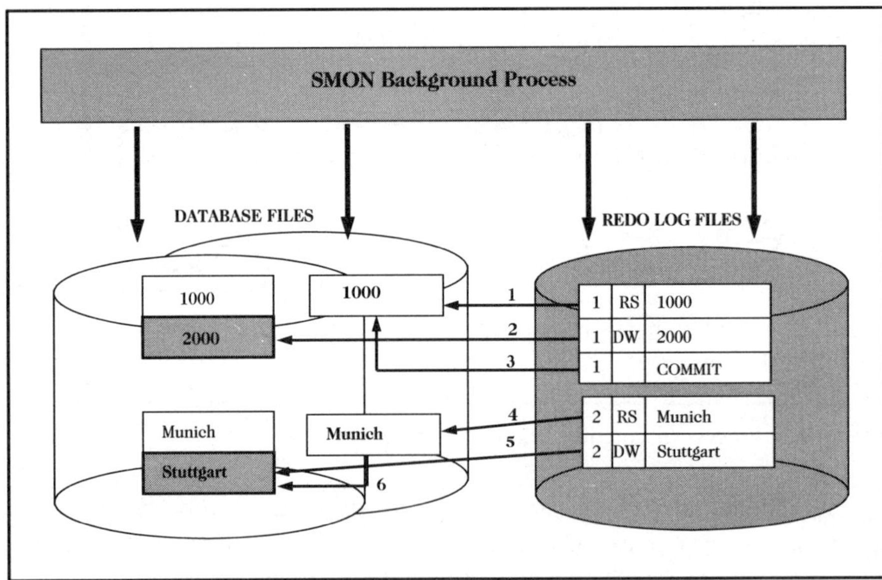

Figure 5.4 Instance recovery by the SMON background process

In order to bring the database files up to date, an instance recovery is automatically carried out by the SMON background process as soon as the instance is started up again. Using information from the redo log files a *roll*

forward is carried out for every completed (committed) transaction and a rollback for every incomplete one.

Thus the following steps will be gone through when the ORACLE instance starts up again:

For transaction T1:

1. The rollback entry, containing the original value of 1000, is written from the redo log file to the rollback segment in the database.
2. The modified value (2000) is written from the redo log file to the database file.
3. The commit record for transaction T1 causes the rollback entry in the rollback segment of the database to be deleted.

After these three steps have been carried out transaction T1 is completely recovered and the new value (2000) is stored in the database file.

For transaction T2:

4. The rollback entry, containing the original value 'Munich', is written from the redo log file to the rollback segment in the database.
5. The modified value ('Stuttgart') is written from the redo log file to the database file.
6. Since no commit record exists for transaction T2 this transaction was uncommitted when the system went down and must be rolled back with the aid of the entries in the rollback segments.

Once the instance recovery procedure is complete the database files are in a consistent state again, that is all transactions which were committed when the crash occurred have been made permanent in the database, all uncommitted transactions have been fully rolled back.

Following this schematic introduction to the process of instance recovery we must turn to the question of how long such a process takes. This is particularly important for a heavily used system in which a large number of transactions are regularly carried out which would all have to be restored via the redo log entries if the instance crashes. In the previous example we also tacitly assumed that the system simply 'knows' the exact point from which the recovery should be started. The recovery process must begin from a point where the database files were consistent with the contents of the database cache. For instance recovery and indeed for all recovery processes it is therefore crucially important to be able to determine this starting point correctly.

In a working system these consistency checkpoints are set by ORACLE when one of the following events occurs:

- whenever one redo log file is completely filled and it is necessary to switch to the next one (redo log file switch);
- whenever a number of blocks defined by the DBA has been written to the redo log file. It should be noted that it is the number of operating system blocks (usually 512 bytes) which is significant in this case and not the far larger redo log blocks (default size 8192 bytes). LOG_CHECKPOINT_INTERVAL, which is the relevant INIT.ORA parameter, has a default value of 20,000 operating system blocks.

Using the LOG_CHECKPOINT_TIMEOUT parameter, it is also possible to initiate a checkpoint which depends on a given interval of time and not on how many write operations have been carried out. This parameter specifies when, that is how many seconds after the last checkpoint, a new checkpoint should be executed.

When a checkpoint is carried out all the data blocks which have been modified up to that point (for data, index and rollback segments) are written by the DBWR process from the database cache to the database and at the same time the checkpoint is logged in the control file. In addition the checkpoint is recorded in the file headers of all database files by entering the number of the current redo log file.

By setting checkpoints at predetermined intervals ORACLE ensures that the maximum length of an instance recovery will always be limited, at most by the maximum size of the redo log file and this period can be shortened by setting the LOG_CHECKPOINT_INTERVAL or the LOG_CHECKPOINT_TIMEOUT parameters accordingly.

A checkpoint always applies to the database as a whole and includes all its data files. However in the course of normal database operations it is also possible to set 'minor' checkpoints which only apply to some of the system's data files. This type of checkpoint can be set when one of the following events occurs:

- when the online backup of a tablespace is about to start;
- when a tablespace is put offline with the NORMAL or TEMPORARY option.

In both cases a checkpoint is carried out for all the data files which belong to the tablespace in question. This means that all data blocks which belong to the tablespace's data files are written back to the data files before the actual operation on the tablespace is started.

5.5 Media recovery

5.5.1 General introduction

We have now seen that process and instance recovery are carried out by the two background processes PMON and SMON, in each case independently and without external intervention being necessary.

A variety of conditions and measures are necessary to enable the restoration of an ORACLE database which has lost one, several or even all data files following a disk failure.

These include the following:

1. The database must be started and run in ARCHIVELOG mode. Process and instance recovery are possible if a database has been started in NOARCHIVELOG mode but media recovery is not possible in this mode.
2. The data files and control files must be periodically backed up using the standard backup programs offered by the operating system in use. We can differentiate between two types of backup:
   - offline backup for when the database is closed,
   - online backup for when the database is in use and all its processes are working while the backup is running.
3. The redo log files which are filled while the database is in use have to be backed up by the archiver background process (ARCH). In most operating systems ARCH is able to carry out this function automatically without the intervention of the DBA. However it is possible (and in a few systems even necessary) to start the ARCH process manually. Each backup will always include a number of archived redo log files.
4. In the case of a media failure where one or more database files are lost the recovery process must be initiated by the DBA and this includes the following steps:
   - restore the backup files;
   - start the recovery operation with the SQL*DBA program;
   - retrieve the archived redo log files which are identified as being necessary for the recovery process.

Which of these steps have to be carried out at which point depends on the specific error situation and on the backup procedures in use.

In the next sections we will look at the basic procedures for backing up a database and for recovering a database following a disk failure.

5.5.2 Backing up an ORACLE database

Creating security copies or backups of sets of data forms the basis for all recovery procedures which become necessary after a disk failure and should be common practice wherever computing systems are in use.

The introduction of database systems which support a growing number of applications programs has led to greatly increased demands on backup and recovery techniques. It has become necessary to provide procedures which can back up even very large databases (possibly larger than 50GB) while those databases are fully operational (online backup). In addition it must be ensured at all times that no error situation can occur which will give rise to an inconsistent database.

In practice of course the type of recovery required differs greatly from system to system. For example a database which is being used to manage a complete spare parts warehouse and which is run around the clock obviously needs different backup procedures from a database which is being used for development and test purposes.

For this reason an ORACLE database can operate in two different modes, namely in NOARCHIVELOG or in ARCHIVELOG mode.

A database should be run in NOARCHIVELOG mode only if it is not essential to recover the full database following a disk failure. If a disk failure does occur while the database is operating in this mode, then it will only be possible to restore the database as it was when the most recent full backup was made. A typical database to run in NOARCHIVELOG mode would be for a development system which as a rule is going to contain only non-critical test data.

However whenever it becomes necessary to recover all possible data in the event of a disk failure then the database must operate in ARCHIVELOG mode. In this mode, and in contrast to NOARCHIVELOG mode, the redo log files are automatically archived once they are filled so that, in the event of a media failure, they can be used together with a full or partial database backup to restore a database file, a tablespace or the full database.

Figure 5.5 illustrates these two modes in which ORACLE can operate. In order to run a database in ARCHIVELOG mode the following INIT.ORA parameters must be set correctly:

- LOG_ARCHIVE_START = TRUE/FALSE
  If this parameter is set to TRUE, the ARCH background process is started together with the instance.

- LOG_ARCHIVE_DEST = <*destination*>
  This parameter specifies the destination to which the filled redo log files should be copied by the ARCH process.

- LOG_ARCHIVE_FORMAT = <*format*>
  This parameter is used in formatting the names of the archived redo log files.

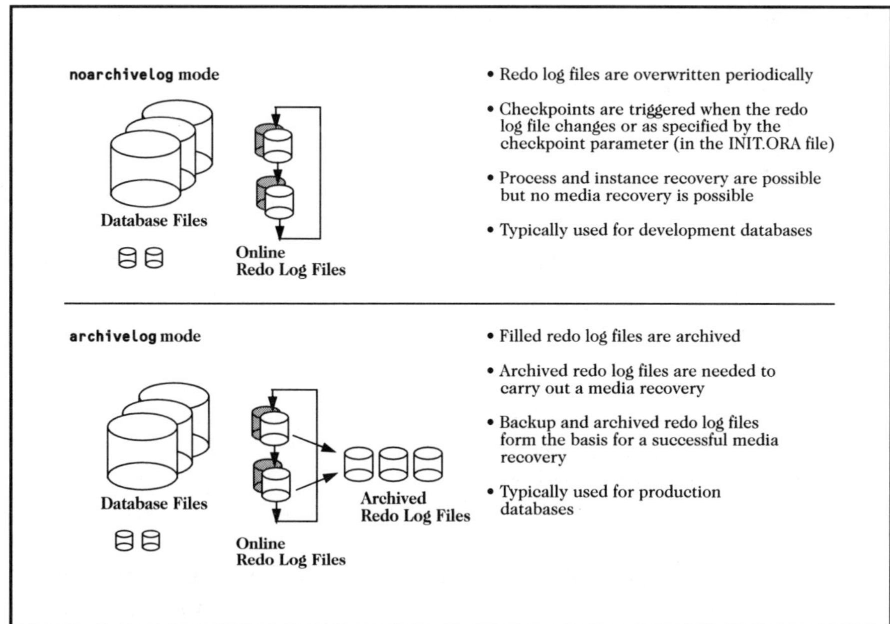

noarchivelog mode
Database Files
Online
Redo Log Files
• Redo log files are overwritten periodically
• Checkpoints are triggered when the redo log file changes or as specified by the checkpoint parameter (in the INIT.ORA file)
• Process and instance recovery are possible but no media recovery is possible
• Typically used for development databases
archivelog mode
Database Files
Online
Redo Log Files
Archived
Redo Log Files
• Filled redo log files are archived
• Archived redo log files are needed to carry out a media recovery
• Backup and archived redo log files form the basis for a successful media recovery
• Typically used for production databases

Figure 5.5 ORACLE operational modes

The mode chosen to run an ORACLE database also influences the choice of backup method. As it is only possible to restore (but not to recover) a database running in NOARCHIVELOG mode, it becomes necessary in this case to make a consistent and complete backup of the whole database. This should include:

- all the data files of a database
- all the online redo log files
- all the control files

A consistent and full backup of all these components is only possible when the database has been cleanly shut down with SHUTDOWN NORMAL.

A database which is operating in ARCHIVELOG mode is also able to make use of additional backup strategies. In this context we should make the basic distinction between a full backup, where the entire database is backed up in one single operation, and a partial backup, where only certain parts of the database are backed up at any one time, for example specific database files or tablespaces.

Using ARCHIVELOG mode means that both full and partial backups can be carried out when the database or the parts of the database to be backed up are either offline or online, thus allowing the following options for carrying out backup operations:

- full offline backup
- partial offline backup
- full online backup
- partial online backup

These options are summarized in Figure 5.6.

In the case of a partial offline backup the database files and tablespaces to be backed up are first put offline. A typical sequence of commands in this case would be as follows:

```
alter tablespace TA offline normal;
$backup <files_from_TA> to <backup_dir>
alter tablespace TA online;
```

If a tablespace is put offline with normal or temporary priority then all active transactions are allowed to complete, following which the data blocks of all the data files involved are written to those files from the database cache (a minor checkpoint). As soon as the system has carried out these preliminary actions the tablespace is in a consistent state and can then be put offline.

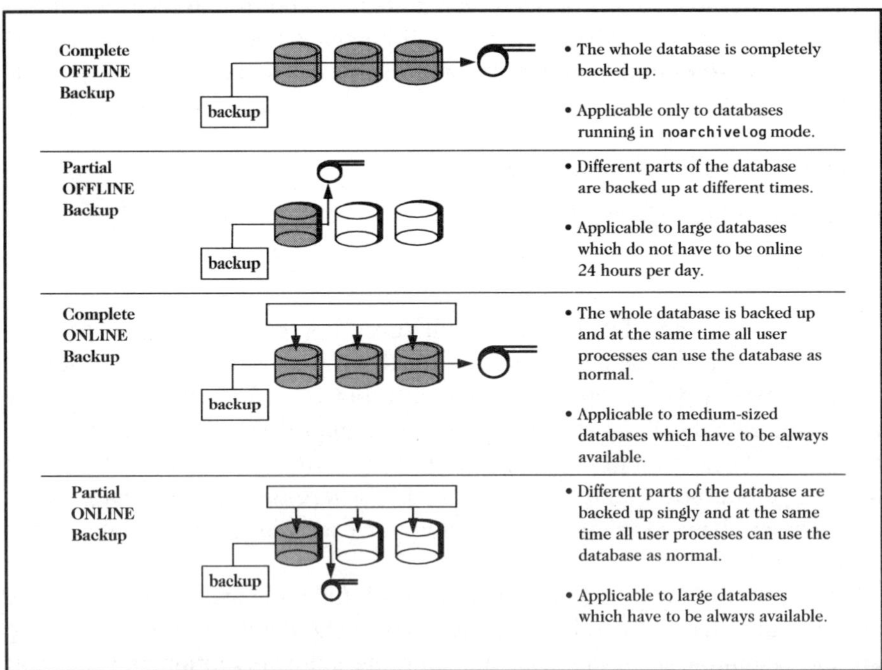

Figure 5.6 Backup strategies for an ORACLE database

During both types of offline backup the data files being backed up are not available to users. This means that if the data must be available at all times the backup must be carried out online. In this case the only difference between a full and a partial backup is in the scope, not in the functionality of the backup operation. During both online backup procedures the database remains open and can be accessed by any user process to carry out all normal database operations.

The beginning and end of an online backup procedure are indicated by the following two SQL statements:

```
alter tablespace <ts_name> begin backup;
alter tablespace <ts_name> end backup;
```

When the statement `alter tablespace begin backup` is entered to initiate an online backup, ORACLE carries out the following actions:

- A minor checkpoint is performed for all the files in the tablespace which is to be backed up. As a result all modified data blocks are written from the database cache to the data files and the fileheaders record the number of the current redo log files.

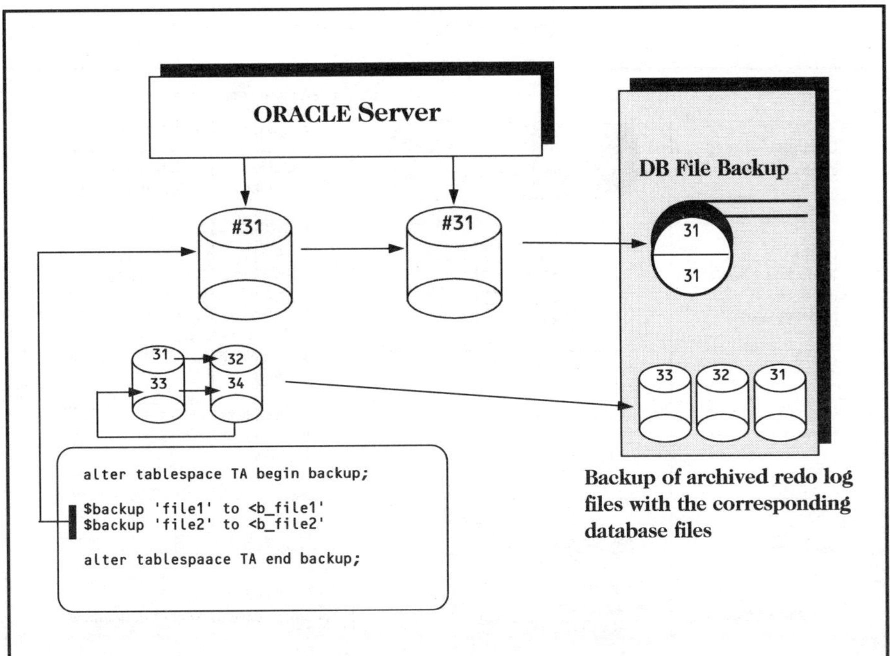

Figure 5.7 The ORACLE online backup method

- In the normal course of events the database fileheaders are always covered by the checkpoint and database cache paging procedures, however they are not modified by any checkpoints which may occur during the online backup. This ensures that all database files included in the online backup contain the same redo log file number thus establishing a common starting point should a recovery become necessary.

In dealing with the question of media recovery, we have so far looked at database files, which can be backed up by a number of different methods, and at redo log files which in ARCHIVELOG mode are archived by ORACLE itself. We must now turn our attention to the third type of file in an ORACLE database, namely the control files.

The primary function of the control files is to record structural information about the database and they are of crucial importance in the task of restoring an ORACLE database. It is therefore very important to make a backup of the control file following any structural changes to a database such as creating or dropping a tablespace, adding a new file to an existing tablespace or transferring a database file. As in the case of database files this backup can be carried out offline as well as online. In the case of an offline backup the control file is copied by issuing the appropriate operating system command when the database is closed. In order to effect an online backup the following SQL statement must be entered:

```
alter database backup controlfile to <filename>;
```

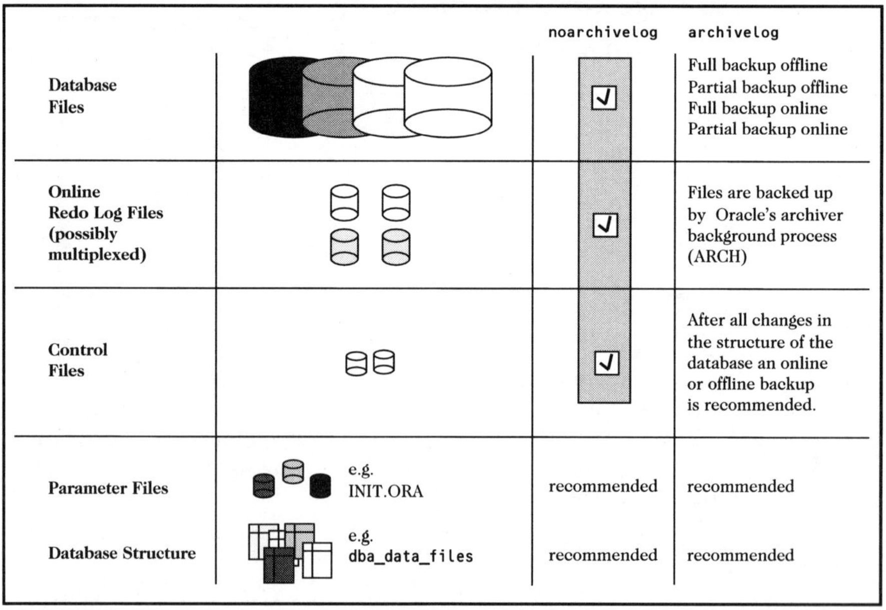

		noarchivelog	archivelog
Database Files		✓	Full backup offline Partial backup offline Full backup online Partial backup online
Online Redo Log Files (possibly multiplexed)		✓	Files are backed up by Oracle's archiver background process (ARCH)
Control Files		✓	After all changes in the structure of the database an online or offline backup is recommended.
Parameter Files	e.g. INIT.ORA	recommended	recommended
Database Structure	e.g. `dba_data_files`	recommended	recommended

Figure 5.8 Backup requirements for ARCHIVELOG and NOARCHIVELOG modes

It is not absolutely essential to back up the parameter files (INIT.ORA, TNSNAMES.ORA etc.) although if a problem with the database does occur, it can be extremely useful to have a backup of these files as well as a complete listing of all the data files in all the tablespaces.

It sometimes (as a result of particular events or actions on the database) becomes absolutely necessary to carry out a backup of some or all the files of a database. Figure 5.9 provides a list of these events and the kind of backup which should be carried out depending on whether the system is running in ARCHIVELOG or NOARCHIVELOG mode.

Database or Operational Events	**Type and scope of necessary backup operation**	
	`noarchivelog` mode	`archivelog` mode
1. A database is newly created.	Complete offline backup.	Complete offline backup.
2. The structure of the database is changed.		
• **A new tablespace is created.**	Complete offline backup.	Offline backup of files in new tablespace. Online backup of the control file.
• **A new database file is defined on a tablespace.**	Complete offline backup.	Offline backup of the new database file. Online backup of the control file.
• **An existing database file is moved or renamed.**	Complete offline backup.	Online backup of the control file.
• **A tablespace is deleted (dropped).**	Complete offline backup.	Online backup of the control file.
3. Normal backup.	Complete offline backup.	Partial or full online or offline backup according to the normal backup schedule.

Figure 5.9 ORACLE backup requirements under normal operating conditions

5.5.3 ORACLE database recovery procedure

If an ORACLE database is run in NOARCHIVELOG mode then a consistent backup is absolutely necessary to restore the database following a disk error. In this mode however it will not be possible to recover all the transactions carried out up to the moment the disk failed as no redo log files have been archived and so the information about more recent transactions is no longer available. This situation is illustrated in Figure 5.10, where at timepoint ***t1*** a full offline backup has been made of all the files in the ORACLE database. As this backup is complete and consistent it can be immediately used at timepoint ***t3*** to provide a fully functional database. However all the changes made to the database between timepoints ***t1*** and ***t2*** cannot be recovered.

A database run in ARCHIVELOG mode has not only this restore function at its disposal but also a range of recovery procedures which enable the complete recovery of a database following a disk error. In this case all transactions can be recovered with the aid of the archived redo log files and a full backup.

Specifically ORACLE provides two different recovery procedures:

- Offline recovery procedure,
  in which case no user program can work with the database during the recovery period.
- Online recovery procedure,
  in which case all tablespaces which do not have to be recovered can be used immediately without any restrictions.

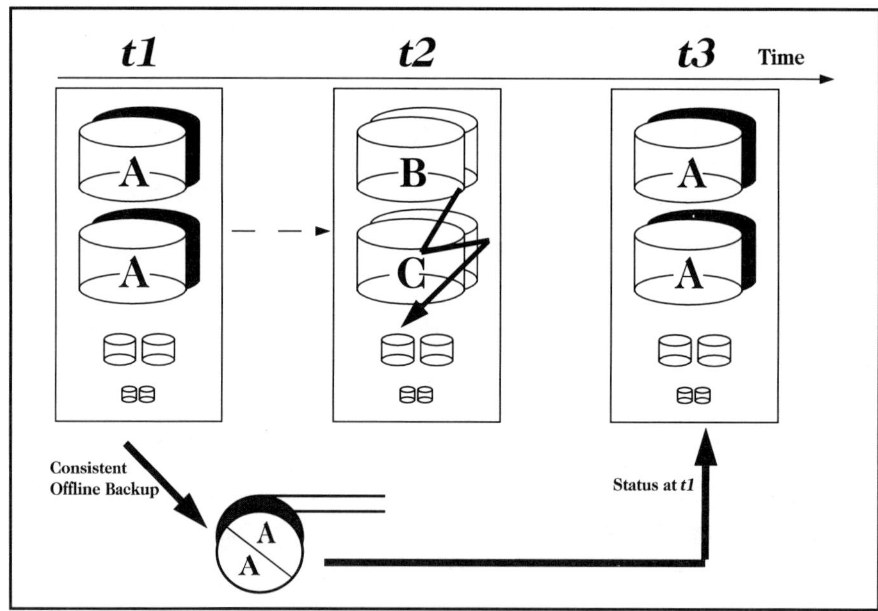

Figure 5.10 Restoring a NOARCHIVELOG database

The online recovery procedure is of particular importance for larger databases which typically consist of a large number of files distributed across many disk drives. For these systems it is often unacceptable if the whole database has to be switched off and recovered as the result of one disk drive failure.

RELEASE 7.1

ORACLE provides the DBA with a number of additional facilities in order to recover all or part of a database: RECOVER DATABASE to recover the whole database, RECOVER TABLESPACE to recover a discrete tablespace, or RECOVER DATAFILE to recover an individual data file. These three options are set out in Figure 5.11 and in the following pages we will look at them in more detail.

If the whole database is to be recovered with the RECOVER DATABASE command, it is also possible to specify that the recovery should be up to a given timepoint or SCN (System Commit Number), the latter being necessary if a global distributed database has to be recovered.

The type of recovery option which is used also depends on the disk failure which has occurred; it is for example not possible to carry out an online recovery with RECOVER TABLESPACE or RECOVER DATAFILE if it is the system tablespace which has been affected by a disk failure. In such cases it is always necessary to carry out a full offline recovery with RECOVER DATABASE.

Operation	Recover mode	Example

`recover database`
`until`
`cancel`
`change<scn>`
`time`
	Offline
	• Database is mounted but not open.
	• The database is not available to users.
		`recover database`
		`recover database until`
		`time '19-apr-92:12:00:00'`

`recover tablespace`	**Online or offline** • Database can be open. • Tablespace being recovered is offline. • All online tablespaces are fully available to all users.	`recover tablespace TA`
`recover datafile`	**Online or offline** • Database can be open. • Database file being recovered is offline. • The database file recovery can be carried out by several processes working in parallel.	`recover datafile <file>`

Figure 5.11 Different types of recovery operation

Figure 5.12 provides an example of the sequence of events in a recovery operation. At timepoint ***t1*** the DBA finds out that disk 2, on which tablespace `TA` is located, has developed a fault so that it is first necessary to stop the ORACLE instance. At the time when the disk error occurred the current redo log number (34) is recorded in the file headers of all three files located in that tablespace. The DBA first restores a backup of the faulty disk to a new disk drive and in our example the redo log number of this backup is 31, which was the current redo log number at the time the backup was carried out.

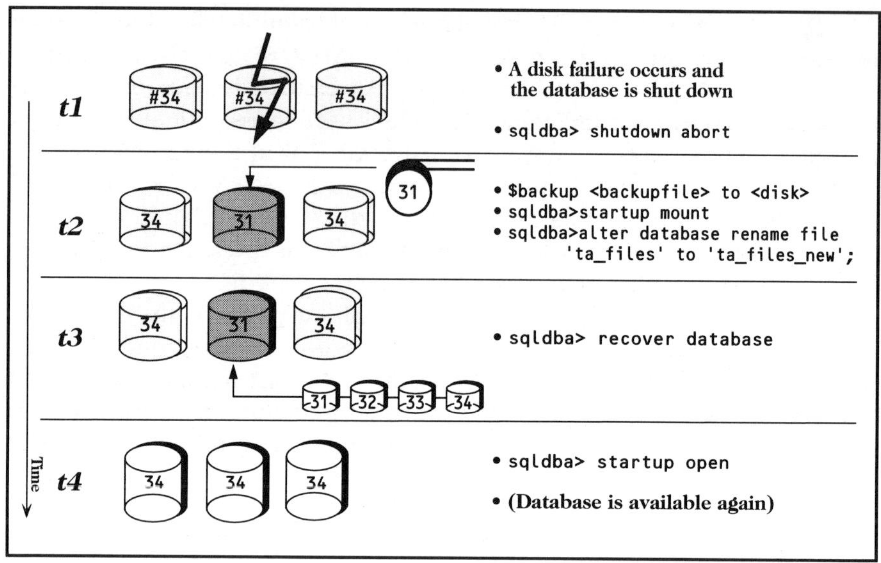

Figure 5.12 Database recovery following a disk failure

If the backup copies of the affected data files cannot be written back to the original file directories then we have a structural change in the database which must be indicated to the control file before the recovery operation is carried out. The required command is:

```
alter database rename file <old_names> to <new_names>;
```

RELEASE 7.1

This completes all necessary preparations and the actual recovery operation can now begin. The RECOVER DATABASE command need only include those data files whose file header contains a redo log file number lower than the redo log number in the current control file; in our example this only applies to the data files of tablespace `TA`. The redo log file number in the headers of the backed up files (`31`) tells the system which redo log file has to be used to start the recovery operation, in our example redo log number `31`. Starting from this point all the archived redo log files are processed and all the changes which have modified the data files of tablespace `TA` can be repeated.

Once all the archived redo log files have been processed the recovery operation is complete and the database can be opened again. The procedure which starts the database will also use the current online redo log file to carry out the final stages of the recovery process. Once the database has been opened it is in exactly the same condition as it was prior to the disk failure and all transactions in tablespace `TA` which had been carried out and committed up to that point will have been completely restored.

Figure 5.13 deals with the same error but in this example a tablespace recovery is carried out (rather than a database recovery). In this case any parts of the database not affected by the error (system tablespace and tablespace TB) can be accessed without restriction while tablespace TA is being recovered.

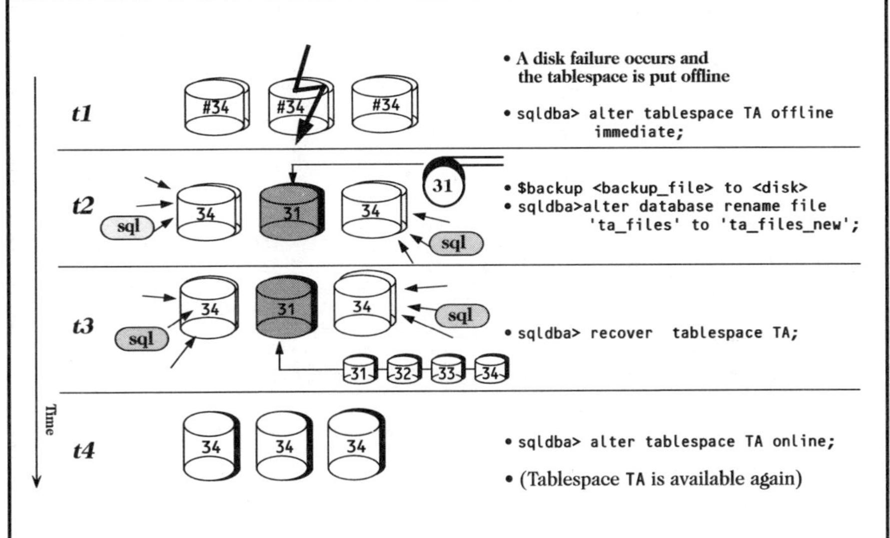

Figure 5.13 Recovering an online tablespace following a disk failure

6

Database tuning

Topics covered in this chapter

- The need for database tuning
- Tuning utilities provided by ORACLE
- The different levels of database tuning
- Tuning data structures
- Tuning SQL statements
- Applications tuning
- Server tuning
- Tuning the database

6

Database tuning

6.1 Introduction

The quality of any database management system is always judged in two crucial respects: in terms of the functionality which it provides and in terms of its overall performance under normal working conditions. So far we have concentrated on the functions provided by the Oracle7 database but in this chapter we will look at how effectively ORACLE can deliver these functions to its users.

Only a few years ago it was unthinkable that relational database systems could break into the domain of hierarchical and codasyl-based database systems, which at that time completely dominated the OLTP market. However the introduction of ORACLE Version 6 demonstrated that relational database servers were also able to achieve good response times for applications where performance is critical.

With Oracle7 we have what is widely regarded as the fastest relational database system currently available. The high level of performance provided by this system has been achieved by a variety of functions, including:

- Optimization of the database servers for different computer architectures, including loosely coupled cluster and massively parallel systems.
- Alternative configuration possibilities to ensure the optimum integration of different applications systems.
- Row locking without escalation to minimize locking conflicts and deadlock frequency.
- Consistent read access without locking with simultaneous modify access.
- Fast commit procedure to minimize physical write and read operations.
- A SQL optimizer to determine the optimum access paths to the data.
- Discrete transactions to optimize systems with extremely high transaction rates.
- Distribution of data across any number of disk drives in one computer system.
- Physical optimization of the database object structures.
- A configurable database cache.

Although ORACLE provides these functions for all computer systems and architectures it is necessary, in order to achieve optimum performance for a specific database system, to ensure that the database server is configured according to the requirements of the applications which are going to use it.

Therefore although in this context we often refer to *database* tuning, we are in fact concerned not just with the database or the database server in isolation, but with all the components of the systems which make use of that database. In order to ensure that optimum performance has been achieved for a database server on a particular platform, we must consider factors such as the system's workload, what types of applications are using it and what data structures have been defined for it.

6.2 Tuning levels

When tuning a database environment it is essential to be able to recognize the system's weak points and at the same time to estimate the improvement in performance which would be gained by eliminating them. If we take as our example the common situation where a given database operation is taking longer than is acceptable to the system's users, one solution might be to define an additional index, which can considerably improve the response time for a SQL operation (by a factor of anything up to 1000) since an index will provide the SQL optimizer with different access paths to the data. Another solution to the same problem, increasing the number of data block buffers in the database cache, may however only result in a performance increase of one per cent. It is therefore always important to establish how effective a given tuning measure has been, whether it has really addressed the existing problem and whether the trade-off between performance and resources justifies the solution. For example before increasing the size of the database cache it is always worth finding out whether the existing database cache area is being fully utilized by the ORACLE Server.

Data structures	• The logical structure of the database contents. • The use/structure of indexes. • The use of clusters (index/hash). • Sequences.
SQL Operations	• SQL optimization (statistical and rule-based methods). • Compiling statistics for database objects.
Applications	• Configuration variants (MTS, DS, client/server). • Integrity constraints at server/application level (declarative and procedural methods). • Stored PL/SQL programs. • Discrete transactions .
Database Server	• Database cache optimization (data block buffer pool, shared pool for SQL objects and the data dictionary). • Checkpoints.
Database	• Distributing the database over a number of disks. • Rollback segment definition (overall number, location, transactions per rollback segment). • Redo log file (size, disks).

Figure 6.1 Tuning levels in an Oracle7 database

Having considered all these factors we can therefore say that a system is well tuned when a given application with a given workload delivers optimum performance using as few computer resources as possible. In this respect we must evaluate the following components of any database applications system:

- the size of the computer system;
- the data structures;
- the SQL commands;
- the application and its configuration;
- the database server including all its components such as the background processes and the database cache;
- the database itself.

6.2.1 Data structure tuning

The foundations for the performance of the whole system are the data model and, in particular, its subsequent implementation as a series of data structures in the ORACLE data dictionary. The logical structure of the database tables and the structure of the corresponding indexes are of crucial importance for all the SQL operations which are carried out on these tables. Whereas a unique index is automatically provided for all primary key constraints, it is important to explicitly create a non-unique index for all foreign key constraints so that when a primary key value is referenced only its index entry is locked, thereby using the lowest possible level of locking granularity (*see also* Chapter 9).

The primary key index and the foreign key indexes of a table represent its primary access paths, however additional indexes can be created on any columns or combination of columns. An important criterion in choosing where to create an index is the selectivity to be expected from an index and the actual need to access a table via the columns which make up an index.

6.2.2 SQL statement tuning

Whether the available indexes are in fact made use of for a SQL operation is ultimately decided by the SQL optimizer. This component of the database server has the task of determining the best possible (that is the most cost-effective or quickest) access path for a given SQL command. The SQL optimizer implemented in Oracle7 differentiates between the following methods:

- rule-based optimization
- cost-based optimization
- cost-based optimization plus hints

If a SQL command is being processed by the SQL optimizer then the access path is determined above all by which database objects are to be accessed and by the WHERE condition of the SQL command.

In the rule-based approach the SQL optimizer determines the access path according to the type of condition in the WHERE clause and depending on which one of a pre-defined set of rules is applicable.

Whereas the rule-based approach relies on a set of rules irrespective of any statistical information about the database objects to be processed, the cost-based approach does consider these statistics when choosing the access path. These statistics for tables, indexes and clusters are compiled using the ANALYZE command and must be periodically refreshed. Some typical ANALYZE commands might be:

```
analyze table TA compute statistics;
analyze table TA estimate statistics;
analyze index TA_PK estimate statistics;
```

The first of these commands returns exact statistics about table TA. The statistical values generated are stored in the data dictionary and can be accessed at any time via the data dictionary view USER_TABLES, which provides us with the following statistical information for a given table:

- number of rows;
- number of the table's data blocks;
- number of the table's data blocks not used;
- average free space available in the data blocks;
- average row length;
- number of chained rows.

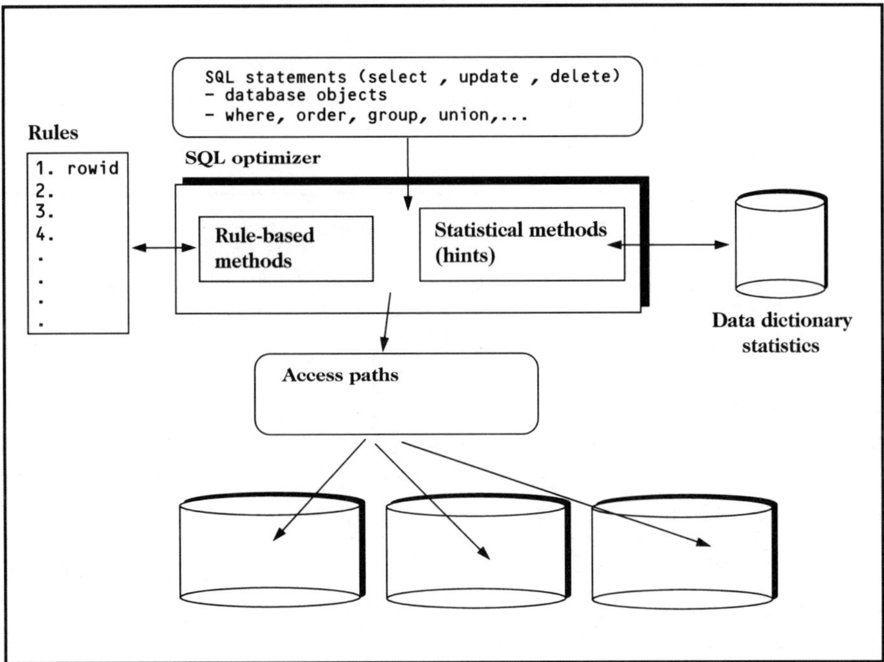

Figure 6.2 SQL optimization methods in Oracle7

In addition the data dictionary view USER_TAB_COLUMNS contains the following statistics for all the columns of a table:

- number of distinct values per column;
- largest and smallest value of a column.

Statistics are also gathered for all indexes and provide the following information:

- depth of B*-tree index;
- number of index blocks at the lowest level of an index (leaf blocks);
- number of keys in an index;
- maximum and minimum values of an index;
- average number of leaf blocks per key;
- average number of data blocks per key.

These values are entered in the data dictionary using the ANALYZE INDEX command and can be displayed using the view USER_INDEX.

The ANALYZE command always returns exact values if it is used with the COMPUTE option but this requires more time, particularly if the tables are especially large, than using the ESTIMATE option; with this latter option only some of the returned values are exact, such as the number of a table's data blocks, the number of unused data blocks and the maximum and minimum values of an index, and the other values are only estimates. In a production environment however it is better to use the estimated values, as these provide an acceptable degree of accuracy and can be generated in far less time than when the COMPUTE option is used.

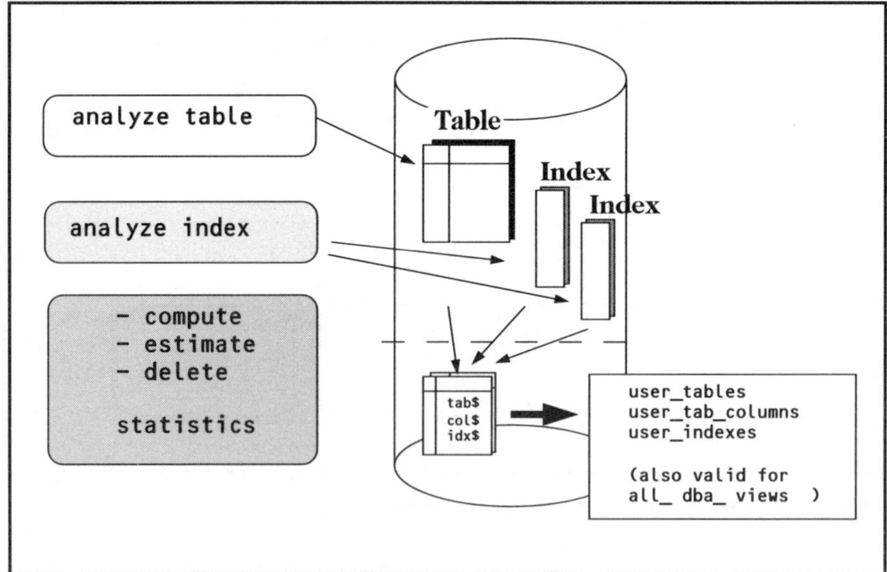

Figure 6.3 Compiling database statistics with Oracle7

Since statistical information for a table, index or cluster is not updated automatically, these values must be periodically generated so that the statistical optimizer is provided with up-to-date statistics. These can be provided either with the ANALYZE command, as we have seen, or with the packaged procedure ANALYZE_SCHEMA which forms part of the DBMS_UTILITY package (*refer also to* Figure 8.16). This procedure gathers statistics on all of the objects in a schema and can be called as follows:

```
dbms_utility.analyze_schema(<schema_name>, <analyze_method>);
dbms_utility.analyze_schema('gstuerner', 'estimate');
```

The cost-based approach to SQL optimization uses the statistics produced by the ANALYZE command for tables, indexes and clusters to find the best possible access path for a given SQL command.

In the Oracle7 database cost-based optimization is the default method. If no statistics are available on tables when a SELECT, UPDATE or DELETE statement is to be executed the SQL optimizer carries out various estimations and determines the corresponding access path based on the resulting statistical data.

Alternative optimization methods can be activated as follows:

- At instance level by assigning one of two values to the INIT.ORA parameter OPTIMIZER_MODE: either CHOOSE for statistical optimization (the default value) or RULE for the rule-based method.
- At session level by use of the SQL command

```
alter session set optimizer_mode = [rule/choose]
```

- At command level by enclosing a hint in a SQL command, for example:

```
select /*+rule+*/ * from tab where no > 4711;
```

The inclusion of hints in a SQL command is not, however, merely of use in redefining the optimization method. It can also be used to give the optimizer various hints and thus to perhaps influence the result of an optimization process. This function, although it is anathema to the relational purist, can be extremely useful in that it makes it possible to develop additional tuning methods (especially for large production systems) so that the user programs are not completely dependent on the SQL optimizer.

In addition to switching from the cost-based to the rule-based method (and vice versa) the following hints are also available to the system user:

- ALL_ROWS
- FIRST_ROWS
- RULE
- FULL(*<table>*)
- ROWID(*<table>*)
- CLUSTER(*<table>*)
- HASH(*<table>*)
- INDEX(*<table> <index> <index>*...)
- INDEX_ASC(*<table> <index> <index>*...)
- INDEX_DESC(*<table> <index> <index>*...)
- AND_EQUAL(*<table> <index> <index>*...)
- ORDERED
  This hint specifies that a join operation is to use the same sequence of tables as that specified in the statement's FROM clause.
- USE_NL(*<table> <table>*...)
  This hint defines the sequence of tables for a nested loops join operation.
- USE_MERGE (*<table> <table>*...)
  This hint defines the sequence of tables for a sort-merge join operation.

These hints can be used on SELECT, UPDATE and DELETE operations and must always be entered as a comment forming the first clause after the command's keyword. The following examples illustrate the typical use of this facility:

```
update /*+rule*/ TA
set ta_text = 'abc'
where no = 35463;
select /*+use_nl(TA TB)*/ TA.*, TB.*
from TA, TB
where ta_no = tb_no;
```

In order to tune SQL statements effectively it is of course necessary to recognize which statements are using up a disproportionate amount of the system's time and resources, and to achieve this ORACLE provides the TKPROF utility, which makes it possible to analyze an ORACLE session in terms of the SQL commands used. This utility can be started by entering the statement:

```
alter session set sql_trace = true
```

After this statement has been entered the information on all SQL statements carried out within the session is recorded and is then stored in a trace file. This information includes the following items:

- the access path of every SQL statement;
- CPU time spent executing a statement;
- CPU time spent parsing a statement;
- the number of physical and logical I/O operations;
- the number of times a statement is executed;
- the number of times a statement is parsed.

With the aid of the TKPROF utility the trace file is formatted so as to present the information in a suitable form, perhaps sorted in different ways if required. The resulting access path information can then be analyzed in order to optimize SQL statements which are very frequently executed within the application.

6.2.3 Applications tuning

In addition to tuning individual SQL commands, as we discussed in the previous section, it is also possible to optimize our system at the applications level. To do this we must look at the configuration type, that is how a particular application is being run. A typical online application should for example be run in Multi-Threaded Server mode as this type of configuration is particularly suited to serving many online applications using only a few database server processes (*see also* Section 3.3). On the other hand an application which makes intensive use of the database's resources should be run in Dedicated Server mode. The user determines in which mode an application should run by entering the required CONNECT clause when logging on to the ORACLE database.

The use of declarative and procedural integrity constraints can have a positive effect on performance; constraints are processed centrally by the database server instead of by the applications program, and they are executed in a highly optimized form.

The use of stored PL/SQL programs produces similar benefits; they are available centrally and already compiled in the database server and once activated are available to all users within the shared pool of the database cache. Declarative and procedural integrity constraints and PL/SQL programs have a particularly positive effect on performance in client/server configurations since the use of these server-resident facilities significantly reduces network traffic.

6.2.4 Database server tuning

When tuning the database server it is especially important to examine the size and configuration of the database cache: the number of data block buffers in the database cache and the size of the shared pool can be of particular significance in determining the performance of an Oracle7 system. The data block buffers in the database cache should be large enough so that each physical read operation will allow about 10 to 20 logical read operations; this corresponds to a data block buffer hit ratio of 90–95%.

The data block buffer hit ratio can be calculated with the aid of the V$SYSSTAT data dictionary view, where the current values are stored for CONSISTENT GETS, DB BLOCK GETS and for PHYSICAL READS. A typical query might be:

```
select name, value
from v$sysstat
where name in ('consistent gets',
'db block gets', 'physical reads')
```

In this example the CONSISTENT GETS and the DB BLOCK GETS represent the logical read operations, that is read operations on data blocks which are already present in the database cache. The values for logical and physical read operations can also be calculated with the aid of the ORACLE Monitor by using the option MONITOR SYSTEMSTATISTICS.

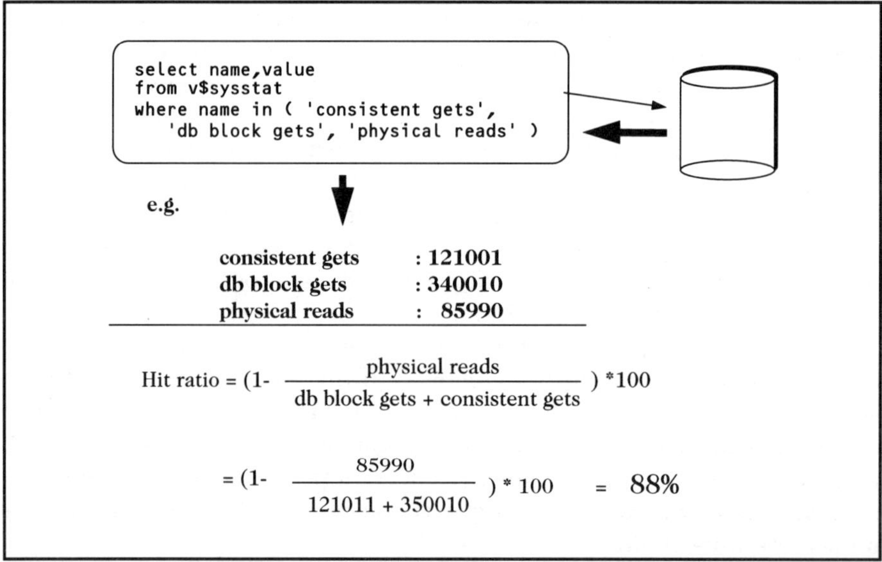

Figure 6.4 Calculating the data block hit ratio from the V$SYSSTAT view

In addition to the hit ratio it is also very important to establish the optimum number of data block buffers in the database cache, since either an under-sizing or an over-sizing of this critical value will have a negative effect on the performance of the whole system.

In order to establish the optimum number of data block buffers for a given application type it is necessary to carry out a data block buffer analysis. In this analysis a typical application is run against the database over a fixed period of time, usually between two and eight hours, and during this period data block access statistics are recorded and can afterwards be evaluated. This analysis has two aspects:

- the utilization of data block buffers present in the database cache;
- the hit ratio to be expected if a different number of data block buffers were in use (a 'what if' analysis).

The first analysis is initiated by the parameter DB_BLOCK_LRU_STATISTICS = TRUE, the second by the parameter DB_BLOCK_LRU_EXTENDED_STATISTICS = n, where 'n' stands for the number of additional data block buffers for which an analysis is to be carried out. Both of these parameters are defined in the INIT.ORA file.

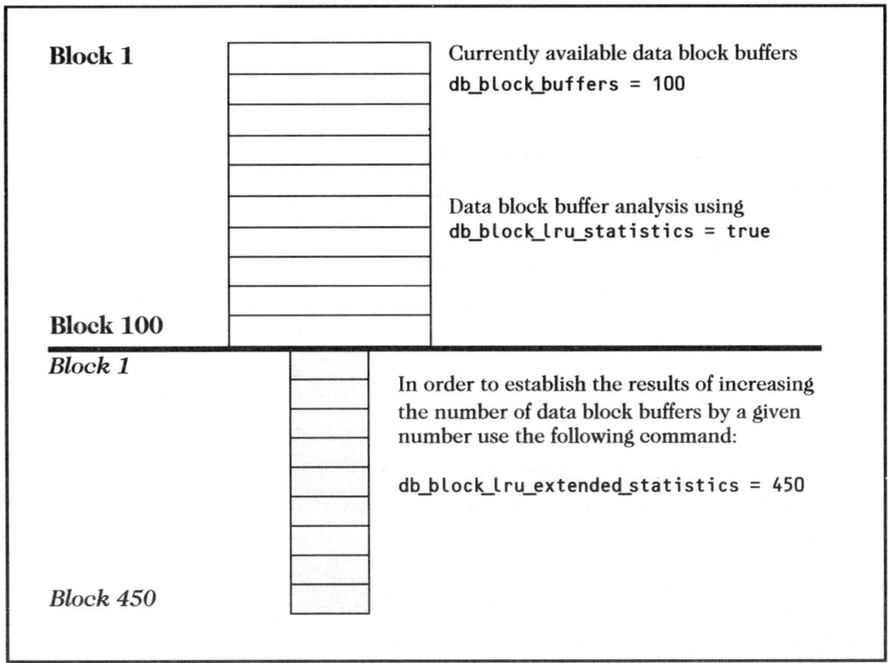

Figure 6.5 Analysing the number of data block buffers

If an ORACLE instance is being run with these two parameters the resulting statistics are stored in the two internal data dictionary tables X$KCBCHB and X$KCNRBH where they can be evaluated as shown in Figure 6.6.

The information stored in the two tables indicates how often a single data block buffer has been accessed or how often a data block buffer *would be* accessed if it were actually present. In the example in Figure 6.6 we can see that of the data block buffers currently available the first thirty are being accessed particularly frequently.

The second evaluation helps us to decide whether to increase the number of data block buffers. We can deduce from it that increasing the number of buffers by 50 data blocks would result in very few additional data block hits. Since the greatest increase in the hit ratio lies in the region of 100–150, the data block buffer should be increased by 150 data blocks. To increase it any further would of course make the database cache larger but it would have no noticeable effect on performance, as these additional data block buffers cannot be used by this type of application.

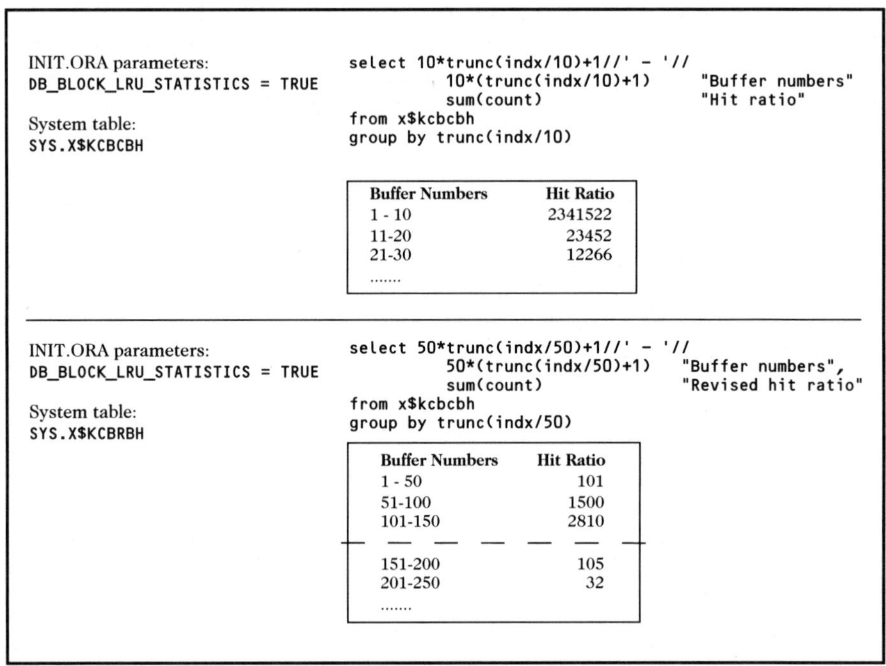

Figure 6.6 Analysing the data block buffer hit ratio

The second important area in the database cache is the shared pool, whose size is specified by the INIT.ORA parameter SHARED_POOL_SIZE, and which contains the following two types of data:

- shared SQL commands, stored PL/SQL programs and database triggers;
- data dictionary information such as table names, column names, index names and constraints.

The amount of space used by both these components of the shared pool can be established by two data dictionary views:

- V$LIBRARYCACHE
  this shows the area given over to SQL commands, PL/SQL programs and database triggers.
- V$ROWCACHE
  this shows the amount of space occupied by data dictionary information.

This same information can also be displayed using the ORACLE*Monitor, for example MONITOR CACHE.

The output of V$LIBRARYCACHE provides statistics on the objects administered in the library cache. An example is shown in Figure 6.7, where the GETS parameter retrieves the number of requests for an object and the PINS parameter returns the number of times an object is executed. At the same time the hit ratio for GETS and PINS is given as GETRATIO and PINRATIO, which in our example is 96%.

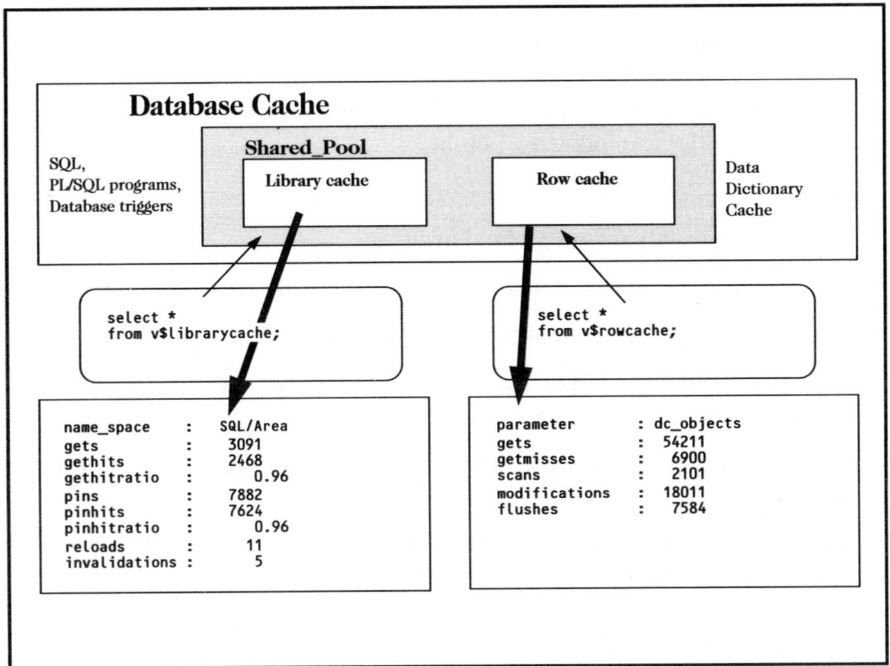

Figure 6.7 Analysing the shared pool in the database cache

Using the view V$ROWCACHE we can find out how often the data dictionary has to be accessed to get the information necessary for processing a SQL statement. In a mature system the dictionary hit ratio and the data block hit ratio should both be around 90%.

In order to get the hit ratio statistics for the whole data dictionary cache the following command must be entered:

```
select (1 - sum(getmisses)/sum(gets)) * 100
from v$rowcache;
```

In order to group the statistics according to the individual data dictionary objects the command is:

```
select parameter, (1-sum(getmisses) /
decode(sum(gets), 0, 1, sum(gets))) *100
from v$rowcache
group by parameter;
```

6.2.5 Database tuning

The most important task in tuning the database is to ensure that the various file types in an ORACLE database and the allocation of database objects to database files are both organized as effectively as possible. In this respect we should consider the following points:

- Redo log files should always be assigned to the fastest disks, whenever possible separately from the database files.
- The system tablespace should only be used for the data dictionary.
- Temporary segments should be stored in their own tablespace.
- Rollback segments should be allocated their own tablespace which is separate from the user data.
- Rollback segments should always be defined with explicit storage parameters.
- The data and index segments of the same database object should where appropriate be stored in different tablespaces on different disks.

6.2.6 Conclusion

Tuning a database system is obviously a very important task, especially for large production systems. At the beginning of any tuning process it is important to establish the weaknesses or limitations of the current system environment and ORACLE provides a range of analytical utilities and methods to facilitate this task. Using the results of such an analysis, it is usually relatively easy to identify simple measures which will significantly improve the performance of the entire system.

7

Introduction to SQL Part 2 (PL/SQL)

Topics covered in this chapter

- The role of PL/SQL in the ORACLE environment
- Processing PL/SQL
- The different types of PL/SQL programs
- The language structures of PL/SQL
- The structure of a PL/SQL module

7

Introduction to SQL Part 2 (PL/SQL)

7.1 Introduction

As we saw in Chapter 2, SQL is the sole means of accessing an ORACLE database and of reading or modifying the data which it contains. A SQL statement is parsed, optimized and executed by the ORACLE Server which then signals to the calling process whether the operation has been successful and, in the case of a read operation, returns the requested data records. If the SQL statement has been generated within a 3GL or 4GL program then the result of the SQL call will normally be used to determine which action the program should next carry out. As SQL is a non-procedural language it provides none of the control constructs common in all standard programming languages.

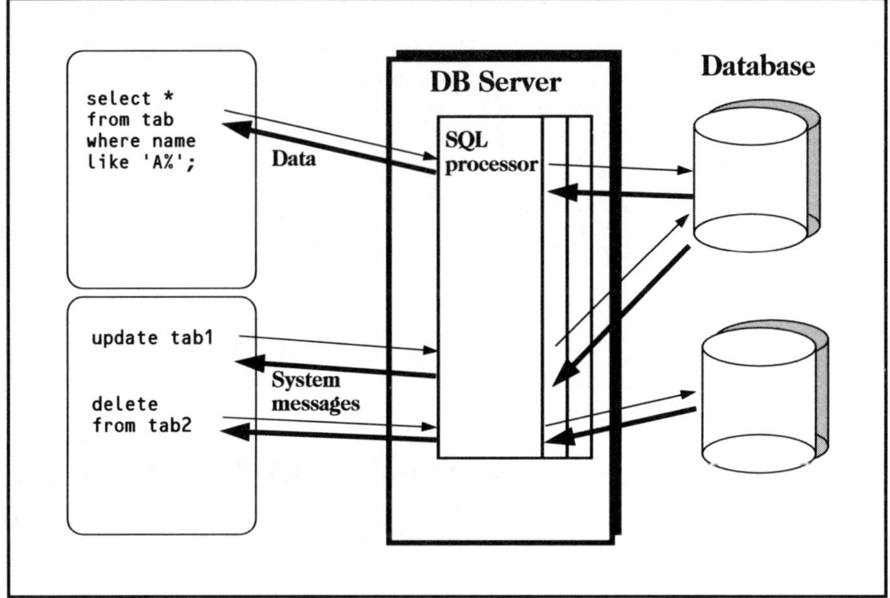

Figure 7.1 Processing SQL statements

The procedural language extension to SQL, PL/SQL, was first introduced with Version 6 of the ORACLE database. It was developed with two primary goals:

1. To make it possible to carry out complex database-oriented operations completely within the database server without having to pass control back to the user program after every single SQL operation (SELECT, INSERT, UPDATE ...).
2. To make a procedural programming language available to all ORACLE programs, both within the ORACLE Server as well as within the ORACLE software development environment.

The first of these goals was particularly concerned with improving overall system performance. When a PL/SQL procedure is called the corresponding block of code, which typically will contain a number of SQL statements and control constructs, is passed in full to the ORACLE Server to be processed. Sending and processing statements in a block significantly reduces the high performance overheads which result when the system has to switch contexts between application and database processes; the resulting improvement is of particular benefit in client/server environments.

The second of the two goals was concerned with increasing software development productivity. The aim was to define a language which could be used to develop complex programs and which would be identical in all ORACLE environments, both within the ORACLE Server as well as within the ORACLE development environments.

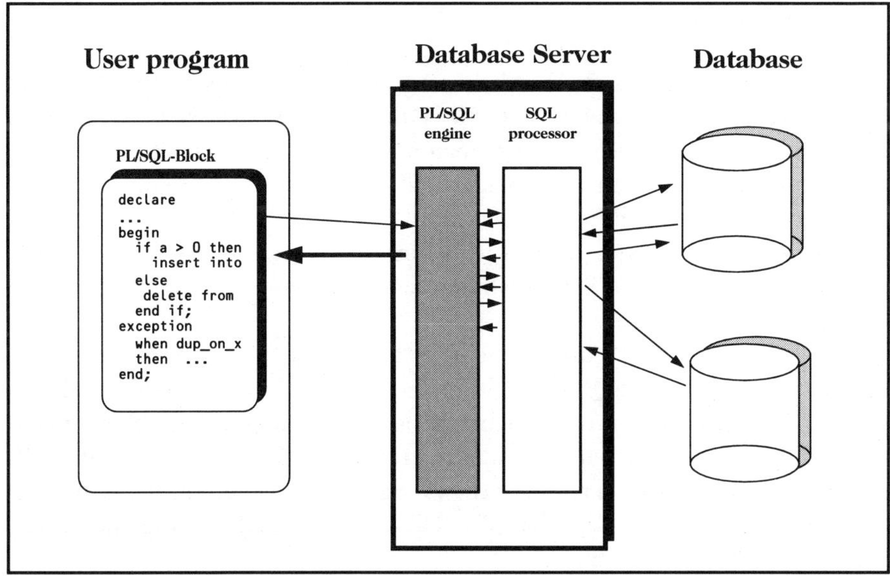

Figure 7.2 Processing an anonymous PL/SQL block in the server

With the aid of PL/SQL procedural functions can be implemented in non-procedural software development tools such as Oracle Forms, Oracle Reports or Oracle Graphics (part of the ORACLE 4GL product range) where they can be executed by event-driven applications triggers. A PL/SQL program is processed by a PL/SQL engine which can be implemented either within the 4GL development tools or as part of the ORACLE Server.

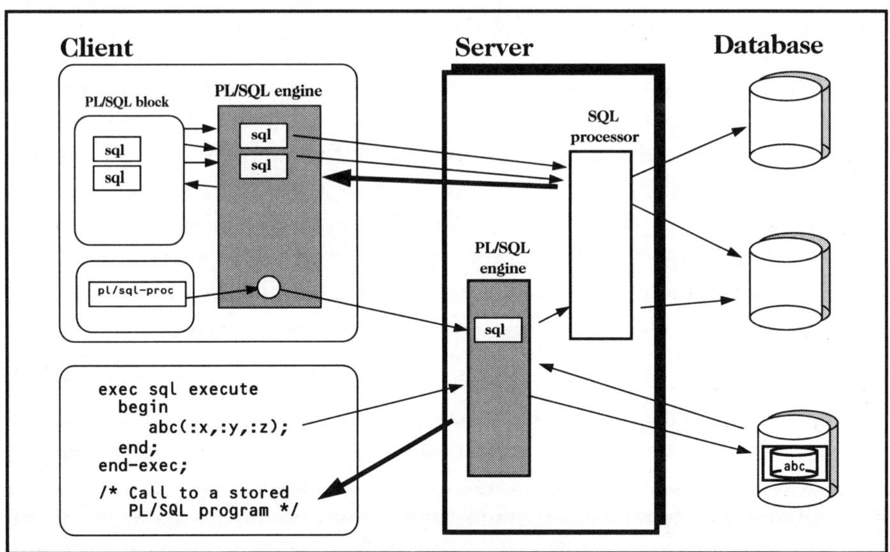

Figure 7.3 Processing PL/SQL in a client/server configuration

This situation is illustrated in Figure 7.3 where the PL/SQL processor of an ORACLE 4GL program executes a PL/SQL program on the user side (the client) and then passes the PL/SQL program's commands to the ORACLE Server. The PL/SQL engine on the ORACLE Server executes PL/SQL programs which have either been transmitted to the Server as PL/SQL blocks (*see* Figure 7.2) or which are already held in the database in a precompiled form as *stored* procedures or functions. In the case of stored PL/SQL programs a call to a given procedure or function is simply sent from the user program to the ORACLE Server which reads the compiled program from the database and executes it.

As we can see in Figure 7.3 it is also possible to combine these two methods, so that a PL/SQL program on the user side can include a call to a stored procedure. This procedure call is passed by the client PL/SQL engine to the ORACLE Server, where it is in turn processed by the server's PL/SQL engine, which returns the result to the PL/SQL client which initiated the call.

In general we can say that PL/SQL can be used to implement the following types of program:

- 4GL procedures and functions which are executed within applications triggers. Examples can be found in all ORACLE 4GL tools where PL/SQL is always used to implement any kind of procedural structures.

- Anonymous PL/SQL blocks which are stored and used as whole blocks within a 3GL environment, being sent as complete units to the ORACLE Server where they are processed. Although widely used with ORACLE Version 6, the introduction of packaged PL/SQL procedures in Oracle7 means that this method is likely to be used far less frequently in future.

- Stored PL/SQL programs: these include stored procedures, functions and also the packages which can be formed from them. A stored PL/SQL program is created as a database object with the aid of the SQL commands CREATE PROCEDURE, CREATE FUNCTION or CREATE PACKAGE and it is then stored in the database in its compiled form. By generating the appropriate call a stored PL/SQL program can be executed on a local or, by means of a remote procedure call, on a remote database server. (Further details on procedures, functions and packages can be found in Chapter 8).

- ORACLE database triggers which are defined on a single table in an ORACLE database and are executed whenever one of the SQL operations INSERT, UPDATE or DELETE is carried out. A database trigger can be used to perform relatively complex operations, including modify operations on a remote database. These would then be automatically secured by the two-phase commit protocol without any further user intervention being necessary (*refer also to* Chapter 9).

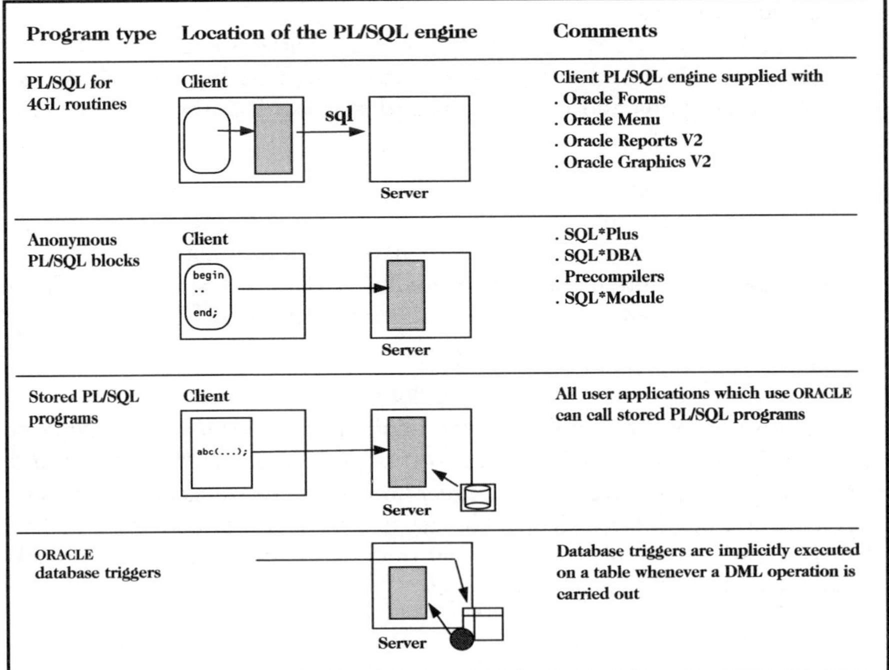

Program type
Location of the PL/SQL engine
Comments
PL/SQL for 4GL routines
Client
sql
Server
Client PL/SQL engine supplied with
. Oracle Forms
. Oracle Menu
. Oracle Reports V2
. Oracle Graphics V2
Anonymous PL/SQL blocks
Client
begin
..
end;
Server
. SQL*Plus
. SQL*DBA
. Precompilers
. SQL*Module
Stored PL/SQL programs
Client
abc(...);
Server
All user applications which use ORACLE can call stored PL/SQL programs
ORACLE database triggers
Server
Database triggers are implicitly executed on a table whenever a DML operation is carried out

Figure 7.4 The different PL/SQL program types and the corresponding PL/SQL engines

These four program types are summarized in Figure 7.4. In the following sections we shall go on to examine the basic characteristics of the PL/SQL language and in Chapters 8 and 9 we shall deal with the specific tasks involved in creating and managing stored programs and database triggers.

7.2 The structure of a PL/SQL block

The definition and implementation of the PL/SQL language owes a great deal to the programming language Ada. In particular features such as the block concept, the definition of data types, the control constructs and error and exception handling all reveal the strong influence of Ada. The implementation of procedures and functions has also taken into account the important concept in Ada of packages and the possibility these offer of overloading functions and procedures, thus providing a modern and very efficient programming aid.

As we have already mentioned, PL/SQL is a block-oriented language and every PL/SQL block basically consists of the following three parts:

- The Declarative Part
  In this part the names and data types of the variables and constants to be used are declared and cursors, which will be used to carry out SELECT operations and to specify user-defined errors or exceptions, are also explicitly defined.
- The Executable Part
  This part contains the actual algorithm code and includes control constructs such as loops, IF-THEN-ELSE constructs, assignment operations as well as the SQL statements which modify or read tables and other database objects and which control database transactions.
- The Error or Exception Handling Part
  An *exception* is an error condition defined either by the user (that is, explicitly) or by the system (that is, implicitly). As soon as an exception occurs (is *raised*) control passes to this part of the PL/SQL block and specifically to the corresponding *exception handler*. An exception handler is a section of code which specifies what actions are to be carried out in response to a particular error so that the processing of the PL/SQL block can be completed in a controlled way.

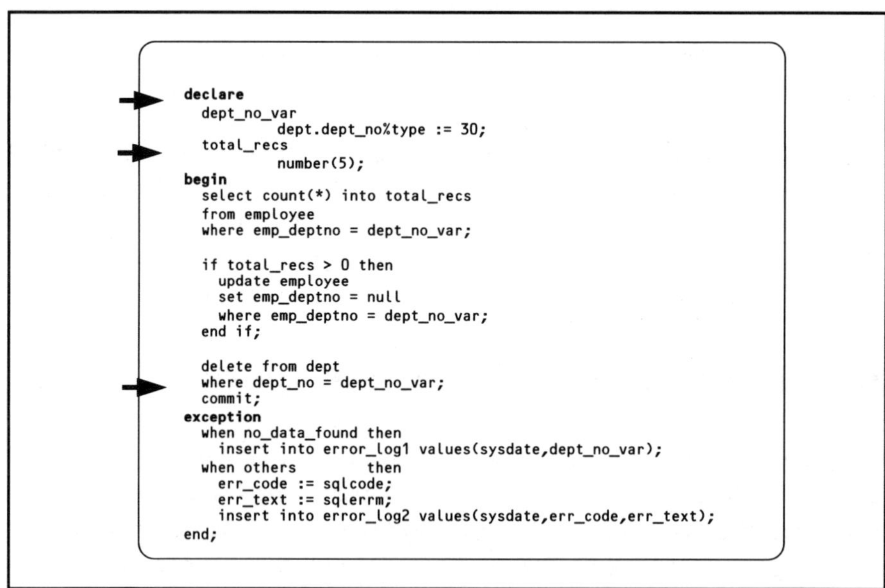

```
declare
  dept_no_var
           dept.dept_no%type := 30;
  total_recs
           number(5);
begin
  select count(*) into total_recs
  from employee
  where emp_deptno = dept_no_var;

  if total_recs > 0 then
    update employee
    set emp_deptno = null
    where emp_deptno = dept_no_var;
  end if;

  delete from dept
  where dept_no = dept_no_var;
  commit;
exception
  when no_data_found then
    insert into error_log1 values(sysdate,dept_no_var);
  when others        then
    err_code := sqlcode;
    err_text := sqlerrm;
    insert into error_log2 values(sysdate,err_code,err_text);
end;
```

Figure 7.5 Example of a simple PL/SQL program

Figure 7.5 shows a typical PL/SQL block with its three component parts. This block structure is evident in all PL/SQL program types, in 4GL procedures, anonymous PL/SQL blocks, stored PL/SQL programs and in ORACLE database triggers. Apart from a few key words which denote the start of the declarative part, all PL/SQL blocks have the same structure, as shown in Figure 7.6.

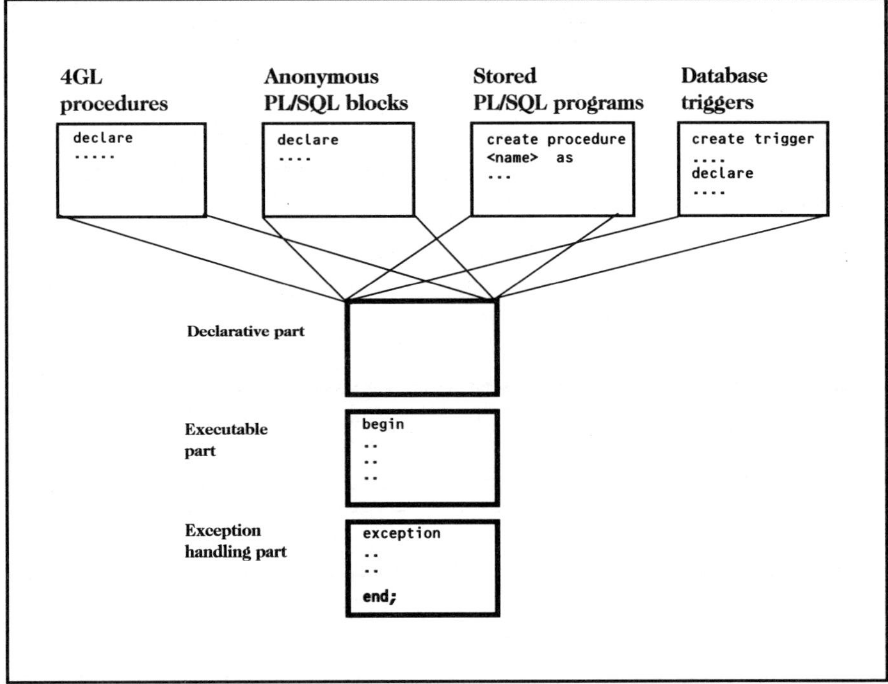

Figure 7.6 The declarative part in the various PL/SQL program types

7.2.1 The declarative part

PL/SQL is a strongly typed programming language in which all variables and constants must be defined and declared before they can be used. In addition the declarative part may also contain any of the following elements of a PL/SQL block:

- explicit SQL cursors, which are needed for set-based SELECT operations;
- user-defined exceptions which are given specific names;
- user-defined error names which are assigned to specific ORACLE error numbers by means of the EXCEPTION_INIT procedure.

Figure 7.7 shows some of the possible variants for the declarative part of a PL/SQL block.

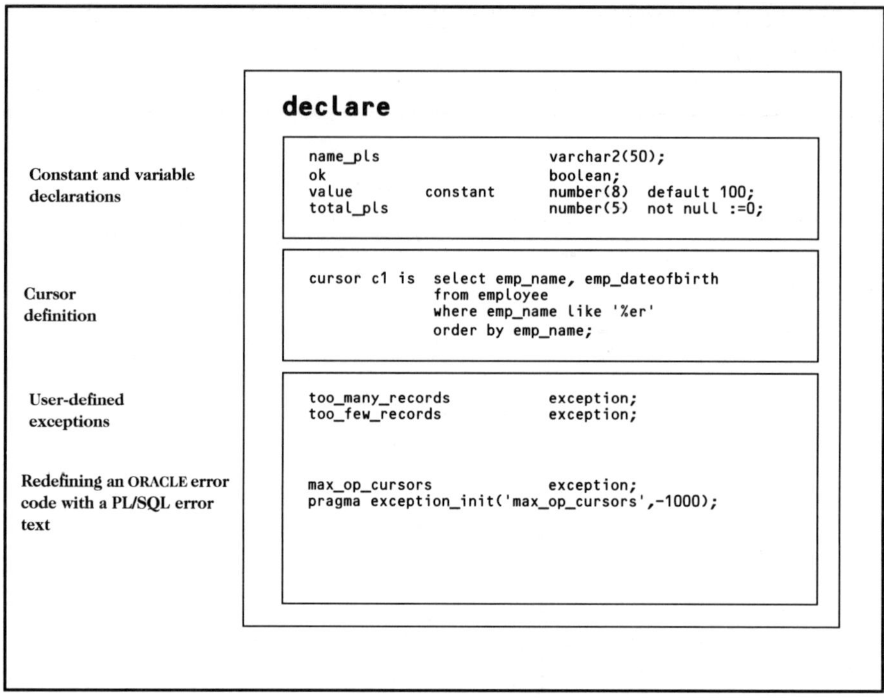

declare
Constant and variable declarations
name_pls varchar2(50);
ok boolean;
value constant number(8) default 100;
total_pls number(5) not null :=0;
Cursor definition
cursor c1 is select emp_name, emp_dateofbirth
from employee
where emp_name like '%er'
order by emp_name;
User-defined exceptions
too_many_records exception;
too_few_records exception;
Redefining an ORACLE error code with a PL/SQL error text
max_op_cursors exception;
pragma exception_init('max_op_cursors',-1000);

Figure 7.7 Examples of the declarative part of a PL/SQL block

Any names can be chosen for variables and constants as long as they do not exceed 30 characters in length (in the rest of this section we shall refer only to variables as the same rules apply to both variables and constants). A variable is defined by a name and a PL/SQL data type, possibly together with a NOT NULL constraint and/or an initial value. Valid variable definitions might be:

```
totalno       number(8)      not null := 0;
text_line     varchar2(80)   := 'PL/SQL is great';
next_date     date;          -- no initialization but a comment
```

Altogether ORACLE provides two composed data types (which we will look at later in this section) and twelve scalar data types, the latter being listed in Figure 7.8, which also shows the range of values for all twelve data types.

It should be noted that the two scalar data types NUMBER and BINARY_INTEGER both incorporate some subtypes (five and two respectively), each of which differs to a certain extent in its range of values and thus imposes certain implicit constraints on the data which can be stored.

Data type	Sub-type	Example	Range of values
char	-	text_1 char(50);	1 .. 32767 bytes
varchar	text_2 varchar(80);	%	
varchar2	text_3 varchar(120);	%	
long	t_long long;	1..64535 bytes	
number		number(10,2);	1e-129 .. 9.99e125
	decimal	decimal;	
	float	float;	
	integer	integer;	
real	real;		
smallint	smallint;		
binary_integer		binary_integer	-2^{-31} .. $2^{31}-1$
	natural	natural;	0 .. $2^{31}-1$
	positive	positive;	1 .. $2^{31}-1$
boolean	-	boolean	true , false
date	-	date;	4712 B.C. - 4712 A.D.
raw	-	raw;	18 bytes
rowid	-	rowid;	4 bytes
mlslabel	-	mlslabel;	255 bytes
raw mlslabel	-	raw mlslabel;	-

Figure 7.8 PL/SQL data types

The two data types MLSLABEL and RAW MLSLABEL can only be used in connection with Trusted Oracle7 (*refer to* Chapter 11).

Up until now we have only looked at explicit type definition, where one of the data types listed in Figure 7.8 is explicitly assigned to a variable. However PL/SQL also makes it possible to define data types implicitly and at runtime by declaring a variable with the data type of a column from a table or view which has already been declared. This type of single declaration is denoted by the keyword %TYPE which is placed after the table and column name, as we can see in the following example.

```
name_var1       employee.emp_name%type;
```

At runtime the variable *name_var1* is assigned the same data type as the *emp_name* column from the *employee* table. In the following declaration:

```
name_var2       name_var1%type;
```

the variable *name_var2* implicitly adopts the data type of the variable *name_var1*, which has already been declared. It should be noted that only backward references are possible in this context.

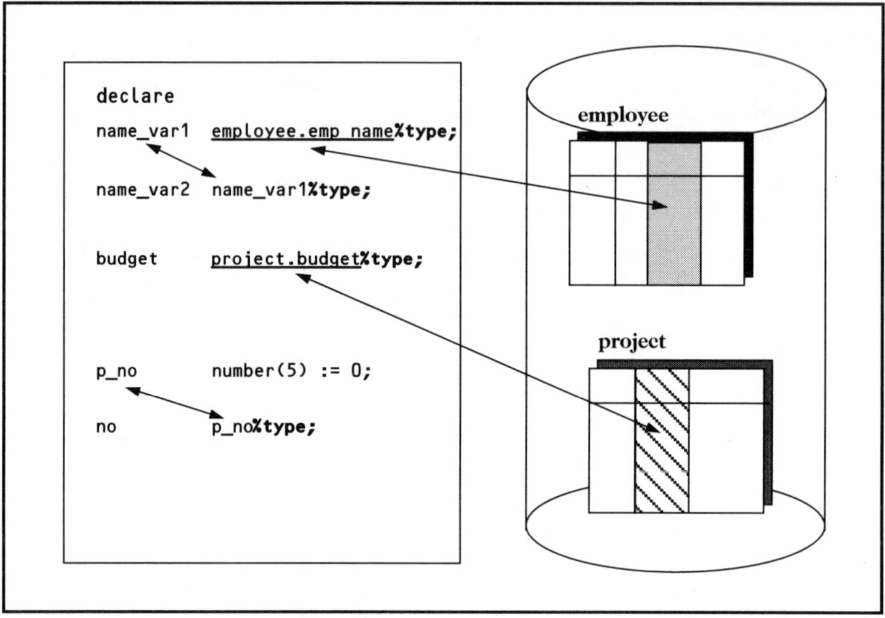

Figure 7.9 Implicit type definitions using the PL/SQL %TYPE attribute

Having seen how an existing column or variable can be used to declare a new variable we can now look at how the same mechanism is used to make use of an entire table structure. When a variable is declared as being of a given rowtype, then a record structure is generated at runtime which exactly matches the referenced table or view. A rowtype declaration is denoted by the keyword %ROWTYPE, preceded by the table or view name. A typical declaration would be as follows:

```
emp_rec     employee%rowtype;
```

The effect of this declaration will be to generate (at runtime) a data structure called `emp_rec` which, in terms of the names and data types of its columns, will correspond exactly to the *employee* table. The individual elements of this record structure are referenced by using the variable name (*emp_rec*) together with the original column name (*emp_name*, *emp_salary*), as in the following example:

```
emp_rec.emp_salary :=   emp_rec.emp_salary * 1.10;
```

In addition to referencing previously declared record structures, the ROWTYPE feature also allows us to reference PL/SQL cursors and to declare a data structure which is composed of the names and data types contained in the cursor declaration (cursors are explained further on in this section). Figure 7.10 shows how both a table and a cursor are used to declare two new record structures.

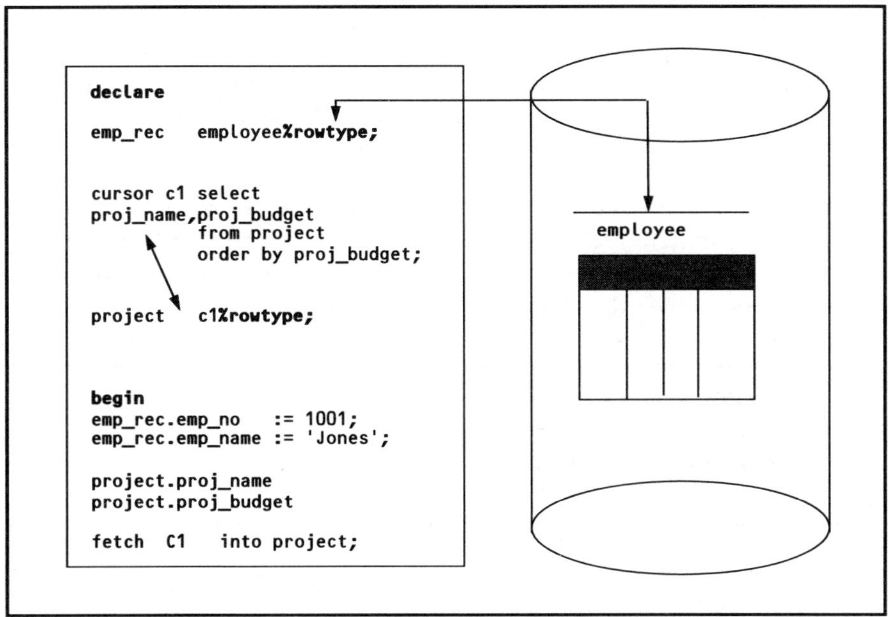

Figure 7.10 Implicit type definitions using the PL/SQL %ROWTYPE attribute

In addition to the scalar data types already mentioned, PL/SQL also provides two composed data types: PL/SQL tables, which are in effect single dimensioned arrays, and PL/SQL records, which are variable data structures that can consist of any number of fields of different data types. Both these data types have to be declared in two stages: first of all the PL/SQL table or record is declared in terms of its own data structure which is assigned a unique name. In the second step table or record variables are declared which are based on the newly defined data structures. The following example shows how the data structure is declared for the PL/SQL table ***text_tab_type***:

```
type text_table_type is table of varchar2(80)
index by binary_integer;
```

In the case of PL/SQL tables (arrays) the individual records are referenced by means of the BINARY_INTEGER data type. Having defined the data type ***text_tab_type*** it is now possible to declare any number of variables which are based on it, as in the following example:

```
text_lines     text_table_type;
error_messages text_table_type;
```

We are now in a position to use these variables as follows:

```
text_lines(1) := 'PL/SQL is the procedural language';
text_lines(2) := 'provided with the ORACLE database';
```

Our second composed data type, the PL/SQL record, which can contain any number of different data types, also has to be implemented in a similar way to the PL/SQL table. First of all we have to define the actual data structure for our record, as in the following example:

```
type emp_rec_type is record
(emp_name          varchar2(30),
 emp_dateofbirth   date,
 emp_deptno        number(8));
```

Here we have defined a simple record structure consisting of three elements (fields) and we can now use this to declare any number of variables which will all have this structure:

```
emp_rec     emp_rec_type;
```

Now we have a variable which contains the three fields and which we would refer to as follows:

```
emp_rec.emp_name        := 'Jones';
emp_rec.emp_dateofbirth := to_date('21-09-1955', 'DD-MM-YYYY');
emp_rec.emp_deptno      := 10;
```

In addition to containing scalar data types as illustrated above, a record can also be defined to include other records, thus allowing the system developer to create sophisticated nested data structures which are able to deal with a wide range of user requirements. In Section 7.2.2 we will look in greater detail at some of the processing options which are available for complex data structures of this type.

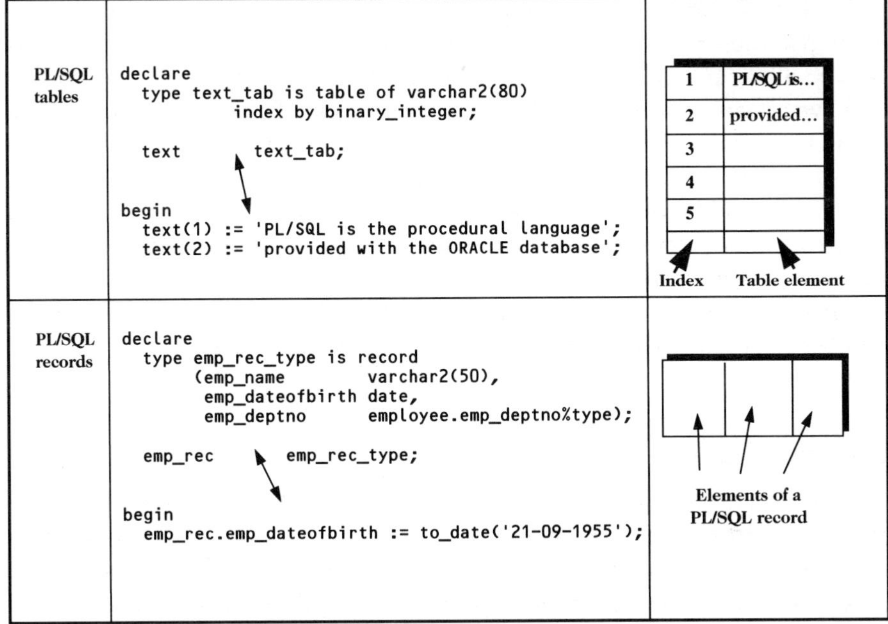

Figure 7.11 Creating user-defined data structures (PL/SQL tables and records)

Defining and using cursors

Whenever a SQL statement has to be processed PL/SQL opens a work area called a *context area* which is used to store all the information needed to process the statement. This context area is referenced by means of a *cursor* and PL/SQL distinguishes between two types of cursors, implicit cursors which are generated by the ORACLE Server, and explicit cursors which must be defined by the programmer whenever a data query is to be carried out which is going to return more than one row of data.

An explicit cursor must first be defined in the declarative part of a PL/SQL block, and this definition consists of three elements: a cursor name (of up to 30 characters in length), one or more input parameters (these are optional) and the SELECT statement which is to be assigned to this cursor. This type of cursor definition is illustrated in the following example:

```
cursor C1(name_var varchar2(30)) is
select emp_name, emp_dateofbirth, emp_deptno
from employee
where emp_name like name_var
order by emp_name;
```

In this example `C1` is the name of the cursor, ***name_var*** is the cursor's input parameter and the SELECT statement specifies the data which this cursor will return. At this stage (in the declarative part of the PL/SQL block) we have of course only defined the cursor; the specific operations which are carried out with a cursor (opening the cursor, reading data with the cursor and so on) will be covered when we look at the executable part of a PL/SQL block. It should be noted however that if an input parameter forms part of a cursor, as in our example, then this parameter must be initialized before the cursor is first activated.

Finally it is important to emphasize that PL/SQL places no limits on the number of cursors which can be open during any one session.

Declaring exceptions

The third PL/SQL component which can be defined in the declarative part of a block is the exception. As we have already mentioned any errors which occur during the processing of a PL/SQL block are always dealt with in the exception part of that same block. More specifically there are three types of error (exception) which can occur during program execution:

- PL/SQL exceptions
  These are ORACLE errors which have been given a specific name for the purposes of PL/SQL, for example DUPLICATE_VALUE_ON_INDEX or ZERO_DIVIDE.

- ORACLE error codes
  These include all the ORACLE error codes not part of the first group; when one of these errors occurs then an error number (as opposed to a name) is returned by the program.

- User-defined exceptions
  These are exceptions which have been defined and named by the programmer. If the PL/SQL program is to branch to the exception part following one of these user-defined errors then it must be explicitly activated (using the RAISE command) in the executable part of the PL/SQL block.

In Section 7.2.3 we will examine in detail the exceptions which are implicitly raised by the system as they have no significance in the declarative part of a PL/SQL block. The user-defined exceptions however are of specific interest to us at this point, as they must be declared in the declarative part before they can be raised in the executable part of the block. We declare an exception by specifying a name for it (which can be up to 30 characters long) followed by the keyword EXCEPTION, as is shown in the following examples:

```
pl_stop      exception;
too_many     exception
too_few      exception;
```

In this example we have declared three exceptions which we can activate in the executable part of our program by using the RAISE command. For example we may decide that we want to raise the exception ***too_few*** if the program variable ***total*** contains a value of less than 50:

```
if (total < 50) then
raise too_few;      -- branch to exception handler for 'too_few'
end_if;
```

It is important to emphasize that, as opposed to system exceptions which are activated automatically, user-defined exceptions must be explicitly raised within the program if control is to pass to the corresponding exception handler in the exception part of the PL/SQL block (*refer also to* Section 7.2.3).

Another feature available to the PL/SQL programmer in this context is the possibility of assigning names to those ORACLE error codes which are not given names by PL/SQL, so that when the error occurs the name and not the number of the error is generated.

A name is assigned to a given ORACLE error code in two steps: first the exception name is declared like any other user-defined exception, then, using the EXCEPTION_INIT command, the exception name is assigned to the error code which is to be replaced, as in the following example:

```
max_open_cursors  exception;
pragma exception_init(max_open_cursors, -1000);
```

In this example the name *max_open_cursors* has been assigned to the ORACLE error number -1000. If this error occurs while the program is being executed then the exception *max_open_cursors* will automatically be raised, control will pass to the exception handling part of the PL/SQL block and the corresponding exception handler (if this has been coded) will be carried out. The keyword PRAGMA in our example signifies that the statement is a compiler directive and is therefore not to be processed when the block is executed.

In concluding our examination of the declarative part it is worth referring once again to Figure 7.7 which contains several examples of the different elements which can occur in this part of a PL/SQL block.

7.2.2 The executable part

The executable part of a PL/SQL program basically contains the actual algorithms or processing logic of the PL/SQL block and specifies what data from the database are to be processed in what way.

In order to carry out these processing operations PL/SQL provides all the control constructs which are available in standard programming languages and these have been fully integrated with all the data manipulation and transaction control facilities which are provided by standard SQL. In addition PL/SQL provides extensive capabilities for creating procedures, functions and packages. Figure 7.12 illustrates some of the control features which are available with PL/SQL.

If we examine PL/SQL in more detail, we can see that there are five basic control structures provided by this language:

- assignments and arithmetic expressions;
- conditional processing (IF...THEN...ELSE) structures;
- loops structures including:
  - infinite or basic loops (LOOP... END LOOP)
  - FOR loops (FOR... END LOOP)
  - WHILE loops (WHILE `<condition>`... END LOOP)
  - cursor loops (FOR `<implicit loop>`... END LOOP);
- cursor control;
- raising exceptions.

The functionality provided by these control mechanisms makes it possible to develop sophisticated and compact programs which are able to carry out all the tasks required of a database server by a 4GL programming language.

We can now examine these control constructs in detail, starting with the assignment operation which is executed using the assignment symbol `:=`. This symbol forms the central part of an expression in which the value on the right-hand side of the expression is assigned to a variable or a PL/SQL table or record element on the left-hand side of the expression, as is shown in the following list of examples. Where necessary ORACLE carries out the required data conversion automatically.

`var := 10;`	(Assigning a constant value)
`var1 := var2;`	(Assigning the value of one variable to another)
`var3 := (var1 * factor1)`	(Assigning the result of an arithmetic expression)
`var4 := substr(var7, 1, 10)`	(Assigning the result of a SQL expression)
`var5 := my_function(var1)`	(Assigning the result of a stored function)
`var6 := (salary > 3500)`	(Assigning the result of a conditional expression)

Another method of assigning values to a variable is by means of the SELECT...INTO command or by means of the FETCH command where a cursor is being processed.

```
begin
if totalno < 0 then
  insert into tab values (...);
else
  delete from tab2 where no = 4711;
end if;
```

if...then...else construct. Each branch of the if statement can contain any PL/SQL or SQL statements

```
test :=  test * 1.1;
var  :=  substr(text,1,20);
cosi :=  cos(...);
```

Assignments, arithmetic expressions, SQL functions

```
for i in 1..end loop
.....
end loop;
```

for loop

```
while totalno < 30  loop
.....
end loop;
```

while loop

```
salary_increase(emp_no, new_salary);
ok := query(emp_no);
```

Calling a stored PL/SQL procedure or function

Figure 7.12 Examples of the executable part of a PL/SQL block

Conditional processing

If a series of PL/SQL statements is to be executed only under certain conditions then these conditions can be defined by means of any one of the following constructs:

```
if <condition(s)> then
   <sequence of statements>
end if

if <condition(s)> then
   <sequence of statements>
else
   <sequence of statements>
end if

if <condition(s)> then
   <sequence of statements>
elsif <condition(s)> then
   <sequence of statements>
end if
```

In each case the specified conditions are evaluated by the system and the result (which can only be either true or false) determines which sequence of statements, if any, is to be carried out. The IF...THEN...ELSE structure has been implemented in all the main programming languages so we shall not examine it in greater detail here.

Loop constructs

Four kinds of loops can be distinguished in PL/SQL:

1. **Unconstrained loops**
   This type of loop (which is also known as a basic or infinite loop) does not have constraints which limit the number of times the loop is executed. An unconstrained loop must be ended from within the loop by means of the EXIT WHEN, GOTO or RAISE commands. An unconstrained loop begins with the keyword LOOP followed by the required statements and ends with the keyword END LOOP, as shown in the following example:

```
loop
   <sequence of statements>
   exit when <condition>
   <sequence of statements>
   exit when <condition>
end loop;
```

```
if name is null or emp_no = 1000 then
   fetch  c1 into rec;
   a := rec.name;
   b := rec.salary;
else
   close c1;
   raise no_more;
end if;
```

if...else contruct

```
if  selected_date < '26-may-93'  then
   insert into tab values (...);
elsif name like 'A%'   then
   a:= first_name;
elsif name like 'B%'    then
   a:= name;
else
   pStoreName(selected_date, name, first_name, status);
end if;
```

if...elsif construct

Figure 7.13 Examples of the IF construct

In this case the conditions in the two EXIT WHEN clauses are evaluated at every iteration. If either condition becomes true the loop is ended and the program continues from the first executable statement following the keyword END LOOP.

2. **FOR loop**

A specified number of loops can be programmed with the aid of the FOR loop. The FOR loop has the following form:

```
for i in <start value>..<end value> loop;
```

In this example *i* represents the variable or index which is increased by 1 for each iteration of the loop. The two values which follow the keyword **IN** specify the first and last value of the variable *i* and the double period **..** denotes the FROM...TO clause in this construct. The first and last values used to determine how many times the loop will execute can be either constant values or can be calculated by an arithmetic expression. The following construct is therefore also a valid FOR loop:

```
for i in (8*factor)..floor(10*factor/0.3) loop
```

If the keyword REVERSE is added after IN the loop's control variable starts with the higher value and is decremented for each iteration of the loop until the lower value is reached, as in the following example where *i* starts with a value of 10 and ends with a value of 1.

```
for i in reverse 1..10 loop
```

3. **WHILE loop**

In a WHILE loop an associated condition is tested before each repetition of the loop. The loop is repeated until the condition tests FALSE. The form of a WHILE loop is as follows:

```
while <condition> loop
<statements>
end loop;
```

4. **Cursor FOR loops**
   The PL/SQL cursor loop is a special type of loop construct within which SQL cursor operations are carried out implicitly, thus allowing very compact programming. However we shall not discuss this type of loop in detail until we have covered the basic procedure for processing set data in SQL read operations.

SQL cursor operations

In Section 7.2.1 we saw that an explicit SQL cursor definition is always necessary when a SELECT statement is going to return more than one row. This type of SQL cursor can be regarded as a link between the set-oriented processing of the ORACLE Server and the record-oriented processing of standard programming languages. In order to implement a cursor we have to make use of four different cursor operations:

- Declaring the cursor
  The cursor is named and the input parameters and the actual SELECT statement are defined.
- Opening the cursor
  The cursor is activated but without data from the ORACLE Server being transferred to the program area. In this phase the database cache is checked to establish whether an identical SQL statement is already present in parsed form or whether the cursor's SQL statement needs to be parsed and an access path defined.
- Retrieving the cursor's data from the database to the cursor's program area
  All rows which fulfil the condition in the SQL SELECT statement are transferred to the corresponding program variables (FETCH). This operation is usually carried out in a loop until all the specified rows have been read.
- Closing the Cursor
  The read operation is ended in a controlled way and all resources are released.

Apart from these four cursor operations the example in Figure 7.14 shows how a cursor can be used to define a variable. In this example the %ROWTYPE qualifier allows us to define a variable which corresponds to the SELECT statement of the cursor `C1`. This structure can then be used in the FETCH statement with the variable's fields corresponding to the individual columns of the underlying database tables.

Together with these cursor operations PL/SQL also provides the following cursor attributes which allow us to check the status of the relevant cursor:

- %FOUND
  Evaluates to TRUE if the most recently carried out FETCH operation found a row.
- %NOTFOUND
  Evaluates to TRUE if the most recently carried out FETCH operation did not find a row.
- %ROWCOUNT
  Returns the number of rows already found.
- %ISOPEN
  Evaluates to TRUE if the cursor is open.

These cursor attributes can be accessed by appending the name of the specific attribute to the cursor's name and they can be made use of in all PL/SQL program constructs. Two examples of cursor attributes are:

```
if c1%found then    select expression has returned data
...
if c1%open then     close cursor before ending procedure
```

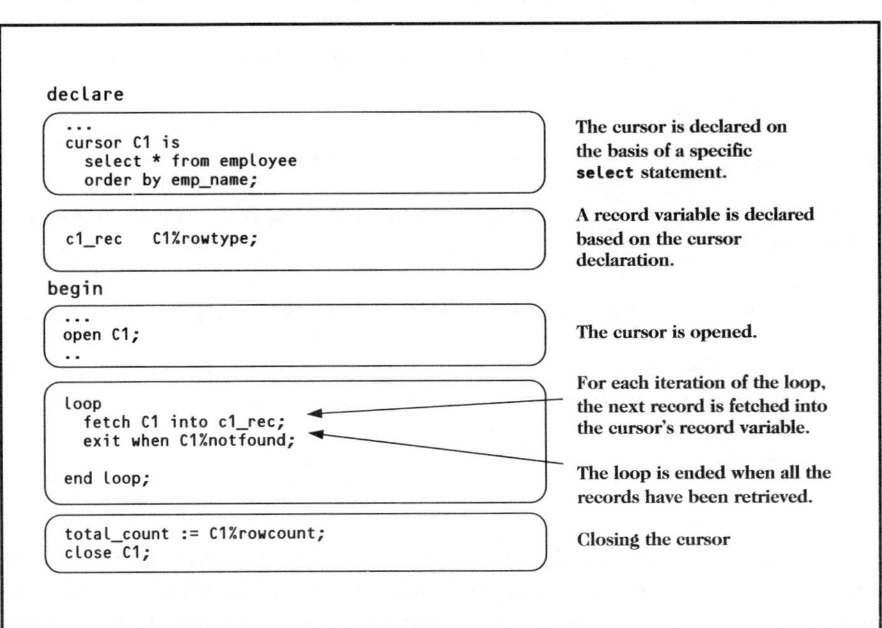

Figure 7.14 Processing a SQL cursor in a PL/SQL program

In Figure 7.14 the cursor attribute %NOTFOUND is used to end the unconstrained loop by checking within the EXIT statement whether or not the last FETCH operation retrieved a row. However these cursor attributes can be used not only with explicit (declared SELECT) cursors but also with all implicit cursors, in which case a cursor name before the attribute is not required. You may, for example, wish to check how many rows have been modified by an UPDATE statement and once the statement has been executed %ROWCOUNT will return the required total and this value can in turn be used in a subsequent SQL statement, as illustrated in the following example:

```
update employee
set emp_salary := emp_salary * 1.05
where emp_deptno = 40;
total_changed := %rowcount;   -- store number of records changed
```

Figure 7.14 illustrates the various steps which have to be taken in processing a subset of the available data with the aid of cursors. Figure 7.15 shows how the same processing could be programmed more concisely by using a cursor FOR loop.

A cursor FOR loop is a particular program construct which is geared to processing sets of data using the cursor operations provided by PL/SQL. This means that a cursor FOR loop implicitly carries out the following operations:

- creating a record data structure on the basis of the cursor definition;
- opening the cursor;
- transferring the rows from the database to the PL/SQL record structure;
- closing the cursor and ending the loop when all the cursor's rows have been read.

The general structure of a cursor FOR loop is as follows:

```
for <record structure> in <cursor name> loop
<statements>
end loop;
```

In this example `<record_structure>` is a name which is assigned to the cursor definition to create a record data type and the data which the cursor returns by an implicit read operation are stored in this structure at every iteration of the loop. The FOR loop is repeated until there are no more rows which satisfy the WHERE condition of the cursor. Figure 7.15 shows a cursor FOR loop which provides the same functionality as the example given in Figure 7.14.

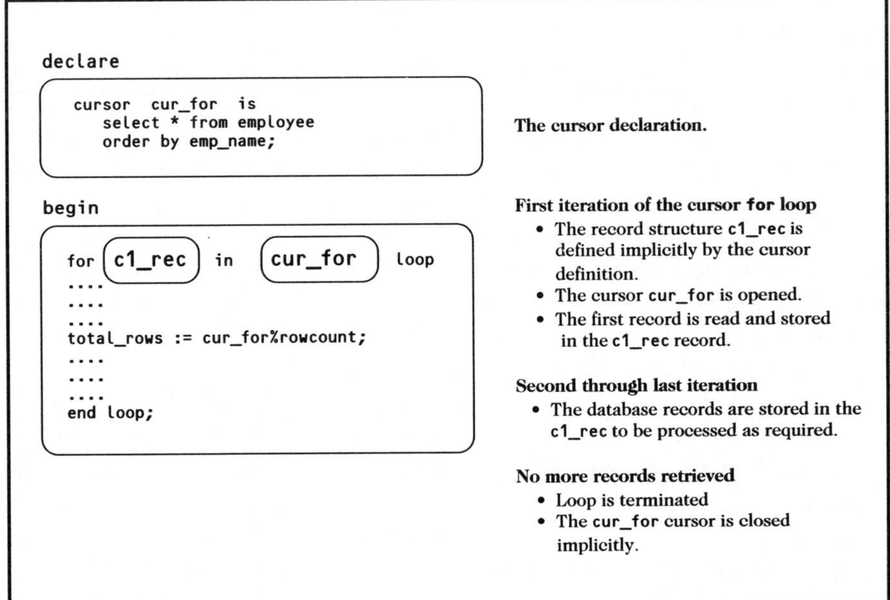

declare
cursor cur_for is
select * from employee
order by emp_name;
The cursor declaration.
begin
for c1_rec in cur_for loop
....
....
....
total_rows := cur_for%rowcount;
....
....
....
end loop;
First iteration of the cursor for loop
• The record structure c1_rec is defined implicitly by the cursor definition.
• The cursor cur_for is opened.
• The first record is read and stored in the c1_rec record.
Second through last iteration
• The database records are stored in the c1_rec to be processed as required.
No more records retrieved
• Loop is terminated
• The cur_for cursor is closed implicitly.

Figure 7.15 Example of a cursor FOR loop

7.2.3 Exception handling

PL/SQL recognizes three types of exception (error) which can arise during the execution of a PL/SQL program:

- internal (system) errors which have been redefined by PL/SQL to return an exception text instead of an error code;
- all other system errors which still return an ORACLE error code. These can also be given an exception name (EXCEPTION_INIT) in which case they will behave like internal exceptions;
- exceptions defined by the programmer which have to be explicitly activated (raised) within the PL/SQL program.

If an internal exception occurs during the execution of a PL/SQL program or if an exception defined by the programmer is activated by the RAISE statement, the program always branches to its exception or error handling section. This part of a PL/SQL program is denoted by the keyword EXCEPTION and it contains routines called *exception handlers* which handle one or more error situations. A typical PL/SQL exception part is shown in Figure 7.16 with each exception handler being defined by the keyword WHEN followed by the name of the exception, as in the following example:

```
when <exception name> then
<statements>
```

If an exception is explicitly raised or if an exception or error occurs during the execution of a PL/SQL program, control branches to the exception handling section. Here the system looks for the exception handler with the same name and carries out the corresponding sequence of PL/SQL statements to deal with the error. It is irrelevant whether the exception has been raised implicitly by one of the predefined error situations or through an exception defined within the program by means of the RAISE command.

All exceptions which do not need to be processed in a specific way can be dealt with by the OTHERS exception handler, which is always used by the system to respond to errors for which there is no specific exception handler.

Figure 7.16 shows four exception handlers which have been defined as follows:

- `dup_val_on_index` and `invalid_cursor` are internal exceptions in PL/SQL.
- `max_op_cursors` is a user-defined exception name which redefines system error code `-1000`.
- `too_many` is a user-defined exception.
- All other exceptions are to be dealt with by the `others` exception handler.

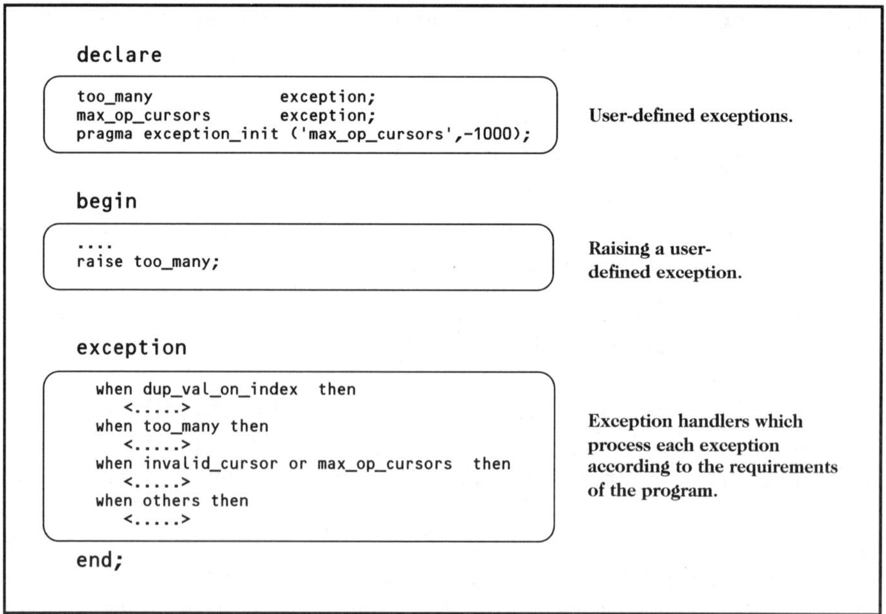

Figure 7.16 The exception handler part of a PL/SQL block

Figure 7.17 provides a list of all the internal exceptions defined by PL/SQL together with their original ORACLE error codes.

Exception name	ORACLE error code
cursor_already_open	ORA-06511
dup_val_on_index	ORA-00001
invalid_cursor	ORA-01001
invalid_number	ORA-01722
login_denied	ORA-01017
no_data_found	ORA-01403
not_logged_on	ORA-01012
program_error	ORA-06501
storage_error	ORA-06500
timeout_on_resource	ORA-00051
too_many_rows	ORA-01422
transaction_backed_out	ORA-00061
value_error	ORA-06502
zero_divide	ORA-01476

Figure 7.17 ORACLE error codes which have been redefined by PL/SQL

In order to create an effective exception handler for the OTHERS exception and to identify what error has occurred, we can make use of two SQL functions, SQLCODE and SQLERRM which return (respectively) the ORACLE error code and the corresponding error text for the exception which has forced the program to branch to the exception part of the PL/SQL block. Thus we might write an OTHERS exception handler which would look like this:

```
when others then
err_code := sqlcode;
err_text := sqlerrm;
insert into program_errors(error_code, error_text, error_time)
values (err_code, err_text, sysdate);
```

After the exception has been dealt with the current PL/SQL block is ended and control returns to the calling program module.

Stored PL/SQL procedures

Topics covered in this chapter

- The features of stored PL/SQL modules
- Stand-alone PL/SQL procedures and functions
- PL/SQL packages
- The benefits of stored PL/SQL modules
- Using stored PL/SQL modules
- Developing stored PL/SQL modules
- Dependency tracking
- Standard PL/SQL packages
- Retrieving PL/SQL modules from the data dictionary

8

Stored PL/SQL procedures

8.1 Introduction

As we saw in Chapter 7 the PL/SQL language forms the basis for the creation of procedures and functions and it is available in all the products of the ORACLE Cooperative Development Environment (CDE) as well as on the ORACLE Server itself.

By making it possible to create anonymous PL/SQL blocks, Version 6 of the ORACLE RDBMS already provided a means of implementing procedures and functions on the server itself, thus improving system performance particularly in the case of client/server applications. Figure 7.2 shows an example of an anonymous PL/SQL block.

Oracle7 has considerably extended the scope of database resident PL/SQL programs by introducing a number of new database objects: in addition to the anonymous PL/SQL blocks of ORACLE Version 6, Oracle7 also makes it possible to create complete packages of user-defined procedures and functions which can be stored in a precompiled form in the database. These stored procedures and functions can be used by any application program which also accesses the ORACLE database. Figure 7.4 provides an overview of the different types of PL/SQL programs.

Figure 8.1 shows what happens when a stored procedure is called by an applications program. The procedure call is first sent to the ORACLE Server where the system checks whether the procedure is already present in the shared pool of the database cache (that is, whether the procedure has recently been executed); if this is the case then the procedure can be executed at once, using the parameters supplied by the current procedure call. If the procedure call is not present in the shared pool area then the procedure code is retrieved from the database in its compiled form, is loaded into the shared pool, is executed and the results are passed back to the calling program.

The options which Oracle7 provides for the creation of database resident PL/SQL programs are based on the latest ideas in the field of modular software development. Thus the user is able to define the following types of PL/SQL constructs:

- functions
- procedures
- packages

PL/SQL packages can contain a number of functions and/or procedures, which are referred to as packaged procedures and packaged functions in order to distinguish them from stand-alone procedures and functions. These three constructs, taken together with the structures provided by PL/SQL itself, provide a framework for developing powerful and sophisticated PL/SQL programs which support recursive programming, which can be overloaded and which can also be accessed on remote ORACLE Servers by means of a Remote Procedure Call. As procedures and functions are processed identically by the ORACLE system we shall use the term 'procedure' in the rest of this chapter to refer to both procedures and functions.

The use of stored PL/SQL procedures can significantly improve the performance of client/server systems; in the first place they are available in a precompiled form on the server where they can be executed without creating any additional traffic on the network and without requiring a context change which would be costly in terms of the system's resources. In addition they can be executed very efficiently while they are still resident in the shared pool of the database cache.

Another important aspect in the use of stored PL/SQL procedures is the possibility they offer to *encapsulate* (group) related procedures, data structures, access privileges and so on. This means for example that if a user is granted the privilege to use a particular PL/SQL package, then the grantee will automatically receive all the other privileges which are implicitly required to make full use of the package. The user is thus able to access data which would otherwise not be available to him or her.

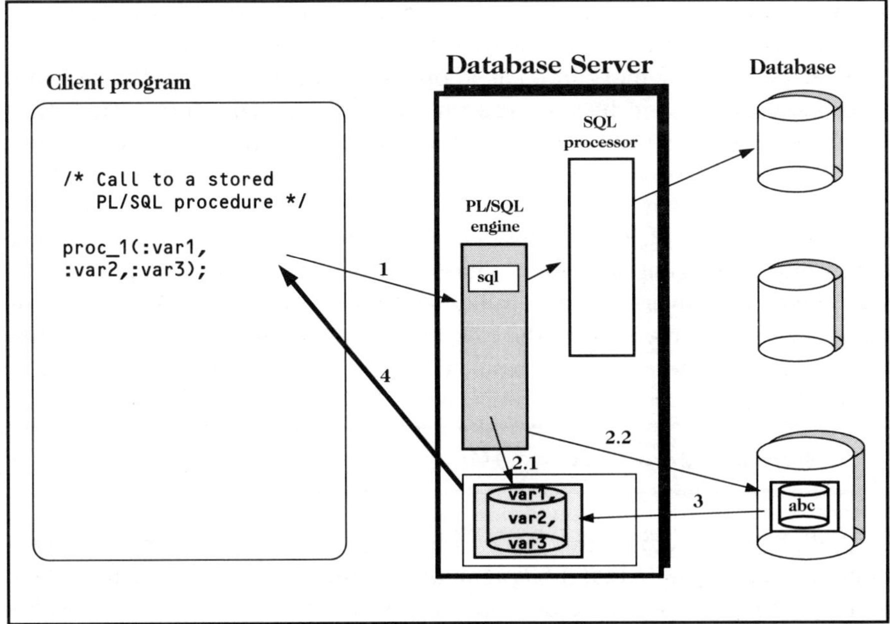

Figure 8.1 Processing a stored PL/SQL procedure

8.2 PL/SQL module constructs

8.2.1 Introduction

As we mentioned earlier there are three basic constructs available for stored PL/SQL modules: procedures, functions and packages. Procedures and functions can be defined either as single objects (CREATE PROCEDURE, CREATE FUNCTION) or within the context of a PL/SQL package (CREATE PACKAGE, CREATE PACKAGE BODY), in the first case we refer to *stand-alone procedures*, in the second to *package procedures*. In functional terms there is no difference between these two types of database object, but as we shall see, the use of packages provides a number of significant benefits derived from modern concepts of software modularity. For the system administrator some of the major benefits include the following:

- Functions and procedures can be packaged according to a system's functional, organizational or security requirements and can then be administered much more easily than if they are stored separately on the server.
- Access privileges can be assigned on the basis of a package so that all the procedures in a package can be made available to a given user as a single unit.

- Packages can also improve system performance. When a package procedure is called for the first time then the entire package to which it belongs is loaded into memory in a single operation, as opposed to the separate loads which would be required for stand-alone procedures. The other procedures from the package can then be called without any further disk I/O being necessary.

A function in PL/SQL behaves in exactly the same way as in other programming languages: it has (optionally) one or more input parameters and it always delivers a return value which can be used in assignment or comparison operations, as in the following example, where `function_1` has three input parameters and its result is assigned to `variable_2`:

RELEASE 7.1

```
<variable_2> := function_1(10, 'Scott', <variable_1>);
```

A PL/SQL procedure also behaves like a procedure in the standard programming languages in that it has a number of input and/or output parameters, as in the following example of a procedure call where `inp_var1` represents the input, `outp_var1` the output and `io_var1` the input/output parameter:

```
procedure_1(<inp_var1>, <io_var1>, <outp_var1>);
```

As we have already mentioned a PL/SQL package is first and foremost a means of grouping a number of procedures and functions together under a package name; the procedures stored in a package still have to be called individually. If the procedure in our previous example were a package procedure then the call would look as follows:

```
package_1.procedure_1(<inp_var1>, <io_var1>, <outp_var1>);
```

In Section 8.2.3 we shall take a detailed look at the structure and functionality of PL/SQL packages but at this point we should note that a PL/SQL package consists of two parts: the *specification* and the *body*. The package specification is in effect the package's interface and declares all the functions, procedures, variables, cursors and exceptions which are available to all users of the package.

The package body contains the actual PL/SQL code for the package's procedures and these include both the *public* procedures, which are those declared in the specification, and the *private* procedures, which are only available to the package's other procedures and cannot be called from outside the package.

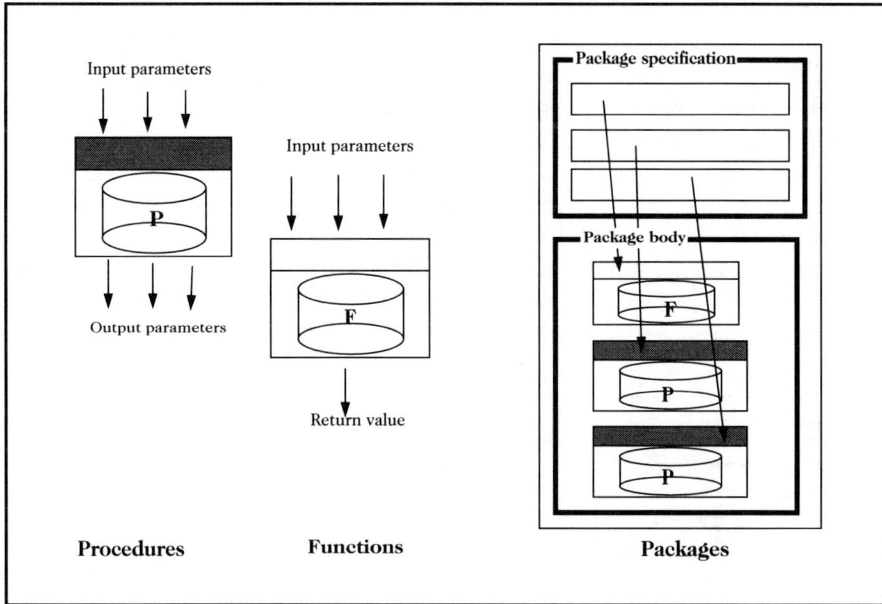

Figure 8.2 Stand-alone procedures and functions and PL/SQL packages

The use of this modular structure also provides the software developer with a number of useful benefits:

- A package can be specified (defined) even though the body (contents) of the package has not yet been programmed. This makes it possible to define the interfaces of a new applications system at an early stage in the development cycle.
- As long as the specification of a procedure does not change, the actual code of that procedure can be altered without the whole package having to be recompiled.
- Any procedures which carry out particularly sensitive processing can be implemented as private procedures so that they cannot be called by any user outside the context of the package.

8.2.2 PL/SQL procedures and functions

Stand-alone procedures and functions in PL/SQL are defined using the SQL commands CREATE PROCEDURE or CREATE FUNCTION, as shown in Figure 8.3. The REPLACE option allows the user to replace an existing procedure with a new version without losing any access privileges which may already have been defined.

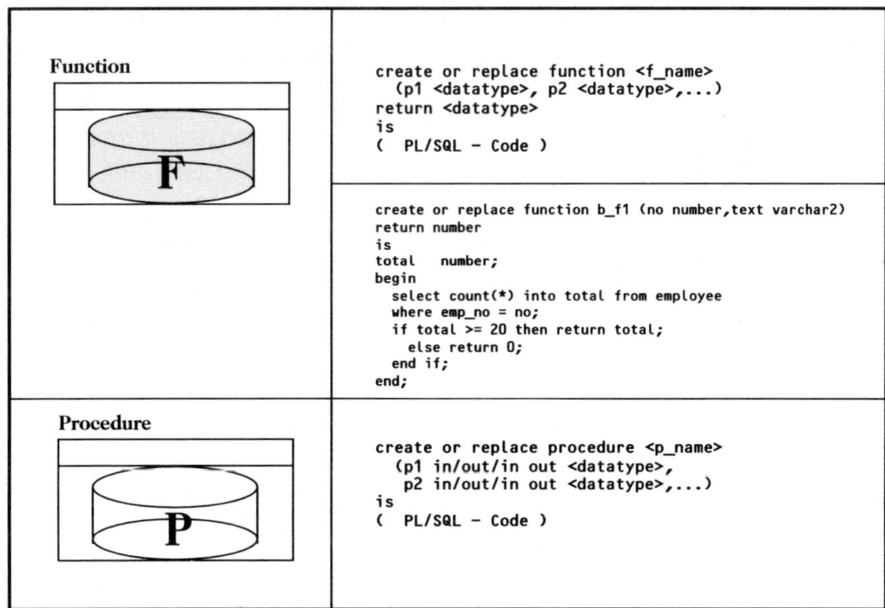

Figure 8.3 Creating stand-alone procedures and functions with PL/SQL

When the CREATE command is executed this causes the corresponding unit of PL/SQL code to be compiled, so that all PL/SQL and SQL constructs and statements are checked in terms of their syntax and semantics. Any errors which are detected are stored in the data dictionary where they can be accessed by means of the views USER_ERRORS, ALL_ERRORS or DBA_ERRORS. These views can also be displayed from SQL*Plus or the SQL*DBA by using the SHOW ERRORS command.

Figure 8.4 shows the sequence of operations which are carried out to create a PL/SQL program. Executing the CREATE PROCEDURE/FUNCTION command causes a complex series of actions to be carried out, as is shown in the following list:

- The PL/SQL compiler checks the unit of PL/SQL code and enters any syntactic or semantic errors in the data dictionary's ERROR$ tables.
- The syntax of any SQL statements within the PL/SQL code is also checked. In addition a pre-parsing check is carried out to establish whether all object names in the code are valid (for example the names of tables, views or columns) and whether all the required access privileges on those objects have been granted to the user. Any errors detected at this stage are also entered in the ERROR$ tables.
- All calls to other PL/SQL procedures are also checked to determine whether the user has the privileges necessary to access them.

- The PL/SQL source code is stored in the data dictionary (in the SOURCES$ table); this takes place even if the code has been found to contain errors.
- The compiled form of the PL/SQL code is also stored in the data dictionary; once again this takes place even if the code has been found to contain errors.
- Finally the user is informed of the final status of the DEFINE operation with a message such as '`Procedure created`', if the compilation was successful, or '`Warning, procedure created with compilation errors`' if any errors were detected.

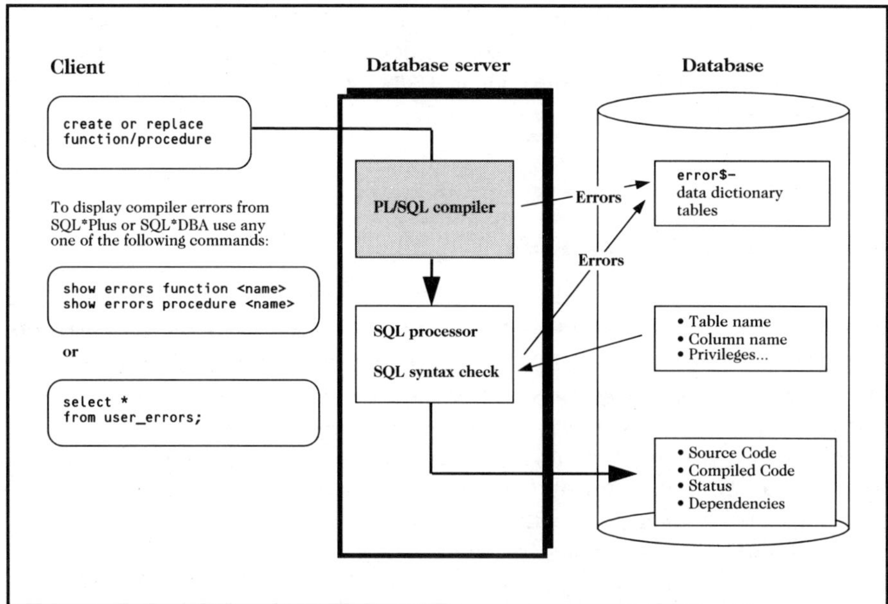

Figure 8.4 Developing a stand-alone function or procedure with PL/SQL

If any errors have been detected during the compilation process, then the PL/SQL unit is given the status 'invalid'. In this case the data dictionary can be accessed as follows to establish the cause of the error(s):

```
show errors function <function_name>
show errors procedure <procedure_name>
```

```
select * from user_errors where name = '<procedure_name>';
select * from all_errors where name = '<procedure_name>';
```

(The first of these commands (SHOW ERRORS) is available only in SQL*Plus or SQL*DBA).

Another very useful way of accessing these error messages would be to create a simple Oracle Forms application based on one of the two data dictionary views ALL_ERRORS or USER_ERRORS. This could be made to run under a second ORACLE session and would allow the user to always see the current error messages generated by the system.

It is worthwhile to remember that the data dictionary stores both the source code as well as the compiled form of each PL/SQL module which has been defined, and this means that it is possible at any time to retrieve the current source code for a particular PL/SQL module as a text file. This facility is of course very useful in the area of software maintenance and before attempting to change or expand the stored PL/SQL modules in a given system, it is always worthwhile to check exactly what is currently available and in use on that system. The source code for a given procedure can be accessed via the data dictionary views USER_SOURCE or ALL_SOURCE (*refer also to* Figure 8.17).

8.2.3 PL/SQL packages

A PL/SQL package is created in two steps: first of all the package specification or header is created using the CREATE PACKAGE command. As we have already seen the package specification contains all the elements by which the package can be accessed by other users. These include the interface definitions for procedures and functions, 'global' constants and variables as well as 'global' exception and cursor definitions. All the procedures and functions in the package specification can be called by any users who have been granted execute privilege on the package.

Any variables and constants which are declared in the package specification are global in nature because once the package has been activated (that is, any one of its procedures has been called for the first time) they retain their values for the duration of the session within which the package was used and can be referenced by all of the package's procedures.

The second step in putting a PL/SQL package together is to create the package body using the command CREATE PACKAGE BODY. This part contains all the actual PL/SQL source code which carries out the processing provided by the package. The objects contained in the body of a package are either private or public: public refers to those objects (procedures, variables and so on) which are also declared in the specification part and are therefore accessible to all users of the package; private refers to those objects which are only used within the package, to carry out internal processing operations, and which are therefore not accessible to external users of the package. In the example in Figure 8.5 for example, the procedure `p_private` can be called by any of the other procedures or functions within the package but, as it is not declared in the package specification, not from outside the package.

Package specification which contains all 'visible' objects:

- Procedures and functions
- Variables
- Exceptions
- Cursors

```
create or replace package pack_1 as
  procedure p1 (a in number, b in varchar2, c out number);
  function  f1 (af in number, bf in number) return number);

  var_1 varchar2(50);
  var_2 varchar2(100);

  too_many exception;
  cursor  C1;

end pack_1;
```

Package body which contains the PL/SQL code for all procedures and functions:

- visible objects (p1, f1)
- hidden objects (p_private)

```
create or replace package body pack_1 as
  procedure p1 (a in number, b in varchar2, c out number);
    pl/sql code
  function  f1 (af in number, bf in number) return number);
    pl/sql code
  procedure p_private(.....)
    pl/sql code
```

The package's initialization block: this block is executed whenever the package is first used (i.e. one of its objects is first called by a new user).

```
begin
 var_1 := '000000';
 ....
end pack_1;
```

Figure 8.5 Creating a PL/SQL package

The process of creating the specification and body of a package follows the same lines as those we have already encountered in creating stand-alone PL/SQL procedures and functions (*refer to* Figure 8.4). In each case the package's code is checked for syntactic or semantic errors and the module is stored in the data dictionary as source code and as a compiled program. When the package body is being stored the individual SQL statements are checked (that is, whether the objects exist and whether the user is entitled to access them), although a full parsing operation is not necessary at this stage. In addition the procedure declarations from the package specification are compared with those in the package body to make sure they match (that is, that both have the same number and type of parameters). Any errors detected when compiling the specification and body of the package are entered in the data dictionary, as with stand-alone procedures, and can be retrieved by means of the three data dictionary views USER_ERRORS, ALL_ERRORS or DBA_ERRORS.

One of the interesting features offered by PL/SQL packages is the possibility of creating overloaded procedure names. This involves defining a number of procedures which all have the same name, but which differ in the number and/or type of parameters they use with each instance of the procedure being programmed separately in the body of the package. This type of programming is typically used where it is useful to have a single function which is able to process a range of different input parameters; one familiar example of this is ORACLE's TO_CHAR function which converts either a numerical or a date input parameter into a character string.

When an overloaded procedure is called the system decides on the basis of the type and number of parameters which instance of the procedure should be executed. Figure 8.6 illustrates an example where a function has been declared in four variants, with each variant being programmed in the package body. Calls to these functions from outside the package might look as follows:

```
i := fget_no(<num_var1>);                variant 1
i := fget_no(<text_var1>);               variant 3
i := fget_no(<num_var1>);                variant 4
```

In each of these calls the correct variant is selected on the basis of the different parameters used.

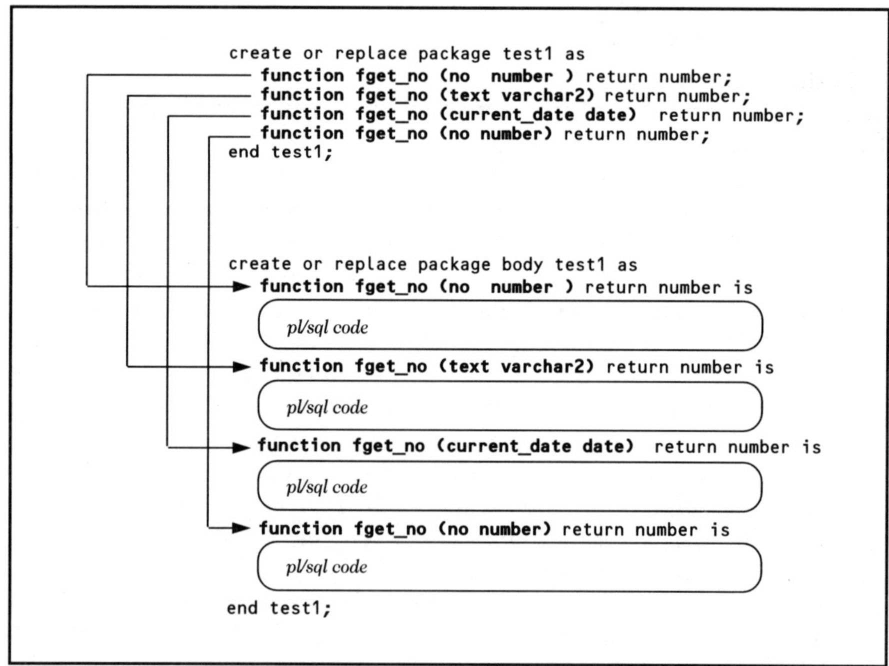

Figure 8.6 Overloading package functions and procedures

The body of each PL/SQL package can contain one block which, like every standard PL/SQL block, starts with the keyword BEGIN. This block is executed once and once only when any one of the procedures in the package is called for the first time by an individual user; the block can therefore be used to carry out any initialization operations which are needed by the procedures in the package body, as is shown in Figure 8.5.

8.2.4 Executing PL/SQL procedures and functions

RELEASE 7.1

When we come to executing PL/SQL programs there are a number of small differences between stand-alone and package procedures and functions. The full name of a stand-alone procedure contains, as well as the name of the procedure itself, also the name of the user who created it. The following lines show the syntax of a stand-alone procedure call together with a specific example:

```
<user_name>.<procedure_name>(<parameter_list>);

gst.sample_proc1(param1, param2, param3);
```

In this example `gst` is the name of the user who created the procedure, and thus forms part of the object name as is the case for all ORACLE database objects.

When a package procedure is called the name of the package must also be added to the object name; if we use our previous example the call is as follows:

```
<user_name>.<package_name>.<procedure_name>(<parameter_list>);

gst.package1.sample_proc1(param1, param2, param3);
```

In order to complete this topic it should be noted that it is also possible to execute a procedure on a remote database. A remote call of this kind can only be achieved by including an ORACLE database link (*refer to* Chapter 14) and the resulting call would look as follows:

```
gst.package1.sample_proc2§stuttgart_link(param1, param2);
```

In this case ***stuttgart_link*** is the name of the database link and this call will execute the procedure on the remote instance specified by the link.

In order to simplify the somewhat lengthy names which result from this naming syntax and in order to conceal the database link names, it is worthwhile defining private and public synonyms for stand-alone and package procedures and functions, as illustrated in Figure 8.7.

RELEASE 7.1

PL/SQL procedure or function call in full	SQL synonym	Procedure or function call using SQL synonym
`gst.b_p1(par1, par2)`	`create synonym b_p1 for gst.b_p1;`	`b_p1(par1, par2);`
`gst.pack_1.p1(par1)`	`create synonym p1 for gst.pack_1.p1;`	`p1(par1);`
`gst.pack1.f1.§stgt(par1)`	`create synonym f1 for gst.pack_1.f1.§stgt;`	`f1(par1);`

Figure 8.7 Defining synonyms for PL/SQL procedures and functions

As we have already seen, the variables and constants which are declared in the package specification are global in nature in that they remain valid until the end of the user session which first used the package. During this time they can be accessed by any other PL/SQL modules which are running under the same session. In this case they have to be referenced in the same way as procedures from the package, for example:

```
i := package1.total;
package1.user_name := 'Scott';
if package2.status = true then...
```

We have already seen that PL/SQL procedures can be called from applications programs as well as from any of the ORACLE development tools (Oracle Forms, Oracle Reports and so on). When we want to call a PL/SQL procedure ORACLE provides us with two methods for defining the procedure's parameters: they can be specified either in terms of their position in the procedure's header or by being explicitly named. Figure 8.8 shows how a procedure can be called using both of these methods.

Regardless of which method is used to specify its parameters, the ORACLE Server carries out the following actions whenever a PL/SQL procedure is called:

- It checks whether the user has the privilege to execute the procedure, either because the user has created the procedure or because he or she has been granted the execute privilege (GRANT EXECUTE).

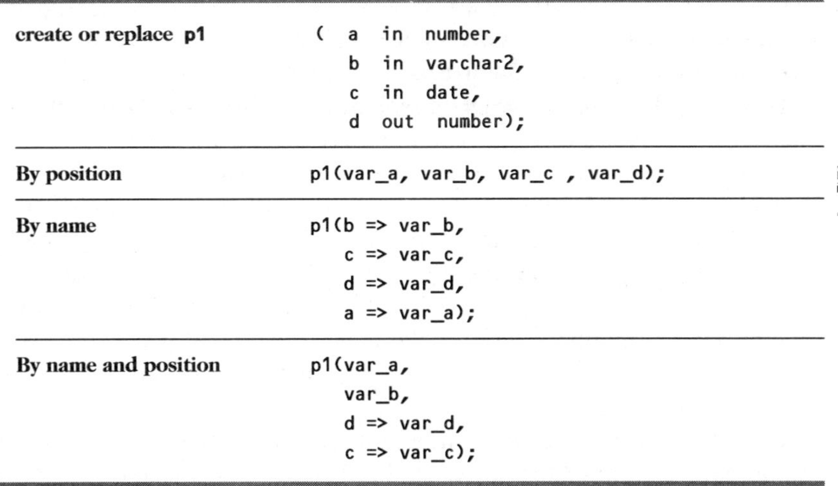

create or replace p1	`( a in number,`
	`b in varchar2,`
	`c in date,`
	`d out number);`

By position	`p1(var_a, var_b, var_c , var_d);`

By name	`p1(b => var_b,`
	`c => var_c,`
	`d => var_d,`
	`a => var_a);`

By name and position	`p1(var_a,`
	`var_b,`
	`d => var_d,`
	`c => var_c);`

RELEASE 7.1

Figure 8.8 Specifying the parameters of PL/SQL procedures and functions

- The server then checks whether the procedure is already present in the shared pool of the database cache, in which case the procedure can be executed immediately, otherwise it must be loaded into the database cache from disk.
- The next check relates to the status of the procedure which can be 'valid' or 'invalid'. The status of a PL/SQL procedure is invalid either because errors were detected when the procedure was compiled or because the structure of any of the objects which the procedure accesses has been changed since the last time that the procedure was executed. If the status of a procedure is invalid then it is automatically recompiled; if no errors are detected then the new version of the procedure can be executed at once (*refer also to* Chapter 8.4).
- The last check carried out by the server relates to whether a package or a stand-alone procedure has been called. In the case of a package procedure all the package's other procedures and functions are also loaded into the database cache's shared pool (if they are not already present there). If the package is being activated for the first time in this session, the server will also execute the package's initialization block.

8.3 Developing and testing PL/SQL programs

The features offered by PL/SQL and by the ORACLE concept of functions, procedures and packages provide us with a set of powerful software development tools for creating applications systems based on stored PL/SQL programs. However this does not mean that we should use stored PL/SQL modules to carry out every single processing task; stored PL/SQL procedures are especially effective whenever a single processing operation needs to make intensive use of the database.

If we decide that a PL/SQL procedure is going to provide an effective solution for a given task, then the next question is whether to implement a stand-alone procedure or a PL/SQL package. On the basis of what we have already covered, it should be clear that a package is more appropriate when the envisaged solution requires a number of separate procedures and functions, all of which should operate within the same overall context. Other reasons for using a package as opposed to a stand-alone solution might be the wish to define a public interface, the need to overload procedure names or to use global variables as well as the additional performance and security features which packages offer.

Developing a PL/SQL program is not any different from using any other standard programming language, the PL/SQL code is entered by means of an editor and is then compiled and executed under a SQL*Plus or SQL*DBA session. Whenever an existing PL/SQL program has to be modified, it can either be first deleted (DROP PROCEDURE/FUNCTION/PACKAGE) or generated with the CREATE OR REPLACE command option.

As with all other programming languages it is of course necessary to test a PL/SQL program before it can be released and this process can be greatly assisted if control or debug information is made available on the status and progress of the program's execution. PL/SQL does not yet include a full development environment with a symbolic debugger although one is currently under development. However PL/SQL does provide a package of procedures which can be used to retrieve certain debug information from the system; this package is called DBMS_OUTPUT and contains the following procedures:

```
ENABLE
PUT(<variable>)
PUT_LINE(<variable>)
NEW_LINE
GET_LINE(<variable>, status)
GET_LINES(<variable>, numlines, status)
DISABLE
```

With the help of these procedures it is possible to retrieve certain debug information via a database pipe, the database pipe being another object which can be defined by means of PL/SQL. When a given procedure or package has to be tested the debug process basically works as follows: the procedures PUT, PUT_LINE and NEWLINE must first be entered at the right points in the PL/SQL source code so that the required status information will be output to a database pipe. Once this information has been entered in the database pipe it can be retrieved using the GET or GET_LINES procedures.

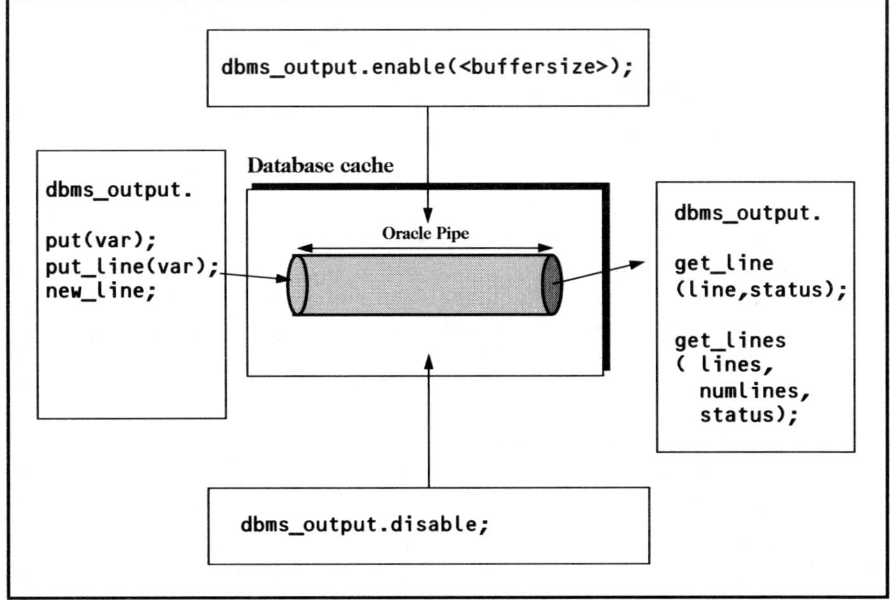

Figure 8.9 Debugging with the DBMS_OUTPUT package and database pipes

Figure 8.9 illustrates the overall operation of the DBMS_OUTPUT procedures. A database pipe for the current session is set up using the ENABLE procedure, this pipe has a default size of 2000 bytes. Once the pipe has been enabled, information can be entered into it: the PUT procedure writes the value of a given variable to the current line; PUT_LINE writes a variable plus a new line to the pipeline and NEW_LINE simply opens a new line.

To retrieve the information stored in the database pipe the user has to use the procedures GET_LINE (to retrieve the next line in the pipeline) or GET_LINES (to retrieve a specified number of lines). It should be emphasized that these read and write procedures will work only if the pipeline has first been explicitly enabled.

Figure 8.10 shows a sample PL/SQL procedure which is being tested with the DBMS_OUTPUT package. As we can see the PUT, PUT_LINE and NEW_LINE procedures have been entered in order to record the status of the procedure at specific points. If we are working with SQL*Plus or SQL*DBA then it is possible, by entering the following commands, to have this debug information output straight to the screen:

```
set serveroutput on
execute proc_to_debug;
```

The first command sends the server's output to the screen and the second executes the *proc_to_debug* procedure.

This method of debugging PL/SQL programs can be used for both stored PL/SQL procedures as well as for PL/SQL triggers (*see* Chapter 9).

```
create or replace procedure proc_to_debug (no number)
is
total    number;
too_many exception;
no_var      number;
begin
  no_var := no;
  dbms_output.put_line('Starting procedure : proc_to_debug');
  for i in 1..10 loop
    select count(*) into total from emp where sal > no_var;
    dbms_output.put('Total number: ');
    dbms_output.put(total);
    dbms_output.new_line;
    no_var := no_var + 1000;
    if (total < 5) then
      raise too_many;
    end if;
  end loop;
exception
  when too_many then null;
  when others then
    raise_application_error (-20100,'Other error');
end;
/
```

Figure 8.10 Implementing debug calls in a PL/SQL stored procedure

Once a PL/SQL procedure, function or package has been sufficiently tested then it can be made available to other users by means of the GRANT command, as follows:

```
grant execute on <procedure> to <user>;
grant execute on <procedure> to <role>;
```

RELEASE 7.1

As we have already mentioned, granting the execute privilege on a package allows the grantee to execute not only all the procedures in the package but also to access all database objects which are processed within the scope of that package. However it is important to note that the privileges needed to access these objects (tables, views etc.) are only granted implicitly and within the scope of the PL/SQL package; this means that the overall security of the database is not in any way affected when other users are allowed to execute the procedures contained in a specific PL/SQL package. As we shall see in Chapter 9 this also applies to the use of database triggers.

This particular feature of PL/SQL packages and triggers can be used to improve and simplify the security management of a given database installation; any information which is highly sensitive, but which must nevertheless be used by less privileged users, can be made available within the highly controlled context of a PL/SQL package, thus ensuring that no illegal operations can be carried out on it.

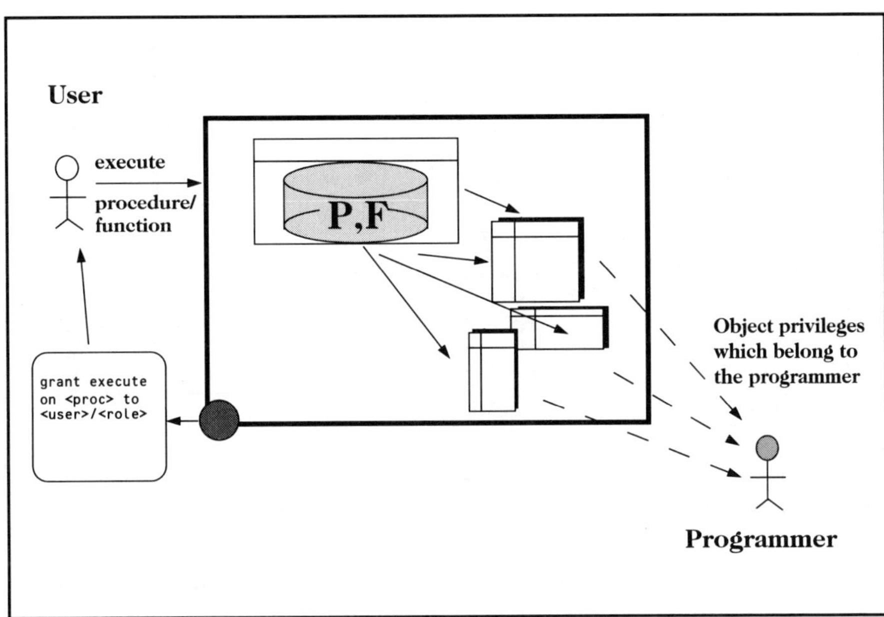

Figure 8.11 Executing a PL/SQL procedure within another user's security context

This situation is illustrated in Figure 8.11, where a user who has been granted the execute privilege is allowed to access the database objects used by the procedure only as long as the procedure is running. As soon as the procedure has been completed all these privileges are revoked from the user.

8.4 Dependency tracking

Database objects may be dependent on each other in any number of ways, and in general we can distinguish between full and partial dependency. A full dependency for example will exist between a table and its indexes, whereas only a partial dependency exists between a table and any views which have been defined on that table. In both cases a change in the structure of a given database object will have direct consequences on all objects which are dependent on it; if a table is deleted for example, then all the indexes on that table will also be deleted, but any views which reference that table will not be deleted but will simply be marked as having an invalid status and will remain as such until a new table is created whose structure is compatible with that of the deleted table.

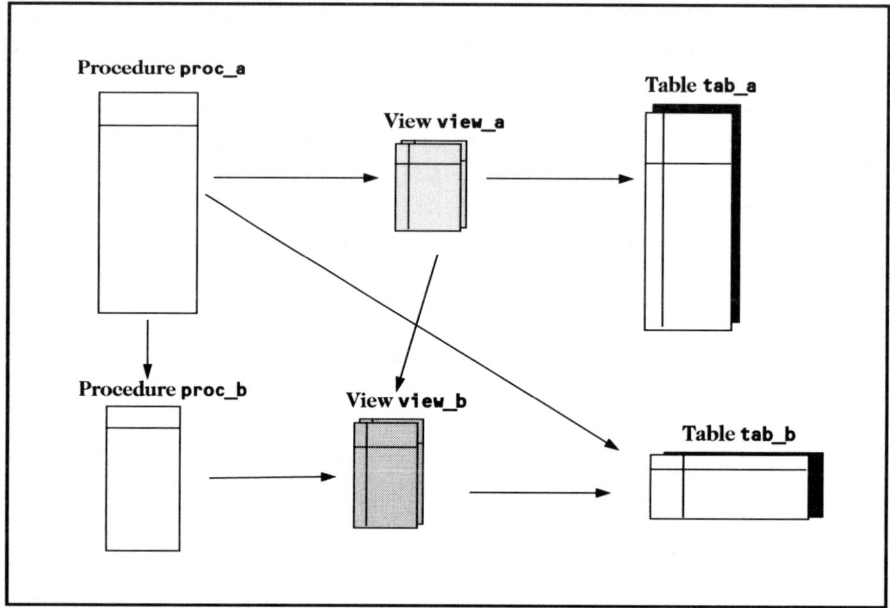

Figure 8.12 Full and partial dependencies in an ORACLE database

The ORACLE Server manages both the full and the partial dependencies which exist between database objects, even when those dependencies extend over several levels of a database's logical hierarchy. Figure 8.12 shows the kind of partial dependencies which can exist in a working system. In this example we can see that a view can be dependent on one or more tables and/or on one or more other views; similarly a procedure can depend on any combination of tables, views and other procedures, and in particular on the database objects which are accessed within the procedure itself.

In view of the complexity of such relationships it is important to know that all aspects of the dependencies between individual database objects are managed automatically and in full by the ORACLE Server. ORACLE does this by assigning a status value of either *valid* or *invalid* to every object in a database schema; whenever the structure of any database object is changed then the status of all the objects which are dependent on it is changed from *valid* to *invalid*. The next time that one of these objects (a view, a procedure) is activated, ORACLE will automatically attempt to recompile it; if the recompilation is successful then the status of the object is reset to *valid* and it can be used as before. If the recompilation detects an error then the status of the object remains *invalid*, an error message is generated and the operation being carried out is aborted.

Thus if the structure of a table is modified by means of the ALTER TABLE command, then the status of all the views, procedures and functions which depend in any way on that table is changed to *invalid*. This situation is illustrated in relatively simple terms in Figure 8.13 in which we take a series of dependencies based on table `table_1`. The view `view_1` is directly dependent on this table as is procedure `tab_proc`; procedure `view_proc` on the other hand is only indirectly dependent on this table because it accesses the view `view_1`. If the structure of `table_1` is changed then ORACLE sets the status of each of these other objects to *invalid* and this new status remains in force for each object until it has been activated and successfully recompiled by the ORACLE Server.

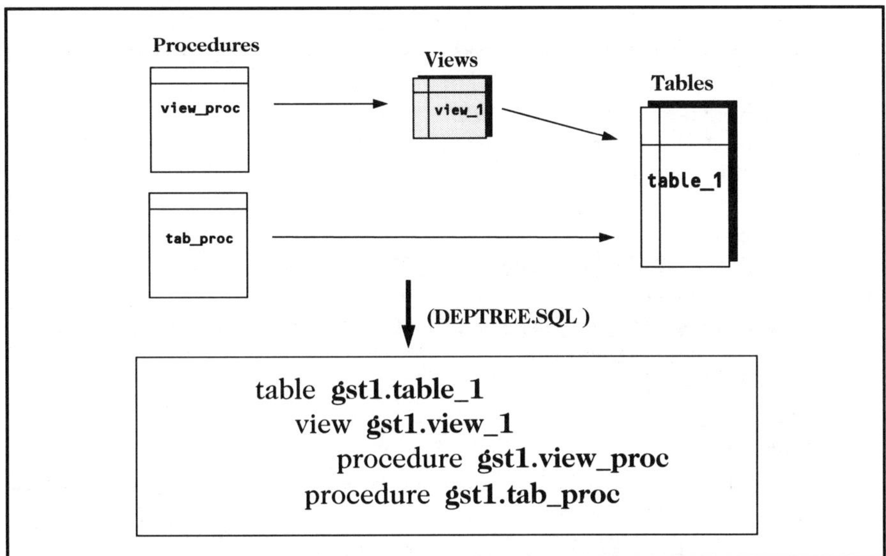

Figure 8.13 Displaying the dependencies between different database objects

The status of each object in a given schema is stored in the data dictionary and we can examine it by means of the data dictionary view USER_OBJECTS. The SQL script in Figure 8.14 will provide us with a compact overview of the status of all the objects of a given user.

Although the server will automatically recompile any object whose status is *invalid*, it does not attempt to do this until the next time that the object has to be used. However following a change to the structure of a given object, it may be necessary to find out as soon as possible whether all its dependent objects can be successfully recompiled. In this case we can carry out the necessary recompilation manually by using one of the following SQL commands:

```
alter procedure         <proc_name> compile
alter function          <func_name> compile
alter package           <pack_name> compile
alter package body      <pack_name> compile
alter view              <view_name> compile
```

```
rem ************************************************************
rem
rem  Procedure: cat_ges.sql  Author: Guenther Stuerner June 1993
rem
rem  Description: shows all the objects belonging to a user
rem
rem  Requirements: the view cat_all must first have been
rem                created using the script cat_all.sql
rem
rem ************************************************************

column object_name format a30
column 'Index/trigger name/status' format a35
spool cat_ges.txt

select
  rpad(substr(object_name,1,18),20,'.')||object_type
       object_name,
  rpad(substr(tr_ind_name,1,25),30,'.')||decode(status,'<v>',
       null,status)
  "Index/Trigger Name"
from cat_all
order by
  decode(object_type, 'TABLE',1, 'INDEX',2, 'TRIGGER',3,
          'VIEW',4,
       'SEQUENCE',5, 'PACKAGE',6, 'FUNCTION',7,
'PROCEDURE',8),
  object_name
/
spool off
prompt
prompt   Results have been spooled to 'cat_ges.txt'
prompt
```

Figure 8.14 Displaying all the database objects which belong to a user

In the normal course of events dependency management can be left entirely up to the ORACLE Server. However it can sometimes be interesting to see which objects are dependent on which other objects and ORACLE provides us with the means to do this quite simply. Every ORACLE Server provides a standard PL/SQL procedure DEPTREE.SQL; when this procedure is executed it generates for that user two views (DEPTREE and IDEPTREE) and a SQL script (DEPTREE_FILL) which when used together will provide all dependency information for the objects owned by that user. Figure 8.15 shows all the steps which have to be taken to create and display this dependency information.

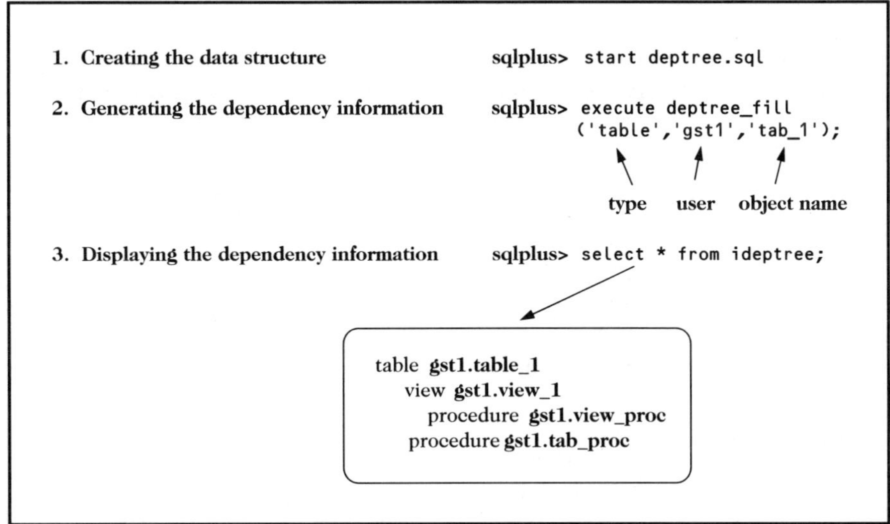
1. Creating the data structure
sqlplus> start deptree.sql
2. Generating the dependency information
sqlplus> execute deptree_fill ('table','gst1','tab_1');
type
user
object name
3. Displaying the dependency information
sqlplus> select * from ideptree;
table gst1.table_1
view gst1.view_1
procedure gst1.view_proc
procedure gst1.tab_proc

Figure 8.15 Retrieving the dependency information for a specific database object

8.5 Stored PL/SQL procedures provided with the ORACLE Server

The ability to create stored PL/SQL procedures, functions and in particular packages provides us with a very effective means of creating database oriented programs. Specific applications can be stored within the database which means that they can be executed very efficiently by any user who has access to the system. It is therefore hardly surprising that the developers of ORACLE have made considerable use of this feature in order to provide the system with new functions very simply and quickly. We have already encountered two of the PL/SQL programs provided with the ORACLE system: the PL/SQL package DBMS_OUTPUT, which can be used for debugging purposes, and the procedure DEPTREE_FILL, which generates and outputs a single table that contains the dependency information for all the objects belonging to a specific user.

Each ORACLE installation provides many other PL/SQL packages (a comprehensive list is given in Figure 8.16) and in the rest of this section we shall have a brief look at some of these and how they can be made use of. The package DBMS_MAIL for example allows us to send mail to any Oracle Mail address and the send procedure (DBMS_MAIL.SEND(...)) can be called from a 3GL or 4GL program as well as from another stored PL/SQL procedure or from a database trigger. One use for this system procedure might be as part of a database trigger which automatically generates an Oracle Mail message whenever certain storage limits in the database have been exceeded.

Package Name	Procedure or function name	Package Name	Procedure or function name
dbms_mail	send	**dbms_lock**	request convert sleep allocate_unique release
dbms_pipe	pack_message (ov) unpack_message (ov) next_item_type(f) send_message(f) receive_message(f) reset_buffer purge unique_session_name(f)	**dbms_output**	enable put put_line new_line get_line get_lines disable
dbms_session	set_role set_sql_trace set_nls close_database_link set_label set_mls_label_format reset_package unique_session_id is_role_enabled	**dbms_alert**	set_defaults register remove waitany waitone signal removeall
dbms_ddl	alter_compile analyze_object		
dbms_utility	compile_all compile_schema analyze_schema format_error_stack format_call_stack is_parallel_server get_time	**dbms_snap**	purge_log refresh refresh_all drop_snapshot set_up wrap_up get_log_age testing
dbms_transaction	read_only read_write advise_rollback advise_nothing advise_commit use_rollback_seg commit_comment commit_force commit savepoint rollback rollback _savepoint rollback_force begin_discrete_transaction purge_mixed		

Figure 8.16 Standard PL/SQL procedures provided with the ORACLE Server

The functionality provided by the procedures in the DBMS_TRANSACTION package corresponds to the SQL commands for transaction management such as COMMIT or ROLLBACK. The same applies for the DBMS_SESSION package which provides functions that match the SQL commands for session management such as SET ROLE or ALTER SESSION.

The DBMS_PIPE package allows ORACLE programs running under the same instance to exchange information and data by means of the database pipe facility in the same way as the DBMS_OUTPUT package which we looked at earlier (*see* Figures 8.9 *and* 8.10). In this case a message is sent to one pipe using the DBMS_PIPE.SEND_MESSAGE procedure and can be read from the pipe by any other ORACLE session with the DBMS_PIPE.RECEIVE_MESSAGE call.

The DBMS_ALERT package provides a means of notifying users or processes of any changes in the status of the database. A typical use for this type of alert function might be where we have a program which has to display current data from the database in a graphical form, so that its display should be refreshed whenever there is a change in the underlying data. In this case we can implement a database trigger which will notify any number of programs (DBMS_ALERT.SIGNAL) that the relevant data have changed. Any programs that need to be informed of such a change can 'register' with the alert facility by means of the DBMS_ALERT.REGISTER call. An ORACLE database alert message is not generated until the change in question has been fully completed (committed).

8.6 Retrieving PL/SQL modules from the data dictionary

As all PL/SQL modules are stored in the data dictionary in both their source and compiled forms, it is of course always possible to retrieve the source code for any PL/SQL program from the database, and this feature can be very useful for developing new PL/SQL programs or maintaining existing ones.

The three SQL scripts which make up Figures 8.17a through 8.17c show how to access the PL/SQL programs which are stored on a given database:

- The first script (`prog_ges.sql`) outputs the status and source code for all the procedures, functions and packages which have been created by the user who runs this script.
- The second script (`prog_sin.sql`) generates the same output (status and source code) for a specific PL/SQL program.
- The third script (`prog_spo.sql`) generates only the source code for a specific PL/SQL program.

```
rem ************************************************************
rem
rem  Procedure: prog_ges.sql Author: Guenther Stuerner June 1993
rem
rem  Description:
rem  Shows all the procedures, functions and packages belonging
rem    to a user together with their status and the program
rem    source code.
rem
rem ************************************************************

column name format a18
column t    format 99
column text format a60
break on name
set pagesize 999
spool proc.txt

select
  name ||
  decode(type, 'PACKAGE','(PS)', 'PACKAGE BODY','(PB)',
         'PROCEDURE','(P)', 'FUNCTION','(F)') ||
  decode(status, 'VALID','[v]', '[inv]'), name, text
from user_source us , user_objects uo
where (us.name = uo.object_name) and (type = object_type)
order by
  name,
  decode(type, 'PACKAGE',1, 'PACKAGE BODY',2, 'PROCEDURE',3, 4),
  type, line
/
spool off
```

Figure 8.17a Retrieving all procedures, functions and packages for a user

```
rem ************************************************************
rem
rem  Procedure: prog_sin.sql Author: Guenther Stuerner June 1993
rem
rem  Description:
rem  Outputs the source code for a given program
rem
rem ************************************************************

column name format a18
column t     format 99
column text format a60
break on name
set heading on

set pagesize 999
spool proc.txt

select
  name ||
  decode(type, 'PACKAGE','(PS)', 'PACKAGE BODY','(PB)',
         'PROCEDURE','(P)','FUNCTION','(F)') ||
  decode(status, 'VALID','[v]', '[inv]')
  name, text
from user_source us, user_objects uo
where (us.name = uo.object_name) and (type = object_type)
and (us.name like upper('&program_name'))
order by
  name,
  decode(type, 'PACKAGE',1, 'PACKAGE BODY',2, 'PROCEDURE',3, 4),
  type, line
/
spool off
```

Figure 8.17b Retrieving a stored PL/SQL program

```
rem ************************************************************
rem
rem  Procedure: prog_spo(ol).sql Author: Guenther Stuerner 06/93
rem
rem  Description:
rem  Outputs the source code for a given program as a text file
rem
rem ************************************************************

set verify off
set heading off
column text format a80
accept name prompt program_name:
set pagesize 999
spool prog_spo.txt

select
  text
from user_source
where name like upper('&name')
order by
  name,
  decode(type, 'PACKAGE',1, 'PACKAGE BODY',2, 'PROCEDURE',3, 4),
  type, line
/
spool off
prompt
prompt Program source is in the text file: PROG_SPO.TXT
prompt
```

Figure 8.17c Generating the source of a PL/SQL program as a text file

9

Semantic data integrity

Topics covered in this chapter

- The need for semantic data integrity
- The ORACLE integrity constraints
- System and user defined constraints
- Declarative integrity in ORACLE
- Referential integrity in ORACLE
- Referential integrity within a transaction
- Procedural integrity in ORACLE
- ORACLE database triggers
- Implementing applications systems with triggers
- How constraints are stored in the data dictionary

9 Semantic data integrity

9.1 Introduction

One of the key tasks of any database management system is to maintain complete data integrity so that it is simply not possible under any conceivable circumstances for the stored data to become inconsistent. This means that the consistency of the data in the database must be ensured regardless of the operation of competing transactions (operational integrity), of user input (semantic integrity) and also in the face of all possible error situations.

We have already looked at operational integrity (Chapter 4) and recovery mechanisms (Chapter 5) in detail. Our aim in this chapter is to examine the methods whereby semantic integrity conditions and integrity actions can be defined within the database itself.

The requirement that a database server should have access to sufficient information about its own data so that it can administer 'central' integrity conditions and ensure that they are being maintained is as old as the relational database model itself. For some time now the ORACLE Database Server has indeed provided sophisticated techniques in the areas of transaction control, locking mechanisms and competing read/write operations, and has thus provided a complete solution to the problems of operational integrity. The question of restoring a database when a given error situation has occurred has also been solved by ORACLE's online backup and online recovery procedures. These solutions also cover the particular demands of distributed databases which we shall examine in detail in Chapter 14.

So far however ORACLE has done little in the field of semantic integrity and this has meant that the rules and actions needed to ensure data consistency have had to be defined within individual applications programs because they could not be specified within the database itself. The responsibility for ensuring data consistency therefore fell to the individual applications programmers who had to implement extensive consistency tests within their programs in order to ensure that the integrity of their data models was being maintained.

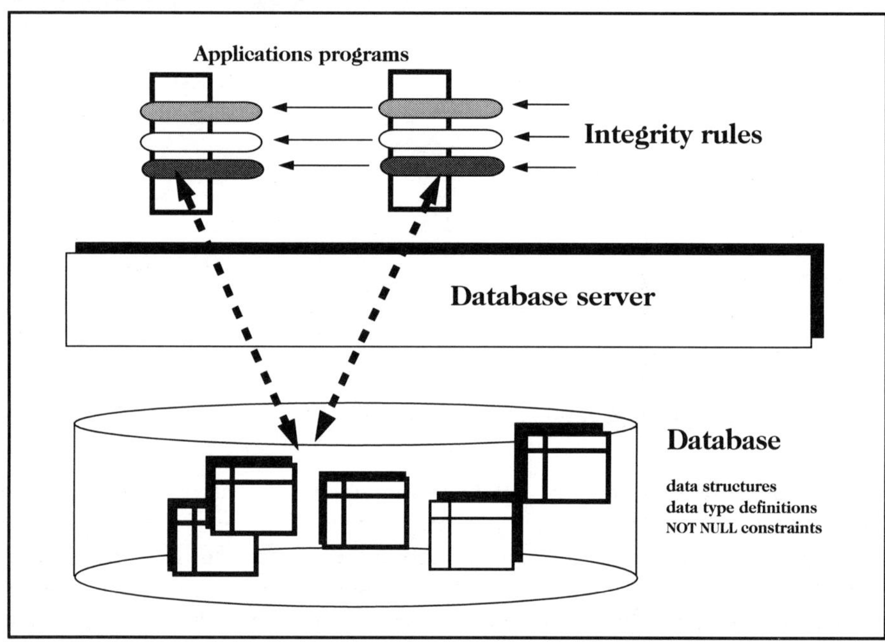

Figure 9.1 Implementing data integrity at application program level

As a result many DBAs were faced with the problem that every new or modified applications program had to be tested to ensure it contained the necessary integrity rules for the data it wanted to access. In addition the DBA had the task of ensuring that any changes to the structure of an existing database did not affect the operation of any consistency checks which were already in place.

In Oracle7 two complementary methods have been implemented to solve all of these problems: the *declarative* method and the *procedural* method.

The declarative method is used to define referential integrity rules, integrity actions and entity integrity rules (*see also* Section 9.2). With this method it is possible to define dependencies between different tables or to specify valid ranges of values when the table is first created.

The procedural method allows the user to define a set of rules which will govern both data structures and data, and to implement these in the form of database *triggers*. Database triggers are programs which are developed in PL/SQL and which are activated automatically whenever a given action takes place in the database. In the case of procedures to ensure data integrity the triggers can be activated whenever a modify operation (INSERT, UPDATE, DELETE) is carried out on the data structures in question.

By combining the declarative and procedural methods it becomes possible to define and maintain all central integrity rules within the database itself.

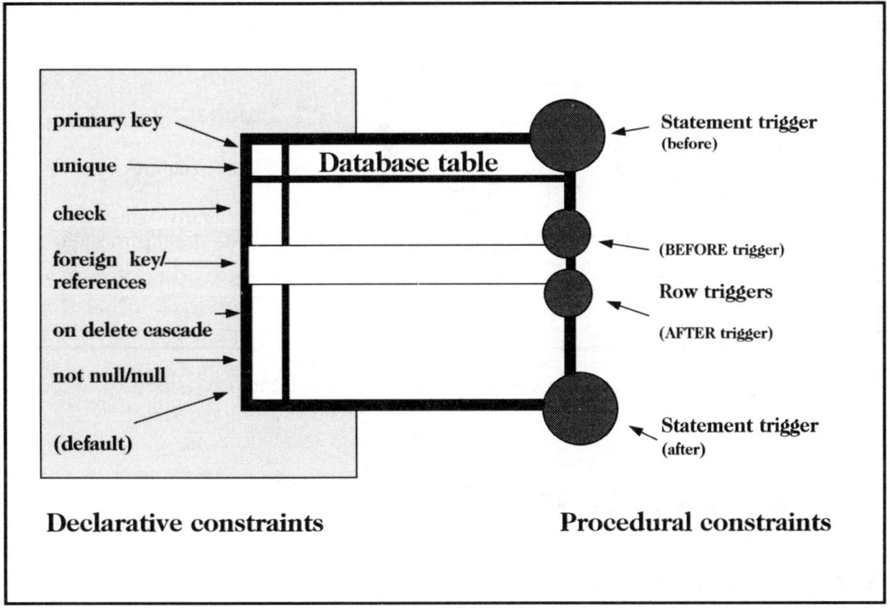

Figure 9.2 Ensuring data integrity with declarative and procedural constraints

This situation is illustrated in Figure 9.3 where the central integrity rules are stored within the database together with the actual data structure, with the database server ensuring that they are adhered to. In this way a data structure is characterized not only by its column names, datatypes and storage parameters but also by its functional context which specifies any rules and their associated actions.

The results of being able to define data integrity in this way are twofold: on the one hand we have a situation where programs which access the database no longer need to carry out their own consistency checking, on the other hand the tasks of integrity testing and integrity management now fall squarely within the traditional area of data structure analysis and design (data modelling) which therefore become even more important than they were in the past.

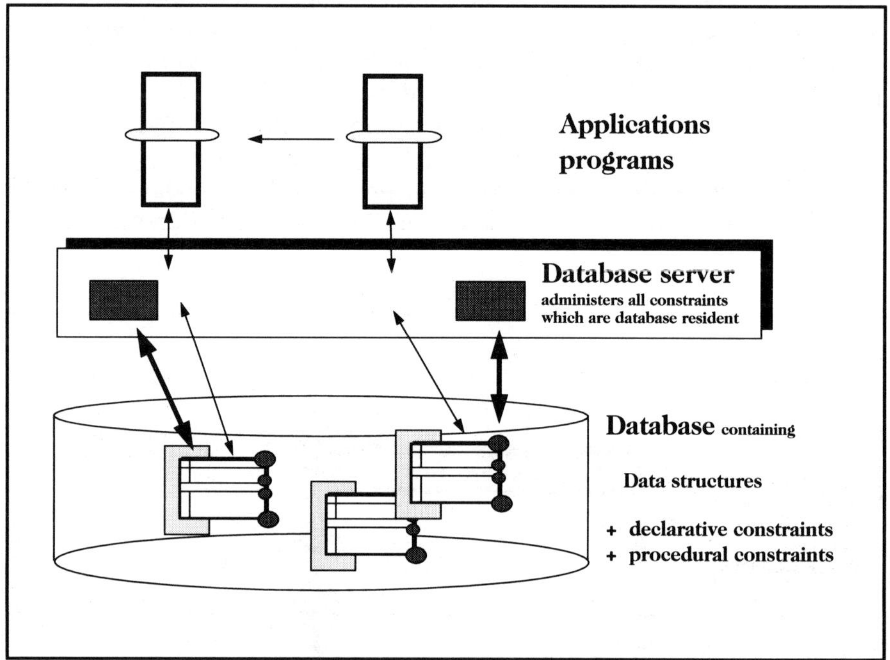

Figure 9.3 Constraint management within an Oracle7 database

9.2 Declarative integrity

9.2.1 Introduction

The declarative method of implementing constraints provided by Oracle7 complies in full with ANSI/ISO standards for defining integrity rules and integrity actions. Declarative integrity rules are specified as part of the table definition and, unless they are explicitly disabled, they remain valid for all modify operations carried out on the database. In general we can distinguish between three types of declarative integrity rules:

- Referential Integrity Rules
  which define the dependencies between different tables in a single database.

- Referential Integrity Actions
  which define the actions to be carried out in one table if a row is deleted within a logically related table.
- Entity or Object Integrity Rules
  which define primary keys, ranges of values and NULL values.

Declarative integrity rules are part of the definition of a database table and are specified when the table is created with the CREATE TABLE or ALTER TABLE statements.

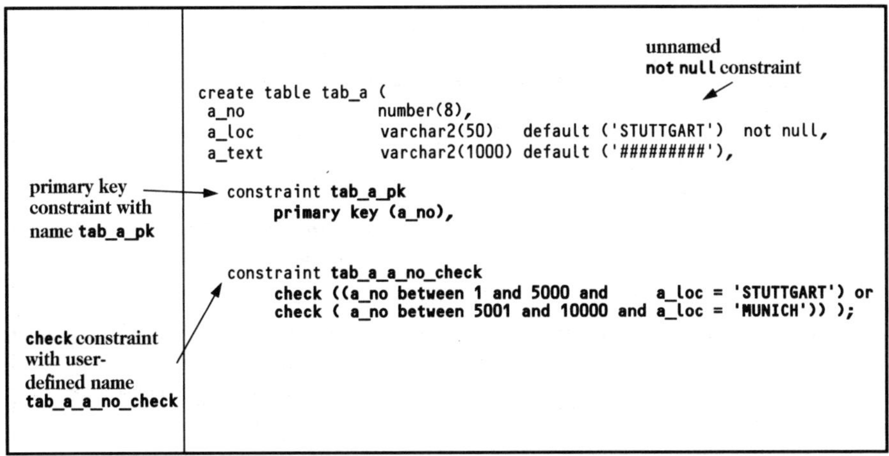

Figure 9.4 Creating a table with declarative constraints

Although it is not absolutely necessary, it is a good idea to give every constraint a name. This is very useful because whenever a constraint is violated the constraint name will be included as part of the error message and this can make it much easier to diagnose the error. Naming constraints also makes it much easier to administer them and we should remember that it is possible not only to define a constraint but also to delete, modify, activate or deactivate it, as shown in the following SQL statements:

```
alter table <table_name> drop constraint <constraint_name>
alter table <table_name> disable constraint <constraint_name>
alter table <table_name> enable constraint <constraint_name>
```

As we can see from these three examples ORACLE does in fact demand that each constraint should have a unique name and any constraints that are not given a user-defined (explicit) name will be assigned an (implicit) name by the ORACLE system. However user-defined names are usually easier to remember and understand and so they should be used whenever the constraint needs to be referenced after it has been defined.

Figure 9.4 shows an example of a table definition which is carried out with a typical mixture of explicit and implicit constraint names. In this example a table *tab_a* is created with three columns and three constraints. The first constraint is a NOT NULL constraint which has not been given an explicit name and which has been defined 'in-line'. System constraint names always have the form and appearance as shown in the following example:

```
sys_c<sequence_number>
sys_c00412
```

Defining a constraint 'in-line' means that the constraint definition is specified as part of the column definition. The following are examples of 'in-line' definitions:

```
a_no  number(8)   not null,
a_no  number(8)   constraint a_no_nn    not null,
a_no  number(8)   constraint a_no_pk    primary key,
```

Figure 9.4 also shows two named and 'out-of-line' constraint definitions. The first defines the column *a_no* as being the primary key of this table, with *tab_a_pk* being chosen as the name of this constraint. Only one PRIMARY KEY (PK) can be defined on any table and this special constraint has the following effects:

- No duplicate values can exist on the specified primary key columns (a primary key can be composed of more than one column).
- When the CREATE TABLE statement is being executed a UNIQUE index is automatically created for the primary key columns.
- All columns defined as primary key columns are not allowed to accept null values, that is these columns have an implicit NOT NULL constraint.

The second constraint definition (*tab_a_a_no_check*) is a CHECK constraint in which ranges of values are defined for the column *a_no*. These values are dependent on the value of column *a_loc*, if for example column *a_loc* contains the value 'Stuttgart' then column *a_no* will only accept values in the range 1 through 5000.

Whenever a modify operation (INSERT, UPDATE) is carried out on columns *a_no* or *a_loc* this integrity rule is checked. Adding a row which violates this rule causes a corresponding error message to be returned. Entering the SQL statement:

```
insert into tab_a (a_no, a_loc) values (1, 'Munich')
```

would result in the following error message:

```
ORA-02290: check constraint (GST.TAB_A_A_NO_CHECK) violated
```

The last two constraint definitions (from Figure 9.4) were defined 'out-of-line', that is they were entered after the columns were defined. Although the way the constraints are written does not affect the way they function, the 'out-of-line' definition is preferable because it makes the statements clearer and easier to read.

The following types of declarative constraints can be defined in Oracle7:

- PRIMARY KEY
- UNIQUE
- CHECK
- DEFAULT
- NOT NULL
- FOREIGN KEY
- FOREIGN KEY REFERENCES
- ON DELETE CASCADE (to ensure the integrity of foreign keys)

All constraint types are listed again in Figure 9.5.

9.2.2 Referential integrity definitions

A relational database will normally contain a series of relationships formed by the mutual dependencies between its individual tables. The rules of referential integrity already take account of this fact when a data structure is being defined and allow us to define relationships which consist of two components:

- a PRIMARY KEY or UNIQUE constraint in one object,
- a FOREIGN KEY in a dependent object.

A FOREIGN KEY must always reference a PRIMARY KEY or a UNIQUE constraint in the same or any other table. However in order to establish a FOREIGN KEY relationship to another table the referenced table (master table) must either be in the same schema as the FOREIGN KEY table or the user creating the FOREIGN KEY table must have been granted the REFERENCES privilege on the master table. A typical PRIMARY KEY/FOREIGN KEY relationship is illustrated in Figure 9.6.

<table>
<tr><th>Constraint name</th><th>Constraint function</th><th>Example</th></tr>
<tr><td><code>primary key</code></td><td>Defines one or more columns of a table as its primary key by which each row can be uniquely identified. A unique index is automatically generated for the primary key column(s). Only one primary key can be generated for each table in an ORACLE database.</td><td><code>a_no number(8)constraint a_pk</code>
<code>primary key,</code>
<code>primary key(a_no),</code>
<code>a_no number(8), ...</code>
<code>....</code>
<code>constraint a_pk</code></td></tr>
<tr><td><code>unique</code></td><td>Defines one or more columns as being unique within the scope of a single table. Unlike the <code>primary key</code> constraint, <code>unique</code> columns may also contain <code>null</code> values and these <code>null</code> value columns may occur more than once within a table.</td><td><code>a_text varchar2(100)</code>
<code>constraint un_1 not null</code>
<code>unique,</code></td></tr>
<tr><td><code>check</code></td><td>Defines a condition which every row in the table must fulfil. This condition can refer to other columns within the same table but not to columns in other tables (e.g. with sub-queries).
Any number of <code>check</code> constraints can be defined on a given table.</td><td><code>constraint salary_check</code>
<code>check</code>
<code>((a_salary > 2000</code>
<code>and a_dept_no = 10) or</code>
<code>(a_salary > 3000</code>
<code>and a_dept_no = 30)),</code></td></tr>
<tr><td><code>default</code></td><td>Defines a default value for a column which will be assigned whenever a new row is inserted which does not have an explicit value for the column in question.
However as this is not a full constraint it is not assigned a system constraint name.</td><td><code>current_date date default(sysdate),</code>

<code>current_time varchar2(12)</code>

<code>default(to_char(sysdate,'hh24:mi')),</code></td></tr>
<tr><td><code>foreign key</code>
<code>references</code></td><td>Defines one or more columns as a key on the <code>primary key</code> or <code>unique</code> columns of another table. 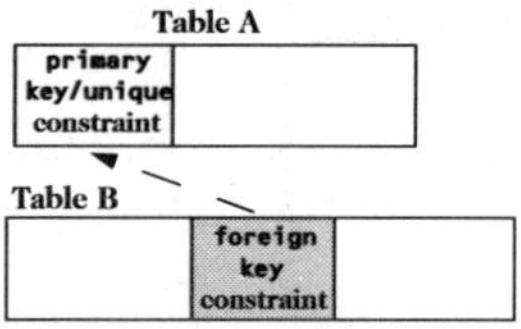

Table A
<code>primary key/unique</code> constraint
Table B
<code>foreign key</code> constraint</td><td><code>b_no number(8), ...</code>

<code>constraint tab_b_fk</code>
<code>foreign key (b_no)</code>
<code>references tab_a(a_no),</code></td></tr>
<tr><td><code>on delete</code>
<code>cascade</code></td><td>Defines an integrity action as an optional part of a <code>foreign key</code> reference clause: if the referenced row (which has a <code>primary key</code> or <code>unique</code> constraint) is deleted then all dependent rows where the <code>on delete cascade</code> option has been set will automatically be deleted. 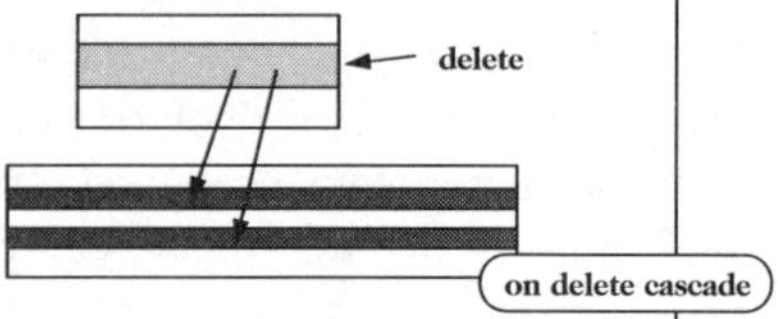

delete
on delete cascade</td><td><code>b_no number(8), ...</code>

<code>constraint tb_fk</code>
<code>foreign key (b_no)</code>
<code>references ta(a_no)</code>
<code>on delete cascade,</code></td></tr>
</table>

Figure 9.5 The Oracle7 declarative constraints

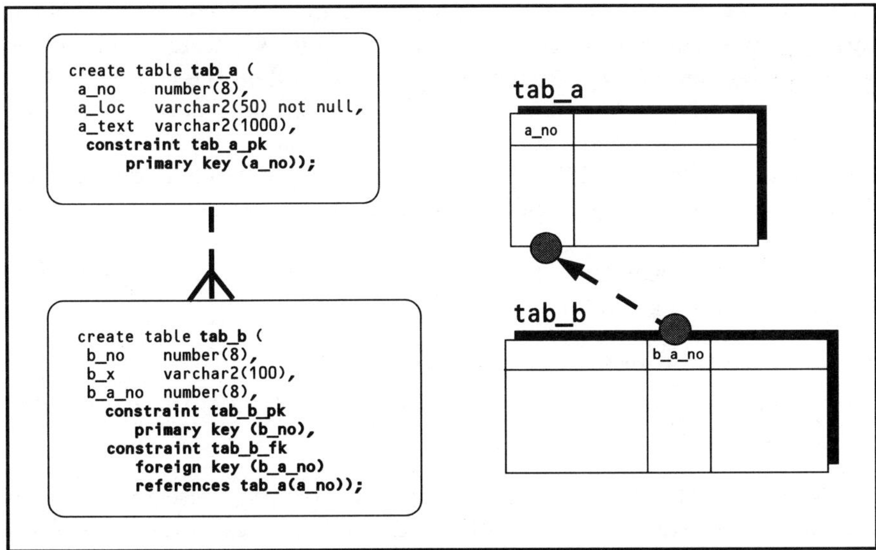

Figure 9.6 Example of a PRIMARY KEY/FOREIGN KEY relationship

In this example the FOREIGN KEY relationship specified for table ***tab_b*** means that all modify operations on table ***tab_b*** must also reference (that is, have a corresponding value in) the master table ***tab_a***. If this is not the case INSERT or UPDATE operations will be rejected. Figure 9.7 illustrates this type of situation.

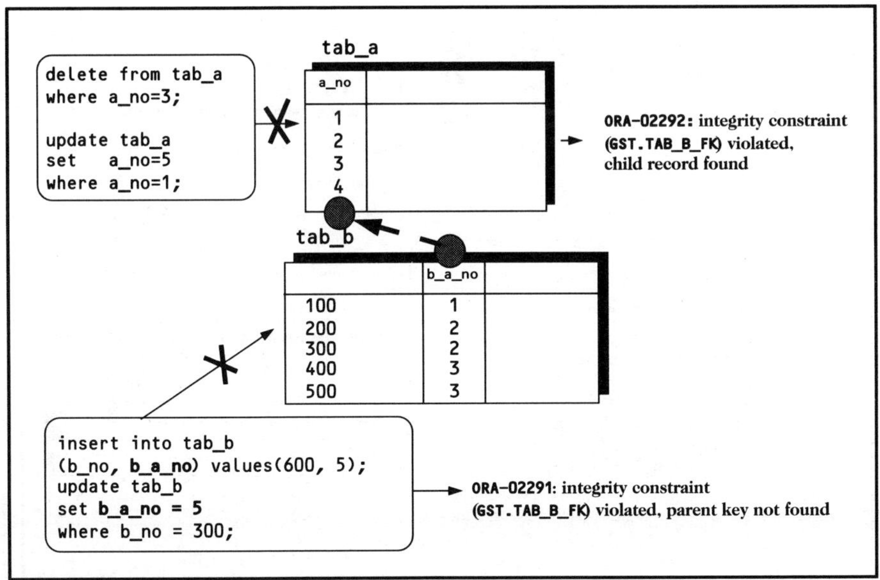

Figure 9.7 Controls on modifying tables with FOREIGN KEY constraints

However this type of referential integrity relationship affects not only the foreign key (dependent) table, but also the referenced (master) table. When a table is referenced by a foreign key relationship then the columns which make up its primary key or unique constraint can only be modified if no dependent rows exist in the corresponding foreign key table. This function is also known as UPDATE RESTRICT. Similarly it is not possible to delete a row from the master table if dependent rows are present in the foreign key table (DELETE RESTRICT).

Thus a delete operation in a referenced (master) table is only possible if one of the following conditions applies:

- No dependent rows exist in a foreign key table.
- The foreign key relationship has been defined using the ON DELETE CASCADE option.

Using the ON DELETE CASCADE option when defining a foreign key means that when a master row is deleted any dependent rows in the foreign key table(s) will be deleted simultaneously. This situation is illustrated in Figure 9.8 where the foreign key definition includes the ON DELETE CASCADE option. If a row is deleted in the master table ***tab_a*** then any dependent rows in table **tab_b** will be deleted before the specified row in the master table is deleted. In the case of multiple dependencies the ON DELETE CASCADE option must be defined on every level, otherwise any dependent rows will not be deleted.

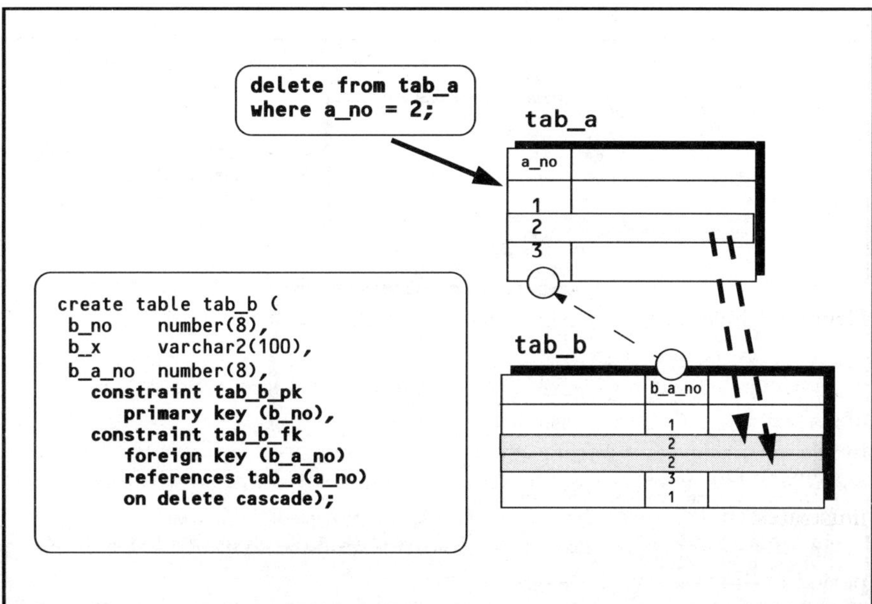

Figure 9.8 A FOREIGN KEY constraint with the ON DELETE CASCADE option

An interesting practical application for this feature is in managing hierarchical structures, such as we often find in bills of materials or in an organigram (*refer also to* Figure 2.6). The implicit dependency which exists between foreign and primary keys can also be depicted as a referential integrity relationship, as shown in Figure 9.9 where the column **b_master** references the primary key row of the same table (**b_*no***).

For every INSERT operation carried out on table ***tab_b*** both foreign key relationships are checked and the INSERT operation is only valid if the following conditions both apply:

- The value entered in **b_*a_no*** has a corresponding value in the table ***tab_a***.
- The value entered in **b_master** has a corresponding value in column **b_*no*** of table ***tab_b***.

If either one of these rules is violated the INSERT operation will be rejected.

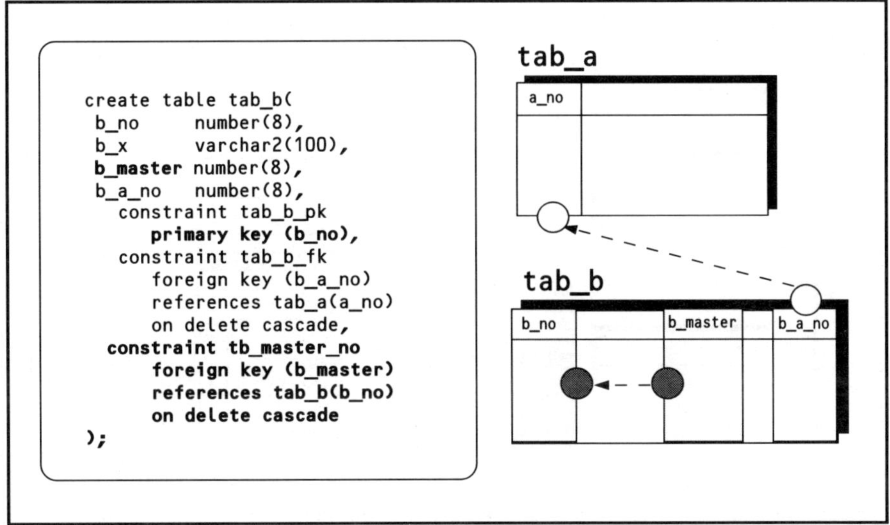

Figure 9.9 Defining a FOREIGN KEY constraint within a single table

However in order to ensure that a foreign key constraint is really being observed it is not enough to simply check for the presence of a given value by means of a read operation. A solution implemented in this way would very soon lead to inconsistencies between dependent tables, as Figure 9.10 illustrates.

In this example we have different transactions being carried out over a period of time.

At timepoint ***t1*** a row is inserted into table ***tab_b*** (Transaction 1) and the system checks whether the corresponding primary key value exists in table

tab_a, in accordance with the constraint which has been defined for table **tab_b**. In our example a read operation carries out the check and confirms the presence of value **4** as a primary key in table **tab_a**. Given that the required foreign key/primary key relationship exists, the INSERT operation is validated and can be successfully completed.

At timepoint *t2* however the row in table **tab_a** on which the check has just been carried out is deleted (Transaction 2). Of course the database server checks whether the primary key value of the row being deleted has any dependent rows in table **tab_b**, but as the insert operation on table **tab_b** has not yet been committed the new row is not yet visible to Transaction 2. The DELETE operation on **tab_a** can therefore be carried out as it appears to be valid.

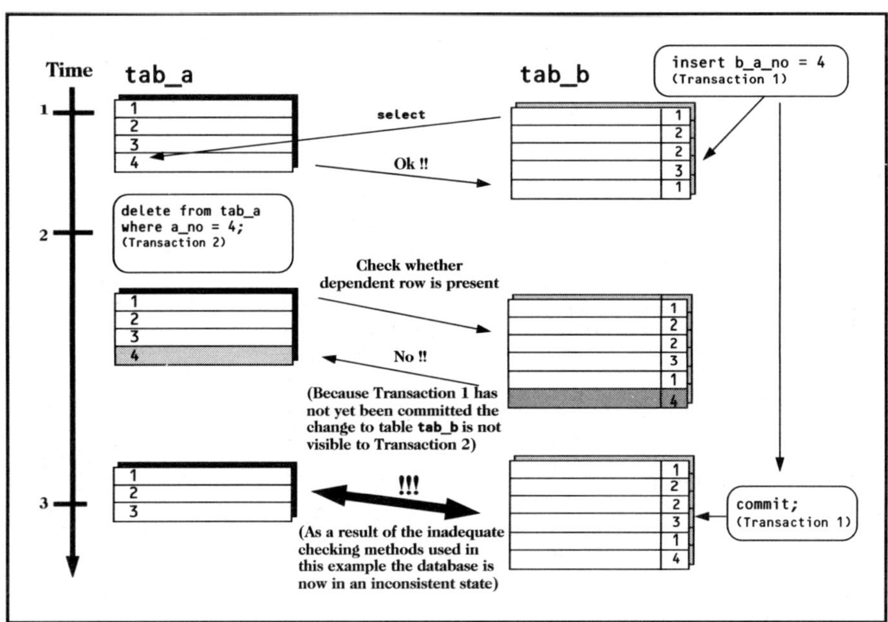

Figure 9.10 Data inconsistency as a result of inadequate integrity checking

At timepoint *t3* the INSERT is committed, which means that a row has been inserted into table **tab_b** for which there is no longer a valid master row in **tab_a** as this was deleted at timepoint *t2*.

On the basis of this example it should be clear that if inconsistencies in the database are to be avoided it is absolutely essential for all referential integrity checks to be embedded in the transaction concept.

In Oracle7 this problem has been solved very elegantly and efficiently by the concept of SHARED INDEX ENTRY locks as illustrated in Figure 9.11. To understand how this feature works we can take our previous example of conflicting operations being carried out on tables **tab_a** and **tab_b**.

When our new record is inserted into table *tab_b*, the system checks for a valid primary key value in table *tab_a* and, if it is present, a SHARED lock is set for this value within the primary key index of table *tab_a*. A SHARED INDEX ENTRY lock represents an even lower level of lock granularity than the standard row lock since, except for changes to the primary key or unique constraint values, it does not prevent the corresponding row in the master table (in this case *tab_a*) from being updated. However this SHARED INDEX ENTRY lock does prevent the deletion of any rows which are being referenced by current transactions.

A SHARED INDEX ENTRY lock is automatically created for any master table when the FOREIGN KEY constraint is defined for the corresponding columns of its dependent tables.

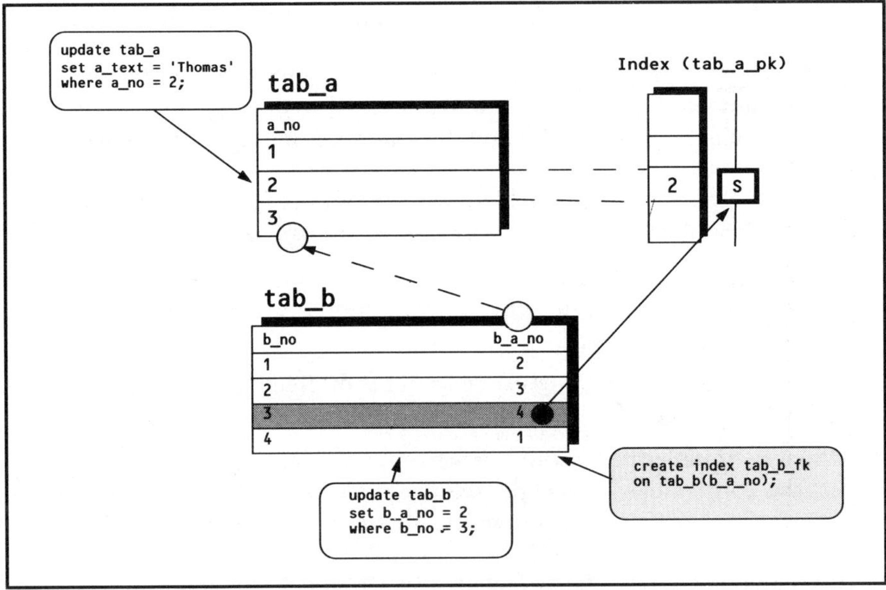

Figure 9.11 Locking mechanisms and referential integrity checking

9.2.3 Entity integrity definitions

As well as referential integrity constraints Oracle7 also provides us with the possibility of defining entity integrity constraints. This type of integrity condition refers to those rules which govern the contents of individual database tables and includes the following:

- PRIMARY KEY constraints
- UNIQUE constraints

- NOT NULL constraints
- CHECK constraints

The PRIMARY KEY and UNIQUE constraints have already been introduced in Section 9.2.2 where we saw how they are used in referential integrity checking to provide reference values for foreign keys in dependent tables. In terms of defining entity integrity constraints we will see that they have a number of additional uses.

A PRIMARY KEY or a UNIQUE constraint is defined on one or more columns of a single table as follows:

```
constraint x_pk primary key (<column1>, <column2>, )
constraint x_uk unique (<column1>, <column2>, )
```

Whereas each table can only have one PRIMARY KEY constraint, it can have any number of UNIQUE constraints. Both types of constraint are managed in a very similar way by Oracle7 and the following rules apply to each of them:

- When the constraint is enabled the system creates a UNIQUE index. If the constraint has been explicitly named the constraint name is used as the index name.
- Both PRIMARY KEY and UNIQUE constraints can be referenced by a FOREIGN KEY constraint.
- If a PRIMARY KEY or a UNIQUE constraint is disabled the associated UNIQUE index is deleted.
- When defining either of these constraints we have the option of specifying the constraint's storage parameters and these will also be used by the index which is generated automatically (*refer also to* Figure 9.12).

Columns which have been included in a UNIQUE constraint can be given null values although this is not possible with a PRIMARY KEY constraint. If nulls are not to be allowed within a UNIQUE constraint then an additional NOT NULL constraint must be defined for each of the columns covered by the UNIQUE constraint, as is shown in the following example:

```
a_no         number(8)         not null,
a_text       varchar2(20)      not null,
constraint   x_un              unique(a_no, a_text);
```

The last of our four entity integrity constraints is the CHECK constraint which is used to define a range of values for a given column. CHECK constraints can be defined for all the columns of a table and can also be used to ensure that a certain range of values in one column will only be accepted in combination with certain values in another column. The following example specifies that the values for the column *a_no* can only be in the range 1 through 5000 if the value contained in column *a_loc* is 'Stuttgart'.

```
constraint tab_a_a_no_check
check (a_no between 1 and 5000 and
upper(a_loc) = 'STUTTGART')
```

```
drop table tab_a cascade constraints;
drop table tab_b;

create table tab_a(
a_no    number(8),
a_loc  varchar2(50)  default('STUTTGART') NOT NULL,
a_text   varchar2(300) default('******'),
constraint ta_pk primary key(a_no),
constraint tab_a_a_no_check
  check ((a_no between 1 and 5000 and a_loc = 'STUTTGART') or
        (a_no between 5001 and 10000 and a_loc = 'MUNICH')))
-- End of tab_a
pctfree 20 initrans 10 pctused 60 tablespace TA
storage(initial 10k next 10k minextents 2 maxextents 99
          freelists 2)
/
create table tab_b(
b_no           number(8),
b_name         varchar2(50) not null,
b_master_no number(8),
b_budget    number(10,2) default 10000 not null,
b_a_no         number(8) not null,
constraint tab_b_pk
  primary key (b_no) using index pctfree 20 initrans 5
     tablespace TA
storage(initial 20k next 10k pctincrease 20),
constraint tab_b_fk
  foreign key (b_a_no)
  references tab_a(a_no),
constraint tab_b_master_no
  foreign key (b_master_no)
  references tab_b(b_no) on delete cascade)
-- End of definition for table tab_b
/
```

Figure 9.12 Creating tables with different types of constraints

Figure 9.12 shows the complete definitions for the two tables *tab_a* and *tab_b* which we have often referred to in our previous examples. Looking at the full SQL syntax we can see that the CREATE TABLE statements can be divided into three broad areas:

- Column definitions
  which specify the names, data types and possibly the default values for the columns which make up each table.

- Constraint definitions
  which specify the various constraints that can be generated on one or more tables; this example makes it clear that out-of-line definitions are far easier to read.

- Storage definitions
  which specify the physical location and structure for storing the table.

The definition of the primary key on table *tab_b* also includes the storage parameters for the UNIQUE index which will automatically be created when the constraint is activated. This means that it is possible to define the optimum storage location (for example a particular tablespace) and structure for the index when it is being created.

9.2.4 Managing declarative constraints

In addition to defining constraints when a table is being created, Oracle7 also provides all the facilities needed to make effective use of them in a working environment. We can distinguish between the following constraint operations:

- defining constraints when a table is created;
- defining constraints on an existing table;
- deleting existing constraints;
- disabling existing constraints;
- enabling existing constraints.

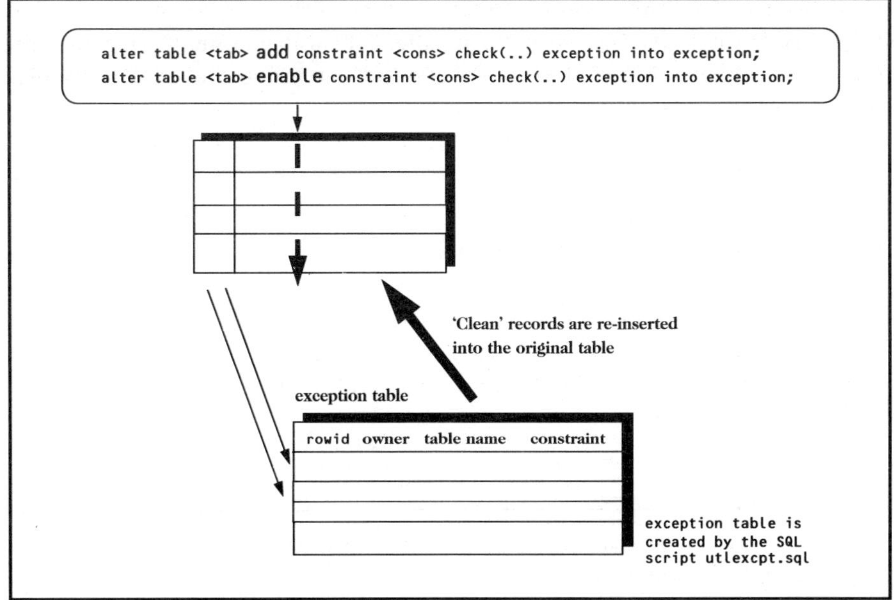

Figure 9.13 Managing non-conforming records in an exception table

A constraint is defined on an existing table with the following command:

```
alter table <table> add constraint <constraint>
```

When this command is executed the whole table will be checked against this new constraint. If any violations of the newly defined constraint are detected an error message is returned and the constraint in question is not enabled. It is however possible for all rows that violate a new constraint to be written to an exceptions table which can then be used as a basis for cleaning up the data in the original table.

Figure 9.14 lists all the possible variations which are available for managing constraints. Please note that carrying out the operations DROP CONSTRAINT and DISABLE CONSTRAINT on primary key or unique constraints will affect not only the actual table being modified but also any other tables that are dependent on that table as a result of a foreign key relationship. This means that the standard DROP or DISABLE CONSTRAINT commands will not work with a primary key or unique constraint that is referenced by one or more foreign key constraints. For these commands to work they must be used with the CASCADE option (as in the example `drop constraint tab_a_a_no_check cascade`), which has the effect of disabling the FOREIGN KEY constraints in all referenced tables before the PRIMARY KEY or UNIQUE constraint is disabled or deleted.

A similar situation occurs when a table with dependent foreign key relationships is to be deleted with the DROP TABLE statement. Here too the table can be deleted only after all foreign key references have been disabled with the CASCADE option. The effect of the statement ***drop table tab_a cascade constraints*** is the same as in our previous example in that first all foreign key relationships on the table are disabled before the table itself is deleted.

Operation type	Example

A constraint is defined as part of the `create table` statement and either immediately becomes active (the default action) or is explicitly deactivated.	`create table tab_a (..`
	`  constraint c1 primary key (a_no),`
	`  constraint c2 unique(a_text)`
	`disable);`

A constraint is defined on an existing table and is:
• activated at once (this is the default action)
• activated at once with all non-conforming records being written to an exceptions table
• made inactive in order to be activated later.
	`alter table tab_a`
	`  add constraint c3 check(a_no > 1000)`
	`  add constraint c3 .. exceptions into`
	`    <exception_table>`
	`  add constraint c3 .. disable`

A constraint is deleted:
• with the `cascade` option (explicitly to disable all associated `foreign keys` in other tables)
• without the `cascade` option.
	`alter table tab_a`
	`  drop constraint c1 cascade`
	`  drop constraint c1`

A constraint is disabled:
• with the `cascade` option (explicitly to disable all associated `foreign keys` in other tables)
• without the `cascade` option.
	`alter table tab_a`
	`  disable constraint c1 cascade`
	`  disable constraint c1`

Existing and deactivated constraints are:
• activated
• activated with all non-conforming records being written to an exceptions file.
	`alter table tab_a`
	`  enable constraint c3`
	`  enable constraint c3 exceptions into`
	`    <exception_table>`

Figure 9.14 Managing declarative constraints

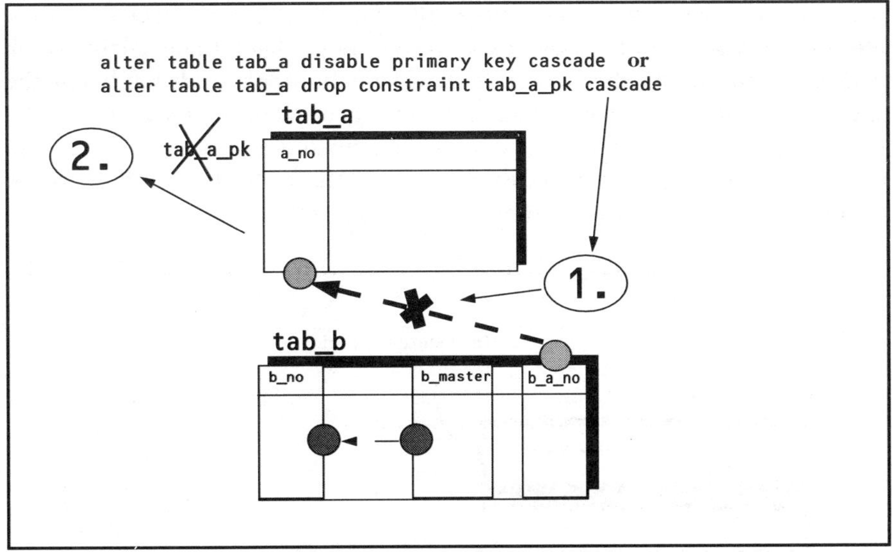

Figure 9.15 Deleting or deactivating a PRIMARY KEY constraint

9.3 Procedural integrity

9.3.1 Introduction

RELEASE 7.1

As we saw in the previous section the declarative integrity method provides an excellent way of implementing and managing simple referential and entity integrity conditions. However for specific data structures it can sometimes be necessary to implement more complex rules which go beyond the limits of declarative constraint structures and in order to do this we have to turn to Oracle7's method of procedural constraint definition in the form of database triggers. A database *trigger* is a procedure written in PL/SQL which is directly assigned to a database table and which is automatically activated by specific actions or events on that table.

Figure 9.16 shows an example of a database trigger which has been assigned to a database table with the statement CREATE TRIGGER. A database trigger can contain any number of PL/SQL statements, of SQL DML operations (SELECT, INSERT, UPDATE, DELETE) and of calls to stored PL/SQL programs; in addition it can access objects on any local or remote databases. Depending on how it is defined a database trigger will fire whenever the table to which it is assigned is changed by an INSERT, UPDATE or DELETE operation.

A typical application for a database trigger might be in a warehouse control system. Whenever parts are checked out of the warehouse we could make the database server check whether the overall stock still available has

fallen below a set minimum. If this is the case then a new order should be placed with the supplier. A database trigger could check the available stock whenever material is checked out and as soon as stock levels fall below the specified minimum a new order could be generated by entering all the necessary details in a corresponding table. By using Oracle Mail to process this table it would even be possible to have the order transmitted to the supplier without any intervention from the system's users.

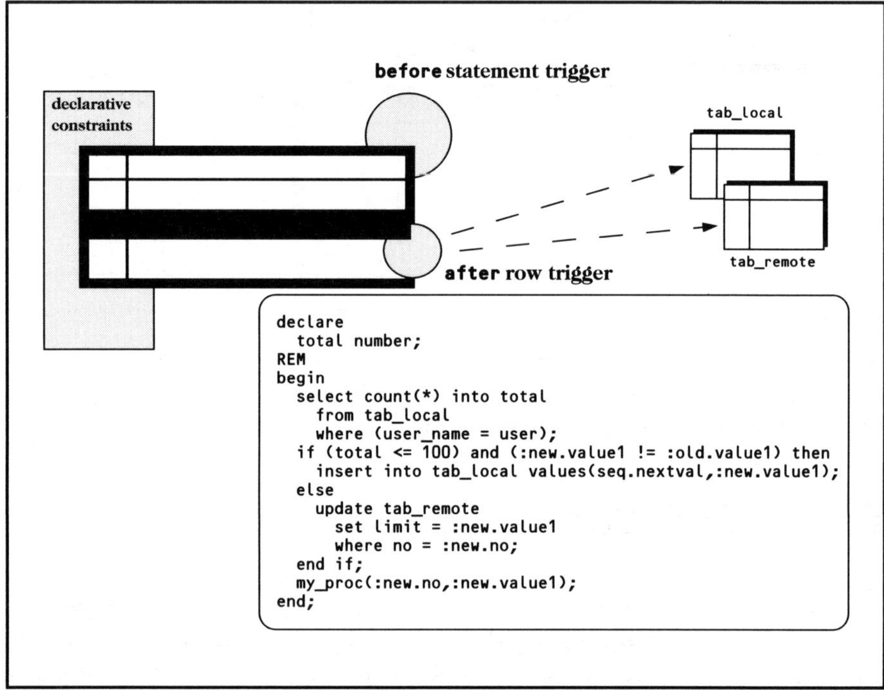

Figure 9.16 Database triggers

It is important to emphasize that all the operations mentioned in our example (checking the stock levels and generating the necessary order) are carried out entirely by the database server with the aid of the corresponding database triggers and that no applications programming is necessary.

Our example for the use of database triggers is illustrated in Figure 9.17. Here we can see that the database trigger is fired by the execution of an UPDATE statement. The trigger establishes that the current stock level is now lower than the set minimum for the part in question and carries out two actions as a result. The first action is to write an order record to the order table which can be situated on the local or on a remote database. The second action initiated by the trigger is to send the order straight to the supplier as an Oracle Mail message, making use of the package procedure DBMS_MAIL.SEND which we looked at in Chapter 8.

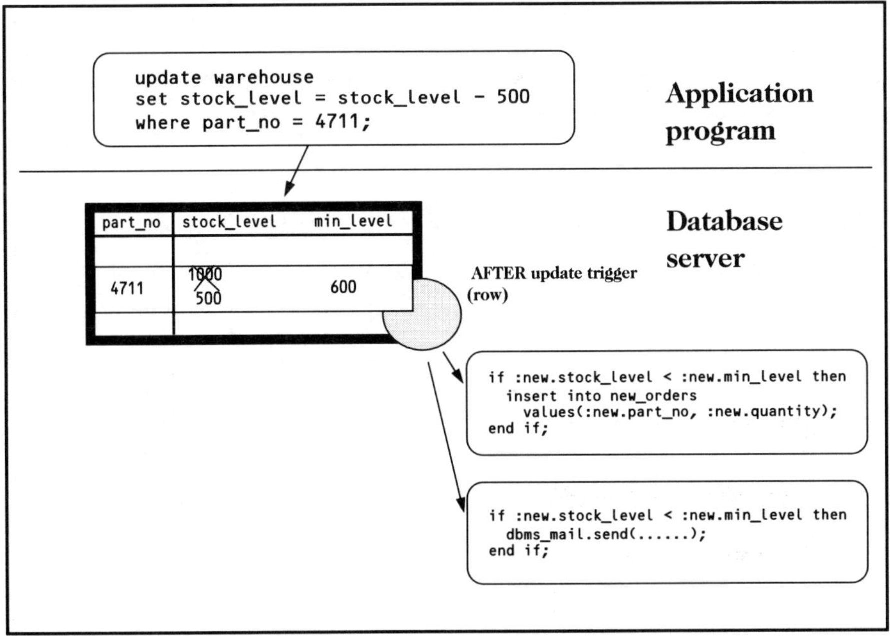

Figure 9.17 Implementing applications with database triggers

9.3.2 ORACLE database triggers

RELEASE 7.1

A defined database trigger always belongs to a specific database table and together with the table's column definitions, data types and declarative constraints forms an integral part of a self-contained and complex database object.

There is a maximum of twelve different types of trigger which can be defined on a database table. The triggers can vary according to the triggering statements (INSERT, UPDATE, DELETE), the trigger timing (BEFORE, AFTER) and the trigger type (statement or row trigger). These different types are summarized in Figure 9.18.

The trigger timing specifies whether the database trigger should be executed before or after the triggering statement; in the example in Figure 9.17 an AFTER UPDATE trigger is used. In addition a distinction is made between whether a trigger should be fired once per statement (statement type) regardless of the number of rows involved or whether a trigger should be fired each time that a row is modified (row type). How frequently a row trigger is fired obviously depends on the number of modified rows. If ten rows are modified by an UPDATE operation a BEFORE or AFTER UPDATE row trigger will be fired ten times.

Event	Trigger timing		Trigger type	
	BEFORE	AFTER	Statement	Row
insert	✓	✓	✓	✓
update	✓	✓	✓	✓
delete	✓	✓	✓	✓

Figure 9.18 The varieties of database trigger

For each triggering event we can therefore distinguish between four types of trigger:

- BEFORE statement triggers
- AFTER statement triggers

- BEFORE row triggers
- AFTER row triggers

It is important to note that a row trigger is executed in one of two contexts in that it is either carried out on a row which is to be modified (BEFORE) or on a row which has already been modified (AFTER). In each case the trigger has access to two instances of the row, the original values and one with the new, modified values. These can be referenced by using one of the two prefixes :OLD or :NEW in front of a column name. This convention is illustrated in Figure 9.17, where the new stock level is read from column `:new.stock_level`. This method can also be used to assign a value within a BEFORE row trigger and the old/new values can be retrieved for each of the individual DML operations which cause a trigger to be fired. In the case of an INSERT operation for example any reference to the :OLD column values will always return the value 'null' as the row did not previously exist.

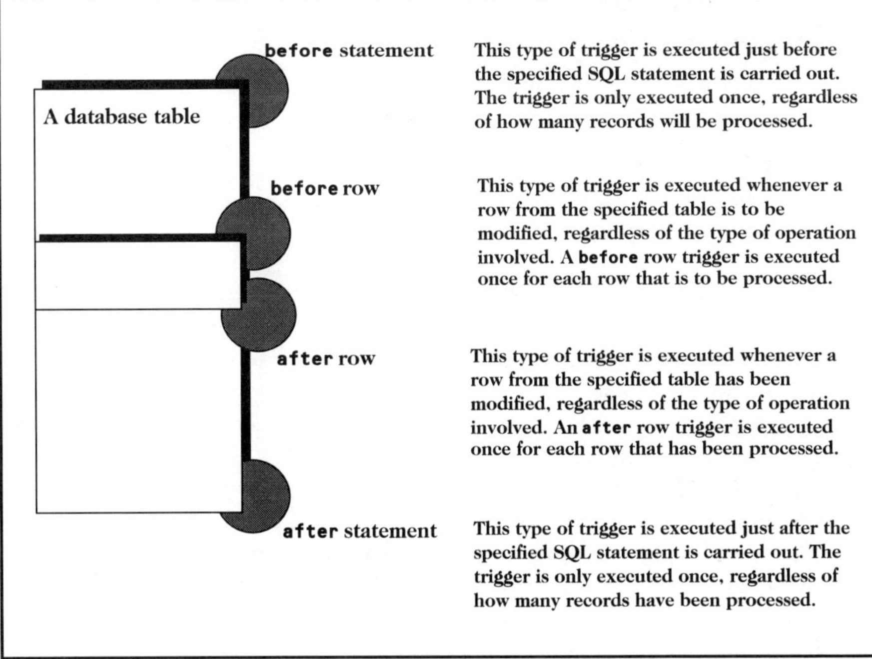

A database table
before statement
This type of trigger is executed just before the specified SQL statement is carried out. The trigger is only executed once, regardless of how many records will be processed.
before row
This type of trigger is executed whenever a row from the specified table is to be modified, regardless of the type of operation involved. A before row trigger is executed once for each row that is to be processed.
after row
This type of trigger is executed whenever a row from the specified table has been modified, regardless of the type of operation involved. An after row trigger is executed once for each row that has been processed.
after statement
This type of trigger is executed just after the specified SQL statement is carried out. The trigger is only executed once, regardless of how many records have been processed.

Figure 9.19 Oracle7 database trigger types

Event	Contents of old and new row instances	
`insert`	old	null values
	new	new row values
`update`	old	original row values
	new	new row values
`delete`	old	original row values
	new	null values

Figure 9.20 Accessing two instances of the same row from a database trigger

The SQL statement CREATE TRIGGER defines the following elements for any trigger which is to be created:

- the name of the trigger;
- the trigger timing (BEFORE, AFTER);
- the triggering event or events;
- the trigger type (statement or row type);
- the trigger restriction;
- the trigger's PL/SQL code which defines the actual processing to be carried out by the trigger.

This basic structure of the CREATE TRIGGER statement is shown in Figure 9.21. It is important to note that each trigger can deal with more than one event; if a number of events are to be dealt with by one trigger they must all be listed in the OR clause.

If an UPDATE trigger is defined without explicitly specifying any columns, the trigger will be executed whenever any of the table's columns are updated. If a trigger should be fired only when certain columns are modified, these columns must be listed within the UPDATE clause. Modifications to columns not listed in the trigger definition will not fire the trigger.

A row trigger is defined by use of the FOR EACH ROW clause.

Oracle7 also makes it possible to define an additional condition within the trigger statement which is evaluated before the trigger is executed. If the condition evaluates to TRUE the trigger is carried out, otherwise the execution of the trigger is ended without any further processing.

create or replace trigger <trig_name>	**Trigger name**
before / after	**Trigger timing**
insert or **update** of <column1>,<column2>,...or **delete** **on <tab_name>**	**Trigger event**
(for each row)	**Trigger type**
when <condition>	**Trigger restriction**
PL/SQL trigger source code	**Trigger body**

Figure 9.21 The structure of an Oracle7 database trigger

The actual trigger program, which resides within the trigger body, is constructed like a standard PL/SQL module and can use all the linguistic elements which we covered in Chapter 7. In addition to these standard PL/SQL constructs however, trigger programs can also make use of special IF constructs which enable a trigger program to be easily structured in cases where

several events are to be dealt with under one trigger. By using these constructs, which are listed below, the trigger can be made to branch to different sections of its code in order to deal with specific events:

```
if inserting then
if updating then
if updating ('<column1>') then
if deleting then
```

Figure 9.22 shows the use of this structure in a trigger definition.

```
create or replace trigger stock_order                Trigger name
after                                                Trigger timing

insert or
update  of s1,s5                                     Trigger event
on warehouse
for each row                                         Trigger type
-----------------------------------------------------------------
declare                                              Trigger body
  total number;
begin
  if inserting then
    <pl/sql>
  if updating ('S1')  then
    <pl/sql>
  if updating ('S5')  then
    <pl/sql>
exception
  when no_data_found then ......
end;
```

Figure 9.22 Processing control within a database trigger

A database trigger is always executed within the context of a specific transaction and is therefore a constituent part of the current transaction or of the triggering DML statement. This is also the case when a DML operation in one database trigger fires a trigger on another table, so that we have a cascade of triggers belonging to one triggering statement.

RELEASE 7.1

A DML operation is not considered to have been successfully completed unless all direct and indirect database triggers can be ended positively and all declarative constraints have also been observed. If any one of the fired triggers ends with an error then all modifications to the data are rolled back, regardless of whether they were initiated by a database trigger or by the original DML statement. This also applies if the modification carried out by a trigger is on a remote database; in this case we have a (implicit) distributed transaction, which is secured by ORACLE's two-phase commit protocol.

Finally we should mention that a trigger is not able to complete its processing if constraint violations or other ORACLE errors have occurred during its execution.

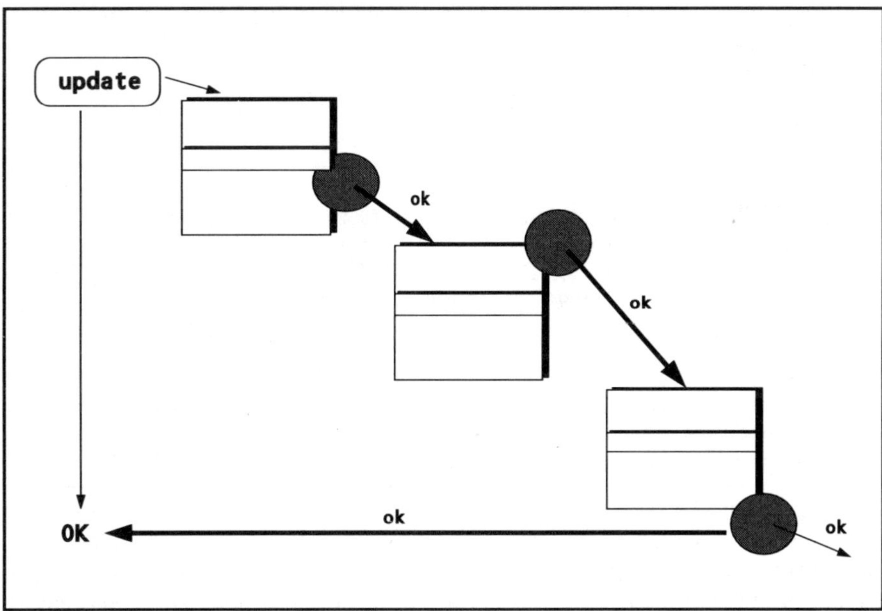

Figure 9.23 Using 'nested' triggers

A trigger program error can also be explicitly generated by calling the procedure RAISE_APPLICATION_ERROR. This procedure has two parameters:

- A user-defined error number
  The user can define error numbers between 20000 and 21000; once this number has been allocated it then behaves like any standard ORACLE error number.
- A user-defined error text
  The user can define a text which describes the error; once the text has been allocated it then behaves like any standard ORACLE error text.

Typical examples for generating a trigger error in this way might be:

```
raise_application_error (-20011, 'invalid input');
raise_application_error (:var_no,:var_error_text);
```

These user-defined error numbers do not have to be unique but it is advisable to work with clearly defined error numbers and error texts within an application system or an ORACLE instance. By managing these error numbers and error texts (which can be in different languages) on a centralized basis, it becomes possible to provide a range of user-defined error tables for different purposes and environments. An individual trigger can then access a specific table to get the correct error number and text which can then be used as parameters for calling the RAISE_APPLICATION_ERROR procedure.

9.3.3 Creating a database trigger

Using the CREATE TRIGGER statement to create database triggers involves a similar process to creating procedures, functions and packages. In each case the code is checked by the PL/SQL and SQL processors and any errors which are detected are recorded in the ERROR$ table. These can be displayed with SQL*Plus or SQL*DBA using the statement (in the case of triggers) `show errors trigger <trigger_name>` (*refer also to* Figure 8.4).

However in contrast to a stored PL/SQL program a database trigger is not stored in the database as a compiled module. As with SQL statements, a database trigger is not compiled until runtime, when it is made available to all users within the shared pool of the database cache.

Since there are so many similarities between how database triggers and stored procedures are developed and tested, the reader should refer back to Chapter 8.3 for any further information on the actual process of implementing database triggers.

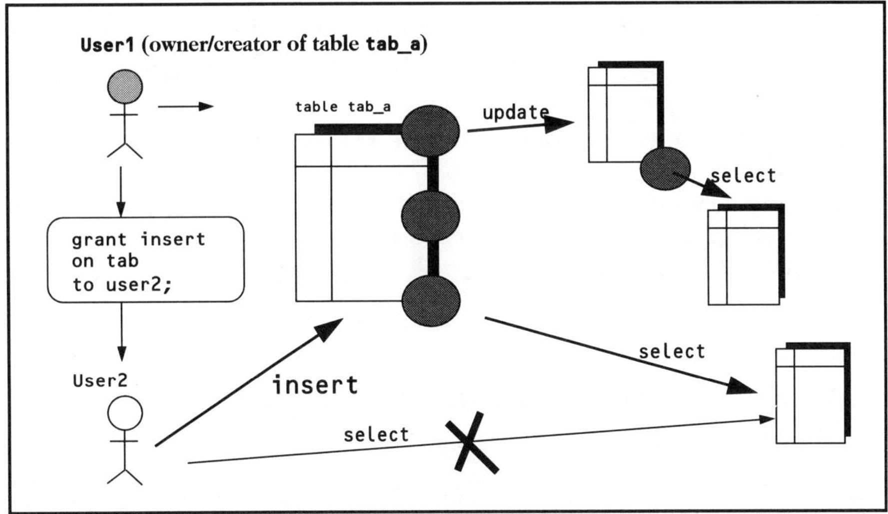

Figure 9.24 Managing access and execute privileges within database triggers

A further parallel to stored PL/SQL packages is to be found in the administration of user privileges. If a user is granted the right to modify a table on which there are database triggers then all the database triggers which have been defined in the security context of the table's owner will also be executed whenever required.

This situation is illustrated in Figure 9.24. In this example a user is given the right to insert new rows into a table. The insert operation causes various database triggers to be fired and these may in turn carry out read or modify operations on additional tables to which the user in our example has no explicit access rights. However since the database triggers are executed in the security context of the table's creator, the new user acquires implicit access rights to these objects via the database triggers.

9.3.4 Managing database triggers

As with declarative integrity constraints, Oracle7 provides all the functions necessary to make effective use of database triggers in a working environment. Specifically we are able to carry out the following operations:

- create database triggers with the CREATE TRIGGER command;
- modify an existing trigger with the CREATE OR REPLACE TRIGGER command;
- disable an existing trigger with the ALTER TRIGGER **<*trig*>** DISABLE command;
- disable all the triggers on a table with the ALTER TABLE **<*tab*>** DISABLE ALL TRIGGERS command;
- enable a single trigger with the ALTER TRIGGER **<*trig*>** ENABLE command;
- enable all the triggers on a table with the ALTER TABLE **<*tab*>** ENABLE ALL TRIGGERS command;
- delete a trigger with the DROP TRIGGER **<*trig*>** command.

When declarative constraints are activated the tables affected are checked completely for constraint conformity. However enabling a trigger does not cause it to be carried out on all the existing records in the table in question.

9.4 Retrieving constraint information from the data dictionary

Information about all database objects is stored in the data dictionary and can be retrieved at any time. In order to retrieve information about the declarative and procedural integrity constraints and actions which have been defined for the objects in a given schema we can access the following data dictionary views:

- USER_CONSTRAINTS
- USER_CONS_COLUMNS
- USER_TRIGGERS
- USER_TRIGGER_COLS

```
rem ********************************************************************
rem  Procedure: cat_comp(act).sql Author: Guenther Stuerner 06/93
rem
rem  Description: Outputs a list of all the indexes, constraints and
rem  triggers for one or more tables. Requires the cat_all view to be
rem  generated first using cat_all.sql
rem ********************************************************************

clear screen
prompt Please enter table name(s) - wild cards (% or _) are OK
accept tab_name char prompt 'Table name: '
break on table_name
column type noprint
column table_name format a15
column 'Index/Cons/Trigger name' format a30
column 'Index/Cons-Ref/Trig-Type' format a30
set linesize 100
set pagesize 60

select rpad(substr(uc1.table_name, 1, 15),17,'.') table_name,
  rpad(substr(uc1.constraint_name,1,18),20,'.') ||
      '('||uc1.constraint_type||')'||
  decode(uc1.status,'ENABLED',null,'[-]') ||
  decode(uc1.delete_rule,'NO ACTION','<nc>', null, null,
           '->cas') 'Index/Cons/Trigger Name',
  decode(uc1.r_constraint_name, null, null,
            uc1.r_constraint_name ||
  ' ('||uc2.table_name||')') 'Index/Cons-Ref/Trig-Type', 2 type
from user_constraints uc2, user_constraints uc1
where uc1.r_constraint_name = uc2.constraint_name(+) and
    uc1.table_name like upper('&&tab_name')
union
select rpad(substr(object_name,1,15),17,'.') object_name,
  tr_ind_name || decode(status,'<v>',null,status)
      'Trigger/Index',
  triggering_event 'Trigger/Index Type,
      decode(type,'I',1,'T',3,4)
from cat_all
where object_type = 'TABLE' and object_name like
    upper('&&tab_name')
ORDER BY 1,4
/
undef tab_name
```

Figure 9.25 Listing all the database objects for one or more tables

In addition to these user-oriented (USER_) views ORACLE also provides, as is the case with all data dictionary views, the corresponding ALL_ and DBA_ views. Whereas in ORACLE Version 6 only the table structure and possibly the index structure were of interest to a programmer, it has become necessary in Oracle7 to provide all the information on a given ORACLE table. As well as the table structure this includes the following elements:

- indexes and index types;
- constraints on the table and their status (enabled, disabled);
- foreign key constraints whereby the names of the referenced tables, the names of the constraints and the status of the ON DELETE CASCADE option are all of interest;
- the names of any triggers as well as their timing, action and type;
- the status of any triggers (enabled, disabled, error).

If we are planning to implement applications programs with a complex table structure which makes use of declarative constraints and database triggers then it is clearly very important to have access to this kind of basic information about our data structures.

The SQL script **CAT_COMP.SQL** which is shown in Figure 9.25 is able to retrieve and output this information in a very compact form. Figure 9.26 shows the output of this script for our two sample tables ***tab_a*** and ***tab_b***.

```
Enter value for tab_name: tab__

TABLE_NAME      Index/Cons/Trigger Name       Index/Cons-Ref/Trig-Type
--------------- ----------------------------- ----------------------------
TAB_A.......... TAB_A_PK..........(Idx)       UNIQUE
                C3................(C)[-]
                SYS_C00622........(C)
                TAB_A_A_NO_CHECK..(C)
                TAB_A_PK..........(P)

TAB_B.......... TAB_B_FK..........(Idx)       NONUNIQUE
                TAB_B_PK..........(Idx)       UNIQUE
                SYS_C00625........(C)
                SYS_C00626........(C)
                SYS_C00627........(C)
                TAB_B_FK..........(R)[-]<nc>  TA_PK (TA)
                TAB_B_MASTER_NO...(R)->cas    TB_PK (TB)
                TAB_B_PK..........(P)
                TAB_B_TR1.........(Tr)[-]     ->B_R_INSERT/UPDATE/DELETE
                TAB_B_TR2.........(Tr)(+)     ->A_R_INSERT/UPDATE

16 rows selected.
```

Figure 9.26 Sample output generated by the procedure '**CAT_COMP.SQL**'

The output tells us for example that two indexes (they can be recognized by the abbreviation '`Idx`') have been defined on table ***tab_b***. In addition a series of check (**C**), foreign key (**R**), and primary key (**P**) constraints have also been defined.

However the foreign key constraint **tab_b_fk** has been disabled, as we can see from the minus sign in square brackets (**[-]**), and the ON DELETE CASCADE option was never specified for it (**<nc>**). All foreign key constraints specify the referenced constraint and the referenced table.

The output also provides us with the status of our database triggers (**(-)** = disabled, **(+)** = enabled and **(err)** = error) and with all the other important trigger details, that is, the timing (**b_** denotes before and ***a_*** denotes after triggers), the type (**r_** = row type) and the triggering events (INSERT, UPDATE, DELETE).

It should be noted that the ***cat_all*** view must be present if the **CAT_COMP.SQL** script is to be used. The structure of the **cat_all** view is shown in Figure 9.27.

```
rem***********************************************************************
rem  Procedure: cat_all.sql  Author: Guenther Stuerner June 1992
rem
rem  Description:
rem  Defines the view 'cat_all' which displays in a single
rem  listing all the indexes and triggers for a given table.
rem  Related to procedure 'cat_comp.sql' which accesses this view
rem ***********************************************************************

create or replace view cat_all as
select
  uo.object_name, uo.object_type,
  rpad(substr(trigger_name,1,18),20,'.') ||
    decode(trigger_name,null,null,'(Tr)')              TR_IND_NAME,
  decode(ut.trigger_type,
    'BEFORE STATEMENT','->B_','BEFORE EACH ROW','->B_R_',
    'AFTER STATEMENT','->A_','AFTER EACH ROW','->A_R_') ||
  replace (triggering_event,' OR ','/')                TRIGGERING_EVENT,
  decode(ut.status, 'ENABLED','(+)', 'DISABLED','[-]',
            'ERROR','(err)',
    decode(uo.status, 'VALID','<v>', 'INVALID','<iv>',
              null))                                    STATUS,
  'T'                                                   TYPE
from user_objects uo, user_triggers ut
where ut.table_name(+) = uo.object_name
union
select
  uo.object_name, uo.object_type,
  rpad(substr(index_name,1,18),20,'.') ||
decode(index_name,null,null,'(Idx)') ,
  uniqueness, null, 'I'
from user_objects uo, user_indexes ui
where uo.object_name = ui.table_name
/
```

Figure 9.27 Creating the '`cat_all`' view

10
Database security

Topics covered in this chapter

- Database security and the ORACLE privilege concept
- Defining object privileges
- Defining system privileges
- The ORACLE concept of privilege roles
- Managing privileges with roles

10

Database security

10.1 Introduction

A standard database will typically contain a large amount of data stored in separate tables which are accessed by a wide range of users in a number of different ways, for example either directly (via SQL) or by means of an application program. The continual increase in the volume and complexity of these data as well as in the number of users using the system means that much greater importance must be given to the twin tasks of maintaining the security of the database objects and of controlling the access privileges of the system's users.

For this reason Oracle7 provides us with two basic types of database privilege: the *object* privileges which define the operations a user is permitted to carry out on a given database object, and the *system* privileges which specify what operations a user is allowed to carry out within the server. Object privileges are allocated for the following types of database objects:

- tables
- views
- PL/SQL programs
- sequences
- snapshots

Examples of system privileges are:

- the right to create a table (CREATE TABLE privilege),
- the right to modify a tablespace (ALTER TABLESPACE privilege),
- the right to create a rollback segment (CREATE ROLLBACK SEGMENT privilege).

The sum of all the privileges which have been assigned to a user describes his access domain or sphere of action within the database. In Figure 10.1 for example `user1` has been granted the necessary privileges to read and modify table **`tab1`** but not however to call procedure **`proc1`** as the necessary EXECUTE privilege has not been granted on this object.

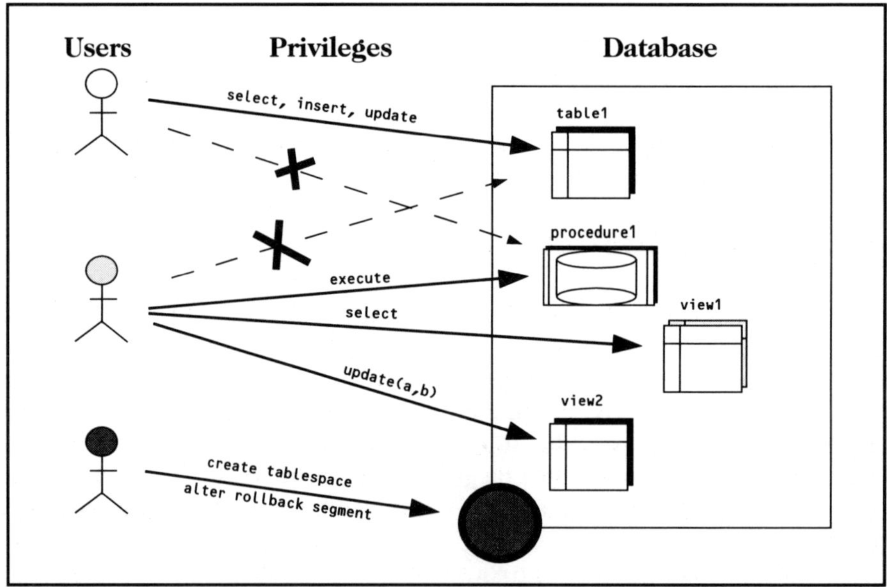

Figure 10.1 Controlling database access through Oracle7 privilege management

When a user is first defined with the Oracle7 database Server (using the statement CREATE USER) he or she starts out with no privileges at all and cannot carry out any operations within the database. Only after the DBA has assigned the CREATE SESSION privilege is the newly created user able to start an ORACLE session (that is, to log on to the ORACLE Server). The CREATE

SESSION privilege is therefore the fundamental privilege without which no ORACLE login is possible. The ORACLE user can then be empowered to make active use of this database by being assigned additional, specific system and object privileges.

All information on the privileges which have been granted to a user is stored in the data dictionary. Whenever a user wishes to carry out a specific operation, the first action of the database server is to check whether the requested action is covered by the user's privilege profile in the data dictionary. If the two do not coincide the operation is aborted with a corresponding error message.

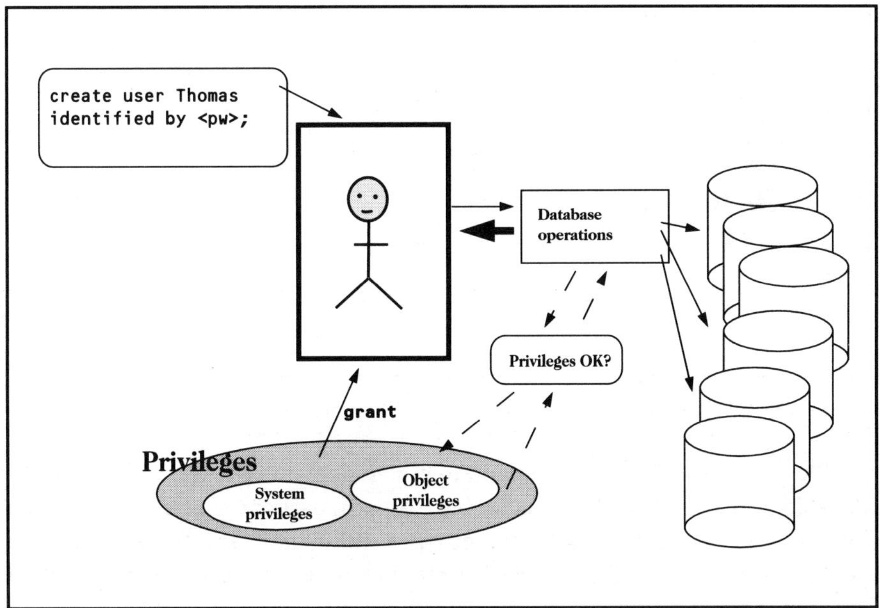

Figure 10.2 Users, privileges and database operations

10.2 The Oracle7 database privileges

As we have already seen, database privileges define the rights of a user to carry out specific actions on existing database objects and to carry out specific actions within the overall database system. Oracle7 therefore distinguishes between two different categories of privileges:

- object privileges
- system privileges

The GRANT command is used to allocate both object and system privileges either to specific users or, as we shall see later in this chapter, to roles which have been defined within the system. However it is important to understand that not all object privileges can be effectively applied to every database object and Figure 10.3 indicates which object privileges are valid for which objects. To access a data snapshot for example only read access is required (*refer also to* Chapter 14) and to make use of a procedure only the EXECUTE privilege needs to be granted.

Object privileges	Database objects: Table	View	Snapshot	Procedure	Sequence
select	✓	✓	✓		✓
insert(col1,.)	✓	✓			
update(col1,.)	✓	✓			
delete	✓	✓			
execute				✓	
reference	✓				
index	✓				
alter	✓				✓

Figure 10.3 Database objects and database object privileges

The use of the GRANT command to assign object privileges is not however the sole preserve of the DBA; as we have seen in earlier chapters, it is possible for the owner of any database object (who will usually also be its creator) to grant other users certain privileges on that object. The following example shows the GRANT statement being used by the owner of a table to pass on SELECT, INSERT and UPDATE rights on it to a second user:

```
grant select,
      insert (col_a, col_b, col_c),
      update (col_a, col_d, col_e)
on    table1
to    user2;
```

This GRANT statement allows `user2` to read `table1`; this user may also insert new rows but may only specify the values for columns `col_a`, `col_b` and `col_c`, and may only modify columns `col_a`, `col_d` and `col_e` in existing rows. All other operations which can be carried out on these tables (*see* Figure 10.3) will not be available to this user until the necessary privileges have been granted (*refer also to* Figure 10.4).

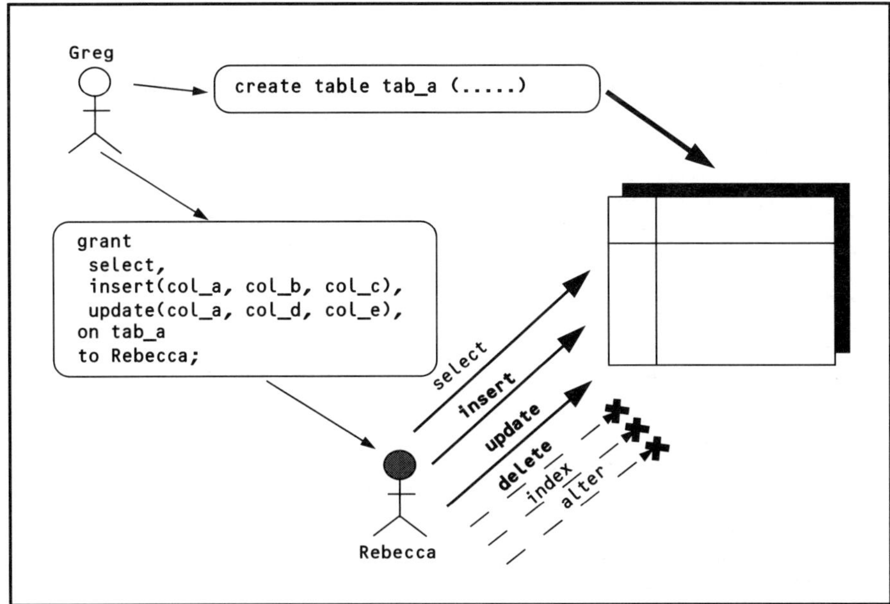

Figure 10.4 Assigning object privileges to another user

Whereas *object* privileges define a user's rights in terms of operations on existing database objects, *system* privileges define what operations may be carried out within the database as a whole, so that for every such database operation there is a corresponding system privilege. A user can therefore only create a table if he or she has been granted the CREATE TABLE privilege and can only define a stored PL/SQL program within the database if he or she has been assigned the CREATE PROCEDURE privilege. Altogether Oracle7 provides over 70 distinct system privileges, thereby allowing user privileges to be assigned in a highly differentiated and tightly controlled framework. Figure 10.5 provides a comprehensive list of all the system privileges available.

It is important to note that any privileges which include the key word ANY should be allocated with particular care as they extend the right to carry out actions outside the user's own schema and should therefore only be assigned to highly privileged users (DBAs). The CREATE ANY TABLE privilege, for example, allows a user to not only create tables in his own schema but to create tables in any schema within the database. The following example of the GRANT statement gives a user the right to log on to the database and to create tables and their attendant indexes:

```
grant create session,
      create table
to    <user>;
```

```
analyze any
audit any
audit system

create cluster
create any cluster
alter any cluster
drop any cluster

alter database
create database link
create any index
alter any index
drop any index

grant any privilege

create procedure
create any procedure
alter any procedure
execute any procedure

create profile
alter profile
drop profile
alter resource cost

create public database link
drop public database link

create role
alter any role
grant any role

create rollback segment
alter rollback segment
drop rollback segment

create session
alter session
restricted session

create sequence
create any sequence
alter any sequence
drop any sequence
select any sequence

create snapshot
create any snapshot
alter any snapshot
drop any snapshot

create synonym
create any synonym
drop any synonym

alter system

create table
create any table
alter any table
backup any table
drop any table
lock any table
comment any table
select any table
insert any table
update any table
delete any table

create tablespace
alter tablespace
manage tablespace
drop tablespace
unlimited tablespace

force transaction
force any transaction

create trigger
create any trigger
alter any trigger
drop any trigger
create user
become user
alter user
drop user

create view
create any view
drop any view
```

Figure 10.5 The Oracle7 system privileges

Figure 10.6 illustrates the basic differences between the two types of privileges which we have been looking at, that is, object and system privileges.

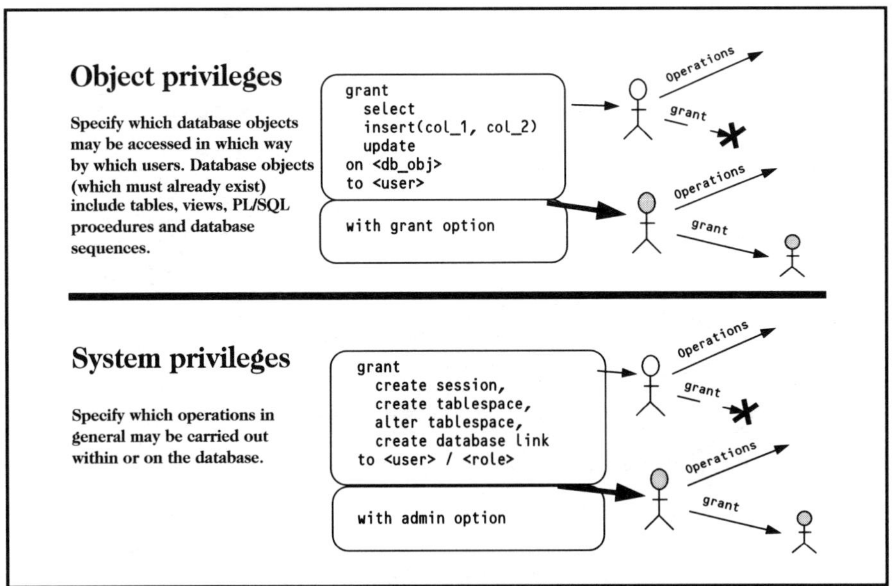

Figure 10.6 A comparison of object and system privileges

Specifying the WITH GRANT OPTION parameter when granting object privileges entitles the recipient to assign the same object privileges to other users. The WITH ADMIN OPTION parameter works in the same way for system privileges: if a user is granted one or more system privileges with this option, he or she is able to allocate these newly acquired privileges to other users. Since system privileges involve operations which affect the database as a whole, the WITH ADMIN OPTION should only be assigned to users who have to carry out some of the functions of a DBA.

10.3 The Oracle7 role concept

As we saw in the previous section, privileges are divided into object and system privileges, and both types can be separately assigned to individual users by means of the GRANT statement. However, bearing in mind the many different system privileges which exist, it is easy to see that administering the privileges for all the users of a working system can quickly become a time-consuming task, particularly if we are dealing with a large number of users.

In order to deal with this problem Oracle7 provides a facility whereby object and system privileges can be grouped and allocated together by creating a user-defined *role*. A role is therefore also a database object which can be created with the CREATE ROLE command by users who possess the corresponding CREATE ROLE privilege (usually DBAs). Privileges are assigned to a role in exactly the same way as they are assigned to users by using the GRANT statement; once a role has been created it can be assigned to a user or to another role. Figure 10.7 illustrates the use of the role concept, with a user being assigned a typical combination of roles and single privileges; all the privileges included in each role are thus allocated to the user in question.

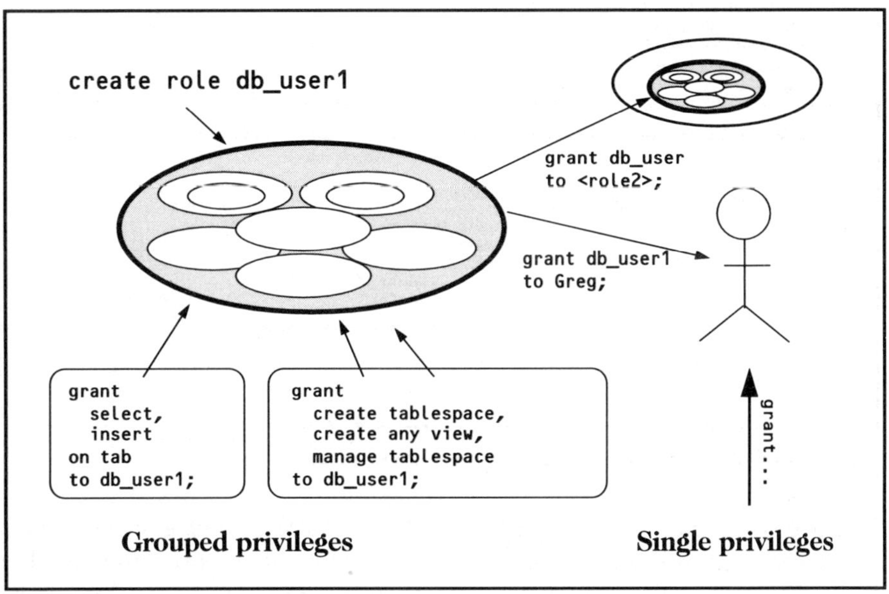

Figure 10.7 Defining and assigning roles

The roles assigned to a user can be divided into the following categories:

- Available roles
  These are all the roles which have been assigned to the user with the GRANT command and therefore represent the maximum scope of a user's role-based privileges.

- Default roles
  These are the roles which are automatically activated as soon as a user logs on to the Oracle7 Server. Default roles are defined for the user with the ALTER USER command but can only be drawn from the available roles which have already been assigned to the user.

- Enabled roles
  These are the roles which are enabled for a user at a given time. Provided that he or she has been granted the SET ROLE privilege then a user can enable or disable any of the roles from the pool of available roles by using the SET ROLE command at runtime, as in the following example:

```
set role role1, role2;
set role all except role1;
```

- Disabled roles
  These are the roles (from the user's pool of roles) which are currently disabled.

Figure 10.8 summarizes these four types of role status.

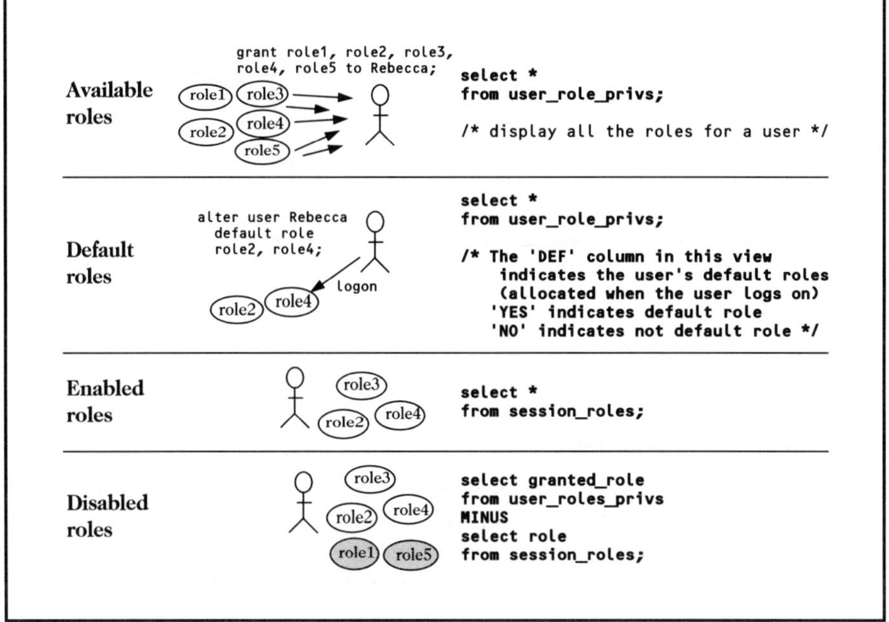

Figure 10.8 Managing the status of a user's roles

Over and above the information on roles and their current status it is often necessary to know on what basis different object or system privileges have been granted to a specific user, that is, whether they have been granted individually or as part of an enabled role. Figure 10.9 shows the SQL statements which are available to retrieve this information from the data dictionary.

The system and object privileges which have been assigned to the roles in an Oracle7 system can be retrieved by accessing the data dictionary views ROLE_SYS_PRIVS and ROLE_TAB_PRIVS respectively. The privileges which have been assigned to individual users can be accessed by means of the two views USER_SYS_PRIVS (system privileges) and USER_TAB_PRIVS_RECD (object privileges).

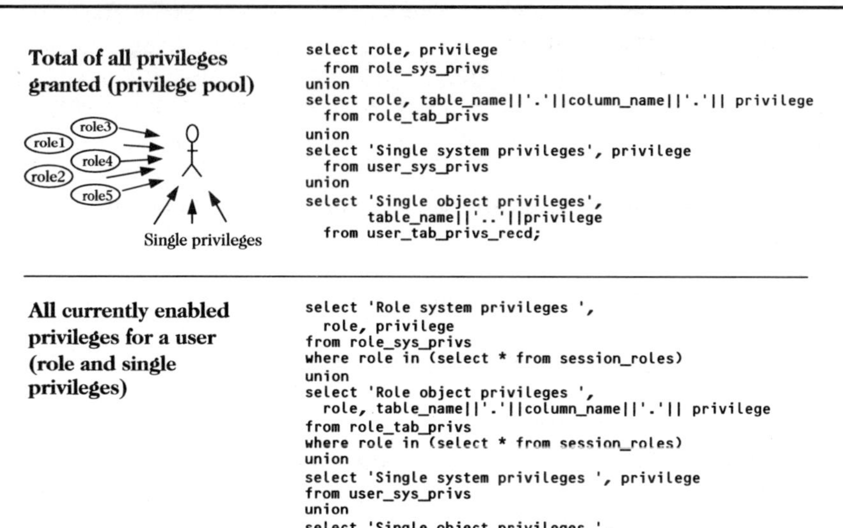

Total of all privileges granted (privilege pool)

```
select role, privilege
  from role_sys_privs
union
select role, table_name||'.'||column_name||'.'|| privilege
  from role_tab_privs
union
select 'Single system privileges', privilege
  from user_sys_privs
union
select 'Single object privileges',
       table_name||'..'||privilege
  from user_tab_privs_recd;
```

All currently enabled privileges for a user (role and single privileges)

```
select 'Role system privileges ',
  role, privilege
from role_sys_privs
where role in (select * from session_roles)
union
select 'Role object privileges ',
  role, table_name||'.'||column_name||'.'|| privilege
from role_tab_privs
where role in (select * from session_roles)
union
select 'Single system privileges ', privilege
from user_sys_privs
union
select 'Single object privileges ',
  table_name||'..'|| privilege
from user_tab_privs_recd;
```

Figure 10.9 Displaying the status of all privileges for a user

Figure 10.9 shows the SQL statements which will provide all the information about the privileges currently available to a given user, both on an individual basis (the first SQL statement) and in the context of a specific role (the second SQL statement).

Creating a role	create role <role_name>;
Assigning privileges to a role	grant <sys_priv>/<obj_priv> to <role>;
Assigning roles to users or to other roles	grant <role> to <user>/<role>;
Revoking roles from users or other roles	revoke <privilege>/<role> from <user>/<role>;
Enabling and disabling roles	set role <role>, <role>,...; set role all; set role all except <role>; set role <role> identified by <password>;
Defining a role as a user's default role	alter user <user> default role <role>;
Deleting a role	drop role <role>;

Figure 10.10 SQL commands for managing roles

It is again worth emphasizing that the Oracle7 role mechanism provides a simple and very effective way of defining and administering user privileges in any working Oracle7 installation, the SQL commands involved are no different from those used to define individual object or system privileges, and roles can be defined to include all the privileges required to carry out specific functions or programs. Another important practical aspect of this feature is that roles can be defined on a hierarchical or modular basis, so that it becomes possible to assign all the privileges of one role to a role at a 'higher' security level; this feature can be very useful in the typical situation where a group of users or developers is working with the same database under a team leader who should at all times have access to the data used by the individual team members.

11

Trusted Oracle7: a brief introduction

Topics covered in this chapter

- The origins of Trusted Oracle7
- Trusted operating systems for Trusted Oracle7
- Security classifications for Oracle7
- Mandatory Access Control (MAC)
- Discretionary Access Control (DAC)
- Defining security labels

11

Trusted Oracle7: a brief introduction

Trusted Oracle7 is a self-contained database server product which has been specially developed for use in environments requiring extremely high levels of data security. Trusted Oracle7 is completely based on standard Oracle7 technology and includes all functions implemented in the Oracle7 Server.

Although the data security mechanisms of the Oracle7 Server are sufficient to guarantee a very high level of data security in the majority of cases (the possibilities available are often by no means fully exhausted) there is an increasing number of cases where an even higher level of data security is required.

The development of Trusted Oracle7 can be traced back to 1988 when Oracle signed a cooperation agreement with the National Computer Security Center (NCSC). The aim of this collaboration was to develop a number of 'secure' or 'trusted' database server prototypes which could be used to evaluate different security concepts in terms of their practical application, benefits and ease of use. Certain features developed as a result of this cooperation, such as the role concept for grouped privileges and the fine granulation of system privileges, were implemented in both Oracle7 and in Trusted Oracle7, but the overall concept which was then formulated for a high-level security database has now been fully implemented in the Trusted Oracle7 system.

However before we can look at the special mechanisms provided by Trusted Oracle7, we must first turn our attention to the overall security context within which the database has to operate, for in order to ensure the complete security of a computing system it is necessary for all the components of that system, and in particular the operating system, to provide the same high level of access security. At the same time as Oracle was developing Trusted Oracle7 the manufacturers of operating systems were also creating high-security versions of their own products and a number of these are now available for the implementation of high-security systems. Some of the more widely used examples of this kind of secure operating system are:

- SEVMS from DEC
- HP/UX BLS from HP
- RISC-ULTRIX MLS+ from DEC
- SUNOS CMW from Sun

In order to implement a database with Trusted Oracle7 it is therefore necessary to be using an operating system which will provide the high-level security functions which Trusted Oracle7 requires (*refer also to* Figure 11.1). In this way we ensure that all aspects of the system provide the required high level of security.

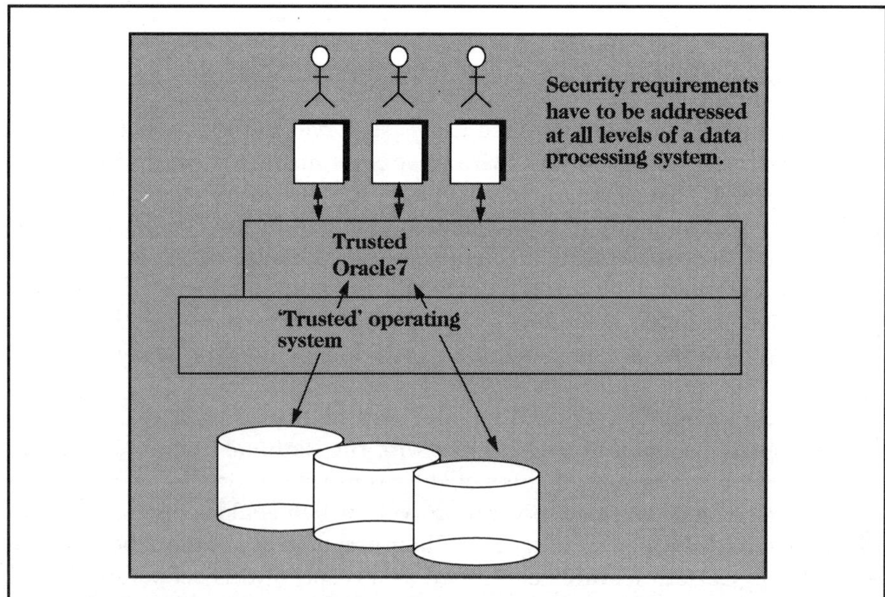

Figure 11.1 Trusted Oracle7 in a high-security data processing environment

In considering the overall security requirements for a specific system it is of course important to know which security functions should be provided by which system components in order to achieve a particular security level; the requirements for the security of operating systems, database systems and networks have all been defined in a number of standard reference works, the best known being the 'Orange Book'.

The standards defined by the TCSEC (Trusted Computer Systems Evaluation Criteria) specify seven levels of security, and these are listed in Figure 11.2 together with the corresponding security levels of the European Security Committees. In the same way as operating systems, database management systems must also undergo an official conformity test if, for example, they want to be rated as fulfilling the standards for a C2 or B1 product.

	NCSC (USA) classifications TCSEC level	European classifications ITSEC level
lowest level of database	D	E0
security	C1	F-C1,E1
Oracle7 →	C2	F-C2,E2
Trusted Oracle7 →	B1	F-B1,E3
	B2	F-B2,E4
	B3	F-B3,E5
highest level of database security	A1	F-B3,E6

Figure 11.2 Security classifications for database systems

In the preceding chapter on Oracle7 security we saw how privileges (individual privileges and roles) and the GRANT statement can be used to assign access rights between individual users, so that the owner of a database object is able to grant different access rights on that object to other users of the database server. This procedure is also known as discretionary access control (DAC), the word 'discretionary' referring to the option which is available to the owner of a database object to assign access rights to any other users.

This option, which is illustrated in Figure 11.3, is also fully available in Trusted Oracle7 but it represents only one of the functions provided for controlling access to a database object.

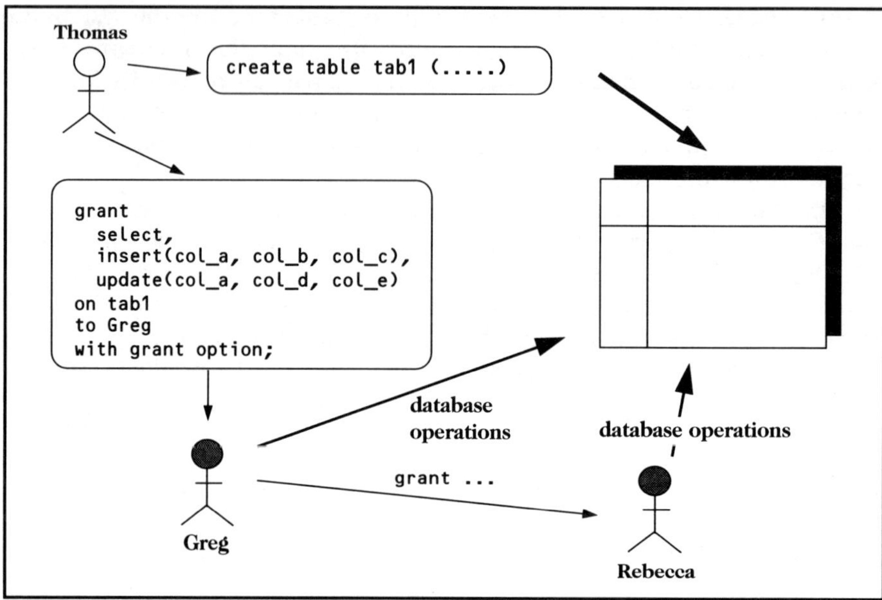

Figure 11.3 Assigning discretionary access control (DAC) with Oracle7

The second procedure required for access control in B1 products is termed mandatory access control (MAC), 'mandatory' in so far as the controls which have been defined are always enforced for all database objects and for all operations with database objects. This second level is basically implemented by the use of 'labels' which are used to control which database objects or parts of a database object are accessible to individual user processes.

Classifications	Categories		
top secret (ts)	**A**	**B**	
secret (s)			
confidential (c)	**P1**	**P2**	
unclassified (u)			

Figure 11.4 Creating security labels with Trusted Oracle7

Within a trusted DP environment every user and every process running under that user is assigned to one or more security levels, which are largely derived from the classifications that represent the hierarchical security levels. The example in Figure 11.4 illustrates four security levels to which four classifications (top secret, secret, confidential and unclassified) have been assigned. However in addition to these primary security classifications, it is possible to define additional access categories within each security level, thus making it possible to differentiate between information which has the same external security level (for example two projects which are both rated as confidential).

Thus if we take the security levels defined in Figure 11.4 together with the additional categories A and B we are able to define ten different labels, using the classifications 'top secret' and 'confidential' in conjunction with the two categories A and B. This method provides us with four label types for each of the two classifications, as we can see for the example of 'top secret':

- top secret:
- top secret: A
- top secret: B
- top secret: A,B

Every user of a trusted operating system works within either a specific security level or a security area, comprising several levels, and that user can only carry out operations which have been assigned to the same security level or area.

This concept of security levels plays a central role within Trusted Oracle7. The database session of every user who logs on to a Trusted Oracle7 database runs under the security label which was defined at operating system level. This label is also assigned to every object which is generated during this database session and, when new rows are inserted into a database table, it is stored with an additional pseudo column, ROWLABEL, which forms one of the distinctive features of the Trusted Oracle7 system. As Trusted Oracle7 is fully based on standard Oracle7 it goes without saying that none of these operations can be carried out unless the corresponding privileges have been granted to the user concerned.

We have already seen how the owner of a database object can make it accessible to other users by granting the corresponding object privileges as in the example `grant select, insert, update on tab_mls to rms;`. However if we are using Trusted Oracle7 we will see that a SELECT operation carried out on table `tab_mls` by user `rms` will return only those rows whose security labels are dominated by the current security labels of user `rms`. This specific function of Trusted Oracle7 is illustrated in Figure 11.5.

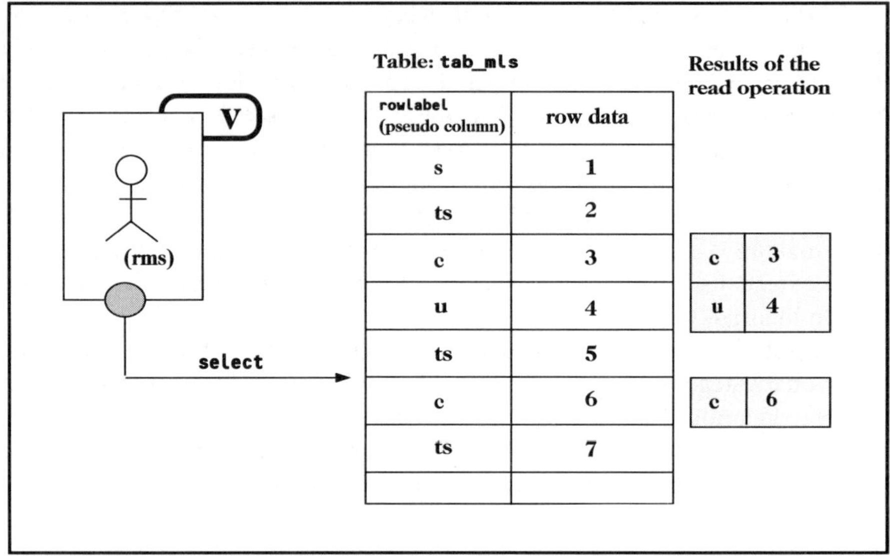

Figure 11.5 Multi-level read operations in Trusted Oracle7

This mechanism for comparing the security labels of user and object is implemented for every operation that is carried out within the context of a Trusted Oracle7 environment, with the system always checking whether the user's security label dominates that of the object. Thus although user `rms` has been granted the SELECT privilege for table `tab_mls` he can only view those rows which are dominated by his own current security label. In our example these are rows 3, 4 and 6 which carry the security labels 'confidential' and 'unclassified'. The 'top secret' and 'secret' rows are not visible to user `rms` at all.

Whereas Trusted Oracle7 allows read access for all rows which are dominated by the current security label of the user, modify operations can only be carried out on rows whose labels correspond exactly to the user's label. Therefore row 4 can be read by `rms` but cannot be modified by him.

On the basis of this simple example we can see that access labels play a central role in the security mechanisms of Trusted Oracle7, being evaluated both at user and at object level and in relation to the question of label dominance.

However Trusted Oracle7 does not only take into account relatively simple read and modify operations on tables but reflects all aspects of a professional high security database. These include, among many other things, the correct handling of:

- PRIMARY KEY and UNIQUE constraints;
- referential integrity conditions;
- multi-level import and export of data;

- multi-level backup and recovery techniques;
- label management.

12

Database administration

Topics covered in this chapter

- The role of the database administrator (DBA)
- The main tasks of the DBA
- Starting up and shutting down a database
- Monitoring system usage and performance

12

Database administration

12.1 Introduction

The use of SQL as a standardized database language is usually seen in terms of its role in providing programmers or end-users with the means to create data structures, to read and modify data in a database or to define data access structures. However a not inconsiderable part of SQL is dedicated to the tasks of administering a database and includes commands to start a database, to define logical structures (tablespaces or rollback segments), and to control access to database objects. In addition it provides a means of managing database resources so that, for example, a database user can be provided with a fixed amount of database space. However since functions of this type depend very much on the specific architecture of the computer being used, the corresponding SQL commands are not covered by the ANSI/ISO standard for SQL.

In addition to these SQL commands which are not or cannot be standardized, ORACLE provides a further series of commands which the DBA can use to administer a database and it is these commands which we shall look at in the rest of this chapter.

12.2 The role of the database administrator

The database administrator plays a central role in the administration of a database, although the need for a DBA and his or her importance are related to the size of the database. This can be measured in terms of:

- the size of the database (as measured in megabytes of data);
- the number of users who work with the database;
- the number of transactions carried out on the database;
- the importance or sensitivity of the database to the organization which uses it.

The importance of the DBA is directly linked to the importance of the data and software stored in a database; where these are crucial to the functioning of an organization it becomes essential that a DBA should always be available to solve any problems that occur with the database as quickly and as comprehensively as possible.

However even in the case of smaller and less 'important' database installations, it is recommended that one person should be given overall responsibility for database management and for carrying out all the necessary functions of a DBA; it is not necessary for this person to always be on site as most DBA operations can be carried out on a remote basis. In the case of such small installations the tasks of the DBA will not take up a lot of time, especially as many of the routine tasks can be automated if required. In larger installations of course the job of a DBA is a very responsible one; he or she not only has to ensure the availability and security of the system's data, but also has to help users and developers to obtain the optimum performance from their own applications systems.

The work of a database administrator includes the following tasks:

- initializing the database;
- starting up and shutting down a database;
- structuring the database, which involves the following specific tasks:
  - defining tablespaces
  - assigning files to the tablespaces
  - distributing database files/redo log files on different disks
  - defining rollback segments in terms of their size, number and location;
- developing and implementing backup and recovery strategies for the database;
- developing and implementing security concepts;
- monitoring database activity;
- tuning the database.

Many of these actions can be implemented as SQL procedures which have to be run at given times (for example starting up or shutting down the database when the computer system is started up or shut down).

The ORACLE utility SQL*DBA represents the primary means by which a DBA will access an ORACLE database, as it provides all the operations necessary to administer one or more ORACLE databases.

12.3 Starting up and shutting down an ORACLE database

As we have seen in earlier chapters an ORACLE database consists of the following components:

- a database cache
- a number of ORACLE background processes
- the three file types:
  - control files
  - database files
  - redo log files

These different components are reflected in the three different states which can exist for an ORACLE database:

- ORACLE instance started
- ORACLE database mounted
- ORACLE database open

If the instance has been started, the database cache has been loaded into the computer's main memory and the ORACLE background processes are running. However the users cannot yet work with the database in the normal way, and only the DBA can access this instance by means of the SQL*DBA program and the corresponding SQL and SQL*DBA statements.

If the database is mounted then the control file has been opened and this can be accessed by the DBA. The operations which can be carried out at this stage include the following:

- modifying the database file names, since if one or more database files are moved to another directory or to another disk this change must be reflected in the control file using the statement ALTER DATABASE RENAME 'old_file' TO 'new_file';
- modifying the names of the redo log files;

- modifying the number of redo log files;
- modifying the operating mode of a database, for example by switching from NOARCHIVELOG to ARCHIVELOG mode;
- database recovery (RECOVER DATABASE).

When an ORACLE database has been mounted the ORACLE instance works only with the control files; the database files with all the user data and the data dictionary are not open and cannot be accessed. For this reason only privileged users can carry out database operations on a mounted database.

In order to access the system at this stage the user has to enter the SQL*DBA command CONNECT INTERNAL, although this will only work provided that the user has been granted the corresponding operating system rights. This means that in this particular case access to the ORACLE system is controlled by the operating system.

Only when the database has been *opened* are the corresponding database files and redo log files assigned to the instance, and all users are then able to work normally with the database's primary resource, namely the tables.

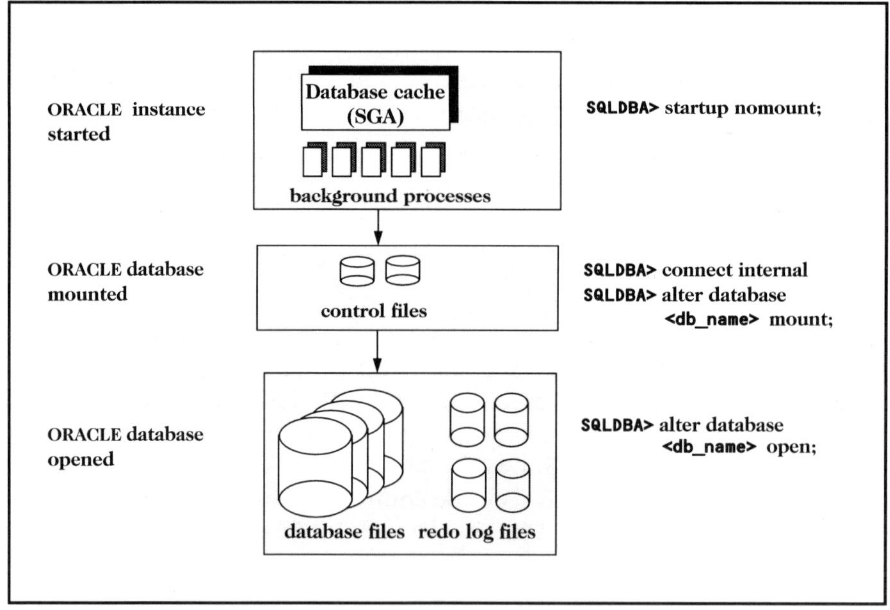

Figure 12.1 The different states of an ORACLE database

In order to start an ORACLE database it is not however necessary to carry out the three separate actions illustrated in Figure 12.1. To start an ORACLE database in one single step it is only necessary to enter:

```
startup open <db_name>
```

The effect of this SQL*DBA statement is to carry out in one sequence the three actions we have just been looking at, that is:

- starting the ORACLE instance,
- mounting the ORACLE database,
- opening the ORACLE database.

An ORACLE database can be started up in other ways too.

```
startup open parallel <db_name>
```

This statement starts an ORACLE instance and opens an ORACLE database with the Parallel Server option which allows several ORACLE instances to work with the same database.

```
startup open restrict <db_name>
```

This statement starts an ORACLE instance and opens an ORACLE database only to users with the RESTRICT SESSION privilege. This is to allow the DBA to carry out work on the database without 'normal' users being active.

The action of stopping a database can also be carried out in a number of different ways, so that the database is put into a specific state by entering the appropriate SQL*DBA command.

- In order to only close the database we have to enter the command:

```
shutdown normal
```

- In order to dismount the database we have to enter:

```
shutdown immediate
```

- Finally in order to close the instance (that is, stopping all background processes and removing the database cache from main memory) we have to enter:

```
shutdown abort
```

The various parameters of the SHUTDOWN statement indicate whether we are carrying out a gradual (NORMAL) shutdown, which will only be completed when all users have logged off the ORACLE Server, or whether the shutdown should be carried out at once (IMMEDIATE/ABORT), in which case all user processes are terminated without warning and the database is immediately closed. Stopping a database with the ABORT option always necessitates instance recovery when the database is reopened.

12.4 Monitoring ORACLE database activity

Another important task of the DBA is to monitor the usage and resources of the database so that any performance bottlenecks can be detected and corrected as early as possible. In order to help the DBA carry out this task Oracle provides three special tools:

- the Oracle Monitor utility which forms part of the SQL*DBA program,
- the views and the dynamic performance tables in the data dictionary,
- the SQL AUDIT statement.

The Oracle Monitor program makes it possible to monitor all current database activity while sessions are running and it provides a wealth of information for the DBA, including the following items:

- which processes and users are currently active;
- which database locks are held by a particular process, that is, exclusive lock, shared lock, waiting for locks to be released;
- the amount of I/O activity being generated by individual processes;
- which tables are being processed;
- what latches are currently active;
- the number of write operations on the redo log file;
- the number of physical read/write operations;
- the hit ratio in the shared pool area for SQL statements, PL/SQL programs or database triggers.

The Oracle Monitor utility does make it easy to retrieve this kind of information about current system activity, but it is also possible to get the same information by using SQL.

ORACLE provides a number of dynamic performance tables for this purpose. These make internal information available in the form of virtual database tables, which can be read and evaluated with the aid of SQL SELECT statements. These dynamic performance tables are not conventional database tables in the sense that they have not been created within a database file and do not require disk space. However the information they provide, which is mainly drawn directly from the database cache, is shown in the form of a normal database table. For this reason they are often called 'virtual' dynamic performance tables.

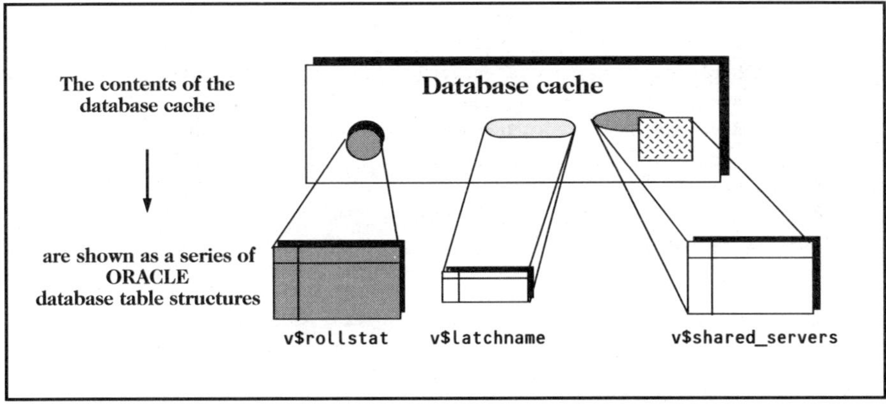

Figure 12.2 Displaying the contents of the database cache by means of the ORACLE **v$** tables

Some examples of these dynamic performance tables (usually referred to as **v$** tables) are:

- V$PROCESS
- V$TRANSACTION
- V$LOGFILE
- V$ROLLSTAT

Figure 12.3 gives the complete list of all available **v$** tables.

The DBA is provided with additional system information by many of the data dictionary views; for example in order to determine how much disk space is currently either used or available the DBA can refer to any of the following views:

- DBA_EXTENTS
- DBA_FREE_SPACE
- DBA_DATA_SEGMENTS

```
v$backup             v$log                v$session_cursor_cache
v$bgprocess          v$logfile            v$session_event
v$bh                 v$log_history        v$session_wait
v$circuits           v$mls_parameters     v$sesstat
v$database           v$mts                v$sga
v$datafile           v$nls_parameters     v$sgastat
v$dbfile             v$open_cursor        v$shared_server
v$db_object_cache    v$parameter          v$sqlarea
v$dispatcher         v$ping               v$statname
v$enabledprivs       v$process            v$sysstat
v$filestat           v$queue              v$system_cursor_stat
v$latch              v$recovery_log       v$system_event
v$latchholder        v$recovery_file      v$thread
v$latchname          v$reqdist            v$timer
v$librarycache       v$resource           v$transaction
v$loadcstat          v$rollname           v$version
v$loadtstat          v$rollstat           v$waitstat
v$lock               v$rowcache
v$lock_activity      v$session
```

Figure 12.3 Dynamic (virtual) performance tables

If information is required which goes beyond the scope of the predefined dictionary views already available, it is relatively easy to define new views, and with the aid of the Oracle Forms system it is also possible to develop an interactive database query utility which allows the DBA to retrieve all information via Oracle Forms masks.

Another tool provided by the Oracle7 Server is the AUDIT facility; this was originally introduced so that all operations on especially sensitive tables could be recorded. However the facility can also be used to monitor system performance with reference to a given table; it is possible to define which tables should be covered by the *auditing* function and to specify which operations on those tables should be recorded in the AUDIT_TRAIL table. The auditing function is switched on as follows:

```
audit select, insert, update, delete
on employee
whenever successful;
```

This example statement will create an entry in the AUDIT_TRAIL table if any one of the four operations SELECT, INSERT, UPDATE, DELETE is carried out on the `employee` table and is completed successfully.

Information recorded in the AUDIT_TRAIL table includes:

- the name of the table;
- the type of operation carried out on it (SELECT, INSERT and so on);
- the user who carried out the operation;
- the terminal on which the operation was carried out;
- the time at which the operation was carried out.

By gathering this information for a specific table over a period of time it becomes possible to build up an accurate picture of how a table is being used, and in particular to establish how frequently a table is being accessed and what kind of operations are being carried out on it. An audit period can be ended at any time using the NOAUDIT statement and the results can be accessed immediately by use of the SELECT command, all of which make the AUDIT statement a very simple tool to use.

An introduction to distributed databases

The next two chapters of this book are concerned with what is one of the most important developments in the world of data processing today, namely the increasing use of distributed processing and distributed data storage technologies. When the first PCs were introduced few people foresaw the revolutionary effect they were to have on established computing practices; since then the market for PCs, workstations and networks has grown to such an extent that hardly any DP project is now undertaken which does not involve the use of distributed applications (client/server), graphical user interfaces (windows based systems) and of database servers.

It is therefore important to be clear about what we mean when we refer to distributed processing (client/server) and to distributed data storage, and to understand the differences between these two technologies.

In terms of the database's role, a typical client/server configuration exists when the application program and the database system run on different computer systems. A SQL statement generated by an applications program is sent on the network to the database system where it is executed, and then data or status information are sent back across the network to the applications program. During this process all database processing is carried out on the database server which does not have to concern itself either with the applications program or with how the data are to be presented (for example on the screen, as a report and so on). Figure 13.1 illustrates this very popular type of configuration.

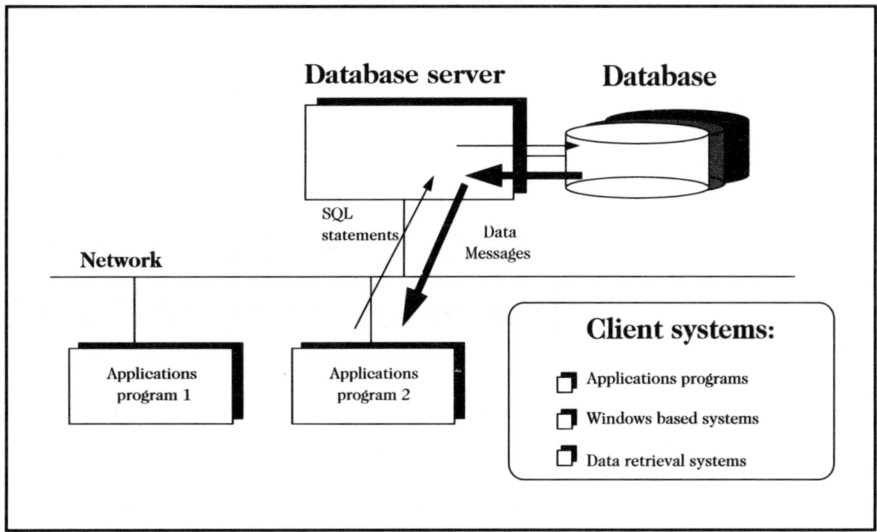

Figure 13.1 A standard client/server configuration

The benefits of this type of system are especially significant where windows based systems are being used, as this kind of graphical interface makes heavy use of a computer's processing and memory resources. However if all such activities are being carried out locally (that is, on the client system) then the performance of the database server will be considerably improved.

We speak of distributed data storage or distributed databases when the data structures being processed are not located on one database but are distributed across several databases on several computers. This type of configuration places far greater demands on the database system than the 'classic' client/server configuration, since SQL statements may have to be forwarded to other database nodes (SQL routing) and complex SQL statements may have to be split up in order to be processed on a number of remote database nodes as partial SQL statements.

Figure 13.2 shows a typical distributed database in which a SQL join is divided into two single statements each of which is individually optimized and executed on two destination databases. However because of the correspondingly greater demands which are placed on the function and design of the database system, this type of configuration is not yet as widespread as the standard client/server configuration with a single database server.

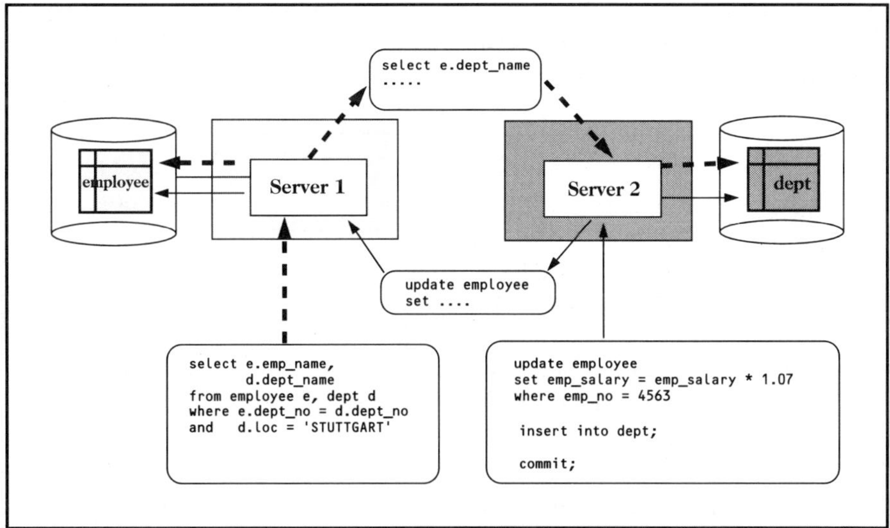

Figure 13.2 Read and modify operations on a distributed database

Another important element of distributed systems, and one which we have not at all considered so far, is the network which is required to link all the components of a distributed system together. As long as we were only dealing with basic questions of database technology we could allow ourselves to ignore this underlying system component, but if we want to understand how distributed systems work, we will see that the role of the network becomes extremely significant in both theoretical and practical terms.

For this reason the whole of Chapter 13 is devoted to the question of network technology. Because a number of different network protocols are covered, the chapter's subject matter does become relatively complex but this is only a reflection of the kind of requirements which arise in practice, where we are increasingly faced with the demand that complex information systems should not only run on different computer platforms with different user interfaces, but that they should also be able to communicate across different network systems.

The use of distributed database technology under ORACLE has been achieved in four phases and these are shown in Figure 13.3.

From this diagram we can see that although Version 6.0 and 6.2 of the ORACLE DBMS supported distributed queries across heterogeneous networks, a client/server configuration was only possible within a homogeneous network, with a point to point connection being necessary both physically and logically. Similarly ORACLE Version 6.0 did not support distributed transactions.

The combination of Oracle7 and Version 2.0 of SQL*Net provides the basis for ORACLE's fourth phase of distributed database technology which supports distributed transactions, client/server configurations in heterogeneous networks and synchronous and asynchronous replication. With the implementation of this phase it is no longer important to know in which network community a client computer or a database server computer is located.

Phase		ORACLE Version
1	Client/server systems in a homogeneous network	5.1
2	Distributed queries and client/server systems in a homogeneous network	5.1
3	Distributed queries in a heterogeneous network. Client/server systems in a homogeneous network	6.0 6.2
4	Distributed transactions, distributed queries and client/server systems in homogeneous and heterogeneous networks. Data replication (synchronous and asychronous)	7.0

Figure 13.3 The development of ORACLE's distributed database technology

As we work through the subject matter of the next sections, it is important to remember that we are examining this whole subject from two different aspects:

- in terms of a network based on SQL*Net Version 2,
- in terms of a database based on Oracle7 functionality.

Of primary importance in our consideration of the network level are the network protocols used and the related ORACLE components which are necessary to create a functioning carrier system that guarantees complete transparency in terms of network protocol and topology. This means that for the user or the application programmer it is no longer necessary to know in which community a database node is located and whether a specific SQL statement has to be sent across several communities to a destination node. In Chapter 13 we will concentrate on the components which make up ORACLE's network technology and on how configurations might vary in a homogeneous or heterogeneous network.

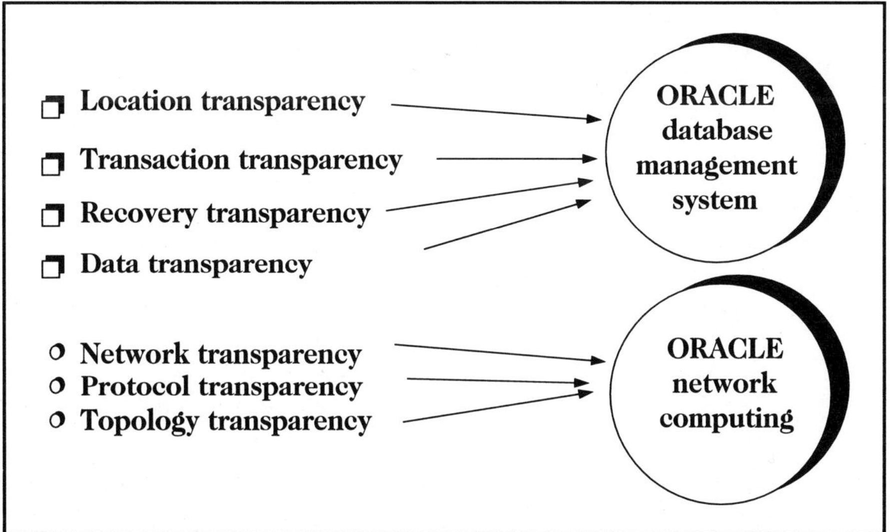

Figure 13.4 The seven key requirements for fully distributed databases

The database level is based on ORACLE network technology, in other words it assumes that the carrier system has been configured and implemented to carry out all necessary distributed database functions. Provided that the carrier system has indeed been correctly set up, the database level is able to provide:

- location transparency
- transaction transparency
- recovery transparency
- data source transparency

Within the database level the user or applications program is able to address any database objects by name with SQL; the routing of the SQL statements to the correct destination node can be left completely to the database system. In Chapter 14 we will look at the database functions which make this possible, these include the functions to carry out distributed read operations, distributed transactions and synchronous and asynchronous replication.

13

ORACLE network technology

Topics covered in this chapter

- The use and significance of networked database systems
- The ORACLE network products
- The structure of an ORACLE network system
- The ORACLE Transparent Network Substrate (TNS) technology
- The TNS node types
- Defining homogeneous and heterogeneous ORACLE networks
- The Oracle MultiProtocol Interchange (MPI)
- Optimizing remote database access

13 ORACLE network technology

13.1 Introduction

Computer networks have become so widely used today that they can be found in almost every professional computing installation in varying degrees of sophistication and on the basis of different network protocols. However this very success has led to a whole new range of problems resulting from the attempt to integrate into a single network hardware and software systems which have many different features and characteristics. Some of these components are often found to be in direct conflict with the integrated solution demanded, and the incompatibility of individual network systems together with the problems caused by moving data across different network communities can sometimes totally undo all the benefits gained by decentralization. If it is not possible for a given organization to integrate a number of independent computer systems into a whole, then the strategic and operational goals of that organization may become impracticable, in which case the overall aim of decentralizing computer resources has to be called into question.

RELEASE 7.1

This is where ORACLE network technology comes in: by providing a range of software products that is able to cope with differing network protocols, network topologies and network access procedures (for applications systems with and without database access), this product group allows us to create a completely transparent network carrier system. The resulting ORACLE network is therefore protocol independent and the instances on the individual computer nodes can be given names by which their databases can be accessed. It is then no longer important in which community a database node is situated, as all protocol dependencies remain completely concealed from the actual applications.

13.2 The network product range

In order to create a fully transparent network ORACLE provides us with the following software components:

- SQL*Net
- ORACLE Transparent Netware Substrate (TNS)
- Oracle Protocol Adapter
- Oracle MultiProtocol Interchange (MPI)
- Oracle Navigator

SQL*Net is responsible for providing a consistent applications program interface (API) for all ORACLE applications and for initiating the connect and disconnect actions with all the necessary parameters. If abnormal conditions occur during the connection process, caused perhaps by a network or computer crash at one of the nodes, SQL*Net informs the relevant ORACLE instances which can then, depending on the status of the transaction, carry out any process recovery which may be necessary.

ORACLE TNS forms the actual core of an ORACLE network. It consists of a number of functions which work independently of protocols and networks and it is responsible for processing the requests generated by the SQL*Net layer. It provides the following functions:

- determining the destination addresses (node name, database instance);
- path optimization with the aid of the Oracle Navigator;
- any code conversion which may be necessary;
- handling BREAK situations.

ORACLE TNS provides an open interface which can be used not only by SQL*Net and the Oracle MPI but by any distributed systems and system functions which run on the distributed network.

RELEASE 7.1

The Oracle Protocol Adapters, Oracle Protocols for short, form the third element in this product architecture, and this layer forms the interface to the actual network protocols being run. Whereas SQL*Net and ORACLE TNS are only present once per instance several Oracle Protocols can be present at the same time for each different network protocol in use. Figure 13.5 illustrates the structure of these layers of software.

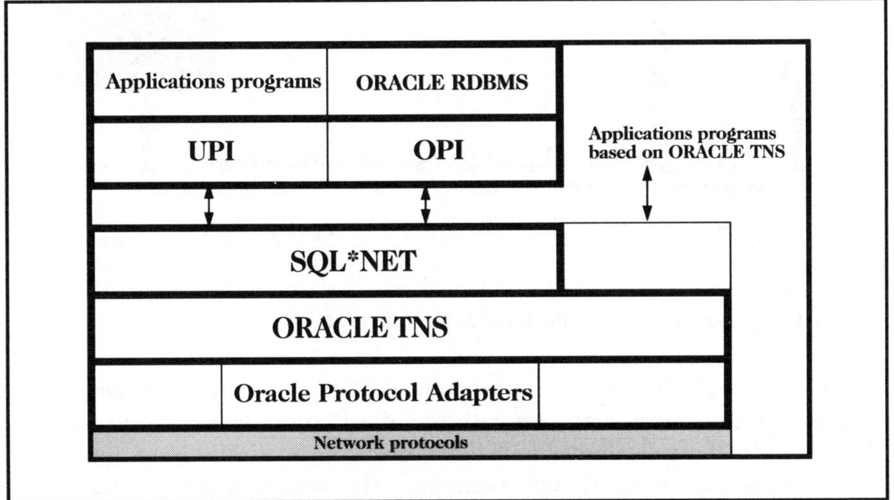

Figure 13.5 The software layers of an ORACLE TNS system

On the client side a database request is passed to SQL*Net via the UPI interface. On the database server side SQL*Net submits this request to the database server via the OPI interface.

If we are dealing with a heterogeneous network then the last two software components, namely the Oracle MultiProtocol Interchange (MPI) and the Oracle Navigator, are particularly important for the functioning of the system. The Oracle MPI is responsible for linking together the different systems on the network. In the simplest case this means creating two point to point connections which link the Oracle MPI to the client system and to the database server. These two physical point to point connections can be treated by the application as a logical point to point connection on the application side therefore making it possible to create client/server configurations beyond the boundaries of the network.

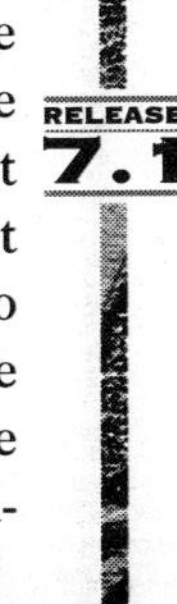

For this reason the Oracle MPI can be regarded as a TNS application system with a software structure whose layers correspond to those of SQL*Net.

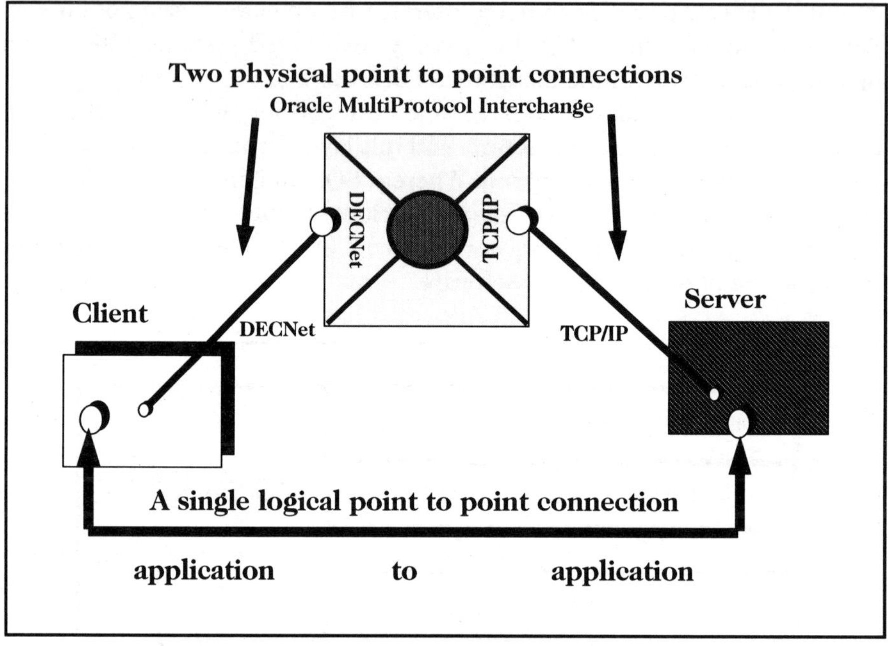

Figure 13.6 The Oracle MultiProtocol Interchange (MPI)

The Oracle Navigator is part of the Oracle MPI and its task is to determine whether there is more than one path to a destination database and which of these paths is the most cost-effective. Whereas an Oracle MPI is always needed in heterogeneous network environments, the optimum use of the Oracle Navigator is only possible on a large heterogeneous network where there may be a number of alternative paths from one network community to another. If we are dealing with a homogeneous network the Oracle Navigator is not needed because the navigation on this type of system is undertaken by the network itself.

Figure 13.8 shows a more complex TNS network which consists of three different networks, DECNet, TCP/IP and SPX/IPX; on each network there are a number of client systems and a number of database servers, and in this example these three networks are linked together by three Oracle MultiProtocol Interchanges.

It is important to emphasize that an Oracle MPI provides a completely software based solution and can therefore be installed on any computer system. The only condition is that at least two Oracle Protocols must be available to the computer which is going to be used as the MPI (Figure 13.7).

Figure 13.9 summarizes the information we have covered so far by illustrating a number of basic network configurations together with the software components necessary for both homogeneous and heterogeneous networks. In practice of course we usually find systems which vary in one way or another from the basic configurations shown here. A fairly standard mixed configuration would be where we have a number of client systems on different networks which all access a central server, or where simultaneous access to several database servers in different networks is required. Fortunately the software components which we have been looking at still provide us with the means to link any common network configuration, regardless of its particular characteristics.

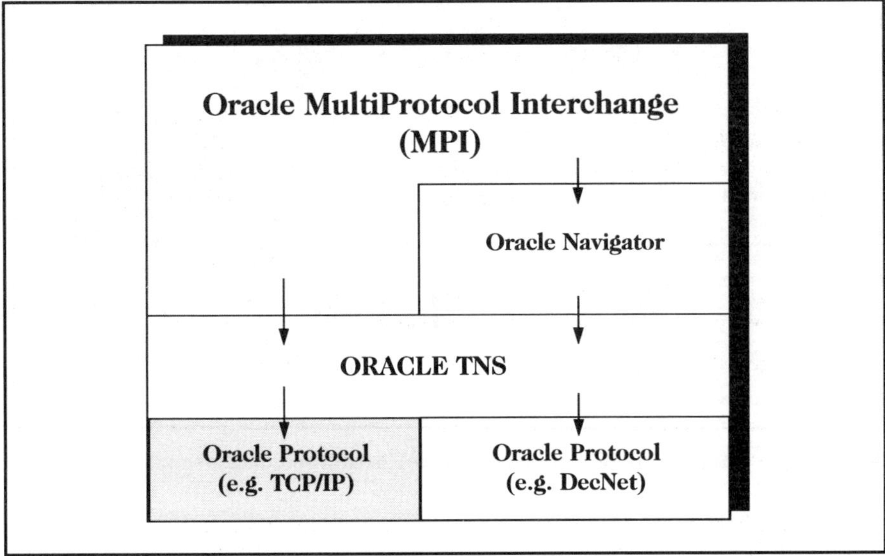

Figure 13.7 The Oracle MultiProtocol Interchange within the TNS software model

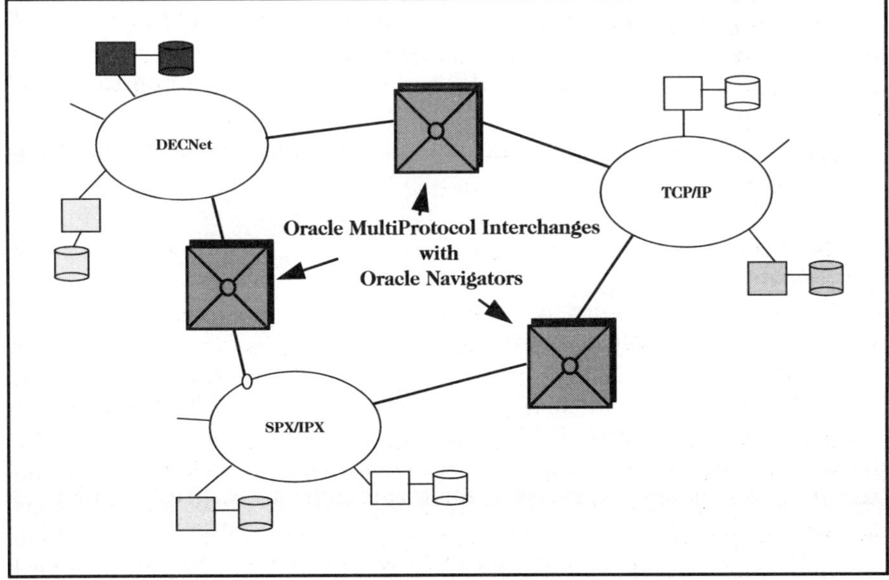

Figure 13.8 Using ORACLE in a heterogeneous network configuration

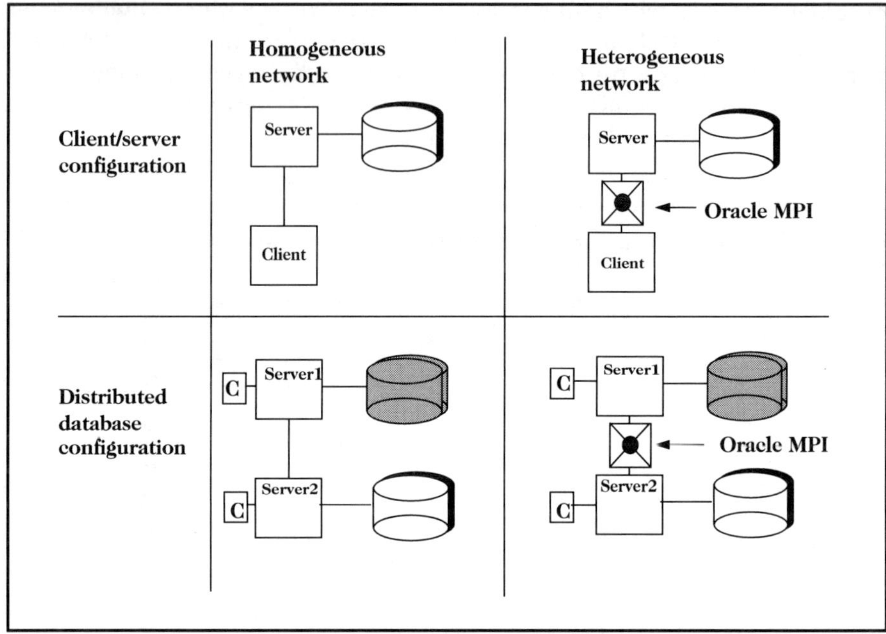

Figure 13.9 Some common configurations for networked database systems

13.3 The TNS node types

In order to carry out their respective tasks the software components which we have just introduced must have access to a description of the whole TNS network, whereby it is important to remember that each network node may have a different perspective on the whole network according to its own specific functions and tasks.

A homogeneous TNS network can comprise three different TNS node types:

- client Nodes (C)
- database Server Nodes (S)
- database Server/Client Nodes (SC)

A client node (C) is the machine on which an application is run, and this type of node does not have its own ORACLE instance with an ORACLE database. A database server node (S) is a computer system which only provides server functions and therefore cannot communicate with other database servers. We speak of a database server with client function (SC) if the database server has access to additional database servers. A SC node can therefore act both as a database server for client programs and as a client which accesses other database servers, so a SC node will always be created where the database server has to pass on a task to another database server, for example reading a table which is not present on its own database. In this case, for the purposes of the second server which receives the SQL statement, the first database server is acting as a client system.

A network node can therefore carry out a number of roles in a heterogeneous network and within a heterogeneous TNS network we can distinguish a total of six different TNS node types:

- client without Navigator (C)
- client with Navigator (CN)
- MultiProtocol Interchange (I)
- Database Server (S)
- Database Server/Client without Navigator (SC)
- Database Server/Client with Navigator (SCN)

Consequently we can add the following node types to those which we already know from homogeneous network environments:

- client with Navigator function (CN)
- MultiProtocol Interchange (I)
- Database Server/Client with Navigator function (SCN)

The task of the Oracle Navigator is to determine what will be the best (most cost-effective) path for a multi-network connection using a number of MPIs. The Navigator function can also be installed on client nodes (these then become CN node types) where its function is to determine the best MPI to use for a multi-network connection; the subsequent path optimization being carried out by the MPI itself. This is always an advantage in cases where a client node needs access to several database servers on different networks and is able to choose between several MPIs. The same applies to a database server/client with the Navigator function; here too the database server's Navigator carries out the initial task of determining the destination address when it is necessary to access more than one network via an MPI.

Figure 13.10 illustrates the individual TNS node types for a homogeneous and a heterogeneous configuration. Perhaps the most important task of all for someone planning a TNS network is to decide which roles a specific network node should fulfil within a TNS network. This decision determines which software components and which TNS data will have to be made available at a later stage.

TNS node type	Abbr	Homogeneous network	Heterogeneous network
Client without Navigator	C	✓	✓
Client with Navigator	CN	–	✓
Oracle MultiProtocol Interchange	I	–	✓
Database Server	S	✓	✓
Database Server/Client without Oracle Navigator	SC	✓	✓
Database Server/Client with Oracle Navigator	SCN	–	✓

Figure 13.10 TNS node types in homogeneous and heterogeneous networks

13.4 Description of an ORACLE TNS network

In order to carry out their respective tasks within a TNS network, the various software components and the nodes must have access to a common data pool in which all necessary information about the TNS network is stored. ORACLE therefore provides a total of three configuration files and one MPI parameter file which between them comprehensively describe all aspects of a TNS network. These files are:

- TNSNAMES.ORA
  This file describes all the computer nodes and their ORACLE databases, which can be accessed by a client node (C, CN, SC, SCN) and defines a TNS alias name which is unique in the TNS network. This TNS alias name addresses exactly one ORACLE instance on one network node in any network community.

- TNSNET.ORA
  This describes a TNS network in terms of its networks and MPIs together with the costs of each network community, for example in terms of transfer speed. This file is used by the Navigator to determine the best connection paths.
- TNSNAV.ORA
  This file describes a Navigator with all Navigator addresses and all networks.
- INTCHG.ORA
  This file describes an Oracle MPI and is used when it is being configured.

Network type	Node type	TNSNAMES.ORA	TNSNET.ORA	TNSNAV.ORA	INTCHG.ORA
Homogeneous network	C	✓	–	–	–
	S	–	–	–	–
	SC	✓	–	–	–
Heterogeneous network	C	✓	–	✓	–
	CN	✓	✓	✓	–
	I	–	✓	✓	✓
	S	–	–	–	–
	SC	✓	–	✓	–
	SCN	✓	✓	✓	–

Figure 13.11 The relationship between TNS node types and configuration files

Figure 13.11 shows which of these files is needed by which network node and specifies the allocation of the TNS configuration files to the various node types in homogeneous and heterogeneous configurations.

From this diagram we can see that if we are dealing with a homogeneous network environment, the only file of any real significance is TNSNAMES.ORA. For a heterogeneous network however, all four files are important, and within this configuration they can be classified as follows:

- TNSNAMES.ORA
  for all TNS nodes with client function
- TNSNET.ORA
  for all TNS node types with Navigator function
- TNSNAV.ORA
  for all node types apart from those which are exclusively database servers
- INTCHG.ORA
  for MPI node types only

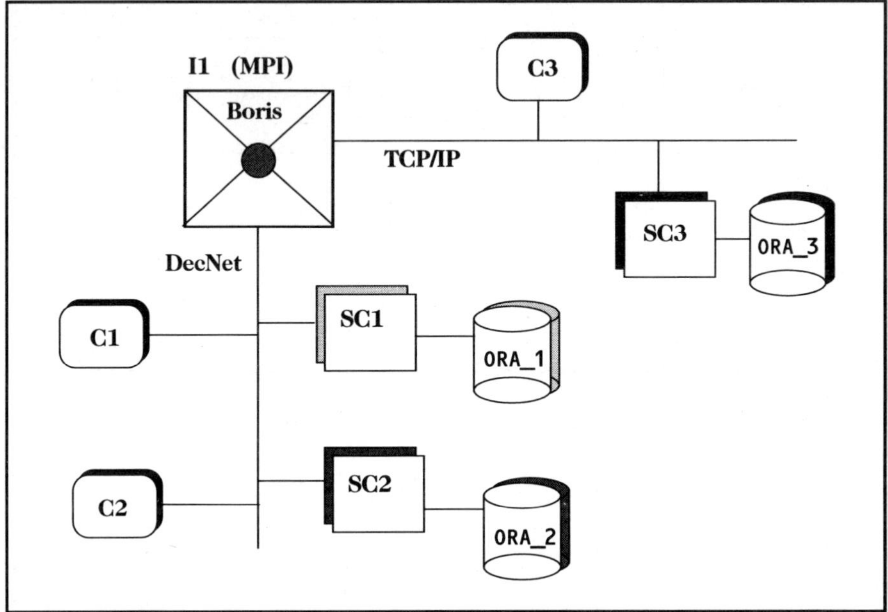

Figure 13.12 Example of a heterogeneous ORACLE TNS network

ORACLE includes a formal TNS description language which is used in the first three configuration files to describe a TNS network. Using the small TNS network shown in Figure 13.12 we shall examine how all the necessary TNS configuration files are created for the corresponding TNS nodes. In this example, the following naming convention has been chosen:

- Each node has been named in terms of its TNS function (C=Client, SC=Server/Client and I=Interchange) together with a number.
- One ORACLE instance is active on each node and these are denoted by `ORA_<node number>`, so that `ORA_1`, `ORA_2` and `ORA_3` are the system identifiers (ORACLE_SID) for the individual ORACLE instances and databases.

Having decided on the naming convention for the different components which make up our sample TNS network, we must first create the correspon-ding TNSNAMES.ORA file which, as we have already mentioned, is needed to describe all the databases with which a client application can work. This file provides the following specific information:

- the TNS alias names of the individual databases;
- the address of the database as follows:
  - the name of the community to which the database node belongs
  - the network protocol being used
  - any network specific details such as node name and port number
  - the ORACLE system identifier (SID).

This will result in a description of the network as shown in Figure 13.13.

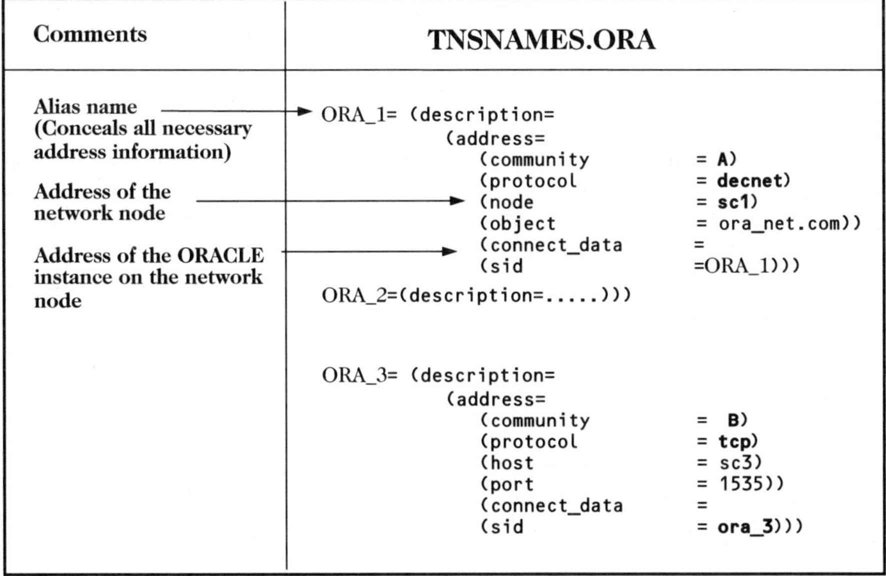

Comments
TNSNAMES.ORA
Alias name
(Conceals all necessary address information)
Address of the network node
Address of the ORACLE instance on the network node
ORA_1= (description=
(address=
(community = A)
(protocol = decnet)
(node = sc1)
(object = ora_net.com))
(connect_data =
(sid =ORA_1)))
ORA_2=(description=.....)))
ORA_3= (description=
(address=
(community = B)
(protocol = tcp)
(host = sc3)
(port = 1535))
(connect_data =
(sid = ora_3)))

Figure 13.13 Example of the configuration file TNSNAMES.ORA

The TNS alias names each refer to a specific ORACLE instance and its database and can, for example, be specified in an explicit SQL CONNECT statement. If `C1` is to be 'connected' to `SC3` the CONNECT statement would be as follows:

```
connect <user_name>§ora_3 / <password>
```

This directly connects the client program on `C1` from community `A` (DECNet) to the database server `SC3` in community `B` (TCP/IP) with a 'logical' point to point connection created by the TNS network. As we shall see later this TNS alias is also used to establish indirect connections with the aid of ORACLE database links.

The TNSNAMES.ORA file must be installed on all nodes which are to function as clients (*refer to* Figure 13.11), but it is important to realize that this file does not have to be identical on all nodes. It is also possible to define system wide or user specific TNSNAMES.ORA files, so that access to individual TNS nodes can be tightly and finely controlled.

It should also be emphasized that a valid TNS alias does not automatically allow access to any databases on that node. Entry to an ORACLE database can still only be gained with a valid username and password. This applies both for local and remote databases. The alias entries in the TNSNAMES.ORA file only provide the basis for working with the databases which are concealed by the alias names.

The example shown in Figure 13.13 for the TNSNAMES.ORA file represents the standard structure for all TNS files. It is only the key words which will differ in specific cases.

RELEASE 7.1

The next file to be defined for our network example (Figure 13.12) is the TNSNET.ORA file. This file type describes the whole TNS network in terms of its Oracle MultiProtocol Interchanges and all the individual networks with their respective protocols; in addition the file defines the costs per community. This file is identical on all TNS nodes which require it (that is, all nodes with Navigator function).

Specifically the TNSNET.ORA file defines the following items of information:

- All MultiProtocol Interchanges with:
    - the names of the Connection Managers
    - the addresses of the Listener processes
    - the details of all the communities on each Interchange
- Community costs
  The costs for all the communities of the TNS network are specified in terms of a relative scale from 1 to 100 where 1 stands for the lowest and 100 for the highest cost.

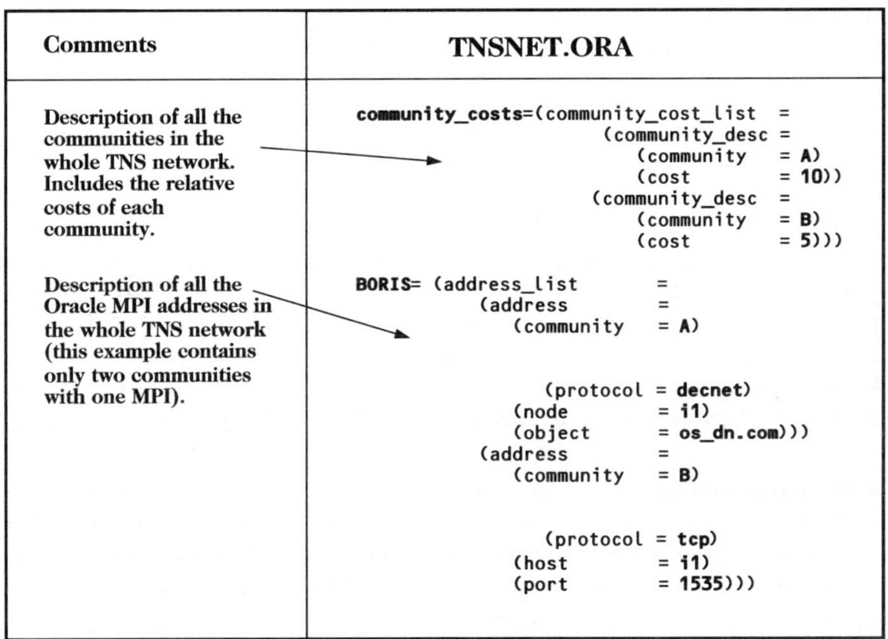

Comments	TNSNET.ORA
Description of all the communities in the whole TNS network. Includes the relative costs of each community.	`community_costs=(community_cost_list = (community_desc = (community = A) (cost = 10)) (community_desc = (community = B) (cost = 5)))`
Description of all the Oracle MPI addresses in the whole TNS network (this example contains only two communities with one MPI).	`BORIS= (address_list = (address = (community = A) (protocol = decnet) (node = i1) (object = os_dn.com))) (address = (community = B) (protocol = tcp) (host = i1) (port = 1535)))`

Figure 13.14 Example of the configuration file TNSNET.ORA

Figure 13.14 shows the TNSNET.ORA file which describes the TNS network from our example in Figure 13.12.

The third file needed for the description of a TNS network is the TNSNAV.ORA file. This file describes a Navigator whose task is to find the most cost-effective path to a destination address within the TNS network.

As we saw from Figure 13.11 the TNSNAV.ORA file is present on almost all TNS node types, the only exception being a database server which does not have any client functions. In this case we are again looking at a file which will have different characteristics on different nodes.

Within a TNS network there are two types of Navigator:

- Interchange Navigator
  This Navigator is part of an MPI and its task is to determine and set up the most cost-effective connection to a destination node in cases where there is more than one possible path. This situation of choosing a path via different communities is illustrated in Figure 13.15.

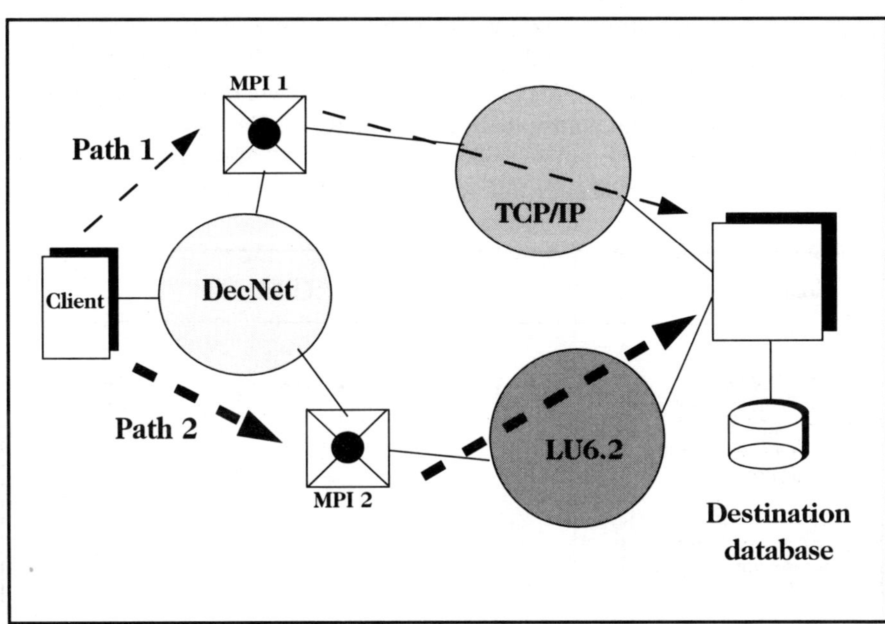

Figure 13.15 Using alternative paths to reach a destination database

- Client Navigator
  This Navigator is part of a client node (CN, SCN) and its task is to determine the best possible Interchange to carry out a required network connection.

Within the TNS nodes which have Navigator functions (I, CN, SCN) the TNSNAV.ORA file fulfils the following functions:

- It describes the Listener addresses on its own node (an Interchange usually has two Listeners, a client usually has only one Listener).
- It describes all the Navigators which are to be found on the other Interchanges of the same community and which of these can be used as backup Navigators.

RELEASE 7.1

- It describes all the communities with which the node is connected.

In addition the TNSNAV.ORA file is also required for TNS node types which have client functions but which do not have any TNS Navigator software installed (C, SC). In this case the choice of path is not left to the Navigator but is predefined in the TNSNAV.ORA file. This is the normal practice in relatively small TNS networks or in networks where there is never more than one possible path between two communities.

This is the case in our example network (Figure 13.12) where we have two communities which are linked only by one Interchange. A request from client `C1` to server `SC3` is always transmitted via Interchange '`Boris`'.

As there are no alternative paths in this example, there is no point in installing Navigators on the individual client or server systems. Figure 13.16 shows the TNSNAV.ORA file for Community **A** which will be found on all nodes (C and SC types) of the community. As there are no Navigators in this case, a list of possible Interchanges is explicitly specified (PREFERRED_CMANAGERS), in other words the file already defines the connection path to be used.

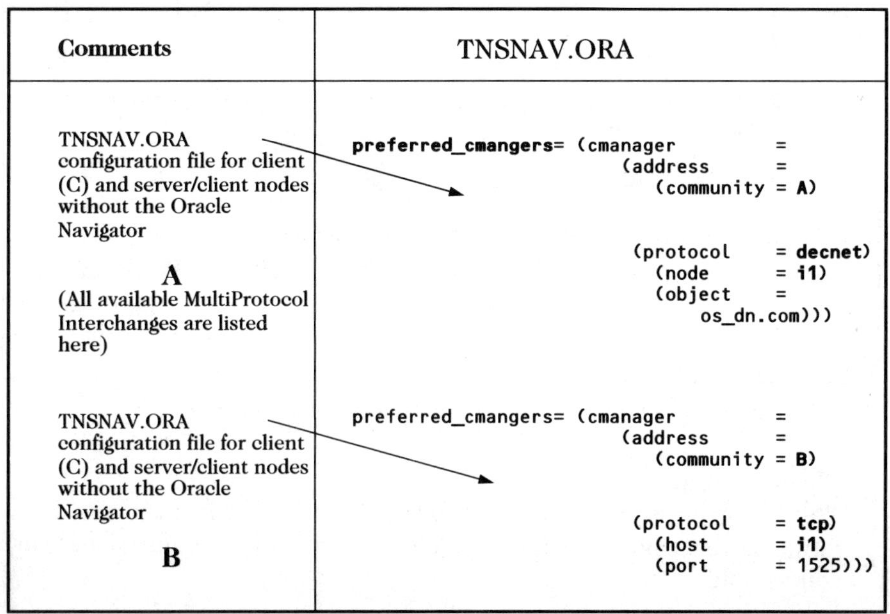

Comments
TNSNAV.ORA
TNSNAV.ORA configuration file for client (C) and server/client nodes without the Oracle Navigator
A
(All available MultiProtocol Interchanges are listed here)
preferred_cmangers= (cmanager =
(address =
(community = A)
(protocol = decnet)
(node = i1)
(object =
os_dn.com)))
TNSNAV.ORA configuration file for client (C) and server/client nodes without the Oracle Navigator
B
preferred_cmangers= (cmanager =
(address =
(community = B)
(protocol = tcp)
(host = i1)
(port = 1525)))

Figure 13.16 Example of the configuration file TNSNAV.ORA for a client without Navigator

Our small example network consists of only two communities and one Interchange. However in the case of TNS networks which contain a number of Interchanges, it is important to ensure that they are defined in the correct order as the first Interchange in a multi-network connection is always used as the *best first hop*. When a connection between two communities is being set up, the Interchange Navigator's search for the optimum connection path always starts with the first Interchange in the list.

RELEASE 7.1

This examination of the three network configuration files (TNSNAMES.ORA, TNSNET.ORA and TNSNAV.ORA) almost completes our look at how a network is defined, and at this point it is worth summarizing their specific functions. The TNSNAMES.ORA file defines the aliases of the individual databases on the different nodes and this file is then copied to all nodes which also function as client systems. The whole network including all Interchanges and network costs is described in the TNSNET.ORA file and this is used by the Navigator to choose a path. Since in our example a Navigator is installed only on the Interchange, the TNSNET.ORA file only has to be stored there. Finally we saw that in order to provide multi-network connections between Community A and Community B, the TNSNAV.ORA file must be installed on all node types with client functions. It is on this file that the preferred Interchange (to be used whenever a multi-network connection is carried out) must be specified.

However so far we have paid relatively little attention to the Oracle MultiProtocol Interchange, but as this product plays a very important role in heterogeneous TNS networks we shall discuss it in greater detail in Chapter 13.5.

13.5 The Oracle MultiProtocol Interchange

13.5.1 Introduction

The task of the Oracle MultiProtocol Interchange is to connect together two or more network communities and to provide the application system with a logical point to point connection across network boundaries, even though a number of physical point to point connections between different networks may already exist.

The three networks and two Interchanges in Figure 13.17 illustrate this type of situation; in order to establish a connection to the destination node and to create a logical point to point connection from application (Initiator) to application (destination database) three physical point to point connections are required. In this situation we can distinguish between four separate tasks that an Interchange has to carry out:

- Establishing a connection
  The Navigator must choose a connection path taking into account both costs and network availability.

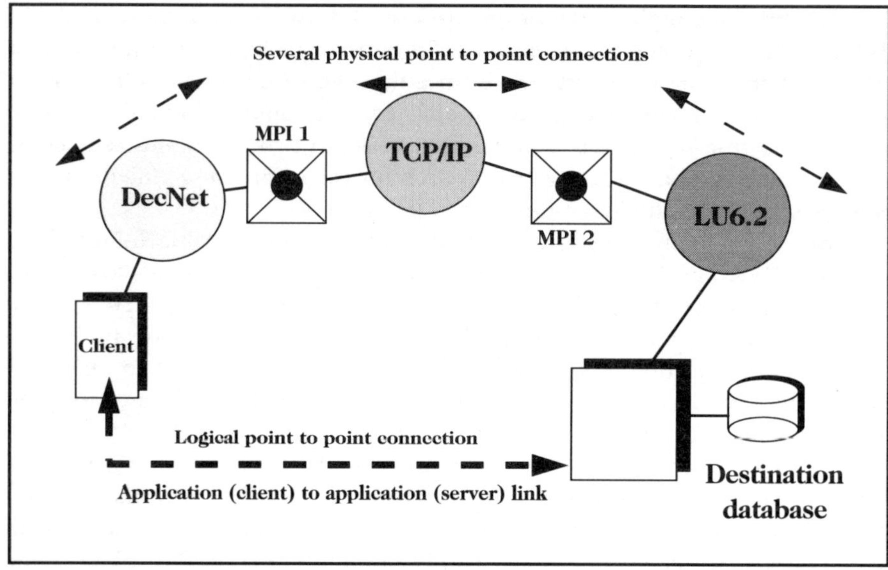

Figure 13.17 Applications oriented client/server configurations

RELEASE 7.1

- Maintaining a connection
  Once a connection has been established the Interchange has to transport data and messages in both directions and to carry out any necessary protocol conversions.
- Terminating a connection
  When a session is ended the connection must be taken down starting with the destination node and working backwards through all the Interchanges involved until the Initiator node is reached.
- Error handling
  If any error conditions occur with an existing connection the relevant information must be relayed from the Interchange to the Initiator node or destination node and the connection is then taken down.

At this point it is again worth emphasizing that the Oracle MPI is a software product based on ORACLE TNS technology, which means that within a TNS network every computer node can adopt the role of an Interchange while at the same time carrying out any other tasks assigned to it.

13.5.2 The structure of an Oracle MPI

In addition to the basic elements of any TNS application (Oracle Protocol and ORACLE TNS) an Interchange also consists of the following software components:

- a Connection Manager with a Network Listener;
- a Navigator;
- a number of data pumps, each one of which is able to handle a number of connections.

RELEASE 7.1

In addition to these software components the Interchange also requires a description of the whole TNS network which also provides the information required by the Navigator. This description is supplied by the TNS configuration files TNSNET.ORA, TNSNAV.ORA and the Interchange configuration file INTCHG.ORA (*refer also to* Figure 13.11).

Figure 13.18 illustrates the structure of an Interchange. In order to understand how the individual components function both individually and together, we shall look at how a connection is established.

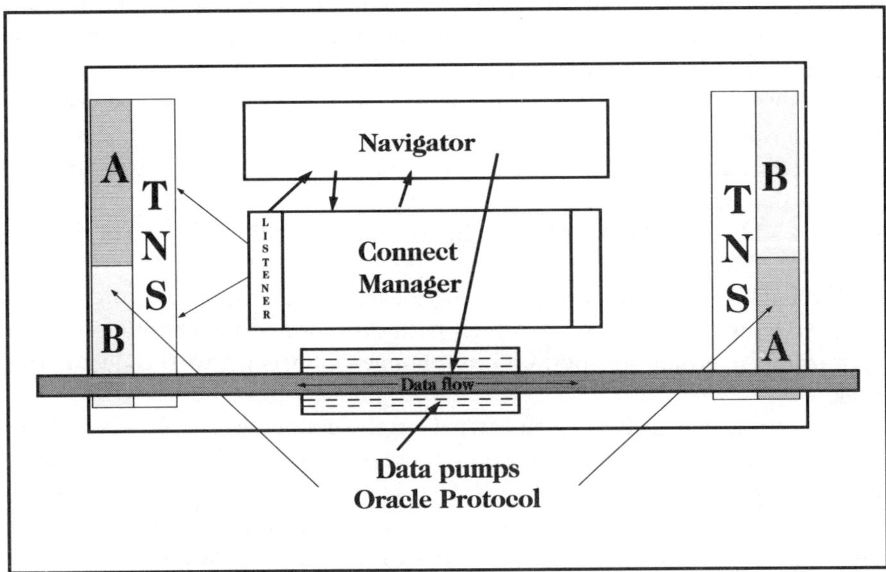

Figure 13.18 An Oracle MultiProtocol Interchange

An Interchange must always be used to make a connection when the database server (destination node) is located in a different network from the client node (Initiator). In order to determine whether this is in fact the case the TNS layer of the client makes use of the two files TNSNAMES.ORA and TNSNAV.ORA; the destination network is determined from the alias of the destination node as defined in the TNSNAMES.ORA file and the network of the client node is read from the TNSNAV.ORA file. If these two networks (Initiator network, destination network) are different then an Interchange must be used, and this Interchange is determined as follows:

- If the client is on a CN node, that is a client with a Navigator function, the client Navigator determines the best possible Interchange for the connection. CN node types should always be set up when a client with several Interchanges can establish connections to several networks. The same applies to SCN types.

RELEASE 7.1

- If the client is on a C node, that is a client without a Navigator function, the sequence of Interchanges specified in the TNSNAV.ORA file decides which Interchange will be used for the connection request. The first Interchange specified under the keyword PREFERRED_CMANAGERS is always the first Interchange to be used.

Once the Interchange has been determined a connection request is sent to it. The Interchange's Listener process detects this request and forwards it with all parameters to the Interchange's Navigator.

The first operation carried out by the Interchange's Navigator is to determine whether it can provide the optimum Interchange for the connection request or whether a better alternative is available. This is particularly important for all requests from clients without Navigators (C and SC nodes) which always select the first Interchange on the PREFERRED_CMANAGERS list, regardless of the actual destination. If the Navigator establishes that another Interchange can provide a more cost-effective path for the connection request then the request is returned by the Connection Manager to the client with the address of the better Interchange. (This is fully dealt with at the TNS level and remains concealed from the application program).

If the connection request is already located on the optimum Interchange the Navigator then determines which path this connection should next take, forwarding it either to another Interchange or directly to the destination node.

After these checks have been carried out the connection request is assigned to a data pump and the Connection Manager initiates the link to the next connection point via the TNS and Oracle Protocol layers. If for whatever reason this connection is not possible then the Navigator works out an alternative path (Re-Navigation). If there is no other possible path for this connection then the operation is aborted with an error message. If the Navigator detects that there is a problem on a given path then it is excluded from the available paths for a specified period of time (TIMEOUT_INTERVAL).

Once a complete connection has been established (that is, from the client to the database server) then all the Navigators involved (both in the Interchanges and in the CN and SCN nodes) have completed their tasks and are no longer required. The Interchanges themselves only have the task of carrying the data streams between the client and server nodes. The task of the Connection Manager at this time is to coordinate and control all activity on the connection such as sending messages or data between the client and the server, carrying out new connection or disconnection requests and converting the data packets according to the protocols being used.

Having seen how an Oracle MultiProtocol Interchange works we can now look at the parameter file INTCHG.ORA, which is used to configure an Interchange and which contains all relevant parameters and reference values. The file includes the following data:

RELEASE 7.1

- the name of the Interchange;
- the address of the Interchange Listener Process;
- the TIMEOUT_INTERVAL for a path on which an error is detected;
- the configuration of the data pumps
  - the number of data pumps
  - the number of connections per data pump (PUMP_CONNECTIONS)
  - the size of a data pump's buffers (PUMP_BUFFERS)
  - the number of minutes after which a pump without a connection automatically switches off (PUMP_UPTIME);
- the number of minutes after which a Connection Manager will switch off an inactive connection (CONNECTION_IDLE_TIME).

13.6 Summary

An ORACLE TNS network provides a carrier system that is independent of networks, protocols and topology and which can be used by applications systems including client and database server applications.

A TNS network is made up of the following components:

- the description of the TNS node types involved
  - in the case of a homogeneous network one or more of the three TNS node types C, S or SC
  - in the case of a heterogeneous network one or more of the six TNS node types C, CN, I, S, SC or SCN
- the required ORACLE software
  - SQL*Net
  - ORACLE TNS components
  - Oracle Protocol
  - Oracle MultiProtocol Interchange (MPI)
  - Oracle Navigator
- the corresponding TNS configuration files
  - TNSNAMES.ORA
  - TNSNET.ORA
  - TNSNAV.ORA
  - INTCHG.ORA

In order to set up a TNS network correctly, it is therefore essential to first define the node types which are going to be included in the network; only once this step has been carried out is it possible to know what software and which TNS configuration files are going to be needed.

14

ORACLE distributed database technology

Topics covered in this chapter

- Implementing distributed database systems
- The ORACLE database link concept
- Defining public and private database links
- Using ORACLE database links for remote database access
- Using global names to define database links
- Distributed database operations
- The ORACLE two-phase commit protocol
- Database replication with ORACLE
- Replication functions used by Oracle7
- Creating and using ORACLE snapshots

14

ORACLE distributed database technology

14.1 Introduction

In the previous chapter we were primarily concerned with the physical implementation of a complex database environment, placing particular emphasis on configuring the network, on identifying the individual communities and their interchanges and on determining individual node types.

The configuration of this type of ORACLE Transparent Network Substrate (TNS) forms the basis for the implementation of client/server applications in homogeneous and heterogeneous network systems and for creating complex databases which are distributed over a number of different computer nodes and network communities.

Having looked at how an ORACLE TNS system is defined in terms of the network structures we can now turn our attention to the actual database itself. In considering this next level we shall assume that a TNS network has been correctly implemented and we shall be looking at the basic functions

RELEASE 7.1

that the Oracle7 system provides which allow us to run several databases on different computer nodes as a single logical database.

The first essential function which our database system must provide is *location transparency*. Anyone who wants to use a distributed database should not have to be concerned with how the system's data and data structures have been distributed over the different computer nodes which make up the overall system. Similarly every user should be able to access the same database objects (tables, views, procedures and so on) on any of the nodes in a production system without having to modify the corresponding SQL statements.

In addition to location transparency a distributed database system must provide the following important functions:

- transparent read operations;
- transparent distributed read operations
  where a read operation accesses a number of database objects which are located on different databases (for example in the case of join, subquery or union operations);
- transparent distributed transactions
  where a modify operation changes a number of database objects which are located on different databases.

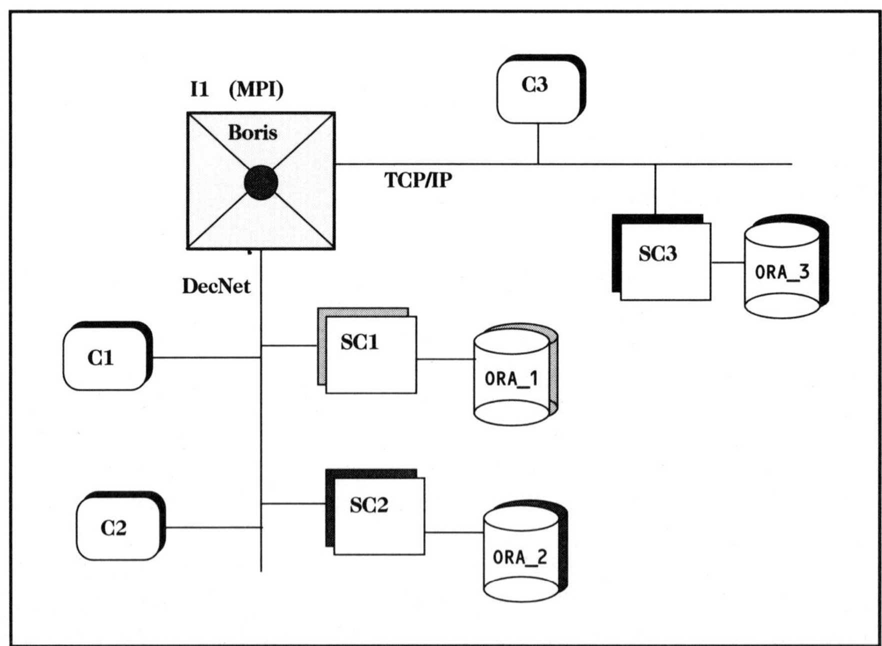

Figure 14.1 A heterogeneous ORACLE Transparent Network Substrate (TNS) network

In the case of distributed transactions it is particularly important to ensure that a programmer does not need to take any special measures to distinguish between a distributed transaction (which involves remote databases) and a non-distributed transaction (which involves only a local database). This transaction transparency must also include implicit distributed transactions which are activated by database triggers.

RELEASE 7.1

In the following sections we shall discuss in detail the database functions which Oracle7 offers for implementing distributed databases and client/server configurations. The configuration shown in Figure 14.1 will provide the basis for the examples which we will use whenever necessary to illustrate specific database functions.

14.2 The ORACLE database link concept

14.2.1 Introduction

Up to this point we have always tended to distinguish between a client/server configuration and a distributed database as though the two types of system were mutually exclusive. However at this point it is important to emphasize that this is definitely not the case. If we refer to Figure 14.1 then we can easily envisage a typical situation where client `C1` logs on to database `ORA_2` and then carries out operations which have to access both the local database and the other two databases (`ORA_1`, `ORA_3`). Here we have a typical client/server configuration which at the same time makes use of a distributed database configuration. In order to deal with this situation adequately ORACLE distinguishes between two types of connection:

- a direct connection
- an indirect connection

In a direct connection the application process connects to a database giving username and password and, at the same time, the corresponding TNS alias name for the required database. Provided that the SQL CONNECT operation is successful the application is then directly connected to the database and is correctly logged in. The TNS alias names are taken from the TNSNAMES.ORA file which we discussed in Chapter 13 and which is illustrated in the example in Figure 13.13. In principle a client can log on to all databases defined in the TNSNAMES.ORA file providing that a valid user account and password exist.

In the case of a direct connection all SQL statements generated by the client are immediately evaluated by the database with which the client program is connected (the direct database). It is completely irrelevant in this case whether or not the direct database server is located in the same community as the client program.

A SQL statement sent by the client to the (direct) database server may of course refer to database objects which are not located on the local (direct) database, in which case the SQL statement must be transmitted to the database which contains the required object(s). The direct database server establishes where the required database objects are located from information in its data dictionary, and having determined the destination address, the direct server establishes a connection to the destination (indirect) database server which it accesses as a client (SC) node.

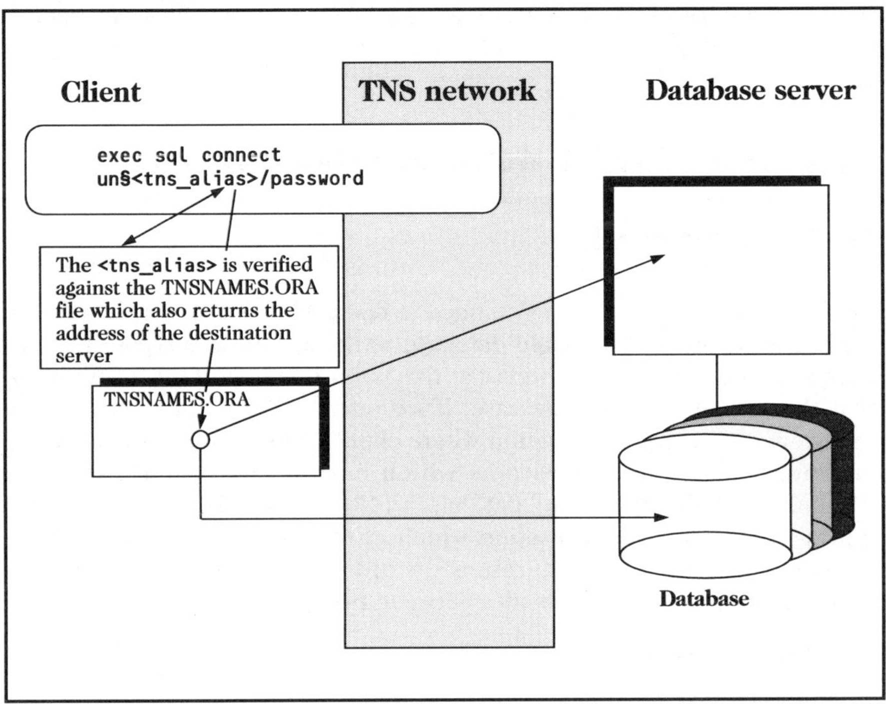

Figure 14.2 Establishing a direct connection with the SQL CONNECT command

14.2.2 Database links without global names

Whereas direct connections are carried out by means of the SQL CONNECT command, indirect connections are based on ORACLE *database links*.

Database links define a schema within a database on any node of a TNS network. They are database objects which are created with the CREATE DATABASE LINK command and we can distinguish between two types of database link:

- database links without global names,
- database links with global names.

The first of these methods, in which any name can be used for database links, is that which was used by ORACLE Version 6. In Oracle7 on the other hand the option of using global names is also available, in which case the database link name must conform to certain naming conventions and must have the same name as the database to which it connects. When global names are being used the name of each database link is checked by the system. In order to guarantee the validity and uniqueness of each database link name, it is a good idea to use global database link names within a production system. Selecting what kind of database link is to be used can be made in one of the following ways:

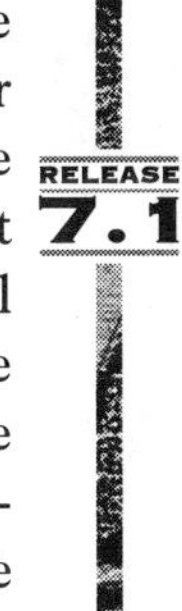

- by setting the corresponding database parameter in the INIT.ORA file for an ORACLE instance

```
global_name=true/false
```

- by changing an ORACLE instance with the ALTER SYSTEM statement

```
alter system set global_name=true/false
```

- by redefining a user session with the ALTER SESSION statement

```
alter session set global_name=true/false
```

We shall take a detailed look at database links with global names in Section 14.2.4.

A database link which is defined in the absence of any global naming convention can have any name and is created with the CREATE DATABASE LINK command. Its form is as follows:

```
create database link <db_link_name>
connect to <user_name> identified by <password>
using <tns_alias>
```

The effect of this statement is to create a database link in the local data dictionary which can then be used in SQL statements following the database object name (tables, view, procedure and so on), as in the following example:

```
select *
from tab_1§<db_link_name>
```

From this statement we can see that table **tab_1** is not in the local database but in the database which is referenced with **<db_link_name>**. The local database server analyses the information behind the database link and then forms the appropriate connection to that database. Figure 14.3 illustrates again the relationship between a database link as used within a SQL statement, a database link as path indicator and the corresponding entry in the TNSNAMES.ORA file. What actually happens with the CREATE DATABASE LINK statement is that the database link string is resolved and the resulting information is stored in the data dictionary.

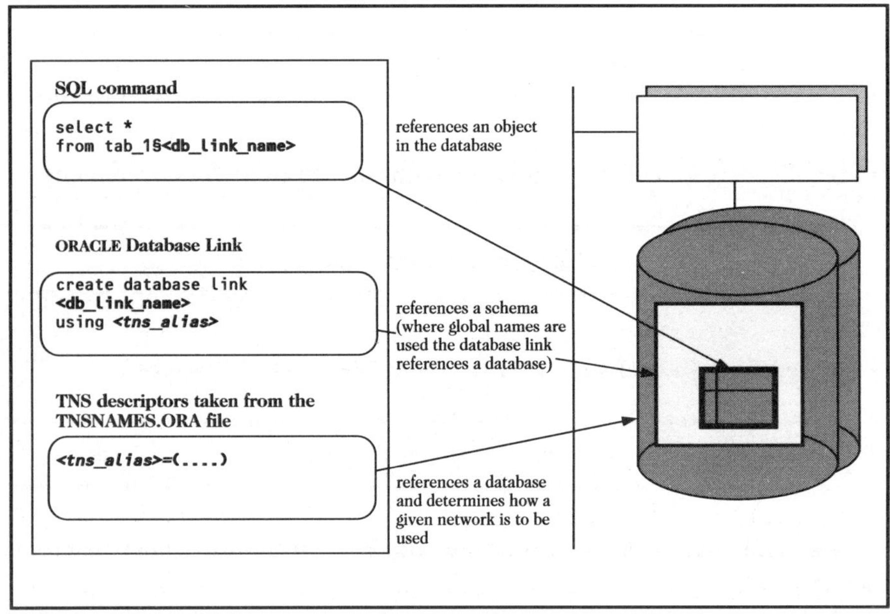

Figure 14.3 Accessing remote databases with ORACLE database links

It is worth noting the hierarchical dependencies which exist here. The TNS alias name from the TNSNAMES.ORA file references a particular database on a specific node, the database link addresses a particular schema in this database and the SQL statement addresses a particular object within the schema.

In order not to have to specify the database link in every SQL statement which accesses a remote database object, or to hide the link from the system's users, it is standard practice to create views or synonyms which can be referenced as though the objects were on the local database, as in the following example:

```
create view tab_1 as
select * from tab_1§<db_link_name>
```

The user of the local database server therefore only needs to know the name of the local view in order to carry out all standard operations on this database object, for example:

```
update tab_1
set a = a + 10
where b like 'Europe%';
```

When this statement is executed the following sequence of actions is carried out:

- The view definition for `tab_1` is resolved by the local database server with the aid of its data dictionary.
- The local server establishes that the view conceals the database link `tab_1§<db_link_name>`. The local database server resolves the database link name and gets the TNS address of the destination computer from the TNSNAMES.ORA file.

- The local database server now has all the destination information necessary to create the connection to the remote database (destination computer, database, schema, object). If this connection has to extend across several communities the relevant Oracle MPIs and, where necessary, Oracle Navigators must also be used (*see* Chapter 13).
- Once a connection to the destination database has been successfully established the local database server sends the SQL statement.
- The destination database executes the SQL statement and informs its client, the local database server, of the outcome of the operation.
- The local database server transmits the retrieved data to its client, the application program.

Figure 14.4 shows the different levels which operate in this kind of transaction as well as the two methods of formulating a SQL statement, that is either by means of a view or synonym or by explicitly specifying the database link name.

The use of views or synonyms for remote database objects makes it possible to achieve complete location transparency since all SQL statements need only refer to the local view names; determining the location of a given database object can be left completely to the respective database server systems which can carry out the routing using the information in the data dictionary together with the structures defined in the TNS network (TNS files).

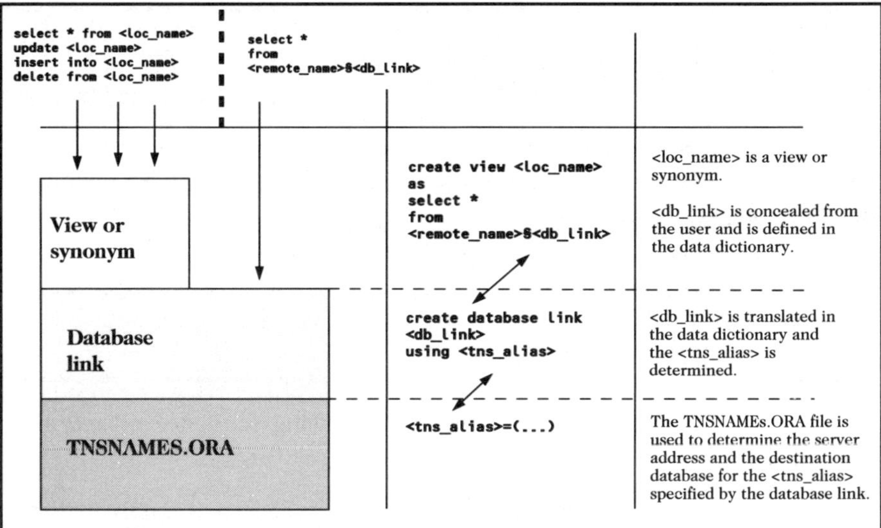

Figure 14.4 Implementing location transparency

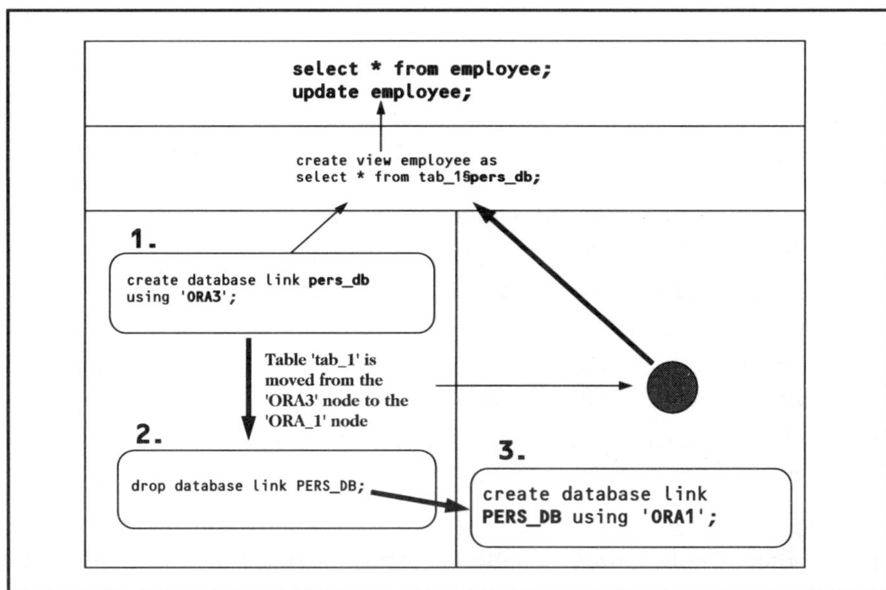

Figure 14.5 Using location transparency in SQL statements

This kind of location transparency also makes it possible to move objects between databases on different nodes without affecting any of the SQL statements which access those objects. All the database administrator has to do is to alter the corresponding database link definition to include the address of the new node or database. The SQL statements within applications programs which access the relocated database object remain completely unaffected.

This situation is shown in Figure 14.5, where table `tab_1`, which was originally created in database `ORA_3`, has now been relocated to database `ORA_1`. Once the database link `pers_db` has been redefined any existing SQL statements can run without having to be modified.

14.2.3 Using database links in practice

The concept of the database link is central to Oracle7's distributed database technology and for this reason we shall examine it in some detail. Figure 14.6 shows the CREATE DATABASE LINK statement with the four possible options it offers for creating a database link object. A basic distinction has to be made between a *public* and a *private* database link; every user who has the CREATE DATABASE LINK privilege can create a private database link which may however only be used by its creator. A public database link is available to all users of a database, who are thus given the right to access the corresponding remote database.

	Definition	Private	Public	Local user	Proxy user	Comments
1	create database link A using 'ora_3';	✓	–	✓	–	Good security Considerable administration
2	create public database AP using 'ora_3';	–	✓	✓	–	Average security Considerable administration
3	create database link B connect to <un> identified by <password> using 'ora_3';	✓	–	–	✓	Good security Minimal administration
4	create public database link BP connect to <un> identified by <password> using 'ora_3';	–	✓	–	✓	Low security Minimal administration

Figure 14.6 Advantages and disadvantages of the different types of ORACLE database link

Another aspect which has to be considered when creating database links relates to how the database referenced by a database link is to be accessed, in other words how to define the user schema for the remote user. Oracle7 provides us with two options in this case, and we can define either individual or central user accounts on the remote system.

For an individual account, the (public or private) database link is defined without explicitly specifying the CONNECT clause (*refer also to* Figure 14.6), in which case the user's (local) username and password are used for logging on to the remote database with the database link. Of course this means that an account with the same username and password combination must have been set up on the destination database, otherwise the login will be rejected.

In the case of a central or proxy account, a username and password are explicitly specified as part of the CONNECT clause when the database link is created, and this user account will always be used for anyone who logs on by means of this database link. This method allows us to define one or more user accounts on the remote database node which can be used as proxy users by any number of other users who need access to the remote database referenced in the database link.

Which of these two methods should be used depends very much on individual circumstances. Basically it is true to say that a combination of public database links and proxy user accounts allows potentially unrestricted access to a remote database as opposed to private links coupled with individual user accounts on the remote system. However the use of individual accounts in particular usually requires more administrative work on the part of the DBA, who has to ensure that the necessary user accounts are also set up on the remote database.

The third of the four possible combinations illustrated in Figure 14.6 provides a useful compromise between security requirements and administrative effort. The use of private database links limits the number of users with access to a remote database, and providing these users with a central account on the remote database reduces the administrative work involved.

This solution is also illustrated in Figure 14.7, where a proxy user account is created on the remote database server and private database links are created on the local database server. In practice of course it may be necessary to create a number of proxy accounts, each of which is allocated different object and system privileges, depending on the particular tasks which have to be carried out by the individual users who need access to the remote database.

In this example all users of database `ORA_1` who need to access database `ORA_3` via their own (private) database link can log in under the user account `ora_3_proxy`; all such users automatically receive all the privileges which the DBA has made available to the user `ora_3_proxy`.

However it is important to remember that, even when no public database links have been defined, remote database access is not limited to those users who are able to create their own database links. Remote access can also be given to users by granting them the right to carry out a view which conceals a private database link created by another user. This feature, which often proves very useful in practice, is illustrated in Figure 14.7 where `user1` creates a view `view_1` which is based on the remote table `tab_1` and on the database link `tom`. After this view has been created `user3` is granted the privileges to read it and to insert rows. The use of this view by `user3` involves the indirect use of the private database link `tom`, although this does not mean that user3 is permitted to execute a direct SQL statement with this database link.

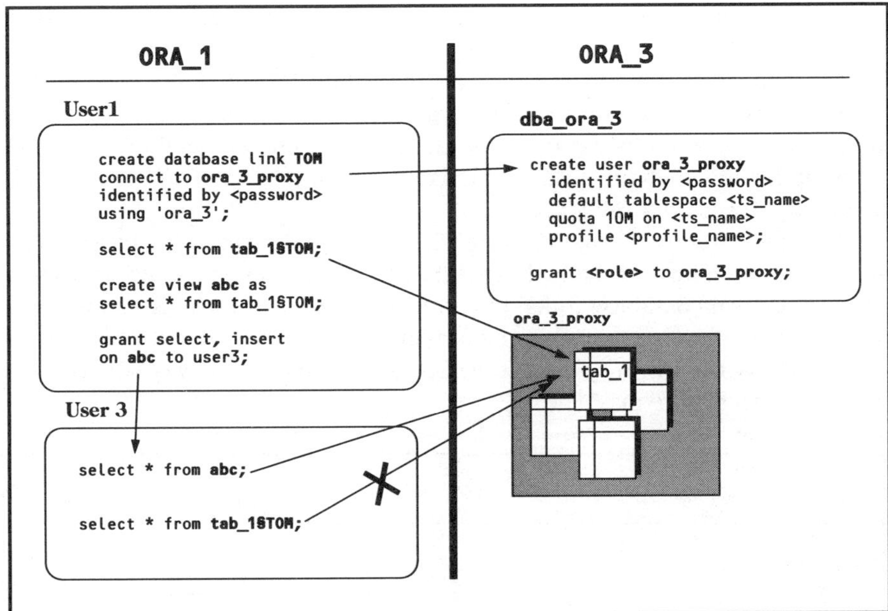

Figure 14.7 Accessing remote database objects using a database link with a central user account

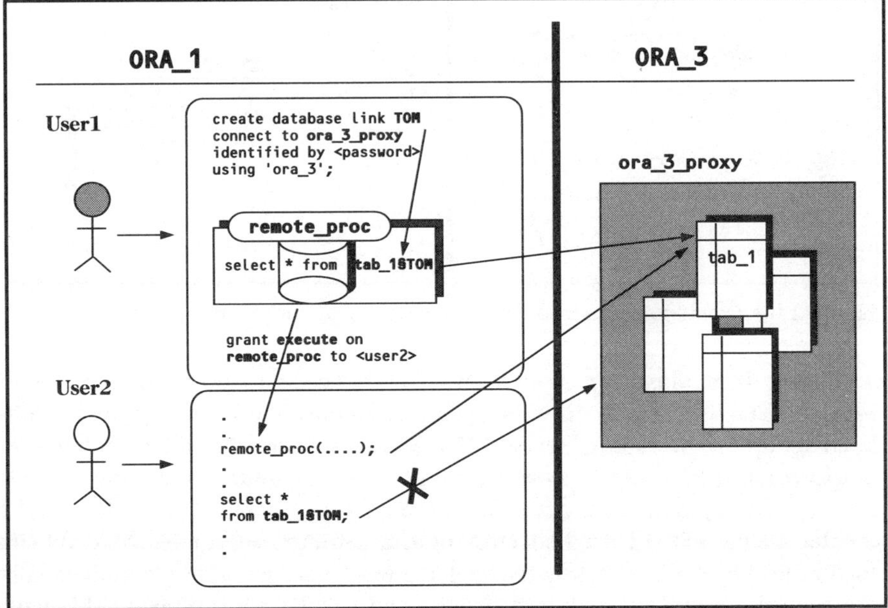

Figure 14.8 Making indirect use of a database link via a stored procedure

Another very elegant way of minimizing the administrative overhead needed for providing users with remote access while still maintaining a high level of database security is to use stored PL/SQL programs, in which case any operations on the remote database are only carried out within a PL/SQL procedure. This means that only the creator of the PL/SQL program has to be given the privileges to create a database link to the proxy user on the remote database. Any local users requiring access to the remote database need only be granted the right to execute the corresponding PL/SQL programs without having to have individual database links set up for them. This solution is illustrated in Figure 14.8.

A further method of maintaining the security of remote databases refers us back to a feature we looked at earlier, that is the use of views and synonyms to conceal database links. In terms of database security it makes more sense to use views rather than synonyms, since the use of a view can be controlled by the DBA (by using the GRANT command) in a way which is not possible with synonyms.

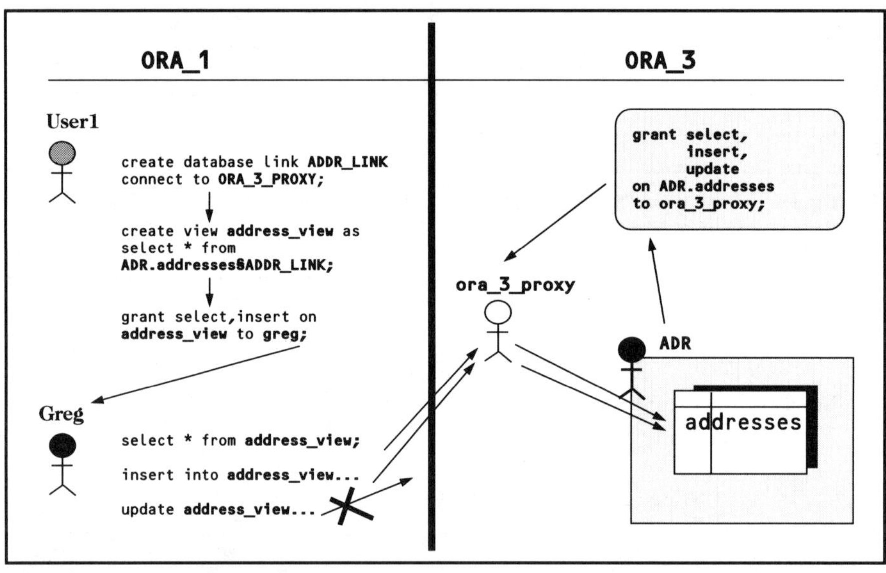

Figure 14.9 Providing enhanced database security by means of local views

Figure 14.9 illustrates how views can be used to control access to a remote database server. In this example a central user `ora_3_proxy` has been set up on the remote server (`ORA_3`), and this user is given a number of object privileges (SELECT, INSERT, UPDATE) on the `addresses` table. On the initiator (local) node a view is defined (`addresses_view`) which conceals the database link `adr_link`. The DBA of the initiator server is then able to further limit the access rights to this local view; user `greg` for example is only assigned the rights to carry out SELECT and INSERT operations on this local view, which means that this local user possesses only a subset of the access rights owned by the user **ora_3_proxy**. Any attempt by user **greg** to carry out UPDATE operations via the view **addresses_view** will be rejected by the local database server.

As we can see from the the various points we have covered in this section, the concept of database links is central to ORACLE's implementation of remote database technology. Database links allow us to both define and control access to all the objects (tables, views, procedures and so on) which are stored on remote database servers. Figure 14.10 summarizes all the SQL statements which are used in conjunction with database links.

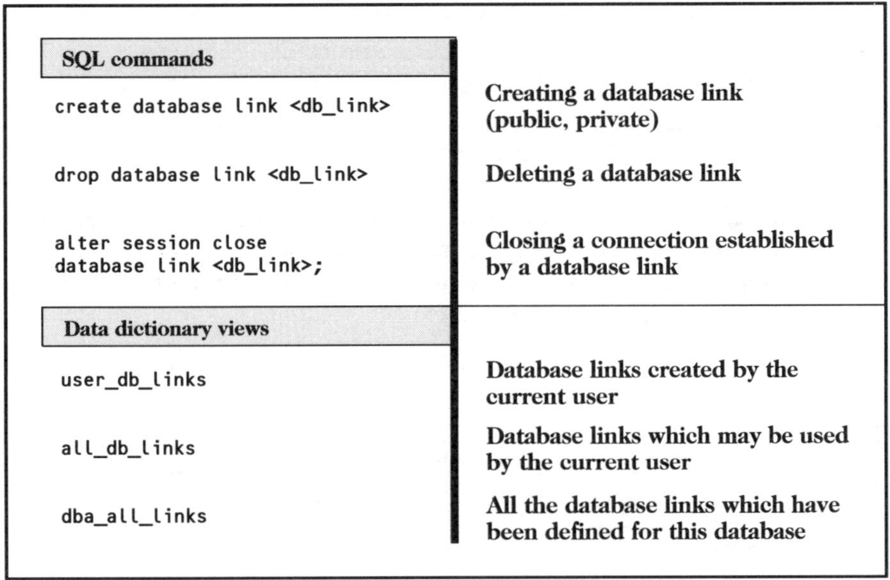

Figure 14.10 Managing and displaying database links

14.2.4 Database links with global names

Oracle7 also allows us to define database links with global names. In this case the database link name is not freely chosen but must contain the correct name of a remote database. A global database link name is made up of three components:

- The name of the remote database (maximum 8 characters). This is the DB_NAME parameter in the database's INIT.ORA file.
- The name of the network domain, with each level of the domain name being separated by a dot (maximum 119 characters). This string represents the DB_DOMAIN parameter in the database's INIT.ORA file.
- The connection name (this part however is optional).

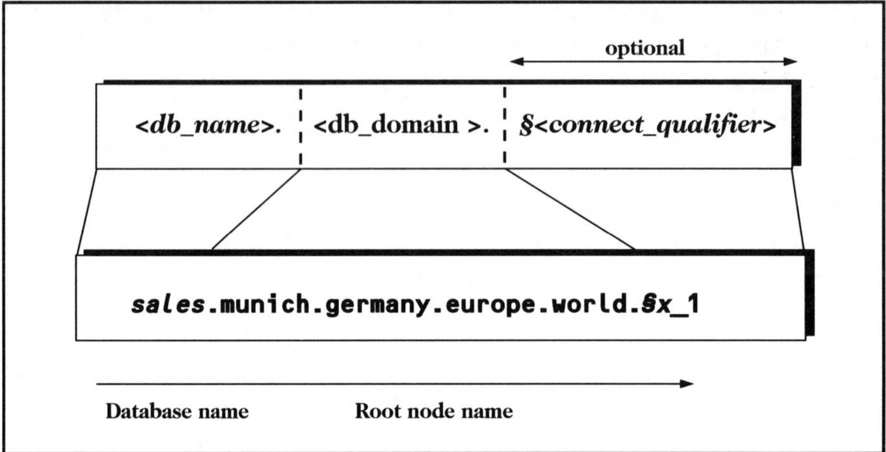

Figure 14.11 The structure of a global database link name

Because global database link names are always checked by the system to ensure that they are both valid (correct) and unique, they are especially useful when different databases are to be addressed within a large network. Figure 14.12 shows a typical large network.

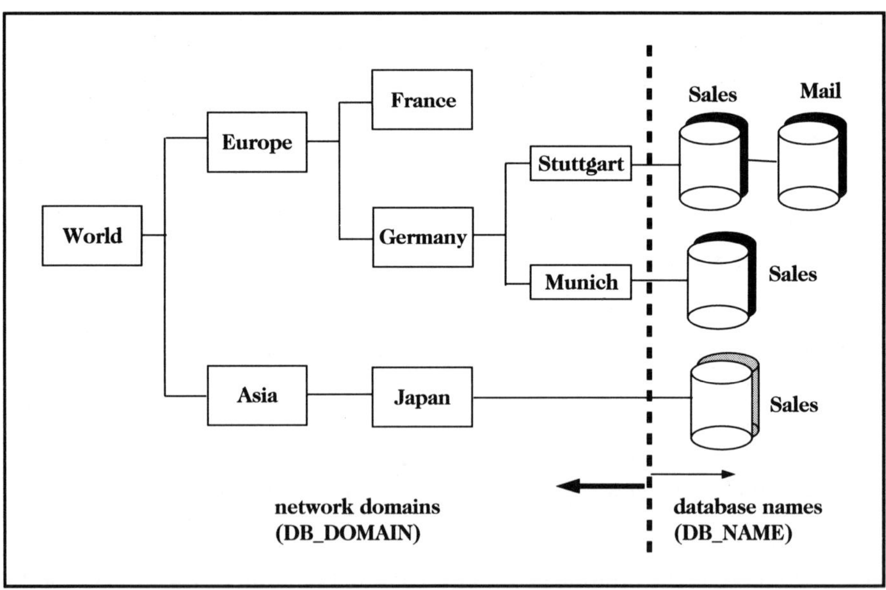

Figure 14.12 Structure of a complex database network showing the network hierarchy

In order to understand the structure of a database link it is easiest to look at how its internal structure (Figure 14.11) relates to the corresponding network (Figure 14.12); here we can see that the address of the database is given starting with the name of the database itself and continuing on to the root node of the whole network (in other words using the standard Internet notation). In this way we get the following global name for the sales database in Munich:

```
sales.munich.germany.europe.world
```

As we mentioned earlier `sales` represents the database name as defined with the INIT.ORA parameter DB_NAME, similarly the network address `munich.germany.europe.world` is defined by the INIT.ORA parameter DB_DOMAIN. We should also remember that global names can only be used if the system has been correspondingly configured in one of the following ways:

- by setting the parameter GLOBAL_NAME=TRUE in the INIT.ORA file for the ORACLE instance;
- by changing the instance with the statement

```
alter system set global_name=true
```

- by redefining a user session with the statement

```
alter session set global_name=true
```

Once a system or session has been configured in one of these three ways then only global names may be used, which means that ORACLE will reject any database links which do not correspond to this naming convention.

Figure 14.13 shows SQL statements which define and use database links based on global names. In the first stage of this example a database link to the `sales` database which is located on a node in Japan is created on the `sales` database in Munich; this database link is supplemented with the CONNECT and USING options. The following SELECT statement then uses this database link name to establish a connection to the remote `sales` database thereby making use of the TNS alias name for the network defined in the TNSNAMES.ORA file. In this case the database link name (`sales.japan.asia.world`) is checked against the DB_NAME and DB_DOMAIN parameters in the INIT.ORA file for the remote server. Only if both parts of the link name are valid will the connection be completed and the requested operation carried out, otherwise the operation is aborted with a corresponding error message.

The connection qualifier, which forms the third and optional part of a database link name, should be made use of whenever access to a remote database is possible in more than one way, for example either by using different network protocols or because a number of proxy user accounts have been set up on the remote database.

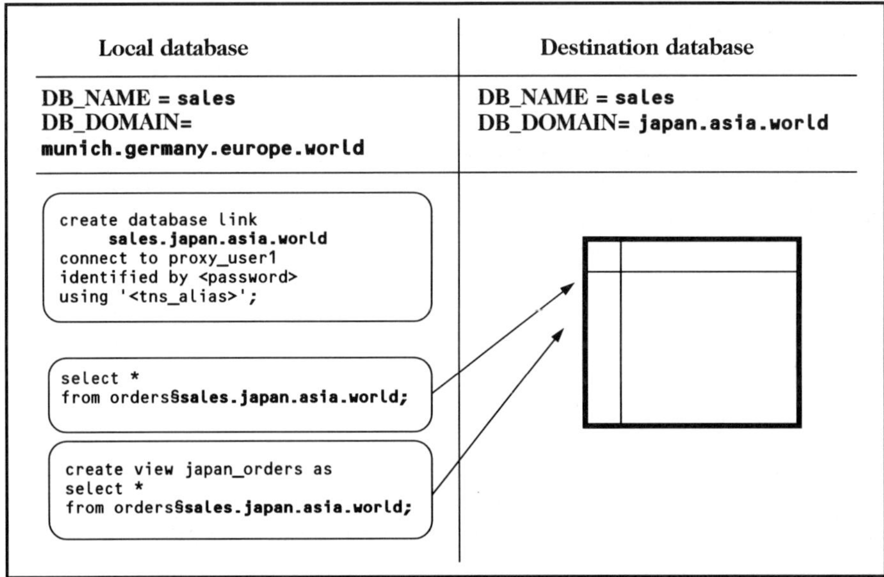
Local database
Destination database
DB_NAME = sales
DB_DOMAIN= munich.germany.europe.world
DB_NAME = sales
DB_DOMAIN= japan.asia.world
create database link
sales.japan.asia.world
connect to proxy_user1
identified by <password>
using '<tns_alias>';
select *
from orders§sales.japan.asia.world;
create view japan_orders as
select *
from orders§sales.japan.asia.world;

Figure 14.13 Creating a database link with global names

One of the useful characteristics of database links is the possibility they offer of combining private and public database link names. This feature results from the way in which ORACLE processes a SQL statement which contains a database link; when a database link is encountered ORACLE first tries to find a corresponding database link name in the user's current schema which exactly and completely matches the link in the SQL statement. If this search is unsuccessful or only partly successful (for example with no match being found for the CONNECT or USING clauses), ORACLE then looks for a corresponding public database link to fill in any of the database link components not found in the user's own schema. This means that a database link can consist of both private and public components, as is shown in the two examples in Figure 14.14.

In the first of these two examples a private database link has been defined without a CONNECT or USING clause; when a SQL statement containing this database link is being processed, the system first retrieves the corresponding private link from the user's own schema. As the database link is not yet complete at this stage, the system looks for a public link with the same name and, in our first example, it uses the public database link to provide the missing USING clause. However since neither the private nor the public database link provides a value for the CONNECT clause, the connection to the remote database is carried out using the same username and password as on the local database.

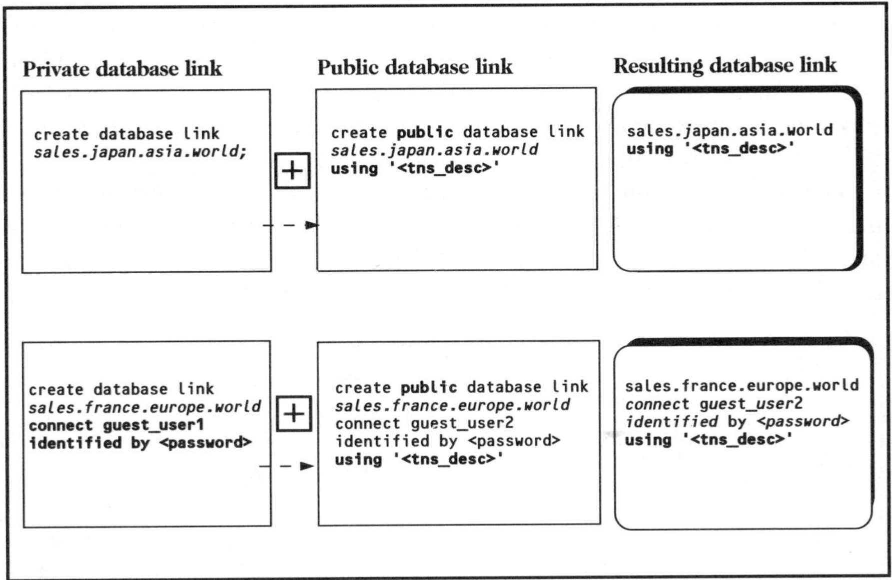

Figure 14.14 Resolving a database link using global names

In the second example the connection to the `sales` database in France is carried out using the CONNECT clause provided by the private database link and the USING clause specified for the public database link.

The flexibility which this method provides can considerably simplify the management of database links, although it is important to note that this procedure for combining private and public database links will only be used when global names have been specified for the current database or session. All the other methods for making use of database links, (which we looked at in Section 14.2.3), such as defining views or synonyms based on database links, providing proxy accounts, providing access by means of stored PL/SQL procedures and so on, can be used for database links with or without global names.

14.3 Distributed database operations

14.3.1 Introduction

ORACLE database links form the basis for the actual operations in a distributed database environment. We can distinguish between two basic operation types:

- distributed read operations
- distributed DML operations or distributed transactions

If data are to be read from one or more remote database servers we speak of a distributed read operation, regardless of whether we have a simple SELECT statement which only addresses one database object on a remote server or complex SELECT statements which reference a number of tables on different database servers.

Figure 14.15 again shows our example network which comprises two individual networks with a total of three database servers each containing one table. On each of these three database servers two database links are needed to provide an access path to the other two servers.

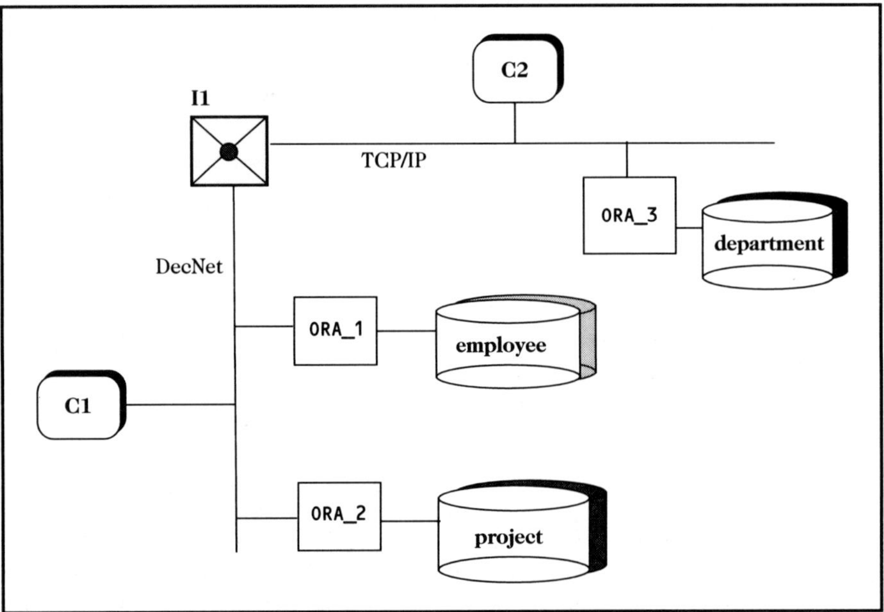

Figure 14.15 Distributed data structures within an ORACLE TNS network

An example of a typical simple distributed SELECT statement would be where the client process logs on directly to the database server and executes the following statement:

```
select *
from employee§emp
where dofbirth > '01-JAN-60'
```

This SELECT statement is parsed by the direct server ORA_2 and sent via the database link emp to the database server ORA_1 to be executed. The result of the operation is sent back from server ORA_1 to the direct database server ORA_2 which in turn makes the results available to the client process. In terms of this process it makes no difference whether the destination database is located in the same community as the direct server or not. In terms of the user process the sequence of events would be identical even if the destination database were on a different network, as in the following statement:

```
select *
from department§dept
where dept_loc = 'Boston'
```

In this case the direct database server again uses the database link to determine the address of the destination server from the data dictionary and sends the SQL statement to the destination server in community B. The connect occurs via the Oracle MPI and the other associated software components described in Chapter 13.

We refer to a complex distributed SQL statement when at least two tables on two different database servers are addressed within the same SELECT statement. The following distributed join command is typical of this type of statement:

```
select e.emp_name, d.dept_name
from employee§emp e, department§dept d
where emp_deptno = dept_no
and emp_name like 'GR%'
and dept_name like 'DP%';
```

The direct server ORA_2 parses this SELECT statement and establishes that neither of the two tables defined in the FROM clause is located on the local database. The analysis of the two database links returns the relevant destination addresses of the remote servers, so that the direct database server has to divide the SQL statement into two individual statements and to send these to the corresponding destination servers where they can be executed. Thus it is the direct server which is responsible for deciding how a complex SQL statement is to be divided and where the join operation is to be carried out; in order to make this decision the direct server is able to access the table statistics for all remote database objects.

It is important to remember that although all these examples use explicit database links (for example, employee§emp), in practice these links should be concealed from the users by defining appropriate views or synonyms, thus providing complete location transparency. The database links are included in our examples simply in order to show how they operate in a distributed ORACLE system.

The ability to carry out transparent distributed read operations was however already provided by Versions 6 and 5 of the ORACLE RDBMS; it is the possibility of carrying out distributed modify operations or transactions (INSERT, UPDATE, DELETE) which is one of the really new features offered by Oracle7.

As we have seen in earlier chapters, the integrity of all the changes to the data in an ORACLE database is ensured by the use of the transaction concept. However this means that in order to carry out a SQL statement which modifies data in a distributed system, the underlying transaction mechanism must be extended to take account of the specific requirements of a distributed database environment. For this reason Oracle7 distinguishes between three types of transaction:

- Local transactions
  Local transactions involve changes only to those tables which are located on the direct (local) server. This type of transaction, which does not require database links, is also encountered in non-distributed systems.
- Remote transactions
  Remote transactions involve changes to tables which are located on one and *only* one remote database server. The remote tables are accessed by means of database links.
- Distributed transactions
  Distributed transactions involve changes to tables which are located on a number of database servers. Remote tables are accessed by means of database links.

However it is not necessary for a programmer or user to know which of these three transaction types is carried out when a particular SQL statement is executed. We can distinguish between these three types in order to better understand how Oracle7 works in a distributed database environment, but for the ORACLE user it is neither necessary nor even possible to specify what kind of transaction is going to be carried out. This decision can be left entirely to the Oracle7 Server.

By providing complete transparency of both location and transaction type, Oracle7 fulfils two of the most important requirements for the effective and simple use of distributed databases. Tables can be moved between databases without any changes being necessary in the SQL programs which access them, and whenever necessary the server will change a local transaction to a remote or distributed one. In Chapter 4 we examined ORACLE's transaction strategy mainly in terms of carrying out local transactions, but now we will extend our examination to cover how Oracle7 deals with the other two transaction types, that is, remote and distributed transactions.

As we have already mentioned a remote transaction takes place when all the data changed by a given command or process are located on one remote database which is accessed by means of a corresponding database link. In this case the direct server plays no part in carrying out the actual transaction, its only function is to transmit all necessary data to the remote server. As for the remote server, it only needs to process the transaction as though it were a local one; any errors which can occur at any stage of the processing (that is, with the client system, the remote or local servers or the network itself) can already be dealt with by the corresponding ORACLE system components which we covered earlier in this book.

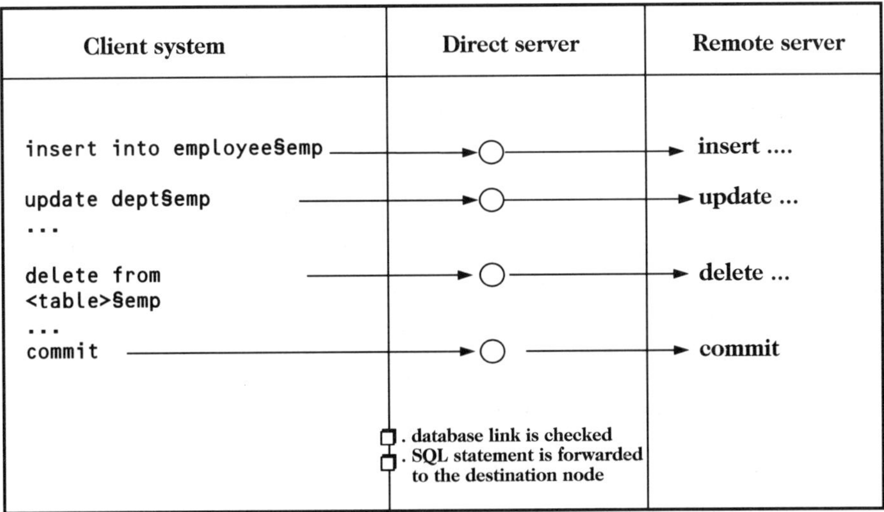

Figure 14.16 Processing a remote transaction

However if we turn to the problem of carrying out distributed transactions, where a single transaction involves changes to the data on a number of databases which are themselves located on different nodes, it soon becomes clear that this type of operation places much greater demands on a database system than 'traditional' transaction types. The reason for this is very simple; if we are to adhere to our transaction concept then we have to find a way of ensuring that all the changes specified within one distributed transaction are going to be carried out either in full (that is, on *all* the databases concerned) or not at all (that is, on none of these databases).

A simple example (*see* Figure 14.17) will serve to illustrate the problems involved in processing distributed transactions; here we have an applications process which generates a transaction to change data on two servers `ORA_2` and `ORA_3`. The client process successfully completes its processing, which means that the changes need to be committed on both database servers. However if in the meantime one of the two servers crashes, how is the system to deal with this situation? When the crashed server restarts the aborted transaction will automatically be rolled back, thus causing inconsistencies in the data on the two servers. It is precisely in order to meet the special requirements of distributed transaction processing that Oracle7 has developed the mechanism of the *two-phase commit*, and in the next sections we shall take a close look at this special feature.

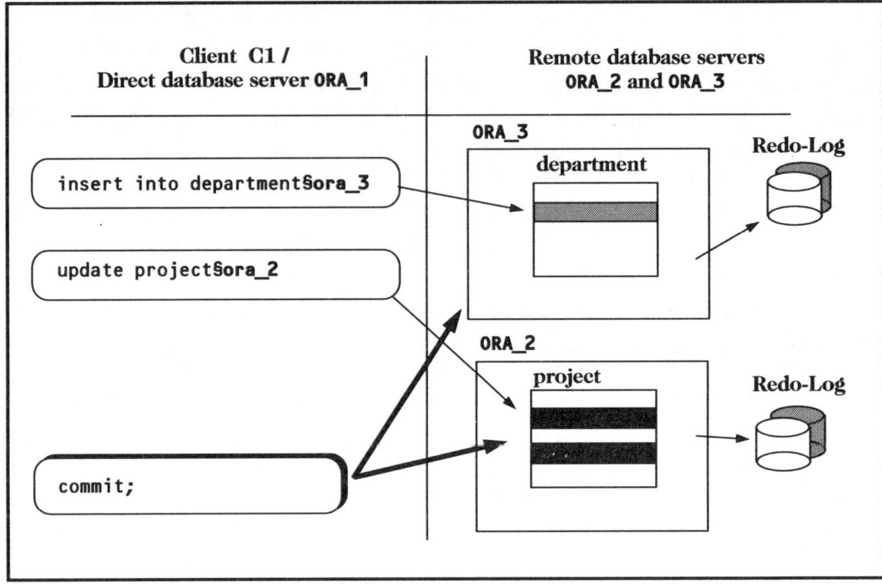

Figure 14.17 Carrying out a distributed transaction

RELEASE 7.1

14.3.2 The two-phase commit mechanism

As we have just seen the (relatively) simple transaction protocol which is perfectly adequate for local and remote transactions is unable to deal with distributed transactions. However the two-phase commit mechanism is able to process distributed transactions by anticipating all the possible error conditions which could occur in the database servers or network components concerned, thereby ensuring secure and consistent transaction processing.

Looking again at the above example we can see that the inconsistencies in that transaction were caused by a non-reversible action (COMMIT) being carried out on server ORA_3 without taking any account of the status of ORA_2, the other server involved in the transaction. The two-phase commit addresses this problem by dividing the commit process of a distributed transaction into two phases:

- the Prepare phase
- the Commit phase

In the Prepare phase all database servers participating in the distributed transaction are 'questioned' about their current condition and the status of their portion of the transaction. If the respective portion is present on the database server then it is 'prepared', which means that it is put into a permanent state which can only be completed by the two-phase commit mechanism issuing a COMMIT or ROLLBACK command. Once a local portion of a transaction is in the prepared state it is able to survive a server failure and the subsequent instance recovery, so that all transaction portions which are in the Prepare phase when a server crashes will still be in that phase when the ORACLE database is opened again.

RELEASE 7.1

The second phase of the two-phase commit, the Commit phase, will only take place if all the local portions of the distributed transaction go into the prepared state. If not all of the participating servers are able to report a successful transition to the prepared state then the distributed transaction is rolled back on all the nodes involved. Figure 14.18 illustrates the basic sequence.

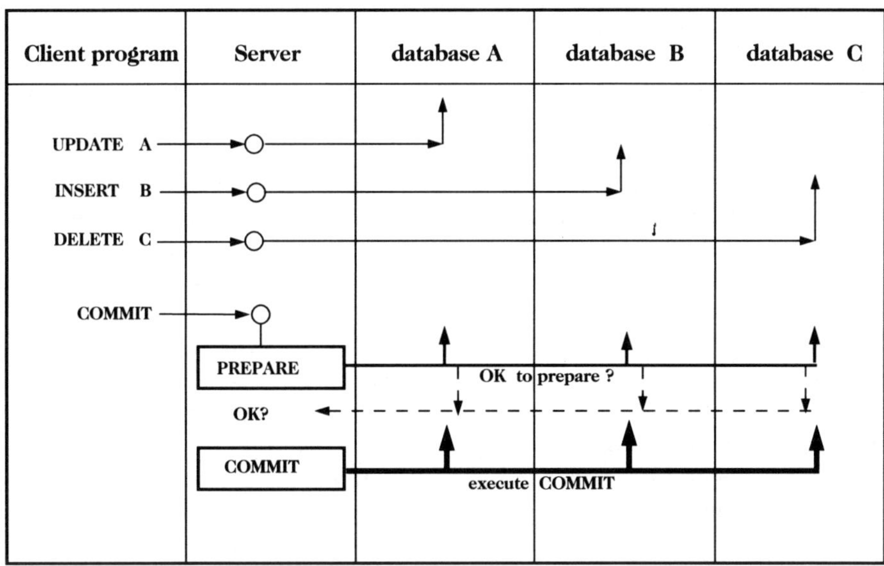

Figure 14.18 Sequence of actions in the two-phase commit mechanism

It is important to emphasize that ORACLE provides complete transparency with regard to the question of when the two-phase commit mechanism is to be activated; in each case it is the direct ORACLE Server which decides whether a simple commit or the two-phase commit mechanism should be used, so that no additional work is required to implement or run an applications program which might have to carry out distributed transactions.

RELEASE 7.1

Having considered the basic functioning of the two-phase commit mechanism we shall now take a closer look at how it has been implemented by ORACLE.

In order to carry out a two-phase commit successfully the participating database servers have to take on certain tasks, so that within the context of a two-phase commit operation we can distinguish between the following types of database server:

- the global coordinator
- the prepare server
- the commit point site
- the local coordinator

The database server at which a distributed transaction is generated (that is, to which the application is directly connected) always assumes the function of *global coordinator* for that transaction. The global coordinator decides whether a two-phase commit has to be used, initiates the Prepare phase and gathers all the 'prepared' messages from the participating database servers; it therefore has overall responsibility for controlling the two-phase commit operation. With one exception (the commit point site) all servers whose databases are modified as a result of a distributed transaction are referred to as *prepare servers*, since the first phase of the two-phase commit involves putting the portions of the transaction to be carried out on those servers into the 'prepared' state.

In terms of the two-phase commit as implemented by ORACLE one of the database servers involved is always assigned the role of the *commit point site*. This database server determines the outcome of a distributed transaction and is the only one not involved in the Prepare phase. When the global coordinator has received the 'prepared' reports from all the prepare servers, the request to commit the transaction is first sent to the commit point site. It is the result of this first commit operation which determines whether the global coordinator will commit or roll back the distributed transaction on all the other (prepare) servers involved in the transaction.

Thus if the commit operation is successful on the commit point site, the global coordinator sends a request to all the prepare servers to commit their portion of the transaction (at this stage still only in the prepared state). If on the other hand the commit point site cannot carry out the commit request, then all the prepare servers are instructed to roll back the prepared transaction.

It is important to note that the role of commit point site is not always given to the same server within an ORACLE network; whenever a distributed transaction is to be carried out, the global coordinator will select a commit point site on the basis of the COMMIT_POINT_STRENGTH parameter in the servers' respective INIT.ORA files. A value for commit point strength, which can be between 0 and 255, is defined for every ORACLE Server and whenever a distributed transaction has to be carried out the server with the highest commit point strength (from all database servers involved) will be chosen as the commit point site.

The ORACLE system documentation provides a detailed explanation of how to set the value for COMMIT_POINT_STRENGTH on a given server. A convenient rule of thumb however is that the value for this parameter should be proportional to the size of a computer, to the number of users it serves, to its

general reliability and to the importance of the data which is stored on that server (thus ensuring that key data are always updated). The greater these factors are, the higher the value which should be set for the commit point strength.

A database server which has other database servers connected to it via database links is referred to as a *local coordinator*. The local coordinator acts as a relay point and is responsible for all the database servers which are directly linked to it, so that during the Prepare phase for example, the local coordinator gathers all the 'prepared' messages from its prepare servers and reports the overall status of its part of the network either to the global coordinator or to another local coordinator, depending on the network's configuration.

Figure 14.19 shows a transaction graph with all the possible two-phase commit node types. In this example database server (1) assumes the function of the global coordinator, as the application program (client process) is directly connected to it. Database server (2) functions both as prepare server and as local coordinator since server (3) is connected to it via a database link. Database server (4) assumes the function of the commit point site and is therefore not involved in the Prepare phase since the commit point site is not addressed until the second phase of the two-phase commit operation.

Having looked at the basic two-phase commit process and at the functions of the database servers involved in a distributed transaction we shall next consider in detail how a two-phase commit is carried out.

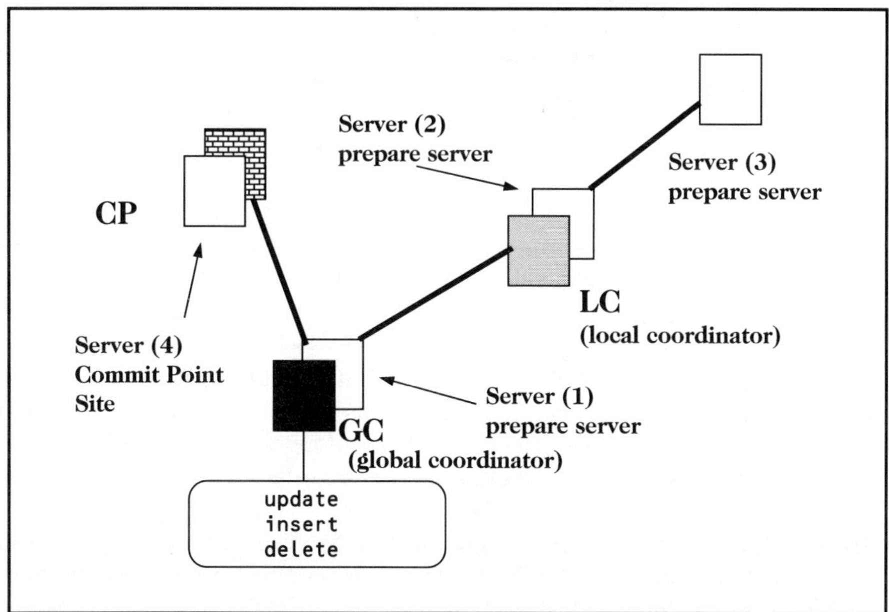

Figure 14.19 Different server roles in the two-phase commit mechanism

14.3.3 The operational stages of the two-phase commit

In order to understand the exact sequence of operations carried out by the two-phase commit mechanism we are going to follow the processing of a relatively simple distributed transaction. Figure 14.20 shows the transaction graph for the three database servers involved in this transaction, with each of the servers carrying out one of the functions necessary within this type of transaction. In this example, server (A) assumes the function of the global coordinator, as the client process is directly connected to this node; server (B) is the commit point site and server (C) is given the role of the prepare server. Figure 14.21 illustrates the exact sequence of actions involved in this distributed transaction during both phases of the two-phase commit mechanism.

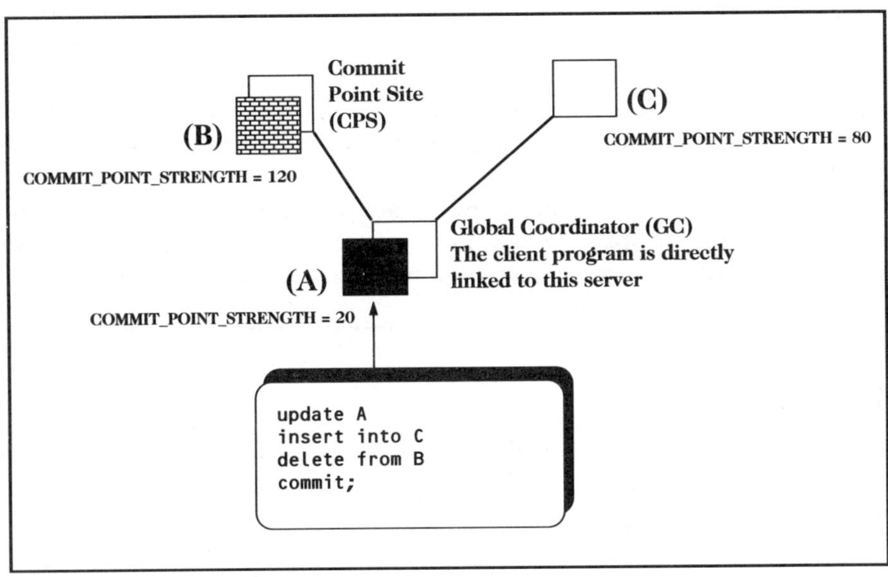

Figure 14.20 Transaction graph for a distributed transaction under Oracle7

At the beginning of the transaction only the global coordinator server is known. By using database links the actual DML operations to be carried out are communicated to the servers addressed by these links. Each server then carries out the first stages of the modify operations in the standard way; the original values of the data to be changed are recorded in a rollback segment, the new and rollback segment values are entered in the redo log buffer and so on.

As is the case with every SQL operation the application program is informed of the operation's status after each statement has been executed, which in this case means that every participating database server sends the corresponding status information back to the global coordinator. In addition to this information however, each database server reports its commit point strength to the global coordinator which uses this information to determine the commit point site. In this example server (B) is designated commit point site since it has a commit point strength of 120, compared with 20 for (A) and 80 for (C).

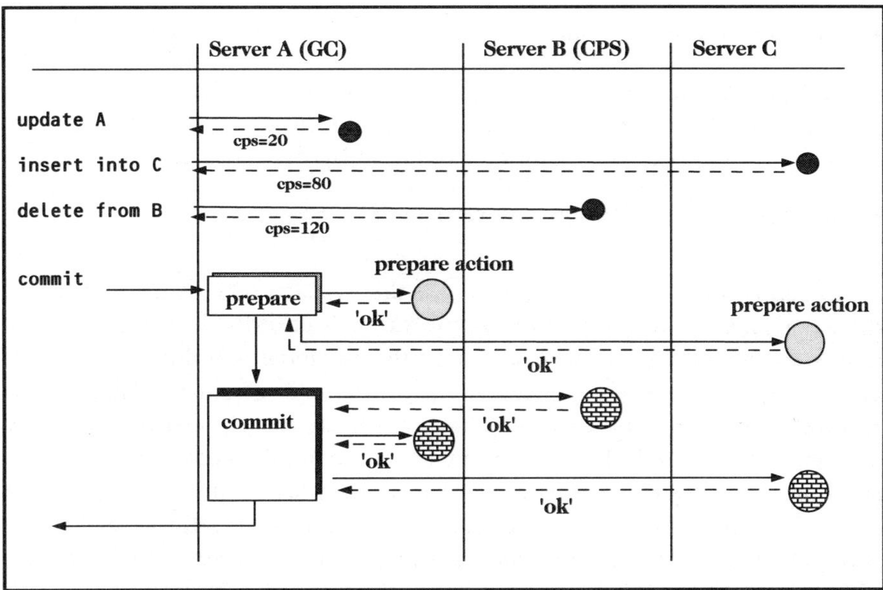

Figure 14.21 Carrying out a two-phase commit with the commit point site

In our example the DML statements from the client process are followed by the COMMIT statement. The direct server (A) recognizes that a distributed transaction has to be carried out and, acting as the global coordinator, it initiates a two-phase commit rather than the standard commit protocol.

In the first phase (the Prepare phase) all the prepare servers, that is, all the servers apart from the commit point site which have carried out modify operations within the transaction, are asked to put their portions of the transaction into the prepared state. The transition from an open to a 'prepared' transaction is carried out by entering the appropriate information in the transaction tables (rollback segment header) and at the same time writing a 'prepare' character to the redo log block. The action of writing a 'prepare' character to the redo log block activates the LGWR process which writes the current redo log block from the database cache to the redo log file; ORACLE therefore processes the prepare record in exactly the same way as it would a commit record. The successful completion of this action means that this portion of the transaction has been prepared and the prepare server informs the global coordinator accordingly.

By recording the prepared status of a transaction in the redo log file ORACLE ensures that the transaction will not lose this status in the event of a system crash and subsequent instance recovery. We have already looked at what happens to different transactions following instance recovery, but now we will look specifically at how distributed transactions are dealt with. The recovery procedure in this case works as follows:

- All open transactions not in a 'prepared' state are rolled back.
- All open transactions in a 'prepared' state are recovered, this means restoring all modifications carried out up to this point and (where necessary) locking any resources required by those transactions.
- All completed transactions are recovered.

To return now to our example, once the prepare servers have prepared their portions of the transaction in the way just described, they are able to report the completion of this operation to the global coordinator, which is awaiting their 'prepared' messages. Only when the global coordinator has received a 'prepared' or 'read-only' message from every prepare server does it initiate the second phase of the two-phase commit mechanism. A 'read-only' message is generated by a prepare server which only has to carry out read operations within the overall distributed transaction; this type of server is not involved in the second phase of the two-phase commit mechanism.

If any one of the database servers participating in this transaction returns an 'abort' message then all the other database servers involved are requested to reverse any changes made so that the whole distributed transaction can be rolled back.

However assuming that 'prepared' or 'read-only' status messages are returned by all prepare servers, the global coordinator is now able to start the second phase of the two-phase commit. This second phase is initiated by sending a request to the commit point site (which has not been involved in the Prepare phase) to commit the changes on its server. Having completed its transaction the commit point site informs the global coordinator of the outcome of this operation, with a positive outcome meaning that the distributed transaction will definitely be completed on all other nodes.

The global coordinator then asks all the other (prepare) servers to commit their portions of the transaction locally; the global coordinator is informed as soon as each portion of the transaction has been committed by the other servers and once it has received all 'commit complete' messages it advises the commit point site that the entire distributed transaction has been completed. Once the transaction has been made permanent in this way, all references to it as a distributed transaction can then be deleted, first in the commit point site and then in the global coordinator.

14.3.4 Error handling during the two-phase commit

The mechanisms of the two-phase commit have been implemented with the sole aim of guaranteeing the integrity of data in a global distributed database even if errors do occur during a distributed transaction. Figure 14.22 lists the most important types of error, the first three of which refer to distributed DML operations and the rest are errors which can occur specifically in the course of a two-phase commit operation.

Error no.	Error description
DML phase	
1	Transaction cannot be communicated to destination server
2	The client program crashes
3	The transaction encounters a DML lock on the remote server
2PC phase	
1	A prepare server crashes before the prepare operation
2	A prepare server cannot be reached by the global coordinator
3	A prepare server crashes during the prepare operation
4	A prepare server crashes after completing the prepare operation
5	The network crashes after completing the prepare operation
6	The commit point site server crashes before the commit operation
7	The commit point site server cannot be reached by the global coordinator
8	The commit point site server crashes during the commit operation
9	The commit point site server crashes after completing the commit operation
10	The network crashes after completing the commit operation

Figure 14.22 Errors which can occur during a two-phase commit operation

During the DML phase of a distributed transaction DML operations (INSERT, UPDATE, DELETE) are sent to the database servers where they are to be executed, so that the following three error types may occur during the DML phase:

- **`DML error 1`: the modify request cannot reach the destination server**
  A modify operation is requested but the destination server cannot be reached because either the network or the remote node is not available. In this case the application program receives the corresponding ORACLE error message and can take the necessary steps to rectify the situation.
- **`DML error 2`: client program crashes**
  An application program has already carried out a number of modifications on database servers within the scope of a single distributed transaction, but before these operations can be committed the client computer crashes.

The transaction in question is still present on the corresponding database servers even though the attendant client process is no longer running.

This type of error condition is handled by the TNS network system comprising the SQL*Net and ORACLE TNS software layers. ORACLE TNS and SQL*Net recognize that a TNS client connection is missing and inform the two nodes at the ends of this logical point to point connection, while at the same time taking down the actual TNS connections. For the two database servers involved there are now open transactions from a user process which does not exist. This type of error is dealt with by the PMON background processes on the two instances concerned, which will detect and then roll back the open transactions on their respective servers.

- **`DML error 3`: A modify operation encounters a DML lock on the remote server**
  Modify operations always entail requests for locks. If a modify operation encounters a DML lock on the remote server and this lock is not released within a given period of time (defined by the INIT.ORA parameter DISTRIBUTED_LOCK_TIMEOUT) the application program receives an ORACLE error message (ORA-2049) describing the situation so that it can react accordingly. This timeout period, whose default value is set at 30 seconds, can be altered if required.

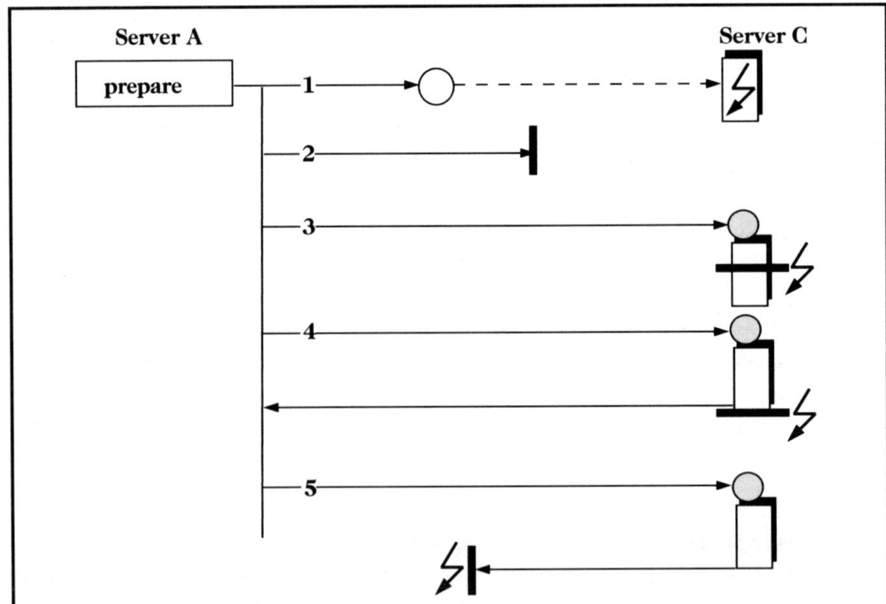

Figure 14.23a Possible error conditions which can affect a prepare server

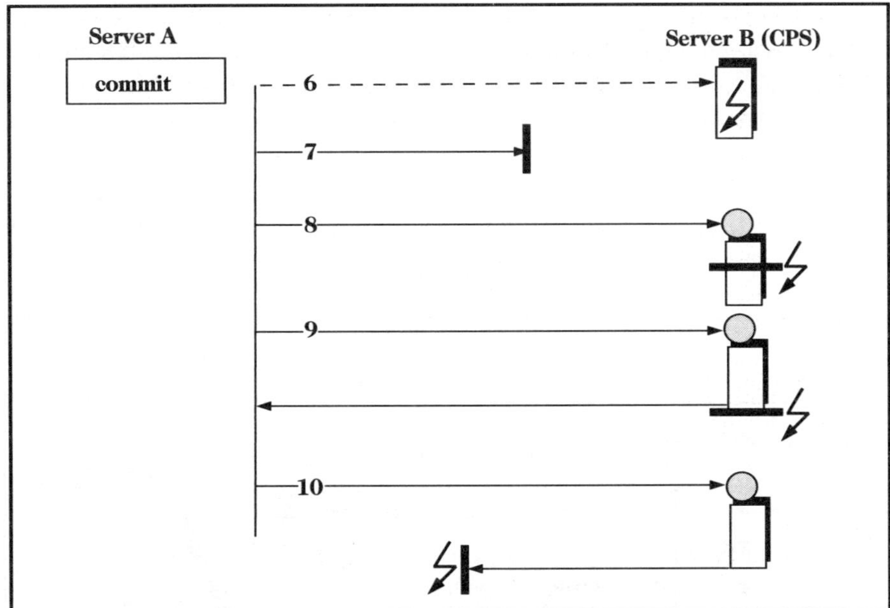

Figure 14.23b Possible error conditions which can affect a commit point site server

The other ten error types which we are going to look at all relate to the two-phase commit operation; Figures 14.23a and 14.23b provide a schematic representation of these errors, which can occur after a client process has carried out one or more DML operations on distributed database servers. Once the client generates a COMMIT statement the direct server, which is also the global coordinator for this distributed transaction, initiates the ORACLE two-phase commit mechanism. Whenever different errors are handled in the same way by the two-phase commit mechanism, these will be looked at together.

- **`2PC error 1`: A prepare server crashes before carrying out the prepare operation**
  In this case at least one prepare server crashes before it receives the request to prepare its portion of the distributed transaction. When the server is started up again the instance recovery process causes all open transactions to be rolled back, and this of course applies to any distributed transactions which are not yet in the 'prepared' state. A subsequent 'prepare' request from the global coordinator to this prepare server causes it to return an 'abort' message to the global coordinator, which as a consequence rolls back the whole transaction. Figure 14.24 illustrates this situation (with reference to Figure 14.21). Exactly the same process occurs if the server crashes during the prepare stage (`error 3`).

A similar process occurs in the case of errors 6 and 8, which concern the server which has been designated the commit point site. If a commit point site crashes before it has carried out the COMMIT operation then its local portion of the transaction will be rolled back on instance recovery. The global coordinator server's request to the commit point site to carry out a COMMIT will therefore be answered with an error message which will cause the global coordinator to roll back the whole transaction.

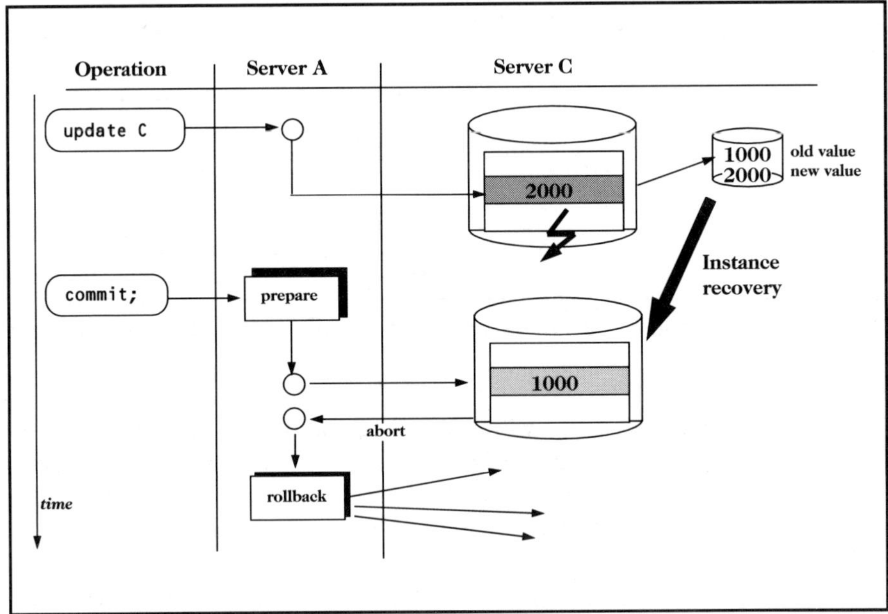

Figure 14.24 Errors during a two-phase commit (prepare server crashes before 'prepare' request)

- **`2PC error 2`: A prepare server is not available to the global coordinator** In this case the global coordinator's attempt to send a 'prepare' request to a prepare server does not succeed due to network failure.

  If a TNS connection fails the TNS components have the task of dealing with this error and rectifying it. In this case the two end points of the application's point to point connection are informed of the failure by SQL*Net. This leads to the prepare server rolling back the local portion of the transaction (process recovery) and to the global coordinator aborting the whole transaction. Consequently the global coordinator requests all database servers involved to roll back their portions of this transaction.

  The error recovery process is similar if, instead of a prepare server, a commit point site cannot be reached (`error 7`).

- **2PC error 4: A prepare server crashes after completing the prepare operation**
  In this case the prepare server, before it goes down, has already recorded its portion of the transaction as 'prepared', has written this record to the redo log file and has informed the global coordinator by sending it a 'prepared' message. After the computer has been restarted an instance recovery is carried out which restores the transaction to its previous status of 'prepared'.

  What then happens to the prepared transaction depends on what has happened to the rest of the distributed transaction during the time that the prepare node was down. Obviously if the transaction is still active, then the overall status of the transaction is exactly as it was prior to the one server going down. If on the other hand the transaction has been completed, either with a ROLLBACK or a COMMIT command, then the global coordinator will have already initiated the second stage of the two-phase commit protocol so that the transaction has already been completed on the other prepare servers involved; in this case the global coordinator will make use of the RECO process to tell the recovered instance how the transaction should be completed.

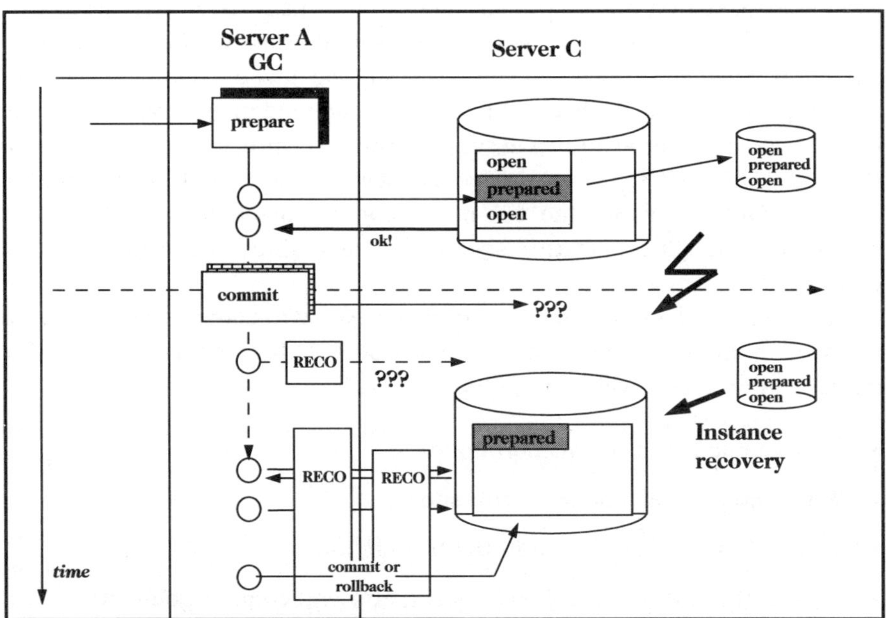

Figure 14.25 Errors during a two-phase commit (prepare server crashes after 'prepare')

Error 9 involves a similar situation, except that in this case it is the server on the commit point site which fails after it has signalled the global coordinator that its portion of the transaction has been committed.

In this situation the global coordinator will nevertheless send a commit request to all the other (prepare) servers, knowing that the committed transaction on the commit point site will be restored when the instance is recovered.

14.3.5 Manual override of the two-phase commit

As we have already seen, any errors which can occur in the course of a two-phase commit transaction are detected by the Oracle7 system which then automatically returns the database to a fully consistent state. Although this automatic recovery process is of course usually a great benefit, there are nevertheless times when it is useful to be able to decide how a specific error is to be dealt with.

Let us for example take the situation where a number of nodes have just prepared their portions of a distributed transaction when the network goes down for what is obviously going to be a longer period of time. Because the distributed transaction cannot now be completed it is going to keep resources locked on all the prepare nodes and this in turn may mean that other (local) users or processes are prevented from working with those databases. Even shutting down and restarting the affected databases will not solve this problem (a method not to be recommended in any case), since the database recovery procedure will simply restore the prepared transactions to their previous state so that the resources will still be locked. In this kind of situation Oracle7 allows the two-phase commit mechanism to be ended manually, although this feature should of course always be used with great care.

However if it does become absolutely necessary to complete a distributed transaction manually (either with COMMIT or ROLLBACK) then the following items of information will be required:

- Which node is the global coordinator?
- Which node is the commit point site?
- Which servers are involved in the transaction?
- What is the status of the global coordinator and commit point site?

These items of information are provided by the following two data dictionary views:

- DBA_2PC_PENDING
- DBA_2PC_NEIGHBORS

Once these two views have been accessed and the exact status of the distributed transaction clarified, it becomes possible to know how the transaction should be ended by using either the COMMIT FORCE or the ROLLBACK FORCE commands on the nodes involved in the transaction. The crucial factor in determining which action to choose is of course the status of the transaction on the commit point site; if it has already committed here, then the COMMIT FORCE command should be executed on each of the prepare servers involved in the transaction, and the local system will record the fact that the transaction has been ended manually in the DBA_2PC_PENDING view (the transaction's status is set to HEURISTIC COMMIT or HEURISTIC ROLLBACK). When the cause of the original error (in our example the network going down) is finally removed, then the RECO recovery process looks for any transactions which have been completed manually and checks whether all the portions of a distributed transaction have in fact been completed in the same way. If this is not the case then this inconsistency is recorded in the DBA_2PC_PENDING view, by setting the value for the column MIXED to YES.

Whenever distributed transactions have been ended manually in this way, it is important for the DBA to check the DBA_2PC_PENDING view as soon as the system is fully operational. It cannot be emphasized too strongly that the use of this option is potentially very risky and that it should only be used after the status of a distributed transaction has been considered and analysed very carefully.

14.4 The Oracle7 replication concept

RELEASE 7.1

The trend towards the use of distributed processing and distributed database configurations is already very strong and the increasing availability of systems which support this kind of system architecture (like Oracle7) is clearly going to accelerate this development. However it is always important to remember that any new technology should be looked at critically and in its context as part of an overall solution before we can determine what real benefits it will provide for the end user. In the case of a distributed database system for example, if we want to know whether we can provide the system's users with an efficient and economical solution for their particular requirements, we need to consider the costs and features not only of the database system but also of the network, and in particular we need to assess the following factors:

- the throughput of the network,
- the stability of the network,
- transmission efficiency,
- location and distribution of the database objects,
- the efficiency of distributed SQL processing.

The location of each database table is of particular importance in determining the efficiency of the overall system. For the ORACLE database itself it is of course irrelevant where a particular table is stored, since the system is able to provide complete location transparency. However in terms of the distributed system as a whole, it is important to realize that some table configurations allow considerably faster and more efficient processing than others.

In order to examine this particular aspect of distributed database systems more closely, we shall consider the example of a company which has a distributed database system which links a network of branch offices (illustrated in Figure 14.26). The database system comprises a central server located at the company's headquarters with a local server at each of the branch offices; the local servers are used to administer data which are specific to that branch (customers, orders and so on) while the central server manages those data which are relevant to the company as a whole, such as the inventory table of all the articles which the company provides. Needless to say, this table is very important to the functioning of the company and all the branch offices are given read access to it so that they can process customers' orders.

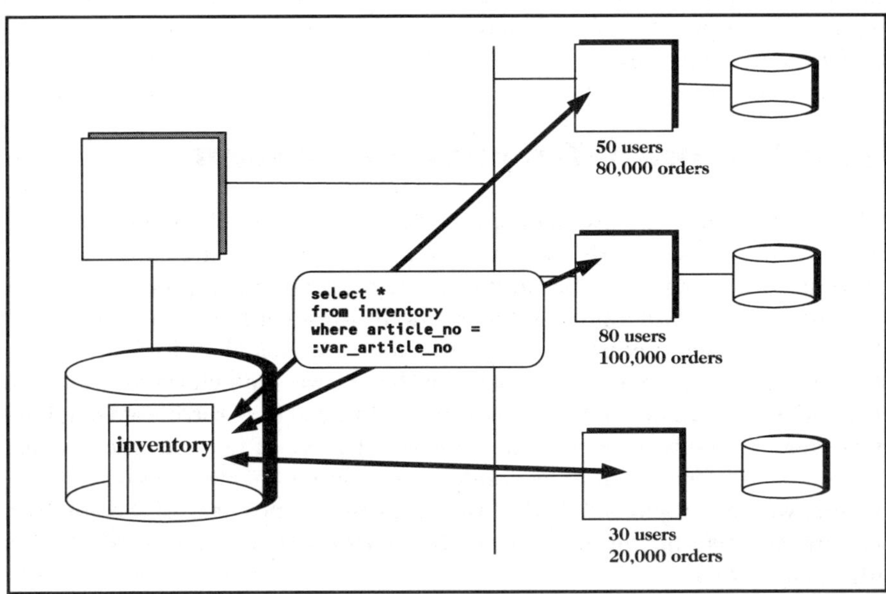

Figure 14.26 Distributed applications system with replication of key data

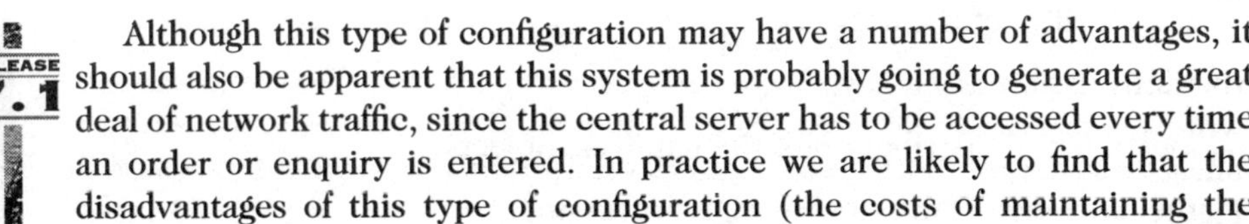

Although this type of configuration may have a number of advantages, it should also be apparent that this system is probably going to generate a great deal of network traffic, since the central server has to be accessed every time an order or enquiry is entered. In practice we are likely to find that the disadvantages of this type of configuration (the costs of maintaining the network, the delays which will occur when a lot of communications activity is going on at once, plus the risk of disabling the entire company if the central server becomes unavailable for any period of time) will combine to outweigh the system's advantages.

However if it were possible to reduce the number of times that the inventory table has to be accessed, then many of these disadvantages would be overcome and the company could gain all the benefits which this type of distributed system definitely has to offer. Of course one answer to this problem would be to provide each branch office with its own inventory table, thus drastically reducing the amount of network traffic which is necessary to maintain normal operations, but this solution presents another problem, which is how to ensure that each local inventory table is up to date and consistent with the 'real' inventory table on the central database server.

RELEASE 7.1

The answer to this very common problem is to use table or data source *replicates*, and Oracle7 provides us with three different types of data replication:

- asynchronous replication
- synchronous (read-only) replication
- synchronous (read-write) replication

The terms 'asynchronous' and 'synchronous' refer in this context to the point in time at which the replicate is modified with reference to the master (or original) table. An asynchronous replication is a copy of remote data which is renewed and brought up to date periodically, at an interval determined by the user (for example once an hour, day or week). A table which is made available by means of the asynchronous replication function is of necessity a read-only table and cannot be modified. A table which is replicated in this way is often referred to as a *snapshot*.

Synchronous (read-only) replication means that any replicate versions of a given table are refreshed whenever and as soon as the original (master) table is modified in any way. Thus there is no set interval at which a replicate table will be updated. As with asynchronous replication, the replicated table can only be read.

The last type of data replication (synchronous read-write) is by far the most sophisticated of the three, since it requires that any change made to any one 'copy' of a replicated table will immediately be transmitted to all the other replicates of that table, that is, within the scope of the same transaction. Indeed in this case it is no longer correct to talk of master and replicate tables, since each instance of a table simultaneously fulfils both of these roles.

Both types of synchronous replication are implemented on the basis of the ORACLE database trigger concept and, in the case of synchronous read-write replication, the integrity of all replicated tables is secured by the two-phase commit mechanism. The three replication types are summarized in Figure 14.27.

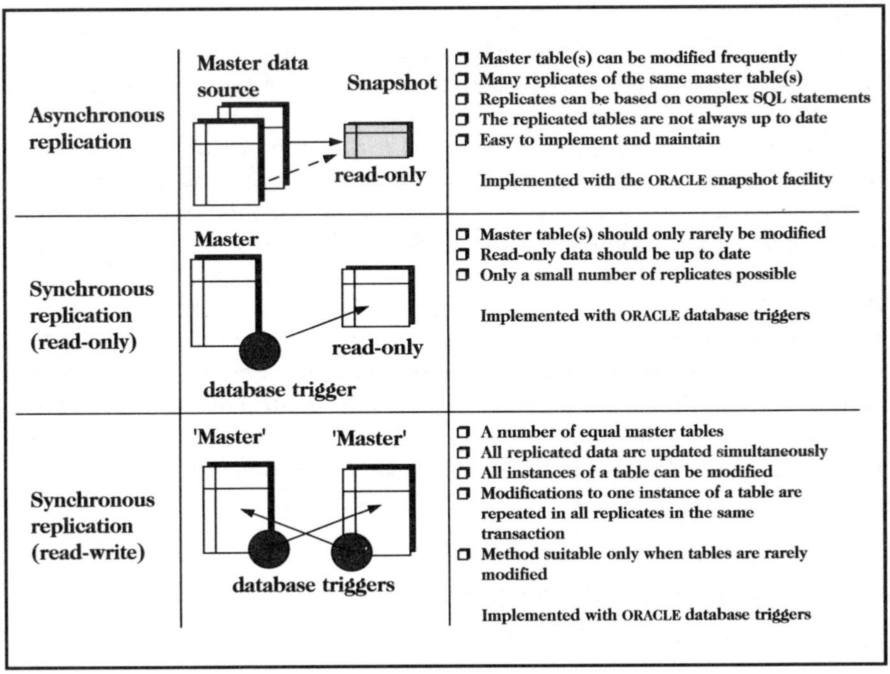

Asynchronous replication	Master data source; Snapshot; read-only	❑ Master table(s) can be modified frequently ❑ Many replicates of the same master table(s) ❑ Replicates can be based on complex SQL statements ❑ The replicated tables are not always up to date ❑ Easy to implement and maintain Implemented with the ORACLE snapshot facility
Synchronous replication (read-only)	Master; read-only; database trigger	❑ Master table(s) should only rarely be modified ❑ Read-only data should be up to date ❑ Only a small number of replicates possible Implemented with ORACLE database triggers
Synchronous replication (read-write)	'Master'; 'Master'; database triggers	❑ A number of equal master tables ❑ All replicated data are updated simultaneously ❑ All instances of a table can be modified ❑ Modifications to one instance of a table are repeated in all replicates in the same transaction ❑ Method suitable only when tables are rarely modified Implemented with ORACLE database triggers

Figure 14.27 The Oracle7 replication types

RELEASE 7.1

With regard to the question of which type of replication should be used for a given configuration, this depends very much on how the tables to be replicated are going to be accessed. The two synchronous methods are appropriate in cases where a table has to be replicated as soon as it has been modified but are perhaps less suitable for tables which are being modified very frequently as the resulting communications traffic can impair the performance of the whole system and increase its overall running costs. In comparison with these two methods, asynchronous replication provides a much greater degree of efficiency in that all the changes made to a table within the specified refresh interval are communicated together in one update process. This greater efficiency of asynchronous replication can be particularly significant when there are a large number of replicate tables to be kept up to date.

A very important difference between these three types of replication is that whereas synchronous replication is based on database triggers and the two-phase commit mechanism, asynchronous replication makes use of a special snapshot feature which undertakes the entire management and control of this function.

A snapshot is created on a database server by means of the CREATE SNAPSHOT statement. This command includes a SELECT statement which specifies the (remote) master table on which the (local) snapshot table is to be based, as in the following example:

```
create snapshot local_inventory
refresh sysdate + 1
as
select * from inventory@headoffice
```

RELEASE 7.1

This statement creates a snapshot object which can be read on the local server as though it were a normal table. The 'refresh' option defines the interval at which the snapshot is refreshed, in the above example an interval of one day has been specified.

Oracle7 distinguishes between two types of snapshots, the simple and the complex snapshot. A simple snapshot is an exact copy of a single master table whereas a complex snapshot includes either more than one table or only part of one or more tables. Therefore a complex snapshot is created when the corresponding CREATE SNAPSHOT statement involves anything more than one simple SELECT command, for example:

- defining an inner or outer join in the SELECT statement in order to create a snapshot on the basis of several tables;
- using any of the ORACLE functions like GROUP BY;
- using any of the ORACLE set operations like UNION or INTERSECT.

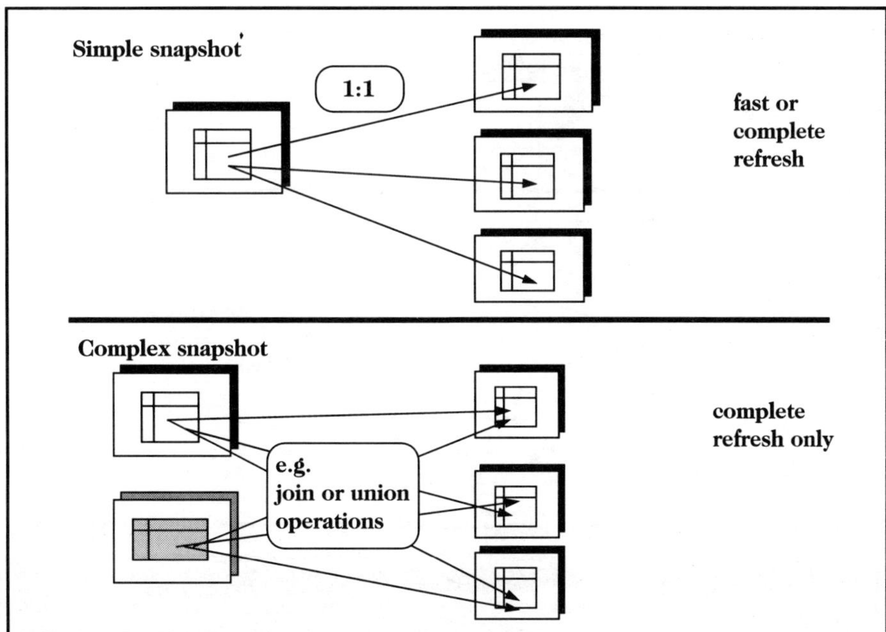

Figure 14.28 Snapshot types and refresh modes

RELEASE 7.1

As we have already mentioned, a snapshot (or asynchronous replicate) is refreshed from the master data sources at an interval of time specified by the user. Oracle7 provides us with additional control mechanisms at this point by making it possible to choose between two refresh modes: *fast* refresh and *complete* refresh.

Where a complete refresh has been specified, ORACLE recreates the entire snapshot by executing in full the SELECT statement on which the snapshot is based, that is, the current snapshot is discarded. In the case of a fast refresh, the existing snapshot is retained and is only updated to reflect the changes to the master table since the previous refresh operation. In order to carry out a fast refresh operation ORACLE records all modifications to the master table in a special snapshot log table, this means however that the fast refresh mechanism can only be used for simple snapshots.

Having dealt with what the snapshot mechanism does, it is now worth looking at how this particular feature works. When the CREATE SNAPSHOT command is entered on a given local server, the system first creates three database objects:

- a table whose name consists of the prefix **snap$** plus the name of the snapshot as defined by the user, that is, **snap$<snapshot_name>**;
- a view with the same name as the snapshot. It is this view which will in fact be read by any user processes on the local server;
- a view with the name **mview$<snapshot_name>**.

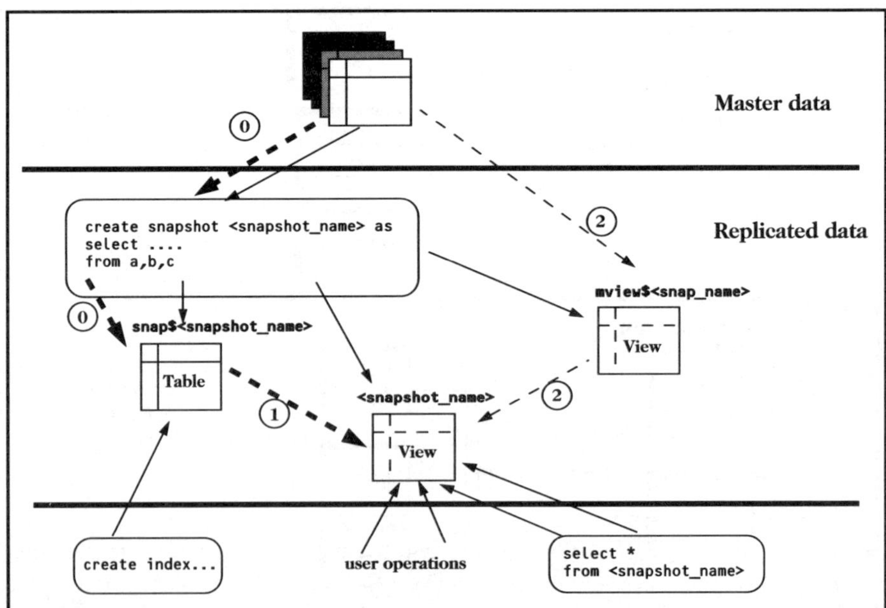

Figure 14.29 Creating a snapshot

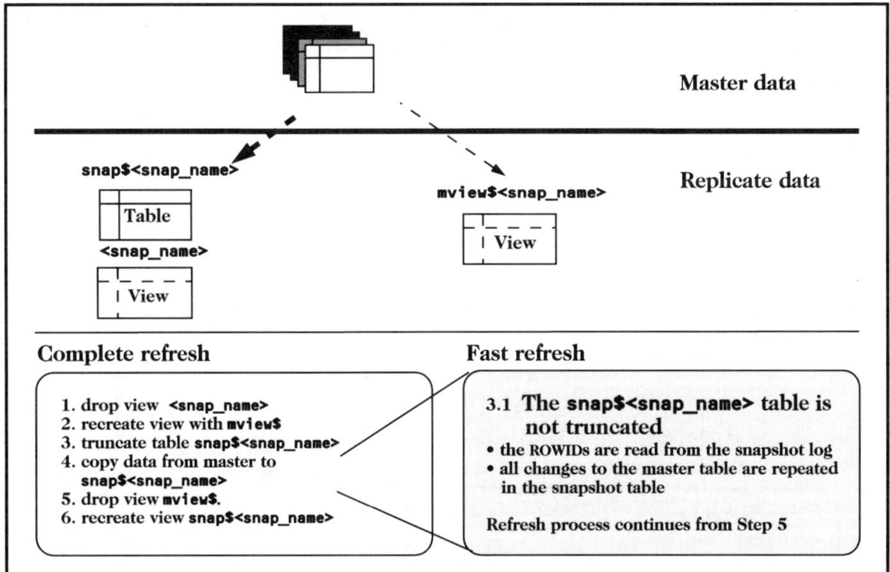

Figure 14.30 Refreshing a snapshot

These three database objects are always stored in the schema of the snapshot's creator and should not be altered in any way. If a snapshot is no longer required then entering the DROP SNAPSHOT command will delete the snapshot and all related objects from the local database. The one exception to this rule is the possibility of creating (additional) indexes on the `snap$<snapshot_name>` table, in order to improve access times.

The function of the view `mview$<snapshot_name>` is to assume the role of the `snap$table` whenever that table is not accessible because it is being refreshed. However this particular view functions differently from standard views in that it references not its own `snap$` table but the actual master table on another server.

Having examined the three database objects on which the snapshot mechanism is based, we will now look at how the refresh process is carried out, starting with the complete refresh mode:

- The first step carried out by the ORACLE system is to recreate the `mview$` view; as already mentioned this view references the original (master) table(s) directly, and all read operations from the local server are carried out via this view until the new snapshot is ready (`path 2` in Figure 14.29).
- In the second step of the complete refresh process all rows are deleted from the `snap$<snapshot_name>` table with the TRUNCATE TABLE statement, which means that all indexes and all GRANTS on the table are retained.

- The third step involves carrying out the SELECT command on which the snapshot is based; all the selected data are copied from the master table(s) to the `snap$` table.
- As soon as all the data have been written to the `snap$` table, the corresponding view is reactivated, the `mview$` view is deactivated and the local snapshot can again be made full use of.

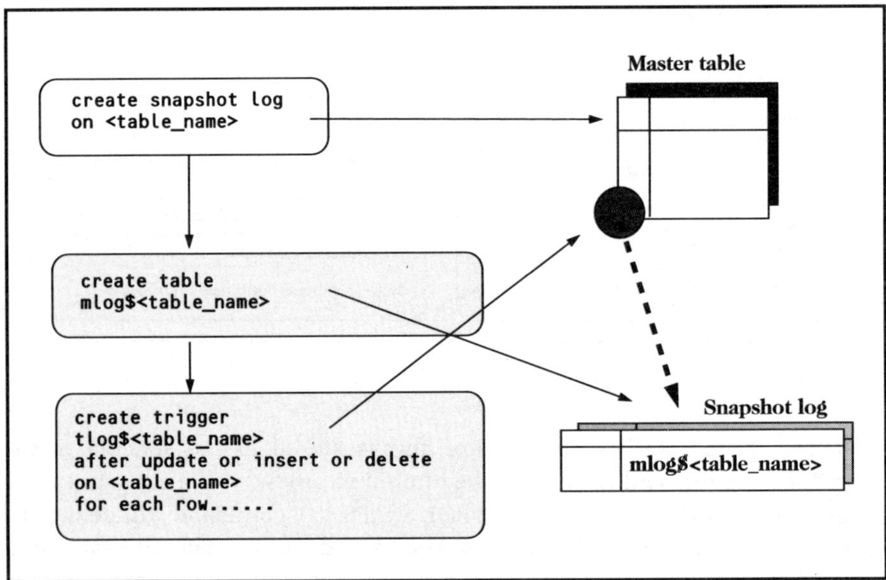

Figure 14.31 Creating a snapshot log table

We have already mentioned that a simple snapshot can be regenerated in fast refresh mode by recording all modifications to the master table in a corresponding snapshot log table which has been created with the CREATE SNAPSHOT LOG command. When this command is executed the ORACLE system creates the following two database objects, both of which refer to the master table:

- a snapshot log table `mlog$<table_name>;`
- an AFTER ROW trigger for all DML operations on that table.

Whenever any data in the master table are modified the log trigger records the ROWID, the current date and the type of operation in the `mlog$` table, so that when the snapshot has to be refreshed it is only necessary to read the log table for the changes which have been made since the last refresh cycle, these changes are then repeated on the replicate table. It is worth pointing out that, in addition to the perhaps more obvious advantages of the fast refresh mechanism in terms of speed and resources, it is also possible to service any number of simple snapshots with the same snapshot log table. Even if the refresh interval for the individual snapshots is different, the ORACLE Server will ensure that all snapshots of the same table are managed correctly.

If we are dealing with simple snapshots it is usually preferable to use the fast rather than the complete refresh method, and this is particularly true if the master table is not modified very frequently or if the snapshot table is very large.

Returning to our original example of the inventory table which is held on a central server, we can now see that the problems posed by the different requirements of the system's users might be solved in the following way:

- A snapshot log for the inventory table could be set up on the central server.
- A simple snapshot of the inventory table could be created on each of the local servers; if these snapshots had a refresh cycle of one day they could be updated at night, thus allowing our user, in addition to the other advantages of this solution, to take advantage of the lower transmission costs which apply after normal working hours.

The overall effect of this solution is to provide a system which offers the security of a centralized system together with the flexibility of a distributed system while at the same time improving system response times and keeping network costs to a minimum. In addition, because of the location transparency provided by ORACLE, it is possible to provide the benefits of a distributed database system without any of the users' existing software having to be rewritten or even recompiled.

15

Oracle7 Release 7.1 – a technological update

Topics covered in this chapter

- The new features of Oracle7 Release 7.1
- ORACLE parallel query technology
- Defining the degree of parallelism
- Parallel recovery mechanisms
- Read-only tablespaces
- Calling stored PL/SQL procedures from SQL
- Using dynamic SQL in PL/SQL
- Extensions to the functionality of database triggers
- ORACLE Open Gateway Technology
- Implementing transparent and procedural gateways
- Release 7.1: new networking features
- New features for database snapshots
- Symmetric replication mechanisms

15

Oracle7 Release 7.1 – a technological update

15.1 Introduction

In recent years downsizing and rightsizing projects have become extremely important to many corporate and government organizations. Many of these, after evaluating their established data processing facilities and systems, have been forced to the realization that much, if not all of their information processing infrastructure needs to be drastically overhauled. Indeed in many cases entire computing systems (that is, hardware, networks as well as applications and system software) are having to be completely replaced.

It need hardly be emphasized that this kind of transition from one system to another is potentially very risky for the organization involved and that careful and comprehensive planning are essential if this change is to be accomplished successfully. Not even the best hardware and software will prevent a downsizing project from turning into a disaster if it has not been planned properly.

A large number of downsizing projects aim to replace existing mainframe systems with client/server configurations based on a server running under the UNIX operating system. These central servers have to be able to provide enormous processing power if they are to service the many client systems and applications which depend on them and it is therefore hardly surprising that the demand for high performance UNIX systems, which can be used as database servers in large client/server configurations, has been growing so quickly in recent years.

The most important computer architectures of this type are symmetric multiprocessor (SMP) systems, which currently dominate this area of the market, cluster systems, which offer enhanced reliability as well as improved performance, and massively parallel systems (MPP) which are considered by many observers to be the mainframes of the future.

All three computer architectures share a common feature, namely the use of several CPUs or, in the case of cluster systems, of several cluster nodes to significantly reduce the amount of processing time taken to carry out a specific task. Whereas SMP systems have in the region of 2–30 CPUs, MPP systems can consist of hundreds or even thousands of processors which can work in parallel.

As we saw in Section 3.3, Oracle7 Release 7.0 specifically supports all three of these architectures (as well as standard single CPU machines of course). Standard Oracle7 makes it possible to implement vary large databases with many hundreds of users on SMP systems and the Oracle7 Parallel Server extension provides additional features to make optimum use of cluster and MPP systems.

However whereas Version 7.0 of Oracle7 was primarily concerned with how effectively to support large numbers of users, Release 7.1 provides new features which aim to make much more effective use of the computing power available with this type of hardware architecture, thereby allowing complex SQL statements to be processed much more quickly than was hitherto possible. Where a number of CPUs are available Release 7.1 divides a SQL operation into sub-components and these are then processed simultaneously by each CPU.

This parallelization of SQL statements is part of the Oracle7 parallel query technology and is available under Release 7.1 as the 'parallel query option'; together with the symmetric replication feature this represents the most important functional extension to the Oracle7 Server technology.

Release 7.1 is of course the first maintenance release for the Oracle7 Server and before examining it in greater detail, we should first look at all the new or enhanced features which this release provides:

- introduction of parallel query technology
- introduction of a parallel recovery procedure
- introduction of read-only tablespaces

- functional extensions for stored procedures
- extensions to database triggers
- extensions to the replication concept

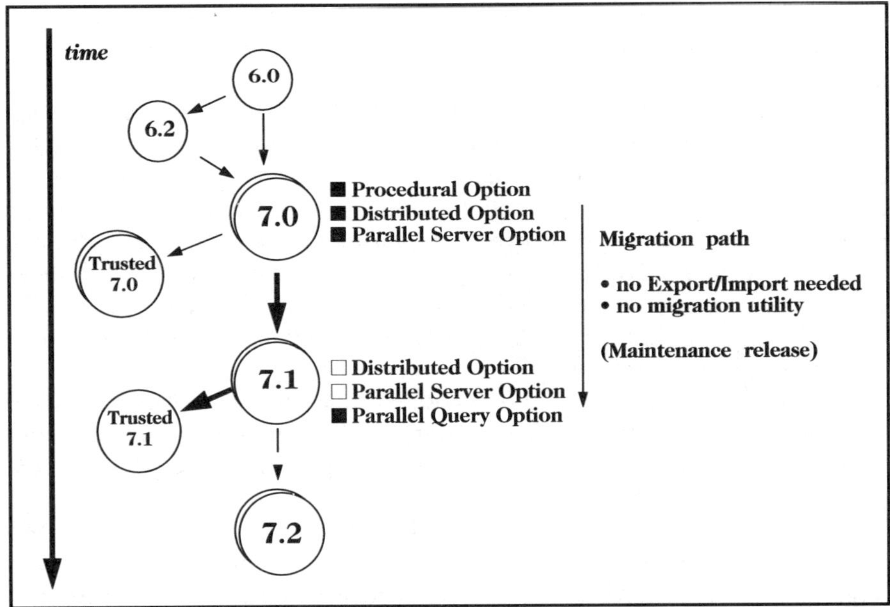

Figure 15.1 The development of the Oracle7 Server products

Release 7.1 of the high level security server Trusted Oracle7 will be available at about the same time as Release 7.1 of Oracle7. For current users of Oracle7 who wish to make the transition from Release 7.0 to 7.1 it is worth pointing out that this latest release does not require any changes to be made to existing Oracle7 databases.

In addition to dealing with the new functions available for the Oracle7 Server we shall in the following sections take a detailed look at ORACLE's Open Gateway Technology which plays a key role in the integration of different data sources and procedural services.

15.2 Oracle7 parallel query technology

15.2.1 Introduction

ORACLE database developers were among the first to recognize the importance of parallel hardware systems, and this resulted in the relatively early availability of database server systems which demonstrate excellent scaling factors on SMP systems and which dominate the growing market for cluster and MPP systems.

In the development of the Oracle7 Server in particular special emphasis was given to increasing OLTP performance for these types of architecture and to improving CPU performance in order to deal with the projected increases in both workloads and the number of users accessing the system.

The feedback from users of large Oracle7 databases has confirmed that to a great extent these goals have been realized; OLTP performance is usually good and nearly all performance problems in this type of environment can be solved by using the various tuning methods provided by the Oracle7 Server. Whenever a point is reached where the workload or the number of users can no longer be managed by the original system configuration, then it is relatively easy to improve overall performance by installing additional CPUs (in the case of SMP and MPP systems) or by adding new cluster nodes to a cluster environment. Such measures are very effective because the Oracle7 Server is able to make nearly optimum use of such additional resources, normally with an efficiency of over 85%.

However although these internal and external measures allow us to deal with the demands of large OLTP environments, the situation is very different when we come to look at how to optimize complex SQL operations, which are often very time-consuming.

Certain SQL operations can take a long time to be processed for two relatively simple reasons; the sheer volume of data to be dealt with is very large and the data have to be processed in a complex way. The kind of complex operation we are referring to includes any one or more of the following:

- sorting data
- grouping data
- join operations
- distinct operations
- creating indexes

Up until now (Release 7.0) any SQL operation could only be processed by one CPU regardless of how many CPUs were in use in the computer system. Figure 15.2 illustrates this situation, where a complex query is being processed by only one CPU because other CPUs in the same system are unable to support the operation.

In this type of *non*-parallel SQL processing the response time, that is the interval of time between the beginning of the operation and the point at which the user is given a result, is directly proportional to the speed of the processor used, which means that the only way to improve performance in this case is to install a more powerful (and therefore more expensive) CPU. However this solution runs counter to all the current trends in hardware development which are attempting to overcome the performance limits of computing systems by using several (SMP) or many (MPP) simple (and therefore cheaper) CPUs in parallel.

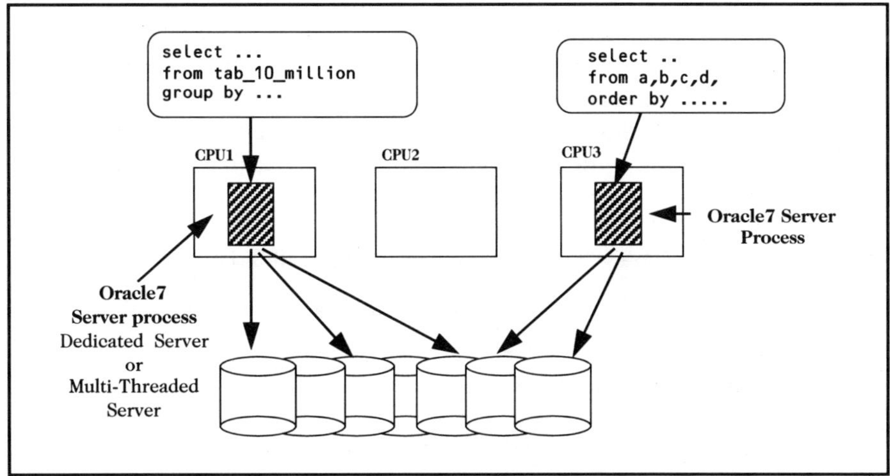

Figure 15.2 Non-parallel SQL processing on a SMP system

Therefore the basic idea for the Oracle7 parallel query technology is both simple and fully in keeping with current developments in computer hardware architecture. Wherever possible or necessary, a given SQL statement is processed not by one CPU only but is split up into smaller units which can be processed by several CPUs in parallel. This type of processing is illustrated in Figure 15.3.

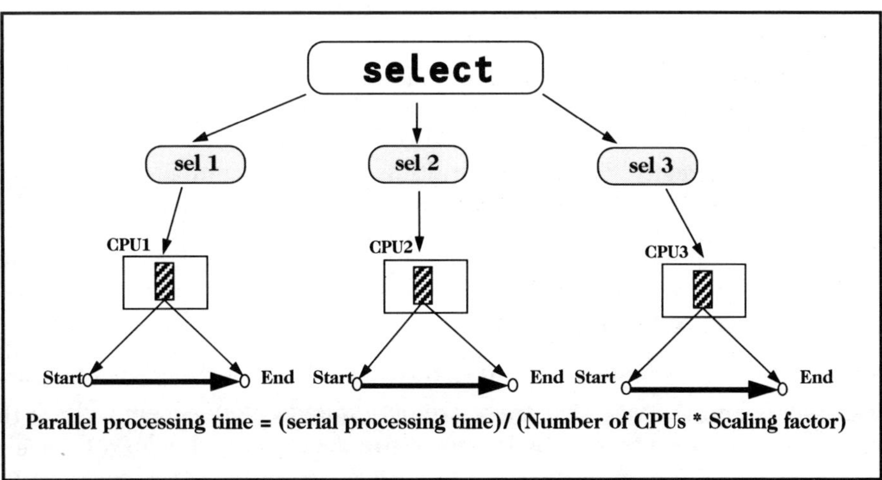

Figure 15.3 Parallel SQL processing

Dividing a SQL operation between several CPUs and processing these SQL sub-statements in parallel will clearly make far better use of a SMP, cluster or MPP system and can therefore drastically reduce the response times for processing complex SQL operations.

We might initially assume that response times in parallel processing will be inversely proportional to the number of CPUs in a given computer system. However this method of calculation, which is shown in Figure 15.3, is a theoretical formula that has little practical relevance and can therefore only be used as a rule of thumb. This is because the response time of parallel processing operations is influenced not only by the number of CPUs but also by any of the other factors listed below:

- the capability of the I/O system to deal with parallel data flows;
- the distribution of the actual data (number of disks, disk striping, tablespace striping);
- the network bandwidth;
- the size and configuration of the database cache;
- parallelization of temporary segments (temporary tablespace) in sorting and grouping operations;
- memory bus bandwidth in SMP systems;
- utilization of individual CPU capacity by SQL sub-statements.

The pragmatic formula for calculating response times, which is illustrated in Figure 15.3, introduces a scaling factor which reflects all the factors listed above. Typical scaling factors found in Oracle7's parallel query technology are in the range 0.7–0.9 depending on the operation itself and on what tuning measures for parallel processing have been undertaken.

Figure 15.4 illustrates the most important factors which influence the use of the Oracle7 Server's parallel query option. In this context it is useful to distinguish between primary factors which have an immediate influence on the effectiveness of parallelization and secondary factors which only affect the system indirectly. The I/O bus width is a typical secondary factor since executing a parallel query can greatly increase I/O requirements, so that the I/O bus width can limit the potential scalability.

Parallelizing a SQL statement

The partitioning of a complex SQL statement into several less complex sub-statements and the way that these are distributed among single CPUs is of decisive importance to the whole area of parallel query technology. Basically there are two different partitioning strategies currently in use, *static* partitioning and *dynamic* partitioning.

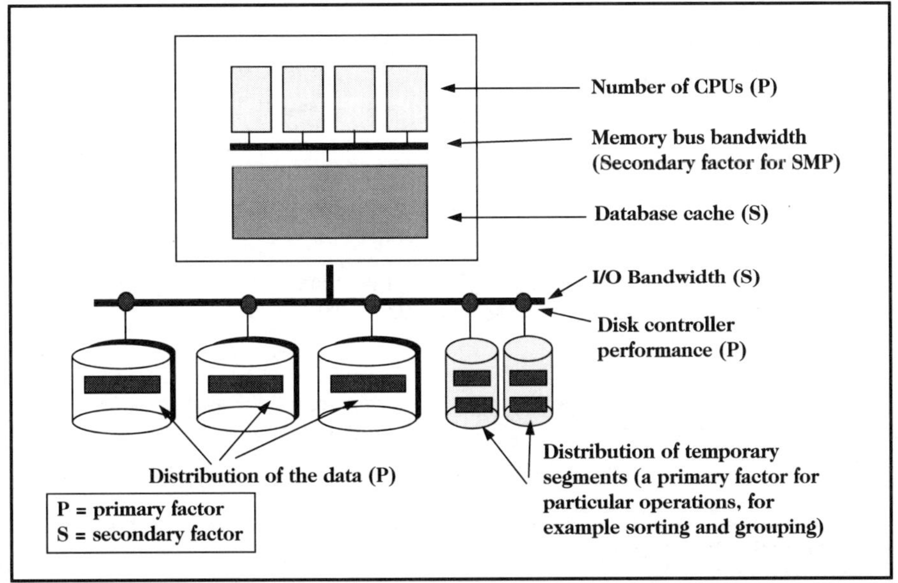

Figure 15.4 Primary and secondary factors which affect the performance of parallel queries

Where static partitioning is in use, a database table is distributed across separate disk drives when it is created, with predefined index ranges being assigned to specific disk drives, and a SQL statement which can be parallelized is split up and processed by different CPUs according to how the tables have been partitioned. This type of partitioning has been developed even further for MPP systems, where each data partition is allocated to a specific CPU.

With dynamic partitioning on the other hand there is no predefined and rigid allocation of the data to specific disk drives and CPUs. What happens instead is that at runtime each SQL operation is partitioned and processed by a number of CPUs on the basis of a factor referred to as the *degree of parallelism*, which can be defined either for the database object (with the ALTER TABLE command) or for the SQL statement (with the aid of SQL hints). The Oracle7 Server sets default values for this factor and these will be used if no explicit values are defined by the DBA or programmer (*refer also to* Figure 15.13).

The degree of parallelism basically specifies how many CPUs should be used to process a SELECT statement on a given database object. Thus if a value of '2' has been defined for a given table, then any SELECT operations on that table will be carried out by two CPUs working in parallel. As we have already mentioned, the improvement in response times which can be gained by using additional CPUs to execute a SQL query is not directly proportional to the number of extra CPUs used. Figure 15.5 shows the same SQL statement being executed under different degrees of parallelism; in this example we assume an overall performance scaling factor of 80%.

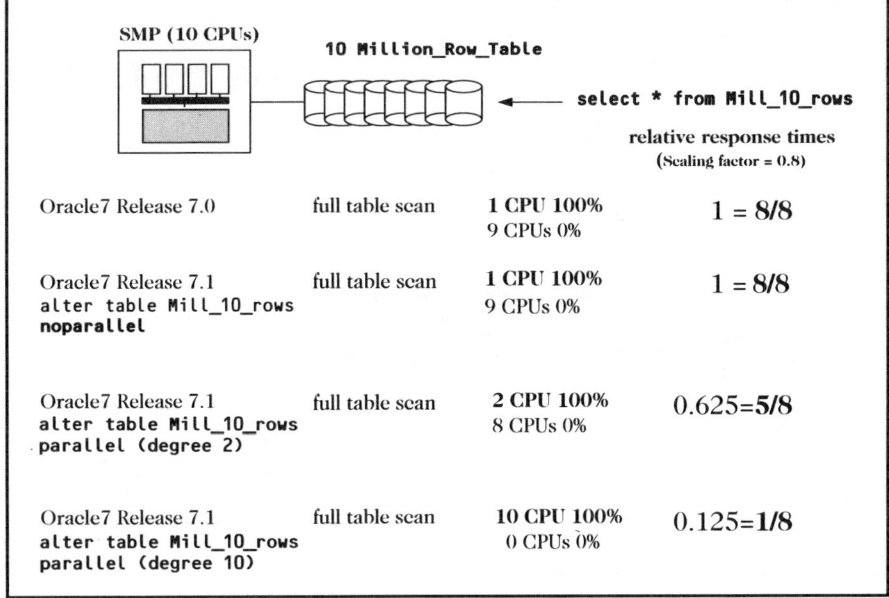

Figure 15.5 Improving response times with parallel queries

Because the decision as to which data are to be processed by which CPU does not depend on the physical location of the data, dynamic partitioning does not require any fundamental reorganization to be carried out before it can be implemented. Dynamic partitioning also has the advantage that any change in the configuration of a system (such as adding further CPUs or cluster nodes) will be fully taken account of the next time that a parallel query is executed. Dynamic partitioning therefore represents a completely transparent implementation of parallel query technology. In Chapter 15.2.2 we will look at other ways in which the execution of parallel queries can be controlled and optimized.

Types of parallelism

Oracle7 distinguishes between two basic types of parallelism:

- horizontal or intra-operation parallelism
- vertical or inter-operation parallelism

Where horizontal (intra-operation) parallelism is used, an operation is divided into several sub-operations and processed by a corresponding number of CPUs in parallel. A typical example for this type of operation would be a full table scan in which the whole table has to be read; using ORACLE's dynamic partitioning facility the table is divided so that it can be read by several sub-operations each of which is processed by a separate CPU.

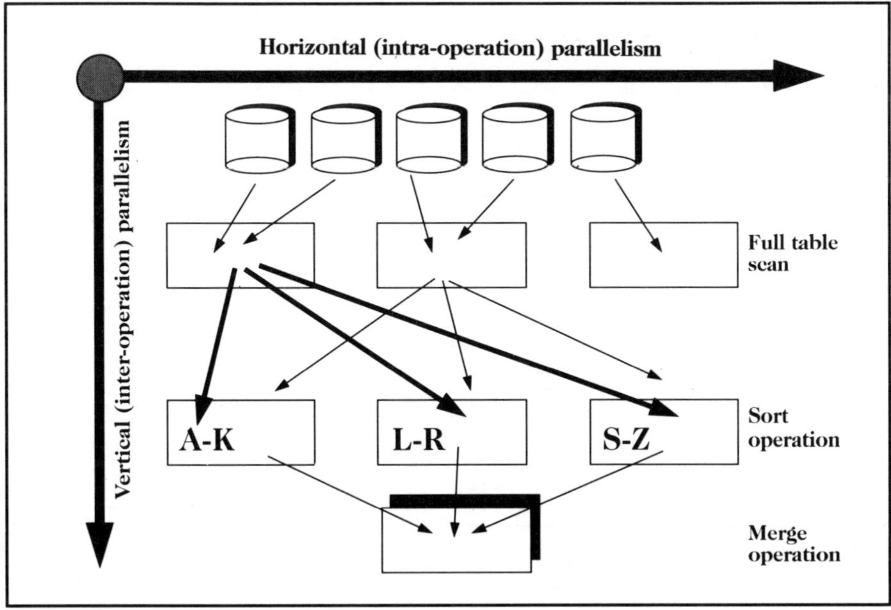

Figure 15.6 Horizontal and vertical parallelism

In the case of vertical parallelism two different types of operation are processed in parallel. Figure 15.6 illustrates this with a sort operation; the data returned by the full table scan processes are simultaneously being sorted by other processes (CPUs) on the basis of the specific sort ranges. Which sort ranges are allocated to which processes is determined at runtime and depends on the degree of parallelism which has been defined for the database objects or operations in question.

Figure 15.7 summarizes the operations which can be carried out using the Oracle7 parallel query technology. Please note that indexed read operations on tables (as opposed to full table scans) cannot be parallelized. On the other hand it is possible to use parallel processing to export all or part of a database much more quickly; in this case all the tables for which a degree of parallelism has been defined will be exported by the Export utility with the corresponding number of CPUs working in parallel.

Hardware requirements

ORACLE's parallel query technology is not limited to any specific computer architecture, although it is primarily aimed at systems which use more than one CPU, that is, SMP, MPP and cluster systems. However experience with this function has shown that very high powered single CPU systems can also benefit from the parallel query feature when carrying out certain tasks.

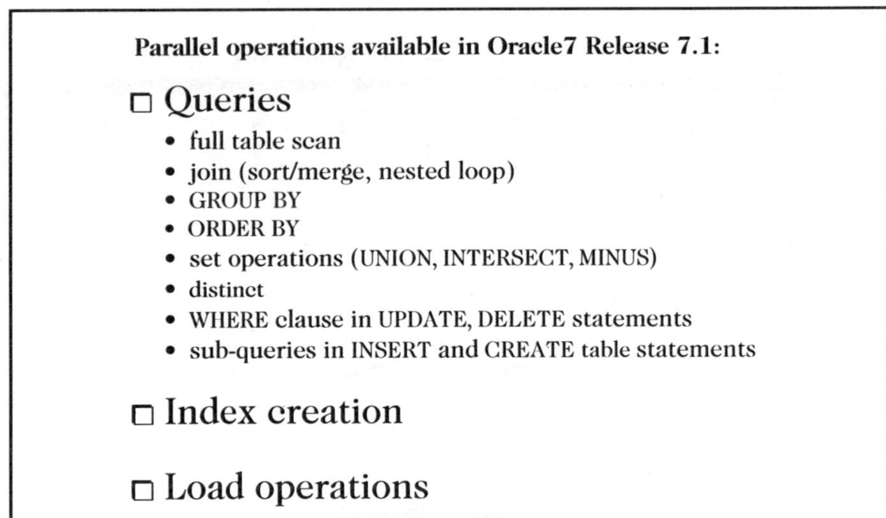

Figure 15.7 SQL operations which can be processed in parallel with Release 7.1

The ORACLE Parallel Server option is still required to run cluster and MPP systems with Release 7.1, as this continues to provide the technological basis for using these types of computer architecture as database servers (*refer also to* Section 3.3.6). The parallel query option therefore represents an addition to the functions of the Parallel Server option, providing parallel systems with the additional benefits of parallel query processing. Figure 15.8 illustrates the relationship between the two parallel technologies of Oracle7 and the different computer architectures on which these products can be used.

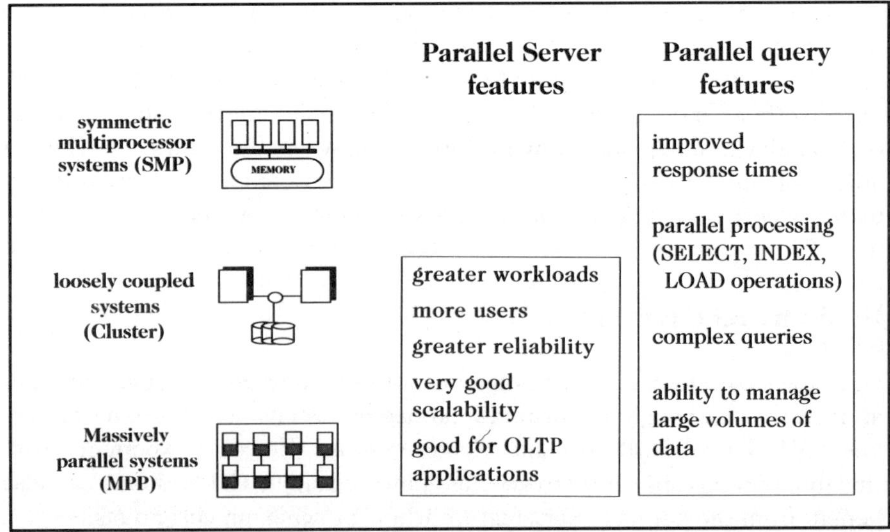

Figure 15.8 Oracle7 parallel processing technologies and hardware architectures

15.2.2 Using the parallel query technology

The parallel query feature forms an optional part of Oracle7, Release 7.1. Once this has been installed then every SQL statement capable of parallelization will automatically be divided into a number of SQL sub-statements for processing. Whether a given SQL statement can in fact be parallelized depends on two factors:

- the type of operation which is to be carried out
- the parameters which control the degree of parallelism

The types of operation which can be parallelized with Release 7.1 have already been listed in Figure 15.7, although it should be pointed out that the SQL*Loader is not affected by the parallel query option as this utility does not use standard SQL statements.

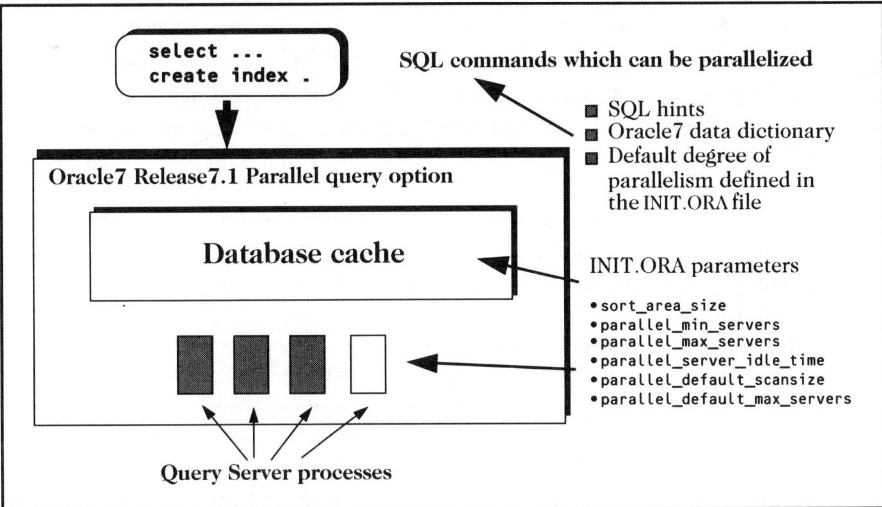

Figure 15.9 The software components of the Oracle7 parallel query option

It is also important to note that the degree of parallelism of a database object (the PARALLEL parameter) can be specified or modified at any time, that is, either when a table is first created or after it has been in use for some time (ALTER TABLE). If it is necessary for any reason to exclude a table from parallel processing the NOPARALLEL parameter should be specified. The following examples show how parallel processing can be managed for individual tables:

```
create table tab_a(...) parallel (degree 2);
create table tab_b(...) noparallel;/* no parallel processing */
create table tab_c(...);/* default degree of parallelism */
alter table tab_a parallel (degree 10);/* degree of parallelism 10 */
alter table tab_d noparallel;/* parallel query disabled */
```

However as we have already mentioned, the degree of parallelism can be defined not only at the object level but also within a specific SQL statement. By using SQL hints within a SQL statement different parallelization values can be assigned to specific SQL operations, and these values will always take precedence over the values defined at object level.

The SQL hint to specify a degree of parallelism (PARALLEL) includes the name of the table to be processed and the value for the maximum degree of parallelism. Similarly a user can specify a switch from parallel to serial processing with the NOPARALLEL hint. The following examples show both hints being used:

```
select /* +parallel (tab_a, 5) */ user_id from tab_a;
select /* +noparallel (tab_b) */ order_no from tab_b;
```

The use of these two new SQL hints, which form part of Release 7.1, is governed by the same rules as for all other SQL hints (*refer to* Section 6.2); they are inserted as a comment after the operator keyword in the SQL statement and they can also be combined with other SQL hints, as in the following example:

```
select /* +full(tab_a) parallel (tab_a, 5) */
user_id, user_name, user_postcode
from tab_a
where user_postcode > 49999
group by user_postcode, user_name, user_id
```

The above example specifies that the required SELECT operation is to be carried out as a full table scan on table `tab_a` (first hint) and also defines parallel processing with a degree of parallelism of 5 (second hint).

Figure 15.10 illustrates the three methods which are available for controlling the parallel query feature for a given SQL operation, and the order in which the three methods are carried out (assuming of course that parallel processing has not been explicitly excluded by the NOPARALLEL parameter). After parsing has been completed the EXECUTE call checks whether the SQL statement contains any hints which define the parallel processing option, in which case the specified value will be used. If no hints are found, the data dictionary is checked to see whether a degree of parallelism has been defined for the object in question. If no value has been specified at this level either then the default, system-wide degree of parallelism is selected. This final value is calculated on the basis of the following two parameters in the INIT.ORA file:

- PARALLEL_DEFAULT_SCANSIZE
- PARALLEL_DEFAULT_MAX_SCANS

The first of these two parameters defines the number of database blocks to be used when calculating the degree of parallelism; the number of data blocks used by a given table is divided by the value of PARALLEL_DEFAULT_SCANSIZE and the result represents the value which will be used for the degree of parallelism. The maximum value which can be set after applying this formula is specified by the second parameter (PARALLEL_DEFAULT_MAX_SCANS), which therefore defines the maximum number of query server processes for an operation.

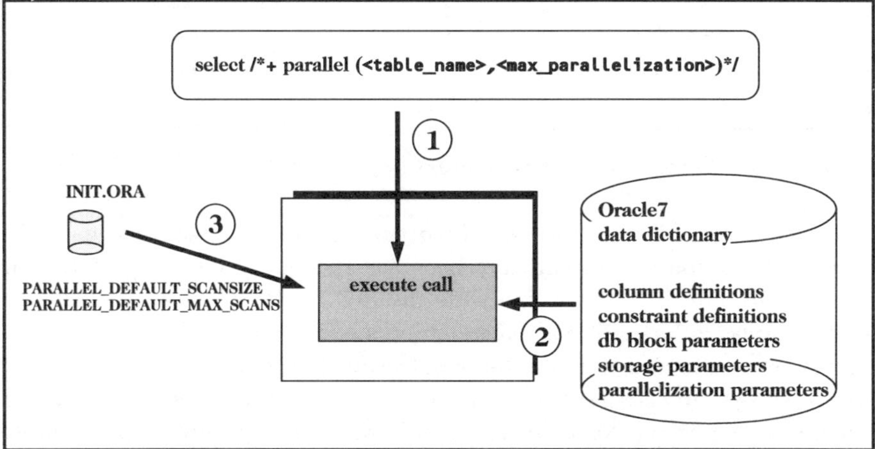

Figure 15.10 Controlling parallel query operations

These two parameters provide an easy method of using the parallel query function without having to modify an established schema or change an existing SQL program. The value for PARALLEL_DEFAULT_SCANSIZE (for a specific table) can be calculated on the basis of the number of blocks used by that table (USED_BLOCKS from the USER_TABLES view), the value for multi-block read operations (MULTI_BLOCK_READ_COUNT) from the INIT.ORA file and the number of CPUs available in the computer system used by the server. A sample calculation which shows how these three values can be used to determine the PARALLEL_DEFAULT_SCANSIZE parameter is given in Figure 15.11.

The second of the two parameters (PARALLEL_DEFAULT_MAX_SCANS) is more simple to calculate, as its value must be determined (in the first place) by the overall number of CPUs which are available on the system in question. However it may prove necessary to reduce this value to take account of other factors such as the overall system utilization, I/O constraints and so on.

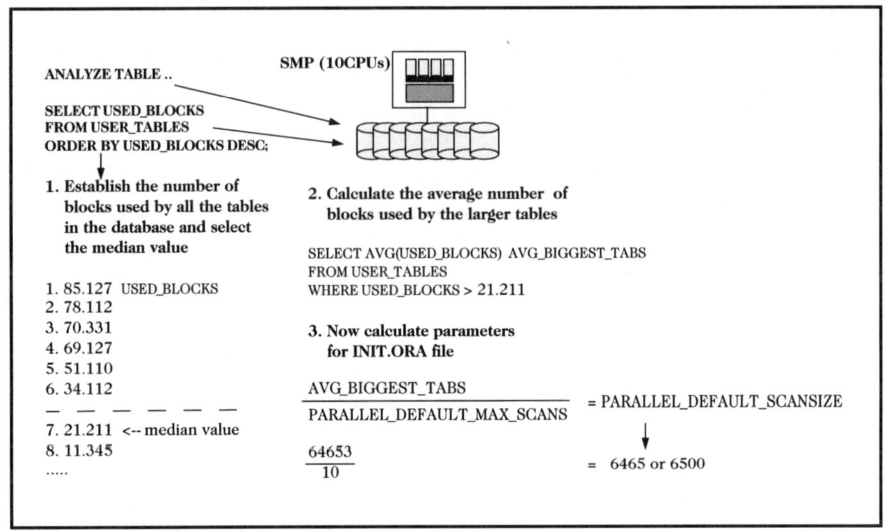

Figure 15.11 Calculating the default degree of parallelism for the INIT.ORA file

The Oracle7 Server process which carries out the EXECUTE call of a parallel SQL query automatically becomes the query coordinator for the whole operation. Its task is to divide the SQL statement into several sub-components, to have the partial statements executed by the Oracle7 query server processes and to make the result available to the user process. The *query server process* represents a new class of Oracle7 process which is created to carry out specific tasks, in a way already familiar from other Oracle7 processes such as DBWR, LCK0 and SNP0.

Query server processes are generated by a query coordinator process as and when they are needed to carry out specific SQL sub-statements. However it is possible to start a number of query coordinator processes as part of an Oracle7 instance; these processes run independently and are therefore immediately available to all query coordinators. The INIT.ORA parameter PARALLEL_MIN_SERVERS specifies how many query server processes should be created when the corresponding Oracle7 instance is started. The query server processes started in this way are referred to as the query server *base* pool (*refer also to* Figure 15.12).

If these existing processes are not sufficient to carry out the number of parallel processing operations required at any one time then new (dynamic) query server processes will be explicitly started by the query coordinators. The maximum number of query server processes which can operate on a given Oracle7 instance is specified by the INIT.ORA parameter PARALLEL_MAX_SERVERS. The total of all the query server processes which have been started in this way form the *variable* query server pool. Query server processes within the variable pool are retained only for as long as they are actually needed, so that if a process from the variable pool has not been activated for a fixed period of time it is terminated. The maximum idle time of a query server process from the variable pool is specified (in minutes) by the INIT.ORA parameter PARALLEL_SERVER_IDLE_TIME.

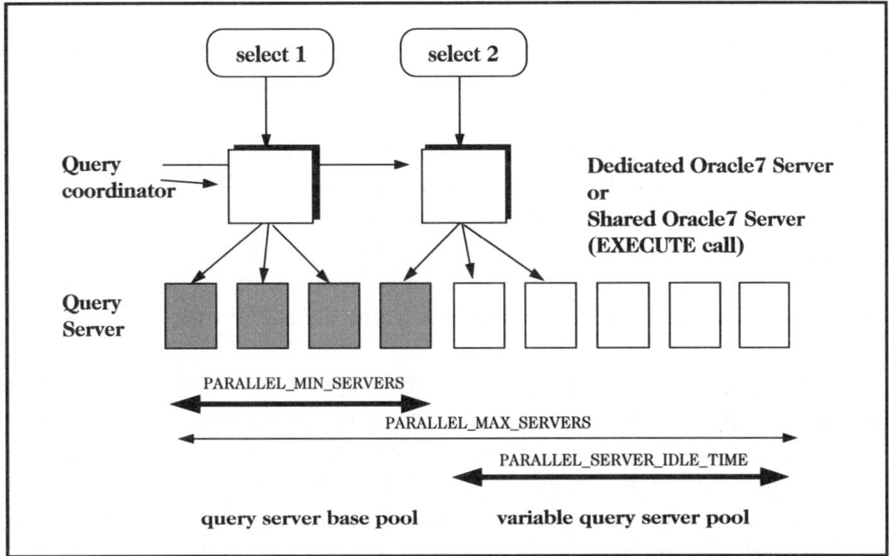

Figure 15.12 Oracle7 system architecture for parallel query processing

There is as yet no precise formula available which can be applied to calculating the degree of parallelism for a given combination of hardware, data and SQL operations. The procedure outlined in Figure 15.11 for defining the default values is a useful first step in this direction and in many cases it provides good results, but if we want to make optimum use of Oracle7's parallel query technology then we have to ensure that all components and aspects of a given system have been quantified and optimized as far as possible. This means being able to answer all of the following questions:

- To what extent is the capacity of the individual CPUs utilized?
- To what extent is the capacity of the I/O channels utilized?
- Which disks have the most I/Os?
- Have any I/O bottlenecks already been identified?
- Which database objects are stored on the most heavily used disks?

The first step in analysing a database is to establish the key reference values for all its tables and the analysis shown in Figure 15.11 can be very useful in this respect, since it allows us to quantify the size and structure of a given table, including the number of used database blocks, number of rows, amount of space used in a database block and so on. Figure 15.16 provides a

SQL script which will return all of these reference values whenever they are needed.

As well as analysing a database's tables in terms of size, it is also useful to find out which tables and which database operations require the longest processing times. By using the ORACLE tool TKPROF, it is possible to establish which SQL statements require very long execute times (for parallelization only the SELECT statements are relevant) and therefore which tables and/or operations should be optimized.

The 'default' degree of parallelism which is derived, as we have seen, from the two corresponding INIT.ORA parameters should not be set at too high a value, otherwise relatively simple operations will occupy an unnecessary proportion of the system's resources. However in the case of tables which are either very large or which are used very frequently, it is important to explicitly define a degree of parallelism which is higher than the INIT.ORA 'default' value.

Once a preliminary reconfiguration of the system has been carried out in this way it is possible to repeat the same sequence of observation and analysis operations; each set of results should be able to provide us with even more detailed information about how the parallel query option can best be used to improve the performance of our system. Equally important of course is to establish which bottlenecks in the system are beyond the scope of this particular feature; it may well be that the solution to a performance problem is to change the workload profile (that is, to create more processes to handle a given amount of data) or to add hints to the corresponding SQL statements.

Of course one of the most effective ways of improving system performance is to create an additional index on a table but, as we mentioned earlier, standard indexes cannot be used by parallel query operations, which will only carry out full table scans. However Release 7.1 of Oracle7 does provide the facility to create indexes which can be used as part of a vertical (inter-operation) parallel processing operation (*refer also to* Figure 15.6). A good example would be a large scale sort operation where the first part (the full table scan) is being carried out by a number of parallel query processes. Release 7.1 makes it possible for the results of these first query processes to be passed to the same number of sort processes which can make use of an index that has been defined on the table being read.

In order to define an index which can be used for this type of parallel processing it is necessary to specify the PARALLEL option when the corresponding index is being created, as shown in the following examples:

```
create unique index tab_a_ind1 on tab_a(user_id) parallel (degree 5);
create index tab_a_ind2 on tab_a (user_name) parallel (degree 20);
alter table tab_a
  enable constraint tab_a_pk using index parallel (degree 10);
```

It is not necessary or indeed even advisable to make every index capable of this kind of parallel processing; in general it is true to say that the primary index of any table should always include the PARALLEL option, as should any index on a medium to large table.

Figure 15.13 summarizes the three levels at which the degree of parallelism can be specified. The higher the definition level, the more specific the definition must be and the greater the resulting administrative workload will be to determine what degree of parallelism is appropriate for a specific database object.

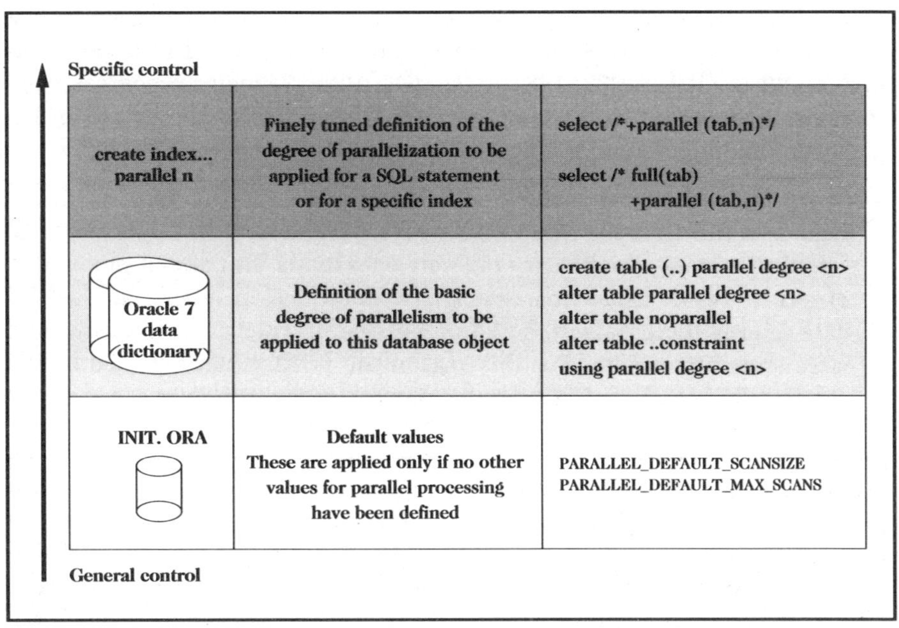

Specific control
create index...
parallel n
Finely tuned definition of the
degree of parallelization to be
applied for a SQL statement
or for a specific index
select /*+parallel (tab,n)*/
select /* full(tab)
+parallel (tab,n)*/
Oracle 7
data
dictionary
Definition of the basic
degree of parallelism to be
applied to this database object
create table (..) parallel degree <n>
alter table parallel degree <n>
alter table noparallel
alter table ..constraint
using parallel degree <n>
INIT. ORA
Default values
These are applied only if no other
values for parallel processing
have been defined
PARALLEL_DEFAULT_SCANSIZE
PARALLEL_DEFAULT_MAX_SCANS
General control

Figure 15.13 The three control levels for parallel processing

We have already mentioned several times that increasing the number of CPUs is not in itself the decisive element in improving the response times of a database system, improved CPU performance should be complemented by increased memory and I/O resources. The I/O of a computer system frequently proves to be a particular bottleneck in the parallel processing of complex SQL statements; database objects often cannot be processed in parallel at a physical level because they are stored on a single disk, so that the disk may be unable to cope with the extra demands being made of it.

However in spite of all these problems and even in cases where the system configuration is far from ideal, parallel processing has still proved itself able to achieve significant not to say dramatic improvements in response times. The following general hints, whenever they can be put into practice, will help towards achieving optimum response times:

- **Disk striping (physical)**
  Database files of the tablespaces with the largest tables can be striped using the available file system; this increases the parallelization at the I/O level.
- **Logical striping (tablespace striping)**
  Different tablespace files can be stored on different disks. The effect is similar to physical disk striping as here too the I/O parallelization is increased.
- **Striping the temporary tablespace**
  Physical or logical striping of the temporary tablespace is a good way of preventing a bottleneck on this internal object. In parallel sort operations (ORDER BY, GROUP BY, DISTINCT, SORT/MERGE) many processes need temporary storage in the temporary tablespace which can lead to an I/O bottleneck if only one disk is used.
- **SORT_AREA_SIZE parameter**
  Bear in mind that the SORT_AREA_SIZE parameter (INIT.ORA) is valid for all processes which carry out sort operations. In parallel mode a lot of sort processes usually carry out sort operations on smaller amounts of data than is the case with serial processing in which few processes sort large amounts of data. For this reason the SORT_AREA_SIZE parameter can usually be reduced in a parallel processing environment.

```
rem Function: db_sum_b.sql
rem
rem Calculates the number of database blocks and the number of extents
rem used by all the segments in a given schema
rem
rem 27.12.93 Guenther Stuerner
rem

create or replace view sum_blocks as
select   segment_name,
         sum(blocks )           sum_blocks,
         count(extent_id)       num_extents
from user_extents
group by segment_name
/
```

The following ORACLE utility carries out an analysis of a given schema

```
begin
dbms_utility.analyze_schema('&schema_name', 'estimate');
end;
/
```

Figure 15.14a Additional SQL scripts required by `db_bl_st` script (*see* Figure 15.14b)

```
rem  ******************************************************************
rem  Function:   db_bl_st
rem
rem  Calculates the block statistics for all the tables in a
rem  given schema
rem
rem  Requirements: 1. The db_sum_b script (generates the view
rem                   'sum_blocks') must run first
rem                2. The script dbms_utility.analyze_schema
rem                   (<schema>, <estimate_or_compute>)
rem                   must also be run first
rem
rem  27.12.93 GStuerner
rem  ******************************************************************

column segment_name    format  a15
column sum_bl          format 99999
column nev_used        format 99999
column del_bl          format 99999
column a_r_l           format 99999
column a_spa_bl        format 99999
column no_rows         format 9999999
column used_bl         format 99999
column num_ext         format 99999

break on Report
compute sum of  sum_bl used_bl nev_used on report

select
   segment_name,
   sum_blocks                      sum_bl,
   blocks                          used_bl,
   empty_blocks                    nev_used ,
   avg_space                       a_spa_bl,
   avg_row_len                     a_r_l,
   num_rows                        num_rows,
   num_extents                     num_ext
from  sum_blocks gb, user_tables
where segment_name=table_name
/
#
#doc  sum_bl    = total number of database blocks per segment
#doc  used_bl   = total number of database blocks which contain data
#doc  nev_used  = total number of unused database blocks
#doc  a_r_l     = average record length
#doc  a_spa_bl  = average free space per database block (in Bytes)
#doc  num_row   = total number of records stored in a table
#doc  num_ext   = total number of extents
#

---------------Results---------------------------------------

Segment_Name Sum_Bl Used_Bl Nev_Used  A_Spa_Bl A_R_L Num_Rows Num_Ext
------------ ------ ------- --------  -------- ----- -------- -------
BIGEMP         3205    2799      405       216    40   114759      15
EMP2             85      69       15       211    40     2744       6
             ------  ------   ------
sum            3290    2868      420
```

Figure 15.14b SQL script to carry out database block analysis

15.3 Parallel recovery procedure

As more and more organizations become increasingly dependent on relational database systems, the performance and stability of these systems assumes correspondingly greater importance. It is therefore essential to know that a given database system provides adequate procedures for both backing up a database and for carrying out all necessary recovery operations should all or part of the database crash.

With regard to any backup procedures in use, one very important requirement is that online backups can be carried out regularly without affecting the overall performance of the system to any noticeable degree, but the speed at which an online backup is carried out is of much less significance. In the case of any recovery procedures on the other hand, speed becomes a critical factor, because if all or part of a database has become inoperative then it is essential to restore the system as quickly as possible.

The time needed to recover a database following a disk failure (for example) can be divided into two stages:

- the restore time
- the recovery time

Restore time is the time needed to physically copy the backup files from the backup medium (such as tape or disk) to the relevant database disks. It is important that the overall recovery process can be confined to the faulty disk drive so that only the backup of the faulty disk is required and the remaining parts of the database system can be used without interruption.

Restore time basically depends on two factors:

- extent of restore granularity
- loading speed of the backup medium

The actual recovery process can be started as soon as the necessary backup copies have been copied to the disk drives. In Oracle7 Release 7.0 a recovery operation was carried out by a single process which had the following tasks:

- to read the redo log entries from the redo log files;
- to write the database blocks, index blocks, rollback segment blocks from the database files to the database cache;
- to carry out the modifications specified by the redo log entry.

How long this recovery process would take depended on the number of redo log files which had to be processed and, since only one recovery process was available, on the performance of the CPUs in the computer system.

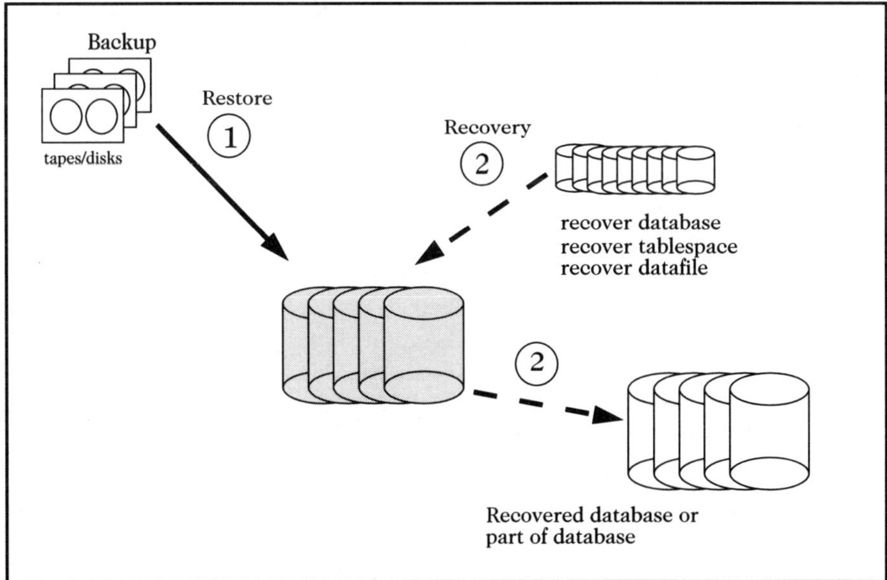

Figure 15.15 Carrying out restore and recovery operations

The number of redo log files to be processed is, in turn, dependent on the transaction rate of the system and on the point at which the faulty disk was last backed up. Systems with higher transaction rates will obviously generate a large number of redo log entries and therefore a large number of redo log files. However it is possible to influence the number of redo log files needed to carry out a database recovery; database objects which are modified relatively frequently can be backed up more often, and objects which are always processed in read-only mode can be assigned to read-only tablespaces which are automatically excluded from any backup and recovery procedures.

A further method of reducing recovery time with Oracle7 Release 7.0 is to parallelize the recovery process manually; this method involves running a number of recovery processes in parallel on a corresponding number of SQL*DBA sessions. Each session recovers one redo log file with the RECOVER_DATAFILE command. However although this method does accelerate recovery, it has the disadvantage of making the DBA completely responsible for the recovery process. In addition the corresponding redo log files have to be read many times as each recovery process only needs those redo log entries which contain transaction protocols for its own database files.

Apart from these organizational measures Release 7.0 of Oracle7 offers no way of improving recovery times for the fundamental reason that the recovery operation on a given instance can only be carried out by the one recovery process, regardless of the hardware architecture in use. However with the introduction of the parallel recovery procedure in Oracle7 Release 7.1, the recovery operation is not limited to one single process but can be carried out by a number of recovery server processes working in parallel. It is important to emphasize that this new feature is not in any way dependent on the Oracle7 Parallel Server and parallel query technologies, but forms an integral part of the basic 7.1 Release.

The distribution of tasks between the available recovery server processes is managed by the recovery coordinator which makes use of a hash function to allocate database blocks (for all three segment types) to the individual recovery servers which are then exclusively responsible for all recovery actions involving those blocks.

We have already looked in some detail at the importance of the transaction concept in ORACLE (Chapter 5) and at how the recovery method depends upon recognizing which transactions have been completed (so that they are entered in the redo log files) and which are still open. Open transactions are of course automatically rolled back when media or instance recovery processes take place.

Similarly we have also examined how redo log files are used to record all the modifications which can be made on a database, including changes in data block values, to indexes, to rollback segments as well as to the transaction table values which form an integral part of the rollback segment header.

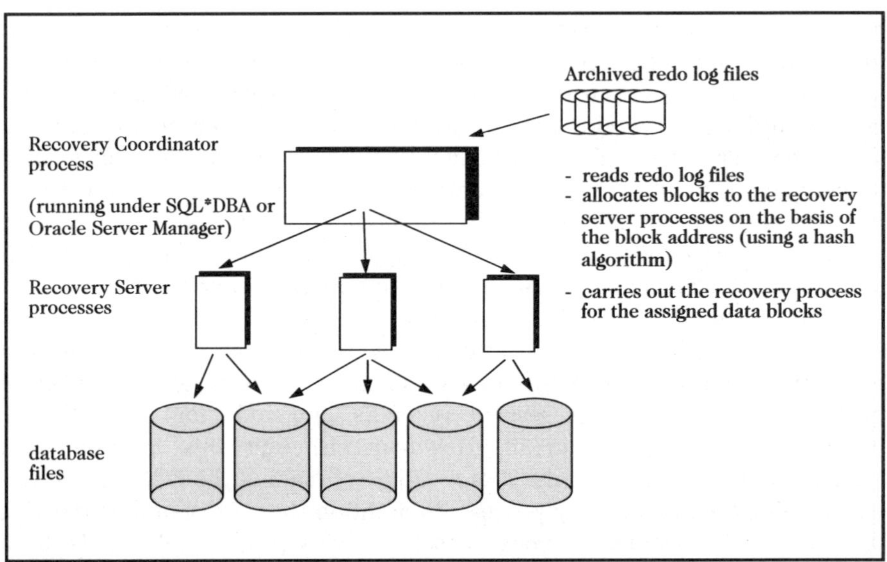

Figure 15.16 The Oracle7 parallel recovery technology

Before we go on to examine Oracle7's new parallel recovery feature, it is important to remember that, for the purposes of the recovery process, there is no essential difference between committing or rolling back a transaction; both measures involve the same basic action of writing rollback segment entries back to the database blocks. This similarity between COMMIT and

ROLLBACK transactions forms the starting point for the parallel recovery procedure introduced with Release 7.1.

A parallel recovery operation involves the following two steps:

- the recovery coordinator process (which runs under the SQL*DBA session) reads the redo log file;
- the individual redo log entries are passed to a recovery server process for processing. A hash procedure ensures that a database block is always processed by the same recovery server.

Figure 15.17 shows a simple transaction being recovered in parallel mode with a total of three recovery server processes operating.

A total of three database blocks are involved in this simple example:

- a database block (data values)
- a rollback segment block for the transaction table
- a rollback segment block for 'undo' values

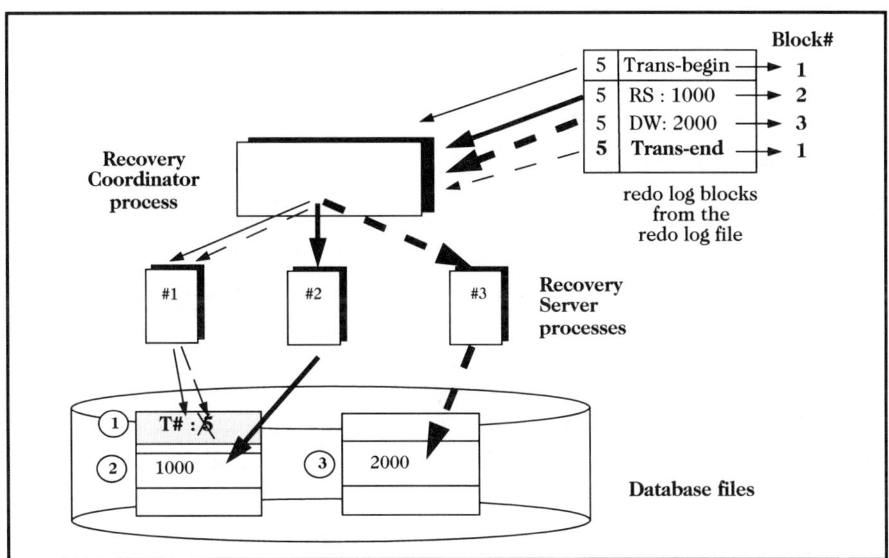

Figure 15.17 Basic recovery processing

For simplicity the content of these three database blocks was shown by allocating the blocks the numbers one to three, which in our example are processed by recovery server processes one to three. In a real situation the allocation of database blocks to the recovery server processes is carried out with the aid of a hash procedure.

The number of parallel recovery processes is controlled in one of two ways: either by means of the INIT.ORA parameter RECOVERY_PARALLELISM or by explicitly specifying the degree of parallelism in the RECOVER statement or with the RECOVER clause of the ALTER DATABASE statement. The degree of parallelism specified in the RECOVERY_PARALLELISM parameter is used only if no value is specified in the RECOVER statement. This parameter also determines the degree of parallelism in an instance recovery.

Figure 15.18 gives an overview of the parameters and statements used in parallel recovery.

The degree of parallelism which should be specified for the parallel recovery operation depends on the following factors:

- the number of disks
- the number of CPUs
- the processing capability of the CPUs

The maximum number of parallel recovery processes which can be started is specified by the INIT.ORA parameter PARALLEL_MAX_SERVERS which depends very much on the number and capability of the installed CPUs.

SQL command/parameter	Defined in/by	Comments
`recovery_parallelism=<n>`	INIT.ORA	Default value for instance recovery Default value for media recovery (where no explicit parallel value specified) <n> = 0 or 1 -> no parallel recovery <n> > 1 use parallel recovery <n> must be less than INIT.ORA parameter PARALLEL_MAX_SERVERS

`recover database`
`tablespace`
`datafile`
`parallel <n>`
 	
or
 	
`alter database <db_name>`
`recover ....`
`parallel <n>`
	SQL*DBA
	Oracle Server Manager
		explicit value for degree of parallelism
		
		recover database ORA71 parallel 20;
		
		recover tablespace TA parallel 5;

Figure 15.18 Commands and parameters for controlling parallel recovery

The degree of parallelism for recovery operations is typically in the region of one to two times the number of disks which make up the database system.

15.4 Extensions to the ORACLE tablespace concept

Until now the ORACLE tablespace concept has been based on the assumption that all database files are stored on read/write media (magnetic disks), and nearly all of the most important internal processing functions carried out by the ORACLE Server involve a write to disk operation. Setting a checkpoint for example involves writing the current checkpoint data structure to the file headers of all database files on the online tablespaces; the very nature of this operation means that it can only be carried out with read/write media.

Due to this method of internal processing it was not possible with previous versions of ORACLE to run parts of the database with read-only media such as compact disks.

With Release 7.1 it is now possible to define a whole tablespace as being read-only and thus to limit all SQL operations which can be carried out on the database objects of this tablespace to read-only operations. This is of particular interest for databases which contain data that need not or must not be modified in the normal way.

All database objects which are located within a read-only tablespace can be processed with any SELECT operations. However contrary to the method used prior to Release 7.1 the database server does not carry out any modifications within the database file header. What this means is that a read-only tablespace can be stored not only on conventional magnetic disks but also on media such as compact disks which can only be written to once.

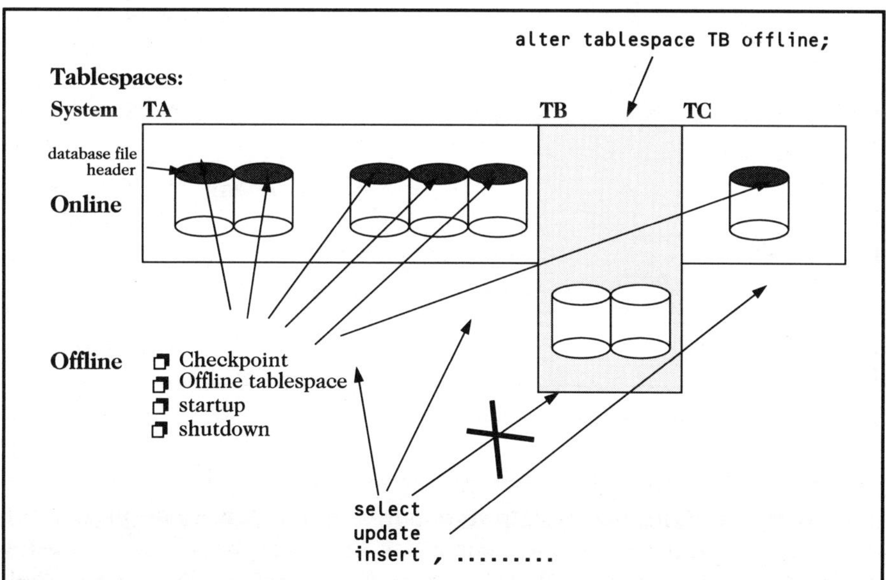

Figure 15.19 Tablespace modes (online/offline) under Oracle7 Release 7.0

Normally a tablespace which has been created with the CREATE TABLESPACE statement together with all its database files will always be in read-write mode. To turn a read-write tablespace into a read-only tablespace the following ALTER TABLESPACE statement must be entered:

```
alter tablespace TC read only;
```

However before this statement can be put into effect the corresponding Oracle7 instance must first be stopped (SHUTDOWN NORMAL) and then re-started in restricted mode. This ensures that there are no open transactions against the tablespace which is to be put into read-only mode and that there are no active rollback segments within this tablespace.

It is only at this point that the ALTER TABLESPACE ... READ ONLY command can be entered; the new definition for the tablespace will be recorded in the data dictionary, the control file and in all the headers of the database files located in the read-only tablespace file. If the database files are to remain on the original disks it is now possible to start the Oracle7 instance and open the database at once.

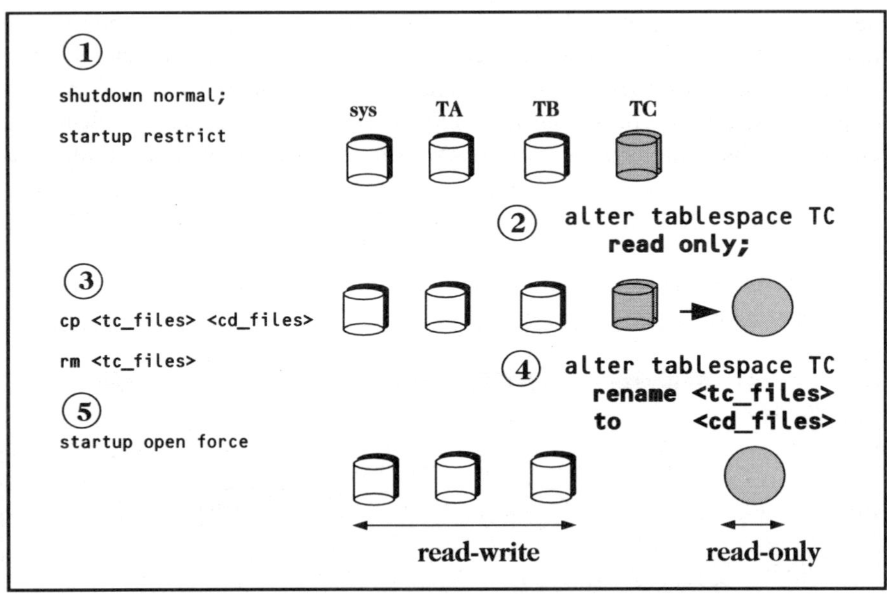

Figure 15.20 Defining a read-only tablespace

Of course it may well be that, having installed a read-only medium, we now want to use this new disk to store our read-only tablespace files; in this case it is only necessary to carry out stages 3 and 4 of the procedure illustrated in Figure 15.20. In stage 3 of this example the physical files of a read-only tablespace are copied to a read-only medium (for example by creating a CD) and in stage 4 the new file names are communicated to the Oracle7 Server by use of the ALTER TABLESPACE ... RENAME statement which will then be recorded in the data dictionary and control file.

Redefining a tablespace from read-write to read-only mode represents a structural change to the database, and therefore requires a backup of the control file and of the database files of the read-only tablespace. However once its database files have been backed up at this point, a read-only tablespace can then be excluded from the normal cycle of backup operations; since a read-only tablespace does not undergo any modifications (neither by SQL statements nor by internal modify operations), the original backup of its database files will be enough to deal with any loss of data caused by medium failure. This also means that a recovery operation does not have to be carried out for a read-only tablespace.

The use of read-only tablespaces should always be considered for large amounts of read-only data. Since read-only tablespaces do not need to be included in backup procedures (apart from the very first backup when the tablespace is created), their use can reduce the time and resources needed to carry out the regular system backups. Because they also make it possible to store parts of the database on CDs (a relatively cheap medium), their use can reduce the hardware costs of running a large database system. These two benefits will often make up for any work which is involved in reorganizing the database in order to set up one or more read-only tablespaces.

One of the potential flaws in this first implementation of the read-only tablespace concept stems from the fact that ORACLE tablespaces cannot be shared between databases, each tablespace, regardless of the type, belongs only to one database. It is therefore not possible to store a given body of common data on a read-only tablespace on CD and then make it available to a number of Oracle7 Servers.

However this type of functionality represents a common requirement of many software producers, who administer the source code of an application system within the database itself. If it were possible to include the same read-only tablespace in any number of databases, then the process of installing new versions of an applications program could be enormously simplified. It would then only be necessary to store the new version of the applications software on a read-only tablespace on CD; this CD could then be sent to any number of customers who would only have to load the new CD in order to have the latest version of their applications software.

Although this particular feature is not available with Release 7.1, Oracle is planning to include it in one of the next Oracle7 releases.

15.5 Additional features for stored procedures

Release 7.1 of the Oracle7 Server has implemented two important extensions to the functionality of stored PL/SQL programs:

- use of PL/SQL functions as SQL functions
- use of dynamic SQL within PL/SQL programs

In Release 7.0 PL/SQL functions and procedures could be called from within stored PL/SQL programs, 4GL procedures (Oracle Forms, Oracle Reports and so on) as well as within 3GL programs (*refer also to* Figure 7.4).

The standard SQL functions provided by ORACLE (altogether numbering more than fifty) form a very powerful extension to standard SQL, and Release 7.0 made it possible to call any of these standard SQL functions from within PL/SQL programs as though they were standard PL/SQL functions. However up until now individual PL/SQL functions which had been developed by a programmer as stored PL/SQL procedures could only be executed in the program environments listed above (PL/SQL, 3GL and 4GL environments) but not from within the server's SQL environment.

This restriction has now been removed with Release 7.1, so that any stored PL/SQL function can now be executed as part of a standard SQL statement as long as the following rules have been observed:

- A PL/SQL function is not permitted to carry out any modify operation on tables using the INSERT, UPDATE or DELETE statements.
- PL/SQL functions which are executed on a remote database server cannot read or modify any global package variables. This also applies to PL/SQL functions which are executed within a SQL statement capable of parallelization.

As we have already seen (*refer to* Chapter 8) PL/SQL functions can be defined as stand-alone modules with the CREATE FUNCTION statement or as part of a PL/SQL package, as Figure 15.21 illustrates.

Figure 15.21 shows a diagrammatic representation of the structure of two PL/SQL functions, both of which can be executed within any SQL statement or as part of a PL/SQL program. As we can see from this example, the package function is called with the package name in front of the function name, otherwise the function is used in exactly the same way as any standard SQL routine. As with other PL/SQL functions it is possible to conceal the full name of the function by using synonyms, as in the following example:

```
create synonym my_func2 for my_package1.my_func2;
```

It is also possible to call a PL/SQL function on a remote Oracle7 Server. A remote PL/SQL function is addressed by using database links in the way already familiar to us from Section 8.2.4. The following statement shows a typical example:

```
select my_func1§stgt(high, low)...from <table_name>
```

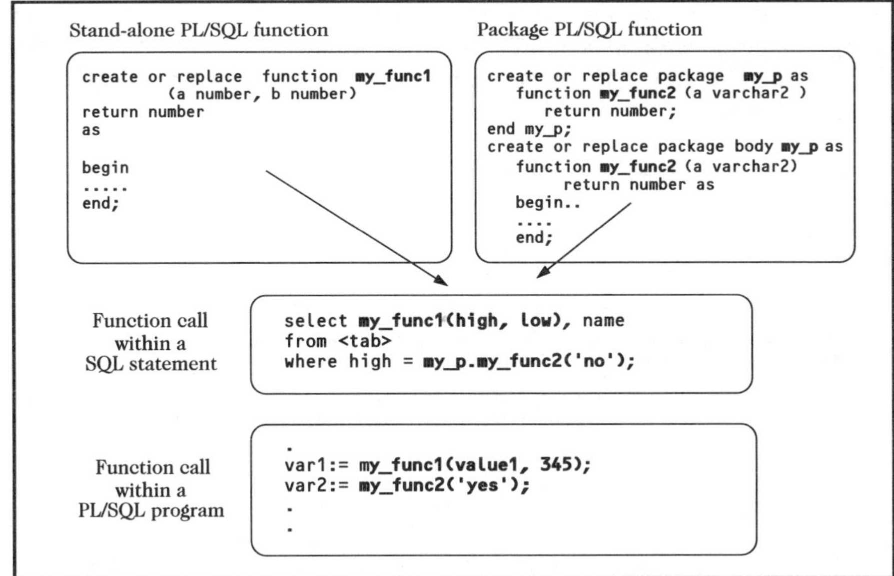

Figure 15.21 Using PL/SQL functions within SQL statements

The function `my_func1` is located on a remote Oracle7 Server, which is addressed via the database link **`stgt`**, and it is executed for all rows which the SELECT statement returns from the local database.

An example of a simple PL/SQL function which can also be used as a SQL function is illustrated in Figures 15.22a and 15.22b with the functions `my_sql_func2` and `my_sql_func3`. Both functions have an identical range, but the first has been defined as a stand-alone function, the second as a package function.

The task of these functions is to multiply a numeric value (the first parameter) with a factor which is not submitted as a parameter but is determined each time that the function is called from the 'factor' table. The factor value to be used is determined by the second parameter which forms an index on the relevant row within the factor table.

As we have already mentioned it is not possible for a PL/SQL function which is being used within a SQL statement to carry out modifications on the database with the INSERT, UPDATE or DELETE commands. In the case of stand-alone functions this is checked at runtime and if this rule has been violated then ORACLE error message **`ORA-06571`** is returned (`Function <function-name> does not guarantee not to UPDATE the database`) and the execution of the statement is aborted.

If a package function is to be called within a SQL statement then the restrictions which normally apply to that function within the PL/SQL environment must be defined by means of the pragma construct as part of the overall package specification. The RESTRICTED_REFERENCES pragma specifies which restrictions are applicable to a particular function and these are checked when the function is compiled. If a package function is called as a SQL function without a RESTRICTED_REFERENCES pragma having been defined then the same ORACLE error message mentioned above (ORA-06571) will be returned.

```
create or replace function my_sql_func2 (num_inp number, var_fac_no number)
return number
as
result              number;
factor_value        number;

begin
select factor into factor_value from factor where fac_no = var_fac_no;
/* factor table: fac_no            factor
                      1              1.500
                      2              4.500
                      3             12.875
*/
result := num_inp * factor_value;
return result;
end;
/
```

```
select    emp_salary,
          emp_deptno,
          my_sql_func2(emp_salary,2)
from employee
/
update employee
set emp_salary = my_sql_func2(emp_salary,
                              decode(emp_deptno, 10,1, 20,2, 30,1, 1))
```

Figure 15.22a Using a stand-alone PL/SQL function within SQL

The RESTRICTED_REFERENCES pragma is defined as part of a package header with the following syntax:

```
pragma restricted_references
(<function_name>,<restriction1>,<restriction2>,...)
```

We can distinguish between two basic types of restriction:

- restrictions against reading or modifying database tables
- restrictions against reading and modifying package variables

Thus we can define any of the following four restrictions:

- WNDS :Write No Database State
- RNDS :Read No Database State (both refer to database tables)
- WNPS :Write No Package State
- RNPS :Read No Package State (both refer to package variables)

In our example in Figure 15.22b the function **my_sql_func3** is not able to carry out any modifications on the tables in the database (WNDS). This limitation is a minimum requirement which must be applied to all PL/SQL functions which are to be used as SQL functions. If this pragma is not implemented for a given package function then it cannot be used as a SQL function.

```
create or replace package  my_package1 as
function my_sql_func3 (num_inp number, var_fac_no number)  return number;
pragma restrict_references(my_sql_func3, WNDS);
end my_p;
/
create or replace package body my_package1 as
function my_sql_func3 (num_inp number, var_fac_no number)
return number
as
result              number;
factor_value        number;

begin
select factor into factor_value from factor where fac_no = var_fac_no;
result := num_inp*factor_value;
return result;
end;
end my_p;

    select my_p.my_sql_func3(emp_salary, 1) from employee
    /

    create synonym my_sql_func3 for my_p.my_sql_func3
    /

    select my_sql_func3(emp_salary,1) from employee
    /
```

Figure 15.22b Using a package PL/SQL function within SQL

The Oracle7 procedural gateway development environment, which we deal with in Section 15.7, offers another interesting feature in this context, in that it makes it possible to integrate any procedural services, for example C programs, into PL/SQL programs.

Using this technology it is possible to implement PL/SQL functions which will execute existing 3GL programs, and these PL/SQL functions can then be called from within SQL statements. We thus have a method of developing relatively complex programs which can easily be called from within the SQL command shell, and of extending and adapting the functions of the SQL environment almost without limit.

Figure 15.23 illustrates an example of how complex functions can be created in this way; a SQL statement contains a call to a stored PL/SQL function which in turn contains a call to a C program which is processed via a procedural gateway.

PL/SQL functions which are called from SQL statements are (of course) still governed by the same object privilege rules which apply to PL/SQL routines in all other circumstances; the user who wishes to call a PL/SQL function from within SQL must have been granted the EXECUTE privilege on that function by its owner.

One final aspect of the use of PL/SQL functions within SQL statements concerns the use of the parallel query option; if a SQL statement which is to be processed in parallel does contain PL/SQL function calls, then those calls will automatically also be executed in parallel. This means that we have in effect the possibility of carrying out PL/SQL procedures and functions in parallel.

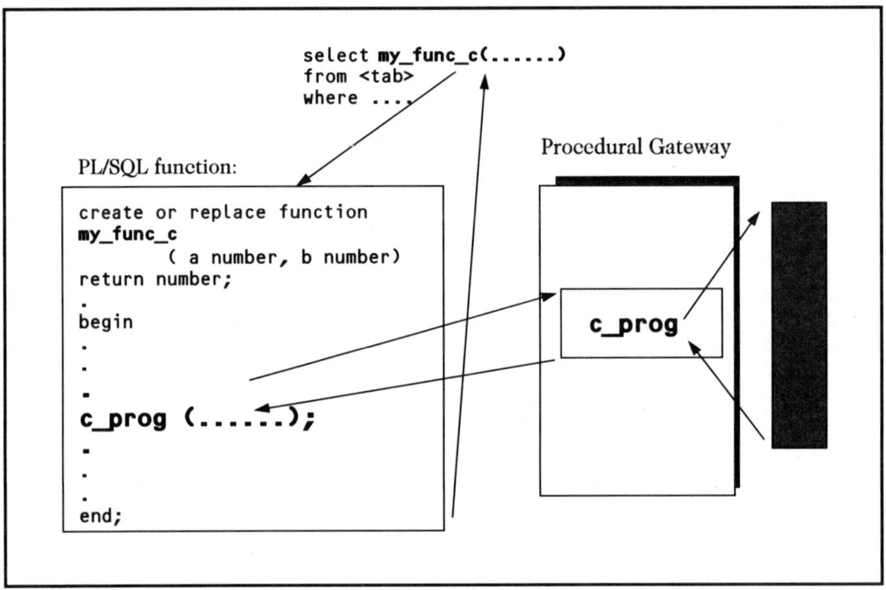

Figure 15.23 Integrating external procedural services in a SQL function call

The second important extension to the functionality of PL/SQL programs, which has been introduced with Oracle7 Release 7.1, is the possibility of using dynamic SQL statements within PL/SQL programs. This new feature means that the full flexibility of SQL programming can be made use of within stored PL/SQL programs.

We looked at the differences between static and dynamic SQL in Chapter 2, but as these differences are relevant to this new feature of Release 7.1, it would be worthwhile to look at them again.

- **Static SQL**
  The structure of a static SQL statement is fixed once it is written and only the SQL statement's bind variables can be assigned variable values at runtime. In the following piece of static PL/SQL code only the bind variable no has a dynamic character, in that it can be assigned different values each time the code is run:

```
declare
no    number;
begin
select emp_name, emp_salary
into name, salary
from employee
where emp_no = no;
end;
```

- **Dynamic SQL**
  A dynamic SQL statement is not fixed when the program is written. The type and structure of the statements to be carried out (SELECT, UPDATE and so on) are generated by the program at runtime on the basis of input parameters or other values which can be read from the database, and in the latter case only if a corresponding database table exists in which executable SQL statements are stored.

Cursor is opened (cursor number is assigned)	`dyn_sql:= dbms_sql.open_cursor;`

SQL statement is parsed	`dbms_sql.parse (dyn_sql,`
	`select emp_name, emp_salary`
	`from employee`
	`where emp_no = :NUM,`
	`dbms_sql.V7);`

Output columns are defined	`dbms_sql.define_column(dyn_sql, 1, emp_name, 20);` `dbms_sql.define_column(dyn_sql, 2, emp_salary);`
Input columns are defined	`dbms_sql.bind_variable(dyn_sql, ':num', <emp_no_value>);`
Statement is executed	`status := dbms_sql.execute(dyn_sql);`
Records are read	`rows   := dbms_sql.fetch_rows(dyn_sql);`
Returned values are assigned to PL/SQL program variables	`dbms_sql.column_value(dyn_sql, 1, ret_name);` `dbms_sql.column_value(dyn_sql, 2, ret_salary);`

Figure 15.24 Using dynamic SQL within PL/SQL programs

Dynamic SQL statements allow very compact and extremely flexible programs to be developed, the major disadvantage with this method of programming is that it is far more demanding and complicated than using static SQL. With dynamic SQL it becomes necessary to explicitly program all the stages of a program's execution which would otherwise (under static SQL) be carried out by the precompiler or the PL/SQL compiler. To give some idea of the difference in complexity between these two types of SQL Figure 15.24 shows a list of the statements which are needed to create the following simple SELECT statement in dynamic SQL:

```
select emp_name, emp_salary
from employee
where emp_no = no;
```

Please note that for the purposes of this example, the SQL statement to be executed has been included as a literal value (`dbms_sql.parse(dyn_sql, 'select emp_name, emp_salary...'`); normally of course it would make sense to pass the SQL statements to be carried out as parameters to the procedure. This is illustrated in Figure 15.24a where a SQL statement forms the second input parameter to the procedure `my_dyn_prog6`, which then executes it dynamically.

It is also possible to actually create dynamic SQL statements within stored PL/SQL programs by putting together predefined sub-commands and SQL statements which have been stored in the database. Figure 15.24b shows how SQL statements can be read from database tables and then carried out within a PL/SQL procedure.

All the operations necessary for carrying out dynamic SQL statements are contained in the DBMS_SQL package (*refer also to* Figure 8.16 which lists all the other Oracle7 PL/SQL packages and their individual procedures). The DBMS_SQL package contains the following PL/SQL procedures (P) and functions (F):

- OPEN_CURSOR (F)
- PARSE (P)
- BIND_VARIABLE (P)
- DEFINE_COLUMN (P)
- EXECUTE (F)
- FETCH_ROWS (F)
- EXECUTE_AND_FETCH (F)
- COLUMN_VALUE (P)
- VARIABLE_VALUE (P)
- CLOSE_CURSOR (P)
- IS_OPEN (F)

```
create or replace procedure my_dyn_prog6 (num_var  in number,
                                          sql_statement  in varchar)
/* Example for how this procedure can be called

my_dyn_prog6(4000,'select emp_name,emp_salary from employee
          where emp_salary > :X')
my_dyn_prog6(7369,'select emp_name,emp_salary from employee
          where emp_no = :X')
my_dyn_prog6(5100,'select emp_name,emp_salary from employee
          where emp_salary <= :X')
my_dyn_prog6(:var_no, :var_sql_state) -- Call for a precompiler
                                      -- or a 4GL program (e.g. Oracle Forms)

*/

as
dyn_sql        integer;
status         integer;
emp_name       varchar(20);
emp_salary     number(8,2);
rows           integer;
log_no         number;

begin
dyn_sql := dbms_sql.open_cursor;
dbms_sql.parse(dyn_sql,sql_statement,dbms_sql.v7);

dbms_sql.define_column(dyn_sql,1,emp_name,20);
dbms_sql.define_column(dyn_sql,2,emp_salary);
dbms_sql.bind_variable(dyn_sql,':x',num_var);

status := dbms_sql.execute(dyn_sql);

select gst_seq.nextval into log_no from dual;

while dbms_sql.fetch_rows(dyn_sql)>0  loop

   dbms_sql.column_value(dyn_sql,1,emp_name);
   dbms_sql.column_value(dyn_sql,2,emp_salary);

   insert into prog_log values (log_no,status,emp_name,emp_salary,null);
end loop;

commit;
dbms_sql.close_cursor(dyn_sql);
end;
/
```

```
rem Calling this procedure from SQL*Plus

begin
my_dyn_prog6(&num_var, 'select emp_name, emp_salary from employee where &where');
end;
/
rem Another way of calling the same procedure

undef sql_st
def   sql_st='select emp_name, emp_salary from employee where &where'
begin
my_dyn_prog6(&num_var, &&sql_st);
end;
/
```

Figure 15.24a A PL/SQL procedure with dynamic SQL calls passed as parameters

```
create or replace procedure my_dyn_prog5 (num_var number,sql_no number)
as
dyn_sql                         integer;
status                          integer;
var_emp_name                    varchar(20);
var_emp_salary                  number(8,2);
rows                            integer;
sql_text_var                    varchar(2000);

begin
/* two sample rows from the 'sql_statements' table:

no(number)  sql_text(varchar2 )
----------  ------------------------------------------------------------
1           select emp_name, emp_salary from employee where emp_no = :x
2           select emp_name, my_sql_func2(emp_salary,fact_no) emp_salary
               from employee where emp_no = :x
*/
select sql_text into sql_text_var from sql_statements
where no=sql_nr;

dyn_sql:=dbms_sql.open_cursor;
dbms_sql.parse(dyn_sql,sql_text_var,dbms_sql.v7);
dbms_sql.define_column(dyn_sql,1,emp_name,20);
dbms_sql.define_column(dyn_sql,2,emp_salary);
dbms_sql.bind_variable(dyn_sql,':x',num_var );

status:=dbms_sql.execute(dyn_sql);
rows:=dbms_sql.fetch_rows(dyn_sql);
dbms_sql.column_value(dyn_sql,1,var_emp_name);
dbms_sql.column_value(dyn_sql,2,var_emp_salary);

/* Record transaction in PROG_LOG table */
insert into prog_log values
    (gst_seq.nextval,status,var_emp_name,var_emp_salary,num_var);
commit;
dbms_sql.close_cursor(dyn_sql);
end;
/
```

```
rem Call procedure from SQL*Plus

begin
my_dyn_prog5(&emp_no,&sql_no);
end;
/
```

Figure 15.24b A PL/SQL procedure with dynamic SQL calls read from database tables

By using these procedures and functions it becomes possible to implement very flexible and compact stored PL/SQL programs and database triggers which are able to provide nearly all of the functionality offered by 3GL programs with embedded SQL. The one major feature not offered by this type of dynamic SQL programming is the possibility to create dynamic SQL statements which work with a variable SELECT and BIND lists. With this (extremely flexible) variant of dynamic SQL programming provided by ORACLE's 3GL environments, the number and type of the parameters for the SELECT or BIND lists do not have to be specified when a routine is being programmed; this means that the procedure or function can be called with a variable parameter list.

In order to make use of the possibilities offered by dynamic SQL programming, it is obviously necessary to provide a method which generates runtime program variables which can be assigned the input values (BIND list) or output values (SELECT list) of a SQL operation. Within ORACLE's 3GL environments (Pro*SQL or OCI) this function is carried out by descriptors; these are data structures which are generated at runtime within a dynamic SQL program and which provide the variable BIND and SELECT lists for the SQL statements to be carried out. The respective commands to create these two sorts of descriptor are DESCRIBE BIND VARIABLE and DESCRIBE SELECT LIST FOR.

15.6 Additional features for defining procedural integrity

As we know from Section 9.3.2 Oracle7 Release 7.0 provides twelve types of database trigger, these twelve triggers can be assigned to any database table but with the restriction that only one of each type of trigger can be defined per table. In Release 7.0 it was therefore not possible to have more than one BEFORE UPDATE row trigger on the same table. However since there is no limit on the size of a given trigger, and since database triggers can also call stored PL/SQL procedures, there was no real limit to the functionality which could be implemented by means of a single database trigger.

However difficulties can occur when different development teams or different software suppliers develop applications systems on the basis of the same data structures and all want to make extensive use of database triggers as part of their system implementation. It is obviously going to prove very difficult to ensure the integrity of a single database trigger if it has to be modified by different teams of programmers.

With Release 7.1 it is now possible to create more than one trigger of the same type on one table; when the triggering event occurs, then all the corresponding triggers are fired in sequence, the sequence being determined by the Oracle7 Server only. It is important to emphasize this fact because, as the order in which the triggers are fired cannot be specified by the user, it is essential that no explicit or implicit dependencies exist between the actions carried out by the individual triggers.

This extension to the procedural integrity methods of Oracle7 makes it possible for different software suppliers to implement database triggers on existing data structures without having to alter any existing database trigger code. This greatly simplifies software integration especially in larger systems and as a consequence has a beneficial effect on the productivity of the developers and the stability of the system as a whole.

Figure 15.25 illustrates a data structure with multiple triggers of the same type.

At this point it is worth referring back to the SQL scripts contained in Figure 9.25, which show how to find out what declarative and procedural constraints have been defined for a given table.

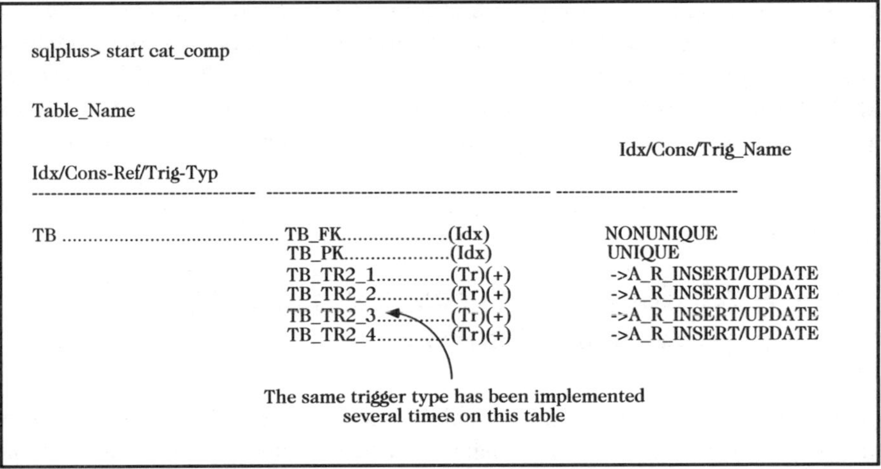

```
sqlplus> start cat_comp

Table_Name
                                                       Idx/Cons/Trig_Name
Idx/Cons-Ref/Trig-Typ
--------------------- ---------------------------- -------------------

TB ....................... TB_FK....................(Idx)      NONUNIQUE
                           TB_PK....................(Idx)      UNIQUE
                           TB_TR2_1..............(Tr)(+)       ->A_R_INSERT/UPDATE
                           TB_TR2_2..............(Tr)(+)       ->A_R_INSERT/UPDATE
                           TB_TR2_3..............(Tr)(+)       ->A_R_INSERT/UPDATE
                           TB_TR2_4..............(Tr)(+)       ->A_R_INSERT/UPDATE
```


Figure 15.25 Using multiple triggers on the same table

15.7 Oracle Open Gateway Technology

15.7.1 Introduction

The need to integrate all available sources of information within any organization has emerged as one of the most important goals of modern data processing systems and is one of the key factors which distinguish a fully developed information technology environment. Needless to say the technical and organizational obstacles which have to be overcome in order to achieve this goal are formidable; data sources will typically be available in a number of formats (relational or hierarchical databases, file systems and so on) and on any number of different hardware platforms.

Particular problems are frequently posed by the introduction of new applications systems; users often want to take advantage of the increased power and flexibility offered by new applications systems, only to find that the new software is unable to access their existing data sources and that to transfer these data to a new system would cost more than the actual applications software.

For these reasons ORACLE has for some years provided the SQL*Connect group of products which allow users to integrate a selected number of database and file systems into an ORACLE environment. The first SQL*Connect products were developed for DB2, SQL/DS and NON-Stop

SQL; these products, which were based on considerably modified ORACLE Version 5 technology, were always developed exclusively for one specific data storage system. Needless to say the development of this type of 'hand-made' SQL*Connect product was extremely labour-intensive and it often required an inordinate amount of time to produce a finished product.

For this reason the second generation of the SQL*Connect products was created with the help of a common development system based on ORACLE Version 6 technology. By using this new development system it was possible to produce a new family of SQL*Connect products within a relatively short space of time.

The introduction of ORACLE's Open Gateway Technology led to a complete redesign of the gateway product range; the experience gained from developing the second generation of SQL*Connect products taken together with the technology incorporated in the Oracle7 database provided the basis for implementing a whole new family of products, all of which are based on the ORACLE Open Gateway Technology. These products can be divided into the following two product classes:

- Transparent (data) Gateways
- Procedural Gateways

Each of these two product classes comprises both ready-made gateway products and development environments which can be used to create individual gateway systems, and the resulting product range (listed below) means that it is possible to integrate a very large number of different data sources and applications into an ORACLE system environment (*refer also to* Figure 15.26):

- Transparent Gateways for some data sources, including DB2, Rdb and DRDA;
- Transparent Gateway Development Environments for customers or VARs who wish to create individual gateway systems;
- Procedural Gateways for some procedural services, for example procedural APPC gateway for CICS or IMS/TM;
- Procedural Gateway Development Environments for integrating C programs and other procedural services.

The basis for all four product groups is the Internal Gateway Developers Kit (IGDK) which is available both to ORACLE developers for the development of transparent data and procedural gateways and to customers who can make use of it to implement their own gateway systems for any data sources or programs.

By making this development system available outside the company, Oracle is helping to provide its users with a much wider choice of gateway systems, and customers who decide to make use of the Gateway Development Environment are given a means of integrating almost any number of different data sources. Furthermore the Development Environment for procedural gateways offers a means of integrating any existing programs and services which are available in a given DP environment. A typical case for program integration would be where a user has a number of complex algorithms (mathematical C routines for example) which are crucial to some aspect of his business processes; ORACLE's procedural gateway technology would allow these software modules to be integrated into a stored PL/SQL program, thus saving the costs and risks involved in rewriting or adapting them for another system environment. This kind of procedural gateway solution is illustrated in Figure 15.30.

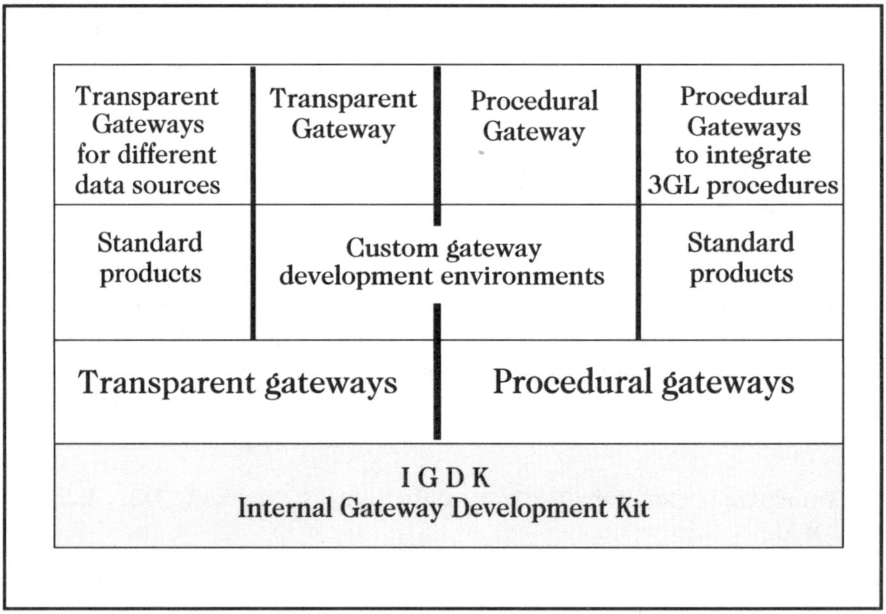

Figure 15.26 The ORACLE Open Gateway product range

15.7.2 The ORACLE Open Gateway products

Transparent Gateways

Transparent Gateway products act in basically the same way as Versions 1 and 2 of the SQL*Connect products in that they too are 'tailor-made' for specific data sources and are developed and marketed by Oracle as separate products. However like all the other products in the ORACLE Open Gateway product range they are based on the IGDK and therefore on Oracle7 technology.

Figure 15.27 shows a typical configuration that includes a Transparent Gateway. In this example the Oracle7 Server acts as the integrating server, analysing all SQL statements and, where necessary, forwarding them for further processing by a remote Oracle7 Server or by a Transparent Gateway. It is important to note that the Transparent Gateway makes use of the same rules which control all distributed databases in an ORACLE system; remote database objects are addressed by means of database links, synonyms or views can be defined to simplify access procedures, access privileges can be defined either centrally or on the remote server. One of the major advantages of applying the same control mechanisms to non-ORACLE data sources is that all access procedures remain completely transparent to the user, who does not need to know what type of data source is being accessed or what type of system is providing it.

Most Transparent Gateway systems are provided with read-write capability and can also make use of the Oracle7 two-phase commit protocol. This is a very important feature of these products since it means that distributed transactions can be carried out in a heterogeneous environment which includes non-ORACLE data sources. However in the case of distributed transactions only one foreign system can be involved per transaction and this system will always be used as the commit point site within the two-phase commit mechanism (*refer also to* Chapter 14).

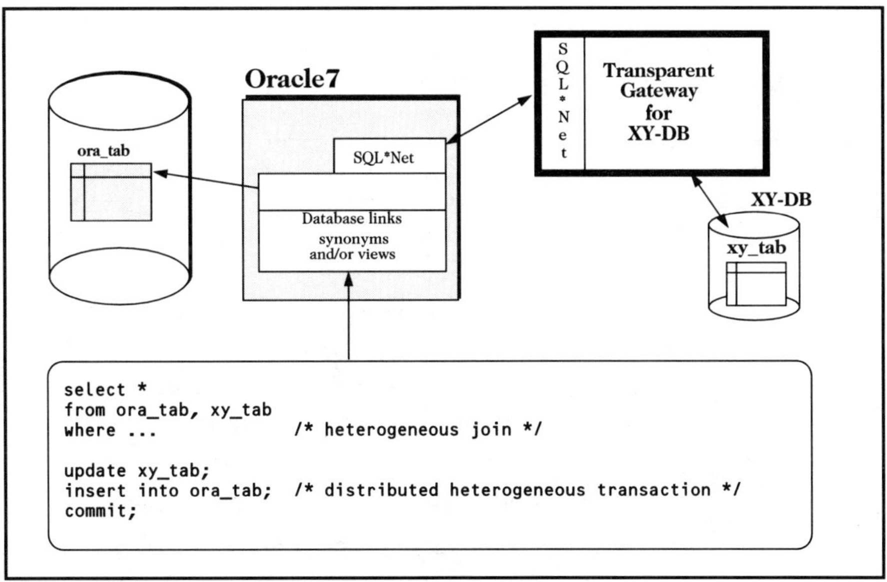

Figure 15.27 Using an ORACLE Transparent Gateway

These new capabilities of the ORACLE database and gateway products represent a major step forward in comparison to the functionality provided by SQL*Connect, and will make it much simpler to carry out migration from one system to another. By using these products it is possible to implement new applications systems which are able to access existing data sources, then when the point is reached for the existing data source also to be replaced, this switch can be accomplished by simply redefining the tables, views and so on which are referenced in the applications program code. Thus it is possible to switch between different data sources without having to alter or even recompile any of the software which accesses them (*refer to* Chapters 13 *and* 14 for more information on this subject).

The Transparent Gateway Development Environment

Whereas ORACLE's Transparent Gateways are ready-made products, the Transparent Gateway Development Environment provides the tools and methods to develop customized gateway systems to specific data sources; this development package consists of a number of interface programs with the corresponding documentation which describes how a Transparent Gateway has to be implemented.

A customized data gateway is basically no different from the ready-made products provided by ORACLE, except that it might not offer all the implementation levels provided by the standard ORACLE gateways; if for example it is only necessary to implement read access to a particular file system then there is clearly no point in programming the functions necessary to carry out any other operations for that gateway. Figure 15.28 shows the typical structure of an individual Transparent Gateway.

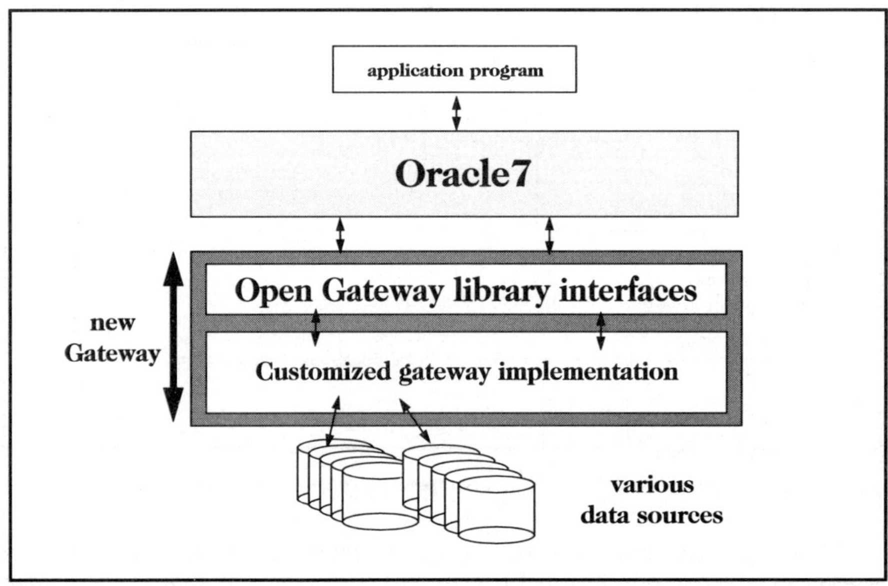

Figure 15.28 The software architecture of a customized Transparent Gateway

ORACLE basically distinguishes between four different Transparent Gateway Development Environments, each of which requires different procedural methods during implementation, thus providing development environments which take account of the specific characteristics of:

- set-based (SQL) systems
- file-based systems
- hierarchical database systems
- Codasyl database systems

As we have already mentioned there is no functional difference between the Gateway systems developed by ORACLE and those produced by users with the Transparent Gateway Development Environment. Nor is there any difference in the way these gateways are configured; the gateway system is always installed on the computer where the data source which is to be integrated is located, and communication between Oracle7 Servers and gateway systems is carried out via SQL*Net and whatever network protocols are required. The only exception to this rule is the ORACLE DRDA Gateway which has to be installed on a dedicated computer system from which it can access all APPC compatible IBM data storage systems via the IBM APPC protocol, although this dedicated system may also be the host system for the Oracle7 Server.

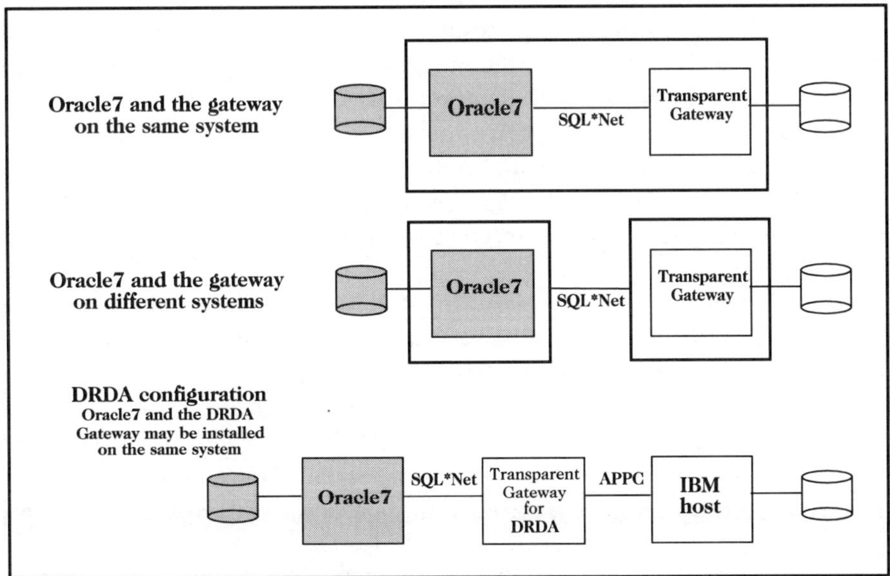

Figure 15.29 Alternative configuration possibilities for Oracle7 gateways

In contrast to the first versions of the SQL*Connect products, the ORACLE Open Gateway Technology systems cannot be used as stand-alone products since they always need the integrating capabilities of an Oracle7 Server to provide the client program with a completely transparent view of all global data structures and to conceal any incompatibilities in a foreign system from the application program.

A data source which has been included in an ORACLE environment by means of a Transparent Gateway does not impose any restrictions on client programs in terms of SQL functionality and syntax. Joins, subqueries, set operations, view definitions and many other standard SQL operations can be carried out via a gateway as though the foreign data source were a normal Oracle7 database. If the gateway has been configured to support write operations, then remote and distributed transactions can also be carried out. However in the case of distributed transactions only one foreign system can be involved per transaction and this system will always be used as the commit point site within the two-phase commit mechanism (*refer also to* Chapter 14).

Procedural Gateways

The SQL*Connect product range has no products comparable with the Procedural Gateways and, as with its Transparent Gateway technology, ORACLE provides both ready-made gateways and a development environment for creating our own customized procedural gateways. The function of a procedural gateway is to make it possible to run any program or procedural service that has been implemented in another (normally 3GL) programming language from within a PL/SQL program and, where necessary, to return the results of that program as PL/SQL parameters. It is important to understand that the 3GL procedures activated in this way are not actually 'included' in the PL/SQL code; the procedural gateway only provides the ORACLE client application with access to the system on which the required routines are located.

As with Transparent Gateways, the ORACLE Procedural Gateway has to be installed on the same computer system which contains the 3GL routines to be used; these routines can then be called from either the local or a remote system (Figure 15.30 illustrates this with a configuration of two nodes connected via SQL*Net). As with other ORACLE products, the location of the procedural gateway and of the corresponding foreign routines can be made completely transparent through the careful use of database links, views and synonyms.

When a 3GL routine is called from a PL/SQL program, as shown in Figure 15.30, the following sequence of actions is carried out:

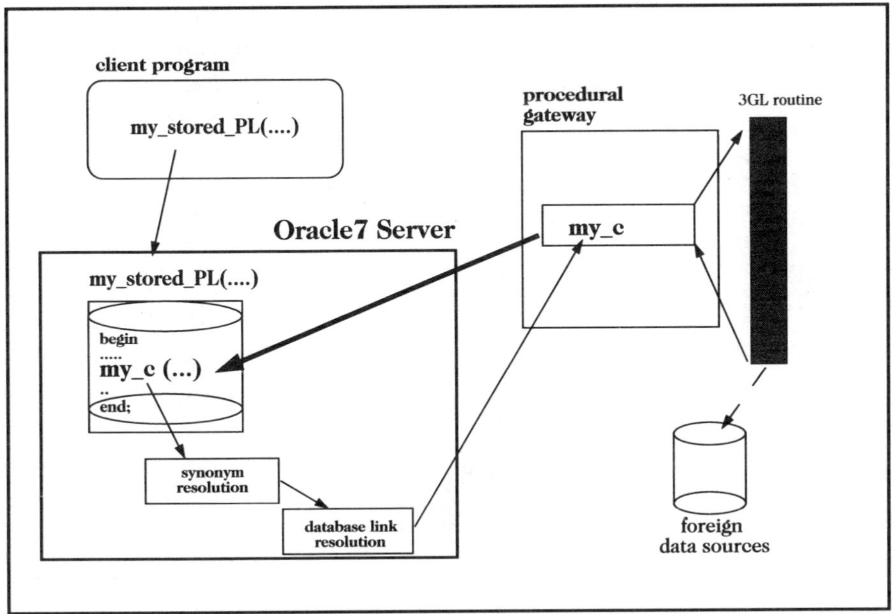

Figure 15.30 Calling a 3GL routine from a stored PL/SQL procedure

- Any synonyms which have been used are resolved.
- Database links are analysed (the database link indicates the procedural gateway into which the 3GL routine has been integrated).
- Any parameters are passed to the procedural gateway.
- The routines are then executed in the context of the procedural gateway.
- Any output parameters are passed back to the calling PL/SQL code.

The Procedural Gateway Development Environment makes it possible to implement custom procedural gateways which have all the functionality of the standard ORACLE products. As with the ready-made products, custom procedural gateways can be used to integrate existing 3GL programs and procedures into PL/SQL programs, which means of course that the procedural gateway can be accessed from within stored PL/SQL programs and database triggers as well as SQL statements which have been developed with PL/SQL.

A customized procedural gateway is defined by means of the Gateway Data Definition Language (GDDL), which maps the 3GL routines on the target system to PL/SQL stored procedures or functions. These procedure definitions are then processed by the Procedural Gateway Builder (PGB) which generates a corresponding interface definition or 'wrapper' that can then be linked with both the ORACLE Procedural Gateway library and with the actual 3GL routine.

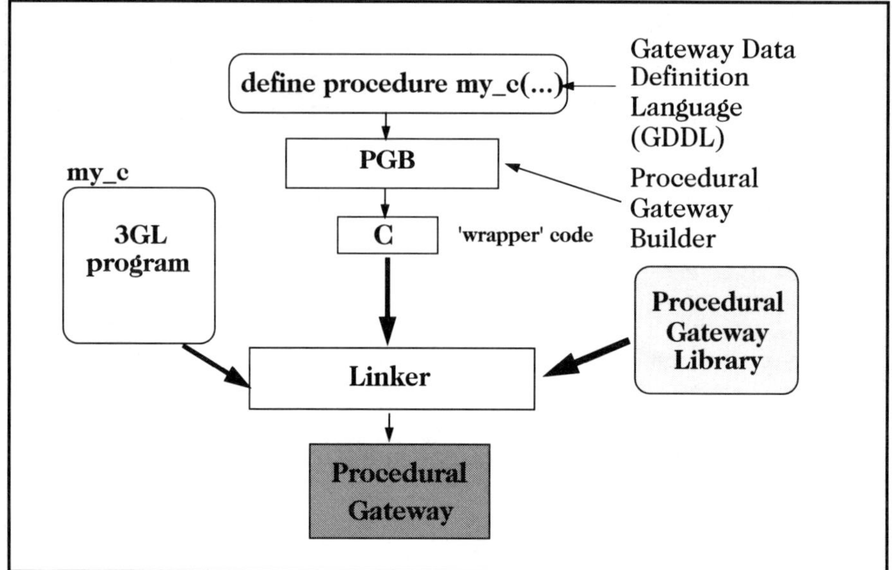

Figure 15.31 Creating a customized procedural gateway

Having looked in general terms at how ORACLE's Open Gateway technology works, it would be useful to examine a specific example of how one of these products works. One of the first procedural gateways to be provided by ORACLE was the APPC Gateway for integrating CICS and IMS/TM transactions into an ORACLE system environment, allowing the kind of configuration shown in Figure 15.32.

Here we can see that, as with the Transparent Gateway for DRDA mentioned earlier, the APPC Procedural Gateway has been installed on a dedicated IBM system (RS/6000). The use of a dedicated system for the gateway has the advantage that no other software components need to be installed on the host system.

Once the gateway has been installed (on the IBM system) and configured (on the ORACLE side) it then becomes possible for any ORACLE application to activate CICS or IMS/TM routines on the foreign system and to make use of the data generated by those routines. Calls to CICS or IMS/TM routines within PL/SQL programs are passed by the Oracle7 Server to the APPC Gateway which makes use of APPC Services to execute the calls on the host system.

It is important to emphasize that the format in which data are held on the IBM host system is completely immaterial in this context, and our ORACLE applications can equally well be provided with data from a file system (VSAM), a hierarchical database (DL/1 or IMS) or any other sort of data storage system which has been implemented on the remote host. The only requirement, as we are dealing with the APPC Procedural Gateway, is that the data are accessed by existing CICS or IMS/TM programs and that the host system is APPC compatible.

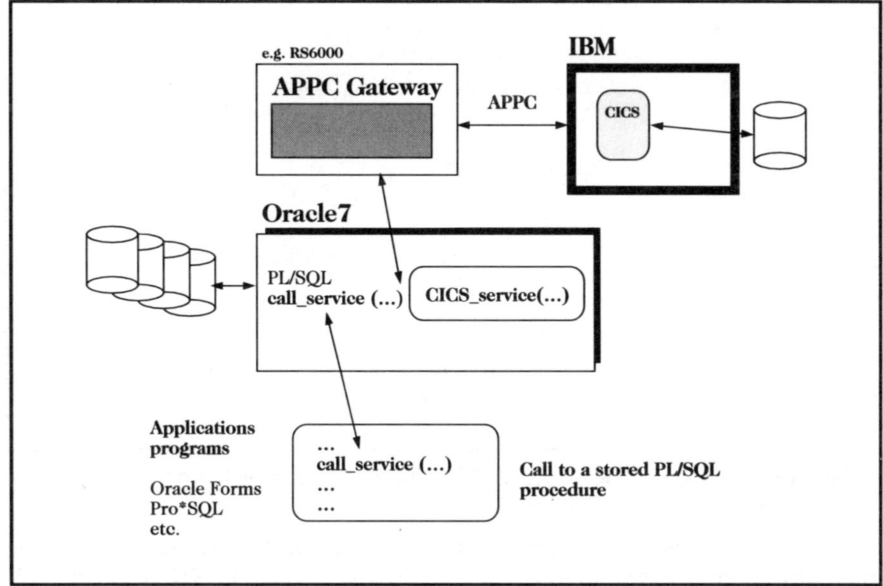

Figure 15.32 Implementing the APPC Procedural Gateway with a CICS host system

15.8 Oracle7 Release 7.1: summary of other new and extended features

15.8.1 Oracle7 Release 7.1 network technology

Because of the increasing importance and complexity of distributed system environments, Release 7.1 includes a number of features which enhance and extend the functionality of the Transparent Network Substrate (TNS) technology that was introduced with Release 7.0 of the Oracle7 Server. The most important of these are listed in Figure 15.33.

Of all the products listed here, it is the Oracle Network Manager which represents the primary means for describing the configuration of a networked system, and it defines the following components of a distributed ORACLE system:

- the ORACLE nodes and instances;
- the MultiProtocol Interchanges;
- the networks and network domains;
- the database links (where the Oracle Name Server is also in use).

Oracle Network Manager	Configuration management for distributed ORACLE systems. GUI based.
Oracle Names	Creates the Name Server for administering all the objects in a distributed ORACLE system. Simplifies the management of large-scale distributed systems.
Secure Network Services	Provides for encryption of all data on a network.
Password Encrytion	Provides password encryption for client/server or server/server logins.
Dead process detection	Generic detection of dead processes independent of the network protocol used
Extended trace features	Improved facilities for tracing and logging error and exception conditions.

Figure 15.33 Oracle7 Release 7.1 TNS Products and the new functions of SQL*Net

This system description can now be used for generating all the configuration files which previously had to be created manually, that is, TNSNAMES.ORA, TNSNET.ORA, TNSNAV.ORA and the Interchange configuration file INTCHG.ORA (*refer also to* Chapter 13).

Another new product provided with Release 7.1 is Oracle Names, which allows us to define one server (the *Name Server*) which can be used to centrally administer all the names which have to be defined within a distributed ORACLE system. An Oracle Name Server will therefore contain:

- all ORACLE node information
- all ORACLE database links
- all Aliases

Oracle Names is an optional product. Database links which are recorded with Oracle Names can be centrally administered by the Oracle Network Manager.

In the field of data security for distributed ORACLE systems there have also been some important extensions. The Secure Network Service, for example, provides an additional level to SQL*Net, and it encodes all data which are being sent to another ORACLE Server via SQL*Net. This possibility of encoding all data which are transmitted via SQL*Net between client systems and Oracle7 Servers or from one server system to another is of particular interest to users who have previously been unable to implement distributed systems because of the sensitive nature of the data which they have to deal with.

Another small but nevertheless extremely important security feature provided with Release 7.1 is the long awaited encryption of passwords for client/server and server/server communication. The use of encrypted passwords can be specified by using the environment variable ORA_ENCRYPT_LOGIN on the client machine and the INIT.ORA parameter DBLINK_ENCRYPT_LOGIN on the server system. This feature is illustrated in Figure 15.34.

It is important to emphasize that password encryption will only take place when the corresponding encryption parameters are set to TRUE at both ends of a communications link; ORA_ENCRYPT_LOGIN must always be set to TRUE on the client side as must DBLINK_ENCRYPT_LOGIN on the server side. The same also applies for password encryption with server to server communication using database links, where the INIT.ORA encryption parameter must be set to TRUE on each server involved in the communication process. If this is not the case the connection attempt must be tried again and a reconnect with unencrypted passwords will automatically be carried out. This automatic reconnect however only happens when both systems are running Release 7.1; an attempt to use encrypted passwords with anything less than a 7.1 server will be aborted with a corresponding error message.

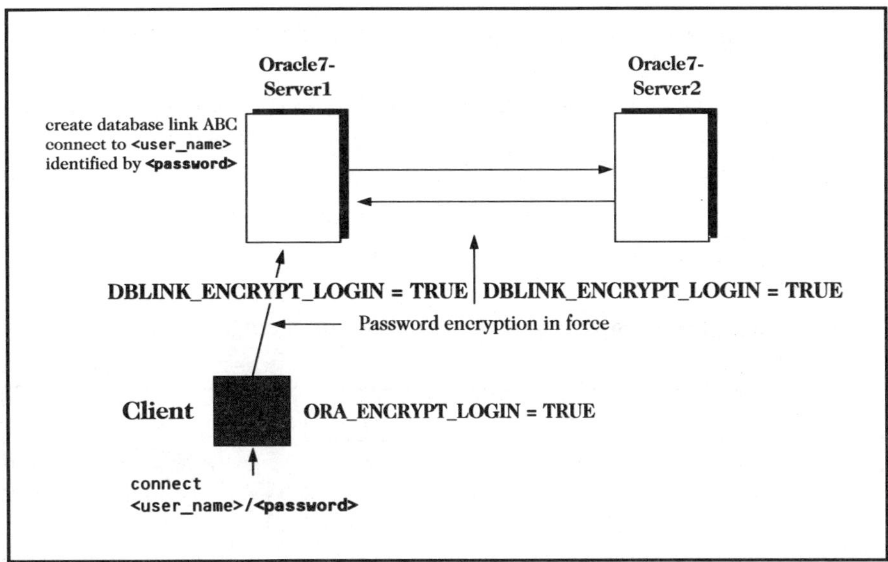

Figure 15.34 Password encryption in client/server and server/server configurations

15.8.2 Extensions to the Oracle7 replication concept

As we have already seen (*refer to* Chapter 14), Release 7.0 of Oracle7 introduced three different types of data replication:

- asynchronous replication (Oracle7 snapshots),
- synchronous (read-only) replication,
- synchronous (read-write) replication.

Release 7.1 of Oracle7 extends this replication technology by making it possible to form a *group* of snapshot tables which can then be processed and accessed as a single unit, instead of having to carry out the same operation on each snapshot table individually. These groups are referred to as snapshot refresh groups.

All operations on snapshot refresh groups are carried out with the DBMS_REFRESH package which provides the following operations:

- MAKE
  to create a refresh group;
- ADD
  to extend a refresh group with additional snapshots;
- SUBTRACT
  to remove a snapshot from the refresh group;
- CHANGE
  to alter a characteristic of the group, for example the refresh interval;
- DESTROY
  to delete the refresh group, that is not to delete the individual snapshots themselves, but to undo the grouping function for all of them;
- USER_EXPORT and USER_EXPORT_CHILD
  to generate SQL scripts which will create another version either of the whole group or one snapshot from the group;
- REFRESH
  to refresh all the snapshots in the group within a single transaction.

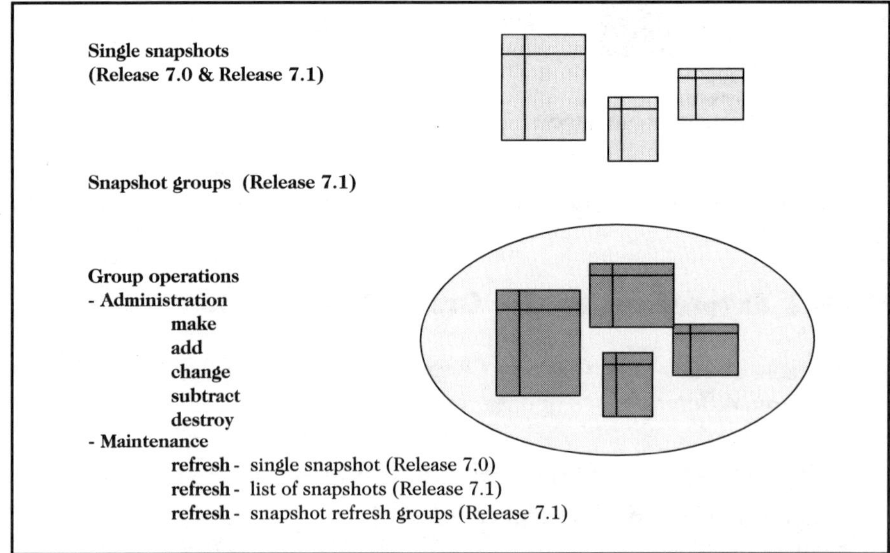

Figure 15.35 Defining and maintaining single and group snapshots with Oracle7

The functions provided by the DBMS_REFRESH package for administering ORACLE snapshots represent an important extension of the functionality already provided (under Release 7.0) with the DBMS_SNAPSHOT package. Figure 15.36 lists the procedures of both packages and also indicates at what point in the snapshot cycle and on which table (that is, the master or the replicate) they are carried out.

Please note that whereas the REFRESH procedure of the DBMS_REFRESH package can only be applied to snapshot groups, the REFRESH procedure of the DBMS_SNAPSHOT package can be used to process both single snapshots and a list of snapshots (LIST REFRESH). When a REFRESH operation is carried out on a group or list of snapshots then all the replicates belonging to that group or list are refreshed in one transaction.

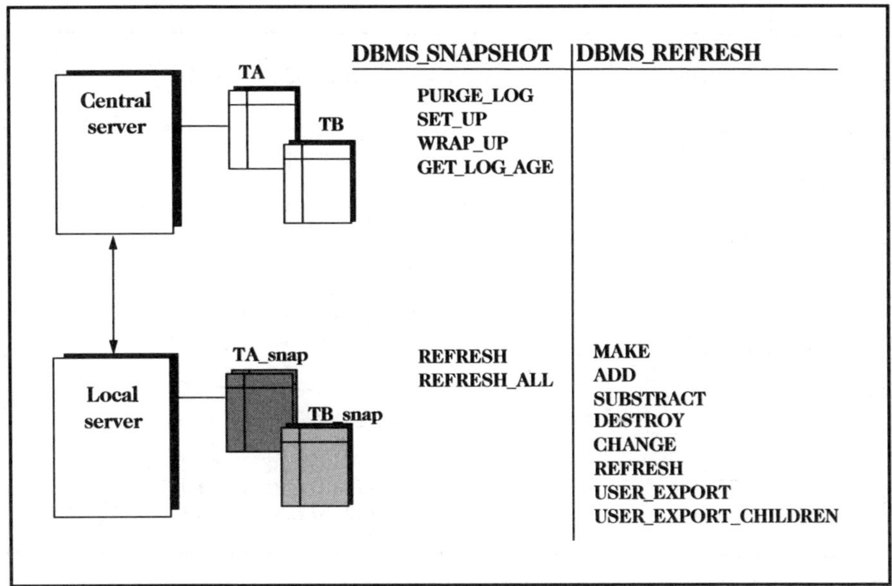

Figure 15.36 Oracle7 snapshot operations

Although it is of course possible to use the procedures of these two PL/SQL packages to carry out manual refresh operations on any replicate tables, this would in practice be a very unusual and repetitive task. As soon as one or more snapshots have been defined, it becomes necessary for them to be refreshed automatically. Every Oracle7 instance makes it possible to control the automatic refresh cycle for snapshot files by means of three parameters in the INIT.ORA file. These parameters are:

- SNAPSHOT_REFRESH_PROCESSES
  This parameter specifies how many background refresh processes should be active per Oracle7 instance, up to a maximum of ten. However more than one refresh process is only necessary if the instance includes a number of snapshots which have to be refreshed at very frequent intervals.

- SNAPSHOT_REFRESH_INTERVAL
  This parameter specifies the interval at which the background refresh processes should wake up to check whether there are any snapshots which need to be refreshed. The default is 60 seconds. If any snapshots have been defined with shorter refresh intervals this parameter must be adjusted to reflect this shortest refresh interval.
- SNAPSHOT_REFRESH_KEEP_CONNECTIONS
  If this parameter is set to TRUE the connection to the remote system containing the master tables will not be taken down after each refresh process has been completed. It is particularly important for this parameter to be set to TRUE when refreshes are carried out frequently so that time spent opening and closing connections is minimized.

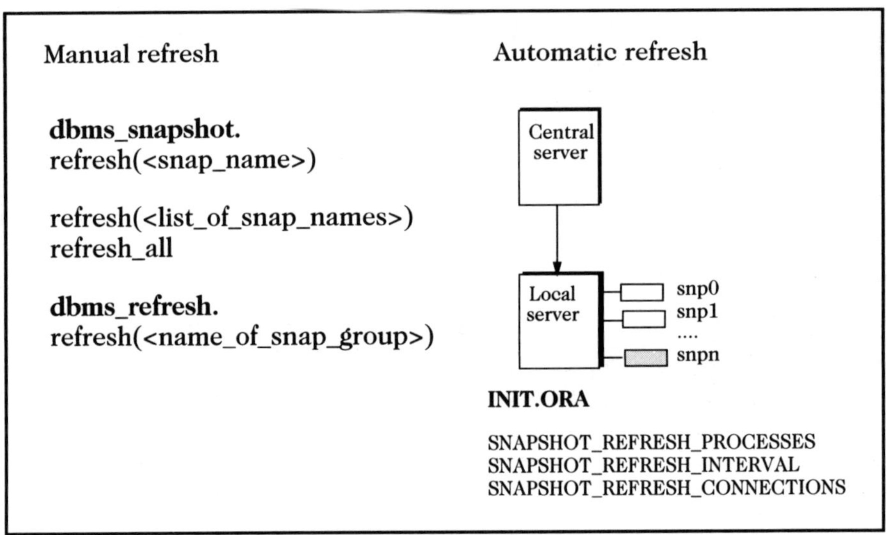

Figure 15.37 Manual and automatic refresh control

If an automatic refresh process cannot be carried out at the specified time due to an error situation (network problem, remote server not accessible, and so on) the refresh background process will still continue to try and carry out the refresh operation at the specified intervals. However if the attempted refresh fails sixteen times in succession, then the refresh process in question will be aborted and a 'broken' flag will be set in the data dictionary for the single snapshot or refresh group concerned. In addition a snapshot trace file is generated. Snapshots or snapshot groups for which the 'broken' flag has been set are no longer included in the automatic refresh cycle.

In order to restart the refresh cycle and reset the 'broken' flag, it is necessary to carry out a successful refresh operation manually, that is, by calling the DBMS_SNAPSHOT.REFRESH package procedure for any single snapshot or DBMS_REFRESH.REFRESH for a snapshot refresh group.

The state of a snapshot or group of snapshots can be examined at any time with the data dictionary views USER_REFRESH and USER_REFRESH_CHILDREN. The 'broken' flag can also be viewed in this way.

Figure 15.38 shows the structure of a simple replication configuration with automatic refresh.

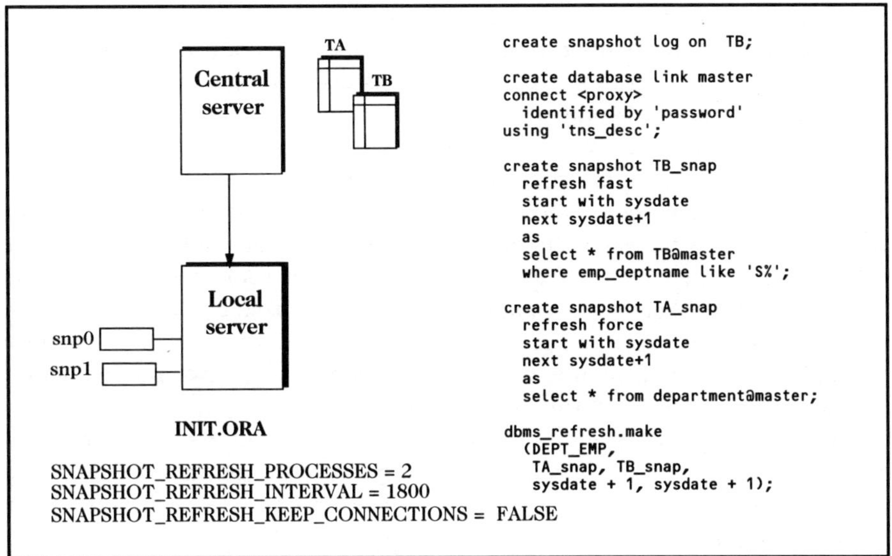

Figure 15.38 Creating a simple replication configuration

15.8.3 Symmetric replication under Oracle7: future developments

Although the increasing availability of network and client/server technologies has made it possible to put together distributed data processing systems which are as sophisticated as they are complex, the technological and organizational demands of developing and maintaining correspondingly sophisticated software systems have proved to be no less formidable, to say the least.

Over the past few years Oracle has introduced a series of products and methods which specifically enable or support the implementation of large-scale distributed database systems. Some of the key technologies to be mentioned here are:

- distributed read operations
- distributed transactions with the two-phase commit mechanism
- client/server configurations in homogeneous and heterogeneous networks

- synchronous and asynchronous replications
- grouped replications (snapshot groups)

Symmetric replication technology represents one of the next major developments which will facilitate the use of distributed database systems.

ORACLE's existing asynchronous replication (snapshot) procedure is characterized by the master-slave principle; one database node has control of the data and modify operations can only be carried out on that node, the replicates (snapshots) derived from the master data can only provide read access and cannot be modified.

As we have already seen (*refer also to* Figure 14.27), Release 7.0 does provide the possibility of implementing a kind of symmetric replication by adapting some elements of Oracle7's distributed processing technology. This solution makes it necessary to create the same table on each database node concerned, so that each table is both master and replicate. Then by the skilful use of database triggers and Oracle7's two-phase commit protocol, it becomes possible to configure these replicates so that any modification carried out on one of them is immediately (as part of the two-phase commit operation) repeated in all the other replicates.

However the problems associated with this particular solution make it unsuitable for wide-scale use, in particular because the amount of time taken to complete each two-phase commit transaction increases with every new replicate which is added.

The symmetric replication procedure implemented with Oracle7 Release 7.1 offers a far more flexible and efficient way of providing true data replication, as it is based on a RPC (remote procedure call) mechanism which executes remote operations asynchronously.

Whereas in synchronous replications the assumption is that all replicates are modified simultaneously upon completion of a transaction, an asynchronous RPC only guarantees that all remote transactions will be carried out at some point in the future, thus allowing the 'local' transaction to be completed very quickly regardless of the number of associated replicates. The distributed part of the transaction is entered in a corresponding RPC queue to be activated by the ORACLE Job Scheduler later on, as illustrated in Figure 15.39.

Release 7.1 of Oracle7 distinguishes between two types of replication:

- updatable snapshots
- N-way replications

The difference between these two types of replication is that snapshots can consist of subsets of a table whereas in N-way replication the whole table must always be present on the various remote nodes. However both types of replication present us with the same problem of how to detect and deal with update conflicts.

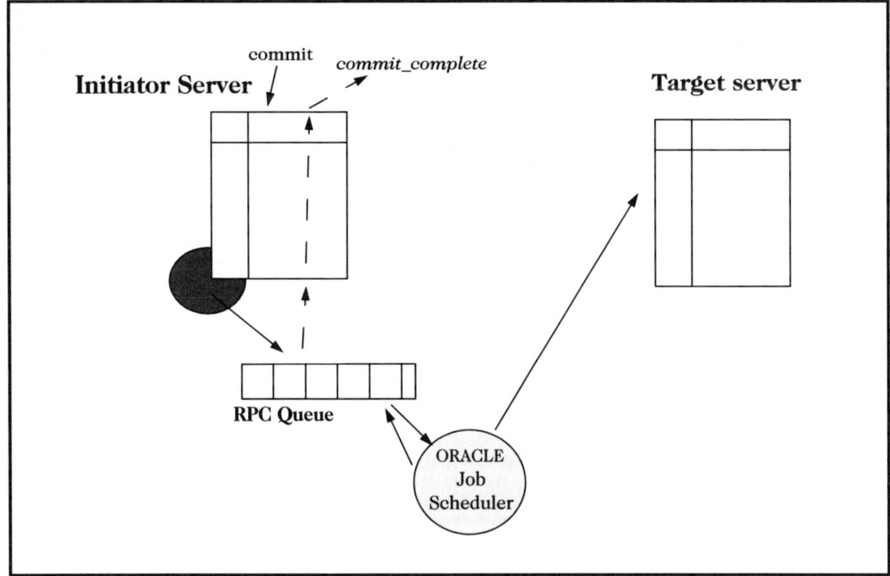

Figure 15.39 Using RPC to carry out symmetric replication

An update conflict becomes inevitable as soon as we make it possible for the same table to be stored and modified independently on more than one database server. If modifications to all replicates of the table are not always going to be carried out within a single transaction, then we will soon have the situation where the replicates of the same table are different from each other, as shown in Figure 15.40.

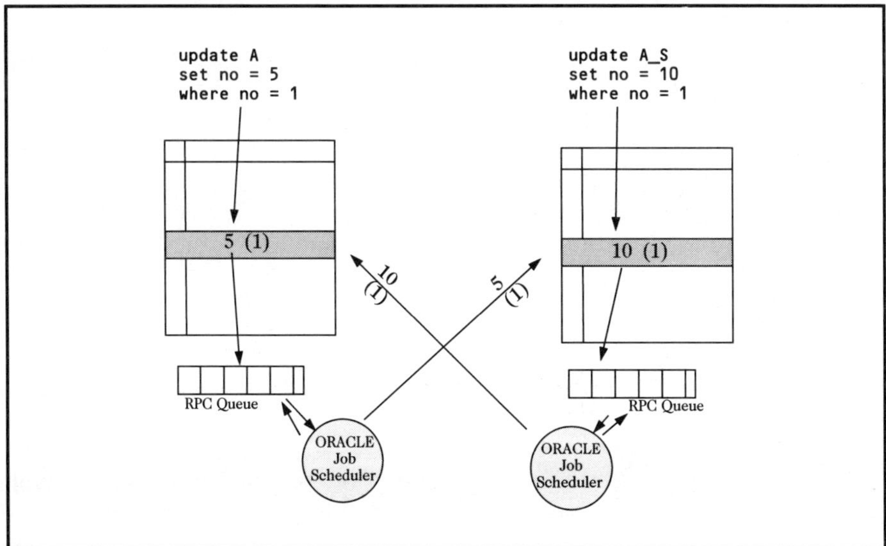

Figure 15.40 Update conflicts with replicated tables

In this example we start with both table A and snapshot A_S containing the same row where the original value for the column no in both cases is 1. A transaction on one node alters this value to 5 and, having been committed, this transaction is then entered in the RPC queue to be repeated on any replicate tables later.

However before the entry in the RPC queue can be processed, the same row is modified in the replicate table (from 1 to 10), the change is also committed and then entered in the RPC queue of the second server.

When the two entries in the RPC queues are to be processed, the ORACLE Server will detect that the value of the row to be modified has already been altered by another transaction. It then invokes a procedure which has been specifically implemented to resolve exactly this kind of conflict for this particular table and column. Needless to say a conflict resolution procedure which deals exactly with this situation cannot be provided as a standard part of the ORACLE Server; what Oracle7 can provide is a set of PL/SQL routines which can be adapted to deal with the specific update conflicts which can arise on a given ORACLE system in terms of nodes, tables and columns.

At the time of writing the final versions of these PL/SQL procedures had not yet been released by the Oracle Corporation, so it has unfortunately not been possible to include them in this version of this book.

Index

Notes

Notes

Notes

Notes

Notes

Notes

Notes

Notes

Books from

International Thomson Publishing

On the Internet

PIECING TOGETHER MOSAIC
Navigating the Internet and the World Wide Web

Steve Bowbrick, 3W Magazine

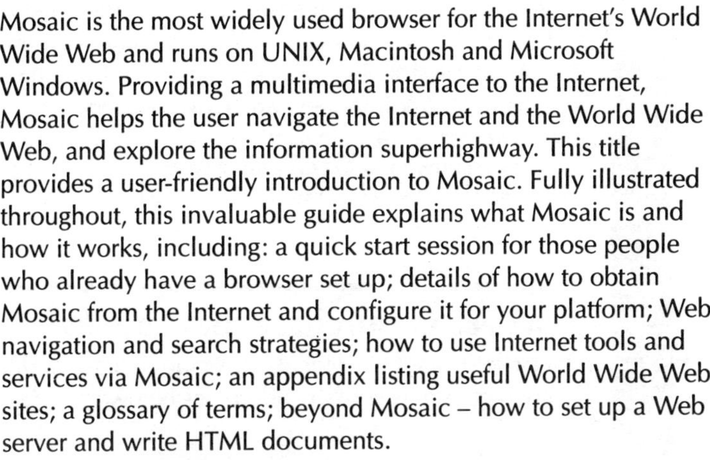

Mosaic is the most widely used browser for the Internet's World Wide Web and runs on UNIX, Macintosh and Microsoft Windows. Providing a multimedia interface to the Internet, Mosaic helps the user navigate the Internet and the World Wide Web, and explore the information superhighway. This title provides a user-friendly introduction to Mosaic. Fully illustrated throughout, this invaluable guide explains what Mosaic is and how it works, including: a quick start session for those people who already have a browser set up; details of how to obtain Mosaic from the Internet and configure it for your platform; Web navigation and search strategies; how to use Internet tools and services via Mosaic; an appendix listing useful World Wide Web sites; a glossary of terms; beyond Mosaic – how to set up a Web server and write HTML documents.

Spring 1995/300pp/1-850-32142-6/paper

SPINNING THE WEB
How to Provide Information on the Internet

Andrew Ford

An indispensable guide for all those who provide or intend to provide information on the World Wide Web, or want to make the most of their existing services, this book for the first time draws together all of the most up to date information and details of contemporary resources into one essential volume. Providing exclusive coverage of Web features, the book includes an overview of Web facilities, how to create hypertext documents, security issues, how to set up a server and the selection and evaluation of software. A variety of examples from current Web sources are included.

December 1994/250pp/1-850-32141-8/paper

On CompuServe

COMPUSERVE FOR EUROPE

Roelf Sluman

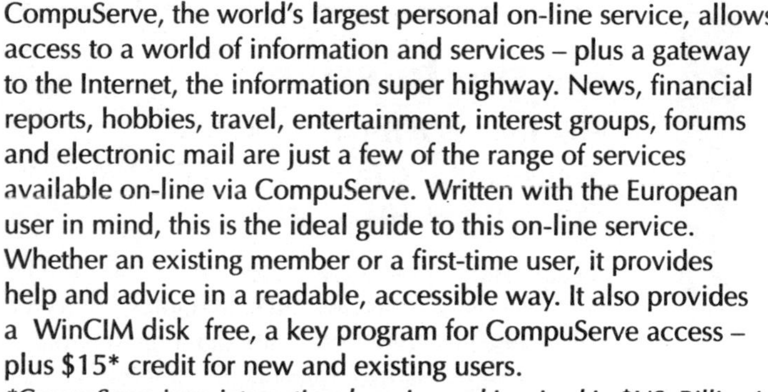

CompuServe, the world's largest personal on-line service, allows access to a world of information and services – plus a gateway to the Internet, the information super highway. News, financial reports, hobbies, travel, entertainment, interest groups, forums and electronic mail are just a few of the range of services available on-line via CompuServe. Written with the European user in mind, this is the ideal guide to this on-line service. Whether an existing member or a first-time user, it provides help and advice in a readable, accessible way. It also provides a WinCIM disk free, a key program for CompuServe access – plus $15* credit for new and existing users.

**CompuServe is an international service and is priced in $US. Billing is in local currency at the prevailing rate.*

December 1994/320pp/1-850-32121-3/paper

Where to purchase these books?

Please contact your local bookshop, in case of difficulties, contact us at one of the addresses below –

ORDERS

International Thomson Publishing Services Ltd
Cheriton House, North Way, Andover, Hants SP10 5BE, UK
Telephone: 0264 332424/Giro Account No: 2096919/
Fax: 0264 364418

SALES AND MARKETING ENQUIRIES

International Thomson Publishing
Berkshire House, 168/173 High Holborn, London WCIV 7AA, UK
Tel: 071-497 1422 Fax: 071-497 1426
e–mail: Information@ITPUK.CO.UK

MAILING LIST

To receive further information on our Networks books, please send the following information to the London address –
Full name and address (including Postcode)
Telephone, Fax Numbers and e–mail address